Microsoft®
Visual Basic® 2010
Step by Step

Michael Halvorson

PUBLISHED BY
Microsoft Press
A Division of Microsoft Corporation
One Microsoft Way
Redmond, Washington 98052-6399

Library of Congress Control Number: 2010924441

Printed and bound in the United States of America.

1 2 3 4 5 6 7 8 9   WCT   5 4 3 2 1 0

Distributed in Canada by H.B. Fenn and Company Ltd.

A CIP catalogue record for this book is available from the British Library.

Microsoft Press books are available through booksellers and distributors worldwide. For further information about international editions, contact your local Microsoft Corporation office or contact Microsoft Press International directly at fax (425) 936-7329. Visit our Web site at www.microsoft.com/mspress. Send comments to mspinput@microsoft.com.

Acquisitions Editor: Ben Ryan
Developmental Editor: Devon Musgrave
Project Editor: Valerie Woolley
Editorial Production: Christian Holdener, S4Carlisle Publishing Services
Technical Reviewer: Technical Review services provided by Content Master, a member of CM Group, Ltd.
Cover: Tom Draper Design

Body Part No. X16-88509

For Henry

Contents at a Glance

Table of Contents

What do you think of this book? We want to hear from you!

Microsoft is interested in hearing your feedback so we can continually improve our books and learning
resources for you. To participate in a brief online survey, please visit:

www.microsoft.com/learning/booksurvey/

Part II Programming Fundamentals

Acknowledgments

Writing a computer programming book is fascinating because the whole process begins well before the software is actually finished. Authors meet with software developers and computer book publishers, explore product specifications and early releases of the software, review the comments and suggestions that readers of previous editions have offered, develop a writing plan and schedule, and begin testing their ideas with beta versions of the product. This iterative process produces important insights and continues (with mounting fervor) until the software is complete and the final books are shipped to the printer.

Microsoft Press is a fantastic place to write a computer programming book. At each stage in the publishing process, talented team members work together to cultivate valuable technical contacts and resources, build visionary product deployment strategies, explore the hidden benefits of emerging technologies, and pick the right words and images to describe them. *Microsoft Visual Basic 2010 Step by Step*, now in its eighth edition, has benefited significantly from this dynamic and innovative publishing environment over the years.

I gratefully acknowledge the support and assistance of the following people who helped to plan, edit, test, produce, and market our book this time (in the order that I worked with them): Ben Ryan, Devon Musgrave, Valerie Woolley, Susan McClung, and Christian Holdener. In particular, Valerie Woolley enthusiastically kept my writing on schedule and insured that our book would fit well in the *Step by Step* series that Microsoft Press is so well known for. I am also very grateful to the Microsoft Visual Studio 2010 development team for providing me with beta and release candidate software to work with.

As always, I offer my deepest gratitude and affection to my family for their continued support of my writing projects and various academic pursuits.

Introduction

Microsoft Visual Basic 2010 is an important upgrade and enhancement of the popular Visual Basic programming language and compiler, a technology that enjoys an installed base of millions of programmers worldwide. Visual Basic 2010 is not a stand-alone product but a key component of Microsoft Visual Studio 2010—a comprehensive development system that allows you to create powerful applications for Windows, the Web, handheld devices, and a host of other environments. Whether you purchase one of the commercial editions of Visual Studio 2010 (described later in this Introduction) or you download Visual Basic 2010 Express for a free test-drive of the software, you are in for an exciting experience. The latest features of Visual Basic will increase your productivity and programming prowess, especially if you enjoy using and integrating information from databases, entertainment media, Web pages, and Web sites. In addition, an important benefit of learning Visual Basic and the Visual Studio Integrated Development Environment (IDE) is that you can use many of the same tools to write programs for Microsoft Visual C++ 2010, Microsoft Visual C# 2010, Microsoft Visual Web Developer 2010, and other popular products.

Microsoft Visual Basic 2010 Step by Step is a comprehensive introduction to Visual Basic programming using the Visual Basic 2010 software. I've designed this practical, hands-on tutorial with a variety of skill levels in mind and by following the premise that programmers learn by doing. In my opinion, the best way to master a complex technology like Visual Basic is to learn essential programming techniques through carefully prepared tutorials that can be completed on your own schedule and at your own pace. And although I have significant experience with college teaching and corporate project management, this book is not a dry textbook or an "A to Z" programmer's reference. Instead, it is a practical hands-on programming tutorial that puts *you* in charge of your learning, developmental milestones, and achievements. By using this book, programmers who are new to this topic will learn Visual Basic software development fundamentals in the context of useful, real-world applications; and experienced Visual Basic programmers can quickly master the essential tools and techniques offered in the Visual Basic 2010 upgrade.

Complementing this comprehensive approach is the book's structure—4 topically organized parts, 20 chapters, and 56 step-by-step exercises and sample programs. By using this book, you'll quickly learn how to create professional-quality Visual Basic 2010 applications for the Windows operating system and a variety of Web browsers. You'll also have fun!

Visual Basic Versions

So how did we get here, anyway? Between 1991 and 1998, Microsoft released six versions of Visual Basic (versions 1.0 through 6.0), which revolutionized software development for Windows by introducing event-driven programming to a wide audience based on the QuickBasic programming language and an IDE. After a significant period of additional development and innovation, Microsoft released Visual Basic .NET 2002, an object-oriented programming language closely related to Visual Basic but implemented on the Microsoft .NET Framework, a comprehensive library of coded solutions intended to be used by most new applications that run on the Windows platform. As improved versions of Visual Basic came out in 2003, 2005, and 2008, Visual Basic became a component within the Visual Studio suite, and significant support was added to the product for database, Internet, and team development projects, as well as continued improvements to the .NET Framework. Visual Basic 2010 is now so tightly integrated with Visual Studio that it is available only as a component in the Visual Studio 2010 programming suite, which includes Visual C#, Visual C++, Visual Web Developer, and other Microsoft .NET development tools. Since 2005, both Visual Basic and Visual Studio have been marketed without the ".NET" moniker, although they are still based on the .NET Framework technology.

Visual Studio 2010 is distributed in several different product configurations, including Professional, Premium, Ultimate, and Express. I've written this book to be compatible with all editions of Visual Basic 2010 and Visual Studio 2010, but especially with the tools and techniques available in Visual Studio 2010 Professional and Visual Basic 2010 Express. Although Visual Basic 2010 is similar in many ways to Visual Basic 2008, there are many important differences and improvements, so I recommend that you complete the exercises in this book using the Visual Basic 2010 software.

Note The Visual Studio 2010 software is not included with this book. The CD distributed with most versions of this book contains practice files, sample databases, and other useful information that requires the Visual Studio 2010 software (sold separately) for use. If you don't have Visual Studio, you can download Visual Basic 2010 Express for free, and it contains an amazing palette of features, though obviously not all the features of Visual Studio Professional, Premium, or Ultimate. As you complete the exercises in this book, I will note from time to time which features are unavailable to you if you are using Visual Basic 2010 Express. Also note that if you are using Visual Basic 2010 Express and you want to complete Chapter 20, "Creating Web Sites and Web Pages by Using Visual Web Developer and ASP.NET," you will need to download Visual Web Developer 2010 Express to complete the exercises. Visual Web Developer is included in Visual Studio Professional, Premium, and Ultimate, but not Visual Basic Express.

Downloading Visual Basic 2010 Express

As noted previously, if you don't have Visual Studio 2010 Professional, Visual Studio 2010 Premium, or Visual Studio 2010 Ultimate, you can complete most of the exercises in this book by downloading Visual Basic 2010 Express from the Web for free. This will give you an opportunity to learn Visual Basic programming and see for yourself if you want to upgrade to a full release of the Visual Studio software.

To download Visual Basic 2010 Express, complete the following steps:

1. Open a Web browser (such as Internet Explorer), and go to *http://www.microsoft.com/ express.*

2. Follow the instructions on the screen to download Visual Basic 2010 Express.

   On the Express Web site, you will also see an Express product feature chart that compares the Express product to the full versions of Visual Studio. Although there are some key differences between the full versions and Visual Basic 2010 Express, many of these differences have no effect on how you learn the essential techniques and features of Visual Basic programming. After you experiment with the Express product, you can decide whether you want to upgrade to one of the full versions of Visual Studio or not. Now, let's get started learning about Visual Basic and how this programming course works!

Finding Your Best Starting Point in This Book

This book is designed to help you build skills in a number of essential areas. You can use it if you're new to programming, switching from another programming language, or upgrading from Visual Basic 2008. Use the following table to find your best starting point in this book.

If you are …	Follow these steps
New to programming	1. Install the practice files as described in the section "Installing and Using the Practice Files," later in this Introduction.
	2. Learn basic skills for using Visual Basic 2010 by working sequentially from Chapter 1 through Chapter 17.
	3. Complete Part IV, "Database and Web Programming," as your level of interest or experience dictates.
Upgrading from Visual Basic 2005 or 2008	1. Install the practice files as described in "Installing and Using the Practice Files."
	2. Complete Chapters 1 through 4, skim Chapters 5 through 17, and complete Chapters 18 through 20.

If you are ...	Follow these steps
Upgrading from Visual Basic 6.0	1. Install the practice files as described in the section "Installing and Using the Practice Files."
	2. Read Chapters 1 through 4 carefully to learn the new features of the Visual Studio 2010 development environment.
	3. Skim Chapters 5 through 13 to review the fundamentals of event-driven programming, using variables, and writing decision structures. Give special attention to Chapters 5, 6, 9, and 12.
	4. Work sequentially from Chapters 14 through 20 to learn the new Visual Basic 2010 features related to user interface design, database programming, and Web programming.
Referencing this book after working through the chapters	1. Use the index to locate information about specific topics, and use the table of contents to locate information about general topics.
	2. Read the Quick Reference at the end of each chapter for a brief review of the major tasks in the chapter. The Quick Reference topics are listed in the same order as they're presented in the chapter.

Hardware and Software Requirements

You'll need the following hardware and software to complete the exercises in this book:

- Windows 7, Windows Vista, Windows XP, Windows Server 2003, or Windows Server 2008

- Visual Studio 2010 (Professional, Premium, or Ultimate) or Visual Basic 2010 Express

- 1.6 GHz processor

- 1 GB RAM

- 3 GB of available hard drive space

- 5400 RPM hard disk drive

- DirectX 9–capable video card that runs at a display resolution of 1024 × 768 or higher

- DVD drive

You also need to have Administrator-level access to your computer.

Note This book and the practice files were tested using Visual Studio 2010 Professional and Visual Basic 2010 Express on Windows 7. You might notice a few differences if you're using other editions of Visual Studio 2010. In particular, if you're using Visual Basic 2010 Express, a few features will be unavailable to you. In addition, all the screen shots in this book were captured using Windows 7. If you are using another version of Windows or Windows Server, you'll notice a few differences in some of the screen shots.

Prerelease Software

This book was reviewed and tested against the Release Candidate of Visual Studio 2010. The Release Candidate was the last preview before the final release of Visual Studio 2010. This book is expected to be fully compatible with the final release of Visual Studio 2010 and Visual Basic 2010. If there are any changes or corrections for this book, they will be collected and added to an easy-to-access Microsoft Knowledge Base article on the Web. See "Support for This Book," later in this Introduction.

> **Digital Content for Digital Book Readers:** If you bought a digital-only edition of this book, you can enjoy select content from the print edition's companion CD.
> Visit **http://go.microsoft.com/fwlink/?LinkId=187514** to get your downloadable content. This content is always up-to-date and available to all readers.

Installing and Using the Practice Files

The CD inside this book contains the practice files that you'll use as you perform the exercises in the book. For example, when you're learning how to display database tables on a form by using the *DataGridView* control, you'll open one of the practice files—an academic database named Faculty2010.accdb—and then use Visual Studio database programming tools to access the database. By using the practice files, you won't waste time creating files that aren't relevant to the exercise. Instead, you can concentrate on learning how to master Visual Basic 2010 programming techniques. With the files and the step-by-step instructions in the chapters, you'll also learn by doing, which is an easy and effective way to acquire and remember new skills.

> **Important** Before you break the seal on the CD, be sure that this book matches your version of the software. This book is designed for use with Visual Studio 2010 and the Visual Basic 2010 programming language. To find out what software you're running, you can check the product package, or you can start the software, open a project, and then click About Microsoft Visual Studio on the Help menu at the top of the screen.

Installing the Practice Files

Installing the practice files on your hard disk requires approximately 10 megabytes (MB) of disk space. Follow these steps to install the practice files on your computer's hard disk drive so that you can use them with the exercises in this book.

1. Remove the CD from the package inside this book and insert it into your CD drive.

> **Note** An End-User License Agreement (EULA) should open automatically. If this agreement does not appear, you can double-click StartCD.exe on the CD. If you have Windows 7 or Windows Vista, click Computer on the Start menu, double-click the icon for your CD drive, and then double-click StartCD.exe.

2. Review the EULA. If you accept the terms, select the Accept option, and then click Next.

   A menu appears with options related to the book.

3. Click Install Practice Files.

4. Follow the on-screen instructions.

> **Note** For best results when using the practice files with this book, accept the preselected installation location, which by default is C:\Vb10sbs. If you change the installation location, you'll need to adjust the paths in several practice files manually to locate essential components, such as artwork and database files, when you use them. Trust me—it is good to use the default installation location.

5. When the files have been installed, remove the CD from your drive and replace it in the package inside the back cover of your book.

   If you accepted the default settings, a folder named C:\Vb10sbs has been created on your hard disk drive, and the practice files have been placed in that folder. You'll find one folder in C:\Vb10sbs for each chapter in the book. (Some of the files represent completed projects, and others will require that you enter some program code.) If you have trouble running any of the practice files, refer to the text in the book that describes those files.

Using the Practice Files

Each chapter in this book explains when and how to use the practice files for that chapter. When it's time to use a practice file, the book includes instructions for opening the file. The chapters are built around scenarios that simulate real programming projects so that you can easily apply the skills you learn to your own work.

> **Note** Visual Basic 2010 features a new file format for its projects and solutions. Accordingly, you won't be able to open the practice files for this book if you're using an older version of the Visual Basic or Visual Studio software. To see what version of Visual Basic or Visual Studio you're using, click the About command on the Help menu.

Visual Studio is extremely customizable and can be configured to open and save projects and solutions in different ways. The instructions in this book generally rely on the default setting for Visual Studio. For more information about how settings within the development environment affect how you write programs and use the practice files, see the section "Customizing IDE Settings to Match Step-by-Step Exercises" in Chapter 1, "Exploring the Visual Studio Integrated Development Environment."

For those of you who like to know all the details, here's a list of the Visual Basic projects included on the CD. Each project is located in its own folder and has several support files. Look at all the things you will be doing!

Project	Description
Chapter 1	
MusicTrivia	A simple trivia program that welcomes you to the programming course and displays a digital photo.
Chapter 2	
Lucky7	Your first program—a game that simulates a Las Vegas Lucky Seven slot machine.
Chapter 3	
Birthday	Uses the *DateTimePicker* control to pick a date.
CheckBox	Demonstrates the *CheckBox* control and its properties.
Hello	A Hello World program that demonstrates the *Label* and *TextBox* controls.
List Box	Demonstrates the *ListBox* control for gathering input.
Radio Button	Demonstrates the *RadioButton* control for gathering input.
WebLink	Demonstrates the *LinkLabel* control that opens a Web browser in your Visual Basic application.
Chapter 4	
Menu	Demonstrates how to use Visual Studio dialog box controls, toolbars, and menus.
Chapter 5	
Advanced Math	Advanced use of operators for integer division, remainder division, exponentiation, and string concatenation.
Basic Math	Basic use of operators for addition, subtraction, multiplication, and division.
Constant Tester	Uses a constant to hold a fixed mathematical entity.
Data Types	Demonstrates Visual Basic fundamental data types and their use with variables.
Framework Math	Demonstrates the .NET Framework classes with mathematical methods.
Input Box	Receives input with the *InputBox* function.
Variable Test	Declares and uses variables to store information.
Chapter 6	
Select Case	Uses a *Select ... Case* decision structure and a *ListBox* control to display a welcome message in several languages.
User Validation	Uses the *If ... Then ... Else* decision structure and a *MaskedTextBox* control to manage a logon process.
Chapter 7	
Celsius Conversion	Converts temperatures from Fahrenheit to Celsius by using a *Do* loop.
Digital Clock	A simple digital clock program that demonstrates the *Timer* control.

Project	Description
For Loop	Demonstrates using a *For … Next* loop to display text in a *TextBox* control, and using the *Chr* function to create a wrap character.
For Loop Icons	Uses a global counter variable in an event procedure as an alternative to loops. This program also displays images by using a *PictureBox* control.
Timed Password	Demonstrates how to use a *Timer* control to create a logon program with a password time-out feature.
Windows Version Snippet	Shows how to use the Insert Snippet command to display the current version of Windows running on a user's computer.
Chapter 8	
Debug Test	A simulated debugging problem, designed to be solved using the Visual Studio debugging tools.
Chapter 9	
Disc Drive Error	Crashes when a CD or DVD drive is used incorrectly. This project is used as the basis of a Visual Basic error handler.
Disc Drive Handler	Completed error handler for loading files that demonstrates the *Try … Catch* syntax.
Chapter 10	
Text Box Sub	A general-purpose Sub procedure that adds items to a list box.
Track Wins	A clean version of the Lucky7 slot machine project from Chapter 2, which you enhance by using public variables and a function that computes the game's win rate.
Chapter 11	
Array Class Sorts	Shows how to create and manipulate large integer arrays. Demonstrates the *Array.Sort* and *Array.Reverse* methods and how to use a *ProgressBar* control to give the user visual feedback during long sorts.
Dynamic Array	Computes the average temperature for any number of days by using a dynamic array.
Fixed Array	Computes the average weekly temperature by using a fixed-length array.
Chapter 12	
Controls Collection	Uses a *For Each … Next* loop and the Visual Studio *Controls* collection to move objects on a form.
URL Collection	Demonstrates a user-defined collection containing a list of Uniform Resource Locators (URLs), or Web addresses, recently visited by the user.
Chapter 13	
Encrypt Text	Demonstrates the *Chr, Asc, Length, Substring,* and *FileExists* methods, as well as a simple encryption scheme to jumble the text in files. Teaches useful text-processing techniques.
Quick Note	A simple note-taking utility that demonstrates the *Clock.LocalTime* property; the *WriteAllText* method; and the *TextBox, MenuStrip,* and *SaveFileDialog* controls.

Project	Description
Sort Text	A text file editor with a menu bar that demonstrates how to manage Open, Close, Save As, Insert Date, Sort Text, and Exit commands in a program. Contains a *ShellSort* module for sorting arrays that can be added to other programming projects.
Text Browser	Displays the contents of a text file in a Visual Basic program. Demonstrates menu and dialog box commands, a *Try ... Catch* error handler, the *ReadAllText* method, and serves as a foundation for the other programs in this chapter.
Xor Encryption	Explores the *StreamWriter* class and the *OpenTextFileWriter* and *ReadAllText* methods for file management, as well as using the *Xor* operator to encrypt files with a hidden code that is entered by the user.
Chapter 14	
Add Controls	Demonstrates how controls are added to a Windows Form at run time by using program code (not the Designer).
Anchor and Dock	Uses the *Anchor* and *Dock* properties of a form to align objects at run time.
Desktop Bounds	Uses the *StartPosition* and *DesktopBounds* properties to position a Windows Form at run time. Also demonstrates the *FormBorderStyle* property, *Rectangle* structure, and *ShowDialog* method.
Lucky Seven Help	The enhanced Lucky7 program (Track Wins) from Chapter 10, which you enhance again through the addition of a second form to display Help information.
Chapter 15	
Draw Shapes	Demonstrates a few of the useful graphics methods in the *System.Drawing* namespace, including *DrawEllipse*, *FillRectangle*, and *DrawCurve*.
Moving Icon	Animates an icon on the form, moving it from the top of the form to the bottom each time that you click the Move Down button.
Transparent Form	Demonstrates how to change the transparency of a form by using the *Me* object and the *Opacity* property.
Zoom In	Simulates zooming in, or magnifying, a picture box object on a form (in this case, a high-resolution image of the planet Earth).
Chapter 16	
Form Inheritance	Uses the Visual Studio Inheritance Picker to create a form that inherits its characteristics and functionality from another form.
Person Class	Demonstrates how to create new classes, properties, and methods in a Visual Basic project. The new *Person* class is an employee record with first name, last name, and date of birth fields, and it contains a method that computes the current age of an employee.
Chapter 17	
Print Dialogs	Demonstrates how to create Print Preview and Page Setup dialog boxes.
Print File	Handles more sophisticated printing tasks, including printing a multipage text file with wrapping lines. Includes lots of code to use in your own projects.
Print Graphics	Prints graphics from within a Visual Basic program by using an error handler, the *Print* method, and the *DrawImage* method.
Print Text	Demonstrates how simple text is printed in a Visual Basic program.

Project	Description
Chapter 18	
ADO Faculty Form	Demonstrates how ADO.NET is used to establish a connection to a Microsoft Access 2007 database and display information from it.
Chapter 19	
DataGridView Sample	Shows how the *DataGridView* control is used to display multiple tables of data on a form. Also demonstrates how navigation bars, datasets, and table adapters are interconnected and bound to objects on a form.
Chapter 20	
Chap20	Demonstrates using Visual Web Developer and ASP.NET 4 to create a car loan calculator that runs in a Web browser, offers Help information, and displays faculty database records.

Uninstalling the Practice Files

Use the following steps to remove the practice files added to your hard disk drive by the Visual Basic 2010 Step by Step installation program. After uninstalling the practice files, you can delete manually any Visual Basic project files that you have created on your own, should you choose to do so.

If you are running the Windows 7 or Windows Vista operating system:

1. In Control Panel, in the Programs category, click Uninstall A Program.

2. Select Microsoft Visual Basic 2010 Step by Step in the list of programs, and then click Uninstall.

3. Follow the on-screen instructions to remove the practice files.

If you are running the Windows XP operating system:

1. In Control Panel, open Add Or Remove Programs.

2. In the Currently Installed Programs list, click Microsoft Visual Basic 2010 Step by Step. Then click Remove.

3. Follow the on-screen instructions to remove the practice files.

Conventions and Features in This Book

Before you start the exercises in this book, you can save time by understanding how I provide instructions and the elements I use to communicate information about Visual Basic programming. The following lists identify stylistic conventions and discuss helpful features of the book.

Conventions

- The names of all program elements—controls, objects, methods, functions, properties, and so on—appear in *italic*.

- Hands-on exercises for you to follow are given in numbered lists of steps (1, 2, and so on). A round bullet (•) indicates an exercise that has only one step.

- Text that you need to type appears in **bold**.

- As you work through steps, you'll occasionally see tables with lists of properties that you'll set in Visual Studio. Text properties appear within quotes, but you don't need to type the quotes.

- A plus sign (+) between two key names means that you must press those keys at the same time. For example, "Press Alt+Tab" means that you hold down the Alt key while you press Tab.

- Readeraids labeled Note, Tip, and Important provide additional information or alternative methods for a step. You should read these before continuing with the exercise.

Other Features

- You can learn special programming techniques, background information, or features related to the information being discussed by reading the sidebars that appear throughout the chapters. These sidebars often highlight difficult terminology or suggest future areas for exploration.

- You can learn about options or techniques that build on what you learned in a chapter by trying the One Step Further exercise at the end of that chapter.

- You can get a quick reminder of how to perform the tasks you learned by reading the Quick Reference table at the end of a chapter. These handy tables are also designed to be used as a topical reference after you complete the book and you need a quick reminder about how to perform a programming task.

Helpful Support Links

You are invited to check out the following links that provide support for the Visual Studio 2010 software and this book's contents.

Visual Studio 2010 Software Support

For questions about the Visual Studio 2010 software, I recommend two Microsoft Web sites:

- *http://msdn.microsoft.com/vbasic/* (the Microsoft Visual Basic Developer Center home page)

- *http://www.microsoft.com/communities/* (the home of technical communities related to Microsoft software products and technologies)

Both Web sites give you access to professional Visual Basic developers, Microsoft employees, Visual Basic blogs, newsgroups, webcasts, technical chats, and interesting user groups. For additional information about these and other electronic and printed resources, see the Appendix, "Where to Go for More Information."

Support for This Book

Every effort has been made to ensure the accuracy of this book and the contents of the companion CD. As corrections or changes are collected, they will be added to a Microsoft Knowledge Base article. Microsoft Press provides support for books and companion CDs at the following Web site:

http://www.microsoft.com/learning/support/books/

If you have comments, questions, or ideas regarding the book or the companion CD, or questions that are not answered by visiting the sites previously mentioned, please send them to Microsoft Press via an e-mail message to *mspinput@microsoft.com*.

Please note that Microsoft software product support is not offered through these addresses, nor does the author of this book offer direct product support.

We Want to Hear from You

We welcome your feedback about this book. Please share your comments and ideas through the following short survey:

http://www.microsoft.com/learning/booksurvey

Your participation helps Microsoft Press create books that better meet your needs and your standards.

> **Note** We hope that you will give us detailed feedback in our survey. If you have questions about our publishing program, upcoming titles, or Microsoft Press in general, we encourage you to interact with us using Twitter at *http://twitter.com/MicrosoftPress*. For support issues, use only the e-mail address shown previously.

Part I
Getting Started with Microsoft Visual Basic 2010

In Part I, you'll receive an overview of essential Microsoft Visual Basic 2010 programming techniques and an introduction to the tools and features that you will work with during most Visual Basic programming sessions. You'll learn to use the Visual Studio 2010 Integrated Development Environment (IDE), with its fulsome collection of programming tools, windows, and menu commands, and you'll receive step-by-step instruction on how to build and run several interesting programs from scratch. This is the place to start if you're new to Visual Basic programming or upgrading from an earlier version.

Chapter 2 introduces how controls, forms, properties, and program code can be used in combination to create an entertaining Lucky Seven slot machine game. Chapter 3 provides an overview of the most useful Toolbox controls, which help you present information or program choices to the user, gather input, work with dates and times, and connect to the Web. Chapter 4 focuses on adding menus, toolbars, and dialog boxes to Visual Basic programs that will give your program the flair of a commercial Windows application.

Chapter 1
Exploring the Visual Studio Integrated Development Environment

After completing this chapter, you will be able to:

- Use the Visual Studio Integrated Development Environment.

- Open and run a Visual Basic program.

- Change property settings.

- Move, resize, dock, and automatically hide tool windows.

- Use the IDE Navigator.

- Open a Web browser within Visual Studio.

- Get Help and manage Help settings.

- Customize IDE settings to match this book's step-by-step instructions.

Are you ready to start working with Microsoft Visual Studio 2010? This chapter gives you the skills you need to get up and running with the Visual Studio 2010 Integrated Development Environment (IDE)—the place where you will write Microsoft Visual Basic programs. You should read this chapter whether you are new to Visual Basic programming or you have used previous versions of Visual Basic or Visual Studio.

In this chapter, you'll learn the essential Visual Studio menu commands and programming procedures. You'll open and run a simple Visual Basic program named Music Trivia; you'll change a programming setting called a *property*; and you'll practice moving, sizing, docking, and hiding tool windows. You'll also learn how to switch between files and tools with the IDE Navigator, open a Web browser within Visual Studio, get more information by using the online Help documentation, and customize the IDE to match this book's step-by-step instructions. These are common tasks that you'll use in most Visual Studio programming sessions, and they will soon become second nature to you (if they are not already).

3

The Visual Studio Development Environment

First, a quick note to readers upgrading from Visual Studio 2008: Although there have been lots of internal improvements to Visual Studio 2010, the Visual Studio 2010 IDE is largely the same IDE that you worked with in Visual Studio 2008. But because you may be new to Visual Studio, I'm going to explain the basics in this chapter. Also, if you're new to Visual Studio, something else that you should know is that although the programming language you'll be learning in this book is Visual Basic, most of the features in the Visual Studio IDE apply equally to Visual Basic, Microsoft Visual C++, and Microsoft Visual C#. All of these programs (or more properly, compiler technologies) are available to you in the same IDE, which you can experiment with now by starting Visual Studio and looking at the product.

> **Important**   But wait a second. If you haven't yet installed this book's practice files, please do so now because we are about to use them. Take a moment to work through the sections entitled "Finding Your Best Starting Point" and "About the CD and Practice Files" in this book's Introduction, and then follow the installation steps. (I recommend that you place the project files and related subfolders in the C:\Vb10sbs folder on your computer.) You also need a current version of Visual Studio 2010 installed, such as Visual Studio 2010 Professional edition. (Most of the exercises will also work with Visual Studio 2010 Express.) Return to this point in Chapter 1 when you're ready to go.

Start Visual Studio 2010

1. On the Windows taskbar, click Start, click All Programs, and then click the Microsoft Visual Studio 2010 folder.

   The folders and icons in the Microsoft Visual Studio 2010 folder appear in a list.

2. Click the Microsoft Visual Studio 2010 icon.

> **Tip**   If you are using Visual Basic 2010 Express, click the Microsoft Visual Basic 2010 Express icon.

If this is the first time you are starting Visual Studio, the program will take a few moments to configure the environment. If you are prompted to identify your programming preferences at this time, select Visual Basic development settings.

When Visual Studio starts, you see the development environment on the screen with its many menus, tools, and component windows, as shown here. (These windows are sometimes called *tool windows*.) You also should see a Start Page containing a set of tabs with links, guidance and learning resources, news, and project options. The Start Page is a comprehensive source of information about your project, as well as resources within the Visual Basic development community. This is one avenue for receiving new information about Visual Studio after you purchase the software. (The screen shown here is probably less detailed than the one you'll see, but I've captured the screens in 800 x 600 resolution so that you can read the text in them clearly.)

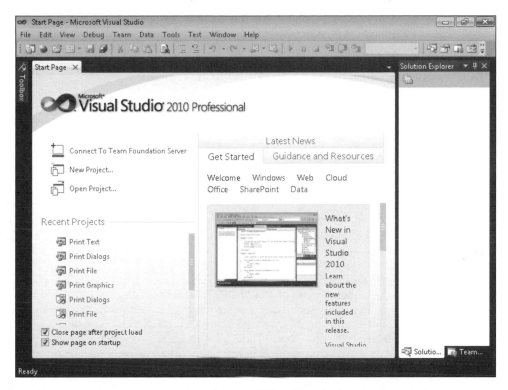

The first thing most developers do when they start Visual Studio is open an existing project—either a completed solution they want to work with again or an ongoing development project. Try opening an existing project that I created for you—the Music Trivia program.

Open a Visual Basic project

1. On the Start Page, click the Open Project link.

   The Open Project dialog box shown in the following screen shot opens on the screen. (You can also display this dialog box by clicking the Open Project command on the File menu or by pressing CTRL+O.) Even if you haven't used Visual Studio before, the Open Project dialog box will seem straightforward because it resembles the familiar Open dialog box in Microsoft Office Word or Microsoft Office Excel.

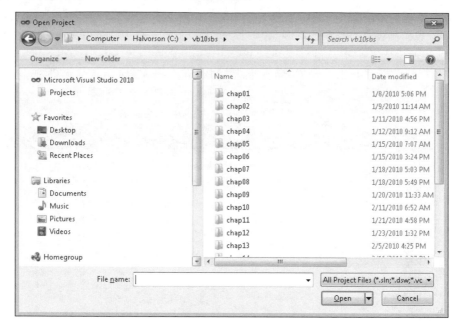

Tip In the Open Project dialog box, you see a number of storage locations along the left side of the window. The Projects folder under Microsoft Visual Studio 2010 is particularly useful. By default, Visual Studio saves your programming projects in this Projects folder, giving each project its own subfolder. We'll use a different projects folder to organize your programming coursework, however, as you'll learn below. Additional locations, such as Favorites and Libraries, will also be available to you, depending on how your computer and operating system has been configured. (The screen shots in this book show Windows 7.)

2. Browse to the C:\Vb10sbs folder on your hard disk.

   The C:\Vb10sbs folder is the default location for this book's extensive sample file collection, and you'll find the files there if you followed the instructions in the section entitled "Installing and Using the Practice Files" in the Introduction. If you didn't install the sample files, close this dialog box and install them now by using the CD included with this book.

3. Open the Chap01\Musictrivia folder, and then double-click the MusicTrivia solution file. (If your system shows file name extensions, this file will end with .sln.)

   Visual Studio loads the MusicTrivia form, properties, and program code for the MusicTrivia solution. The Start Page may still be visible in the center of the screen. In the upper-right corner of the screen, Solution Explorer lists some of the files in the solution.

> **Troubleshooting** If you see an error message indicating that the project you want to open is in a newer file format, you might be trying to load Visual Basic 2010 files into an older version of the Visual Basic software. (Earlier versions of Visual Basic can't open the Visual Basic 2010 projects included on the companion CD.) To check which version of Visual Basic you're using, click the About command on the Help menu.

Visual Studio provides a special check box named Always Show Solution to control several options related to solutions within the IDE. The check box is located on the Projects and Solutions/General tab of the Options dialog box, which you open by clicking the Options command on the Tools menu. If the check box is selected, a subfolder is created for each new solution, placing the project and its files in a separate folder beneath the solution. Also, if you select the Always Show Solution check box, a few options related to solutions appear in the IDE, such as commands on the File menu and a solution entry in Solution Explorer. If you like the idea of creating separate folders for solutions and seeing solution-related commands and settings, select this check box. You'll learn more about these options at the end of the chapter.

> ## Projects and Solutions
>
> In Visual Studio, programs under development are typically called *projects* or *solutions* because they contain many individual components, not just one file. Visual Basic 2010 programs include a project file (.vbproj) and a solution file (.sln), and if you examine these files within a file browsing utility such as Windows Explorer, you'll notice that the solution file icons have a tiny 10 in them, an indication of their version number. (Visual Basic 2010 is referred to as VB 10 internally.)
>
> A project file contains information specific to a single programming task. A solution file contains information about one or more projects. Solution files are useful to manage multiple related projects. The samples included with this book typically have a single project for each solution, so opening the project file (.vbproj) has the same effect as opening the solution file (.sln). But for a multi-project solution, you will want to open the solution file. Visual Basic 2010 offers a new file format for its projects and solutions, but the basic terminology that you might have learned while using Visual Basic 2005 or 2008 still applies.

The Visual Studio Tools

At this point, you should take a few moments to study the Visual Studio IDE and identify some of the programming tools and windows that you'll be using as you complete this course. If you've written Visual Basic programs before, you'll recognize many (but perhaps not all) of the programming tools. Collectively, these features are the components that you use to construct, organize, and test your Visual Basic programs. A few of the programming tools also help you learn more about the resources on your system, including the larger world of databases and Web site connections available to you. There are also several powerful Help tools.

The *menu bar* provides access to most of the commands that control the development environment. Menus and commands work as they do in all Windows-based programs, and you can access them by using the keyboard or the mouse. Located below the menu bar is the *Standard toolbar*, a collection of buttons that serve as shortcuts for executing commands and controlling the Visual Studio IDE. My assumption is that you've used Word, Excel, or some other Windows-based application enough to know quite a bit about toolbars, and how to use familiar toolbar commands, such as Open, Save, Cut, and Paste. But you'll probably be impressed with the number and range of toolbars provided by Visual Studio for programming tasks. In this book, you'll learn to use several toolbars; you can see the full list of toolbars at any time by right-clicking any toolbar in the IDE.

Along the bottom of the screen, you may see the Windows *taskbar*. You can use the taskbar to switch between various Visual Studio components and to activate other Windows-based programs. You might also see taskbar icons for Windows Internet Explorer, antivirus utilities, and other programs installed on your system. In most of my screen shots, I'll hide the taskbar, to show more of the IDE.

The following screen shot shows some of the tools and windows in the Visual Studio IDE. Don't worry that this screen looks different from your current development environment view. You'll learn more about these elements (and how you adjust your views) as you work through the chapter.

The main tools visible in this Visual Studio IDE are the Designer, Solution Explorer, the Properties window, and the Toolbox, as shown here. You might also see more specialized tools, such as Server Explorer and Object Browser, or they may appear as tabs within the IDE. Because no two developers' preferences are exactly alike, it is difficult to predict what you'll see if your Visual Studio software has already been used. (What I show is essentially the "fresh download" or "out-of-the-box" view.)

If a tool isn't visible and you want to see it, click the View menu and select the tool. Because the View menu has expanded steadily over the years, Microsoft has moved some of the less frequently used View tools to a submenu called Other Windows. Check there if you don't see what you need.

The exact size and shape of the tools and windows depend on how your development environment has been configured. With Visual Studio, you can align and attach, or *dock*, windows to make visible only the elements that you want to see. You can also partially conceal tools as *tabbed documents* along the edge of the development environment

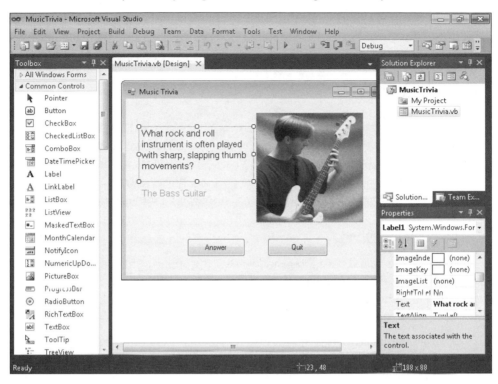

and then switch back and forth between documents quickly. Trying to sort out which tools are important to you now and which you can learn about later is a difficult early challenge when you're learning the busy Visual Studio interface. Your development environment will probably look best if you set your monitor and Windows desktop settings so that they maximize your screen space, but even then things can get a little crowded.

> **Tip** Although I use a screen resolution of 800 × 600 for most of the screen shots in this book—so that you can see the IDE clearly—I usually use 1280 × 1024 for writing code. You can change the screen resolution in Windows 7 by right-clicking the Windows desktop and clicking Screen Resolution. In Windows Vista, you right-click the Windows desktop and click Personalize.

The purpose of all this tool complexity is to add many new and useful features to the IDE while providing clever mechanisms for managing the clutter. These mechanisms include features such as docking, auto hiding, floating, and a few other window states that I'll describe later in this chapter. If you're just starting out with Visual Studio, the best way to deal with this feature tension is to hide the tools that you don't plan to use often to make room for the important ones. The crucial tools for beginning Visual Basic programming—the ones you'll start using right away in this book—are the Designer, the Properties window, Solution Explorer, and the Toolbox. You won't use the Server Explorer, Class View, Object Browser, or Debug windows until later in the book.

In the following exercises, you'll start experimenting with the crucial tools in the Visual Studio IDE. You'll also learn how to display a Web browser within Visual Studio and how to hide the tools that you won't use for a while.

The Designer

If you completed the last exercise ("Open a Visual Basic project"), the MusicTrivia project is loaded in the Visual Studio development environment. However, the user interface, or *form*, for the project might not yet be visible in Visual Studio. (More sophisticated projects might contain several forms, but this simple trivia program needs only one.) To make the form of the MusicTrivia project visible in the IDE, you display it by using Solution Explorer.

Display the Designer

1. Locate the Solution Explorer window near the upper-right corner of the Visual Studio development environment. If you don't see Solution Explorer (if it is hidden as a tab in a location that you cannot see or isn't currently visible), click Solution Explorer on the View menu to display it.

   When the MusicTrivia project is loaded, Solution Explorer looks like this:

2. Click the MusicTrivia.vb form in the Solution Explorer window.

   All form files, including this one, have a tiny form icon next to them so that you can easily identify them. When you click the form file, Visual Studio highlights it in Solution Explorer, and some information about the file appears in the Properties window (if it is visible).

3. At the top of the Solution Explorer window, click the View Designer button in Solution Explorer to display the program's user interface.

The MusicTrivia form is displayed in the Designer, as shown here:

Notice that a tab called MusicTrivia.vb [Design] is visible near the top of the Designer. You can click this tab to display the program code associated with the MusicTrivia form, and as other tabs appear at the top of the Designer, you can switch back and forth among them by clicking the desired tab. You'll learn more about program code and the Code Editor tab in Chapter 2, "Writing Your First Program."

Now try running a Visual Basic program with Visual Studio.

Running a Visual Basic Program

Music Trivia is a simple Visual Basic program designed to familiarize you with the programming tools in Visual Studio. The form you see now has been customized with five objects (two labels, a picture, and two buttons), and I've added three lines of program code to make the trivia program ask a simple question and display the appropriate answer. (The program "gives away" the answer now because it is currently in design mode, but the answer is hidden when you run the program.) You'll learn more about creating objects and adding program code in Chapter 2. For now, try running the program in the Visual Studio IDE.

Run the Music Trivia program

1. Click the Start Debugging button (the green right-pointing arrow) on the Standard toolbar to run the Music Trivia program in Visual Studio.

 Tip You can also press F5 or click the Start Debugging command on the Debug menu to run a program in the Visual Studio development environment.

Visual Studio loads and compiles the project into an *assembly* (a structured collection of modules, data, and manifest information for a program), prepares the program for testing or *debugging*, and then (if the compilation is successful) runs the program in the development environment. While the program is running, an icon for the program appears on the Windows taskbar. After a moment, you see the MusicTrivia form again, this time with the photograph and answer label hidden from view, as shown here:

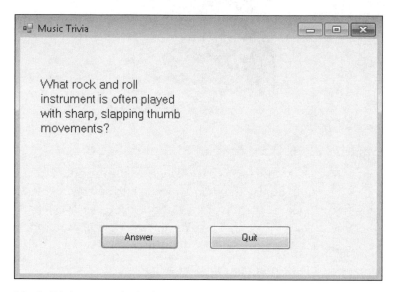

Music Trivia now asks its important question: "What rock and roll instrument is often played with sharp, slapping thumb movements?"

2. Click the Answer button to reveal the solution to the question.

The program displays the answer (The Bass Guitar) below the question and then displays a photograph of an obscure Seattle bass player demonstrating the technique, as shown here. The test program works.

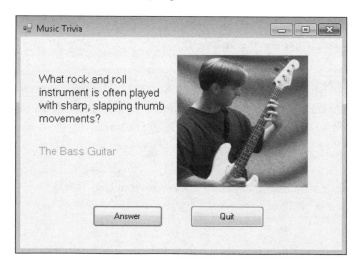

3. Click Quit to close the program.

The form closes, and the Visual Studio IDE becomes active again.

Thinking About Properties

In Visual Basic, each user interface (UI) element in a program (including the form itself) has a set of definable properties. You can set properties at design time by using the Properties window. Properties can also be referenced in code to do meaningful work while the program runs. (UI elements that receive input often use properties to convey information to the program.) At first, you might find properties a difficult concept to grasp. Viewing them in terms of something from everyday life can help.

Consider this bicycle analogy: a bicycle is an object you use to ride from one place to another. Because a bicycle is a physical object, it has several inherent characteristics. It has a brand name, a color, gears, brakes, and wheels, and it's built in a particular style. (It might be a road bike, a mountain bike, or a tandem bike.) In Visual Basic terminology, these characteristics are *properties* of the bicycle *object*. Most of the bicycle's properties were defined when the bicycle was built. But others (tires, travel speed, and options such as reflectors and mirrors) are properties that change while the bicycle is used. The bike might even have intangible (that is, invisible) properties, such as manufacture date, current owner, value, or rental status. And to add a little more complexity, a company or shop might own one bicycle or (the more likely scenario) an entire fleet of bicycles, all with different properties. As you work with Visual Basic, you'll set the properties of a variety of objects, and you'll organize them in very useful ways.

The Properties Window

In the IDE, you can use the Properties window to change the characteristics, or *property settings*, of the UI elements on a form. A property setting is a *quality* of one of the objects in your program. You can change property settings from the Properties window while you're creating your user interface, or you can add program code via the Code Editor to change one or more property settings while your program is running. For example, the trivia question that the Music Trivia program displays can be modified to appear in a different font or font size or with a different alignment. (With Visual Studio, you can display text in any font installed on your system, just as you can in Excel or Word.)

The Properties window contains an Object list that itemizes all the UI elements (objects) on the form. The window also lists the property settings that can be changed for each object. You can click one of two convenient buttons to view properties alphabetically or by category. You'll practice changing the Font property of the first label in the Music Trivia program now.

Change a property

1. Click the *Label1* object on the form. (*Label1* contains the text "What rock and roll instrument is often played with short, slapping thumb movements?")

   To work with an object on a form, you must first select the object. When you select an object, resize handles appear around it, and the property settings for the object are displayed in the Properties window.

2. Click the Properties Window button on the Standard toolbar.

   This button depicts a hand pointing and is on the right side of the toolbar. The Properties window might or might not be visible in Visual Studio, depending on how it's been configured and used on your system. It usually appears below Solution Explorer on the right side of the development environment. (If it is visible, you don't need to click the button, but you should click the window to activate it.)

   You'll see a window similar to the one shown in the following screen shot:

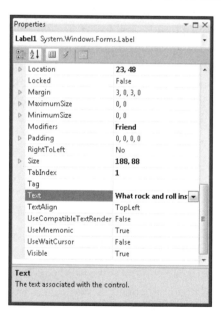

The Properties window lists all the property settings for the first label object (*Label1*) on the form. (In Visual Basic 2010, more than 65 properties are associated with labels.) Property names are listed in the left column of the window, and the current setting for each property is listed in the right column. Because there are so many properties (including some that are rarely modified), Visual Studio organizes them into categories and displays them in outline view. If a category has a triangular arrow sign (>) next to it, you can click the arrow to display all the properties in that category. If a category has a dark rotated arrow next to it, the properties are all visible, but you can hide the list under the category name by clicking the arrow again.

> **Tip** The Properties window has two handy buttons at the top of the window that you can use to further organize properties. Clicking the Alphabetical button lists all the properties in alphabetical order and puts them in just a few categories. Clicking the Categorized button organizes the property list into many logical categories. I recommend Categorized view if you are new to Visual Studio.

3. Scroll the Properties window list box until the *Font* property is visible.

   The Properties window scrolls like a regular list box. If you are in Categorized view, Font is in the Appearance category.

4. Click the *Font* property name (in the left column).

   The current font (Microsoft Sans Serif) is partially displayed in the right column, and a button with three dots on it appears by the font name. This button is called an *ellipsis button* and indicates that a dialog box is available to customize the property setting.

5. Click the Font ellipsis button in the Properties window.

   Visual Studio displays the Font dialog box, shown here, which you can use to specify new formatting characteristics for the text in the selected label on your form. The Font dialog box contains more than one formatting option; for each option you select, a different property setting will be modified.

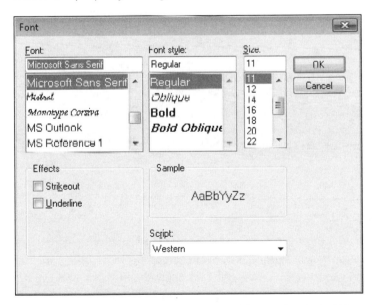

6. Change the font style from Regular to Oblique (that is, Italic), and then click OK to confirm your changes.

   Visual Studio records your changes and adjusts the property settings accordingly. You can examine the changes by viewing your form in the Designer or by expanding the Font property in the Properties window.

Now change a property setting for the *Label2* object (the label that contains the text "The Bass Guitar").

7. In the Designer, click the second label object (*Label2*).

   When you select the object, resize handles surround it.

8. Click the *Font* property in the Properties window.

   The *Label2* object has its own unique set of property settings. Although the property names are the same as those of the *Label1* object, the values in the property settings are distinct and allow the *Label2* object to act independently on the form.

9. Click the Font ellipsis button, set the font style to Bold and the font size to 12 points, and then click OK.

10. Scroll to the *ForeColor* property in the Properties window, and then click it in the left column.

11. Click the ForeColor arrow in the right column, click the Custom tab, and then click a dark purple color.

    The text in the *Label2* object is now bold and purple on the form, as shown here.

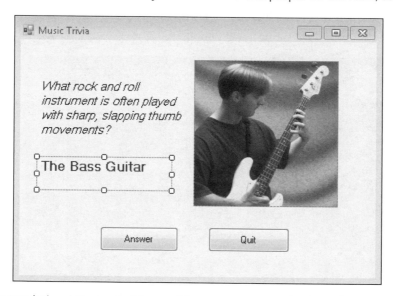

Congratulations! You've just learned how to set properties in a Visual Basic program by using the Visual Studio Properties window—one of the important skills in becoming a Visual Basic programmer.

Moving and Resizing the Programming Tools

With numerous programming tools to contend with on the screen, the Visual Studio IDE can become a pretty busy place. To give you complete control over the shape and size of the elements in the development environment, Visual Studio lets you move, resize, dock, and auto hide most of the interface elements that you use to build programs.

To move one of the tool windows in Visual Studio, simply click the title bar and drag the object to a new location. If you align one window along the edge of another window, it attaches to that window, or *docks* itself. Dockable windows are advantageous because they always remain visible. (They don't become hidden behind other windows.) If you want to see more of a docked window, simply drag one of its borders to view more content.

If you want to completely close a window, click the Close button in the upper-right corner of the window. You can always open the window again later by clicking the appropriate command on the View menu.

If you want an option somewhere between docking and closing a window, you might try auto hiding a tool window at the side of the Visual Studio IDE by clicking the tiny Auto Hide pushpin button on the right side of the tool's title bar. This action removes the window from the docked position and places the title of the tool at the edge of the development environment in an unobtrusive tab. When you auto hide a window, you'll notice that the tool window remains visible as long as you keep the mouse pointer in the area of the window. When you move the mouse to another part of the IDE, the window slides out of view.

To restore a window that you have auto hidden, click the tool tab at the edge of the development environment or hold your mouse over the tab. (You can recognize a window that is auto hidden because the pushpin in its title bar is pointing sideways.) By holding the mouse pointer over the title, you can use the tools in what I call "peek-a-boo" mode—in other words, to quickly display an auto hidden window, click its tab, check or set the information you need, and then move the mouse to make the window disappear. If you ever need the tool displayed permanently, click the Auto Hide pushpin button again so that the point of the pushpin faces down, and the window then remains visible.

Another useful feature of Visual Studio is the ability to display windows as tabbed documents (windows with tab handles that partially hide behind other windows) and to dock windows by using the docking guides that appear as tiny squares on the perimeter of the IDE, as well as a centrally located "guide diamond," as shown on the next page.

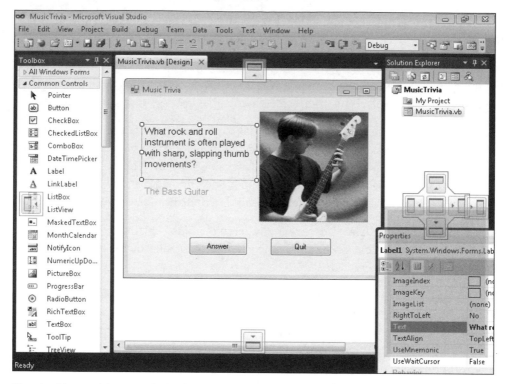

The docking guides are changeable icons that appear on the surface of the IDE when you move a window or tool from a docked position to a new location. Because the docking guides are associated with shaded, rectangular areas of the IDE, you can preview the results of your docking maneuver before you actually make it. In Visual Studio 2010, this feature has significantly improved, and you can preview a variety of different configurations with the docking guides, none of which remain permanent until you release the mouse button.

Because docking and auto hiding techniques take some practice to master, I recommend that you use the following exercises to experiment with the window-management features of the IDE. After you complete the exercises here, feel free to configure the Visual Studio tools in a way that seems comfortable for you.

Moving and Resizing Tool Windows

To move and resize one of the programming tool windows in Visual Studio, follow these steps. This exercise demonstrates how to manipulate the Properties window, but you can work with a different tool window if you want to.

Move and resize the Properties window

1. If the Properties window isn't visible in the development environment, click the Properties Window button on the Standard toolbar.

   The Properties window is activated in the IDE, and its title bar is highlighted.

2. Double-click the Properties window title bar to display the window as a floating (undocked) window.

3. Using the Properties window title bar, drag the window to a new location in the development environment, but don't dock it (yet).

   Moving windows around the Visual Studio IDE gives you some flexibility with the tools and the look of your development environment. Now you'll resize the Properties window to see more object property settings at once.

4. Point to the lower-right corner of the Properties window until the pointer changes to a double-headed arrow (the resizing pointer). Then drag the lower-right border of the window down and to the right to enlarge the window, as shown here.

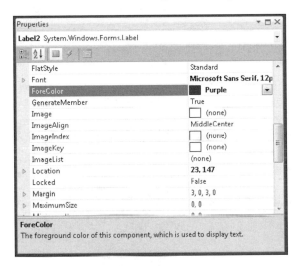

You can work more quickly and with more clarity of purpose in a bigger window. Feel free to move or resize a window when you need to see more of its contents.

Docking Tool Windows

If a tool window is floating over the development environment, you can return it to its original docked position by holding down the CTRL key and double-clicking the window's title bar. (Notice that in the previous exercise, you double-clicked the title bar to undock a docked window.) You can also attach or dock a floating tool in a different place. You might want to do this if you need to make more room in Visual Studio for a particular programming task, such as creating a user interface with the Designer. Try docking the Properties window in a different location now.

Dock the Properties window

1. Verify that the Properties window (or another tool that you want to dock) is floating over the Visual Studio IDE in an undocked position.

   If you completed the previous exercise, the Properties window is undocked now.

2. Drag the title bar of the Properties window to the top, bottom, right, or left edge of the development environment (your choice!), taking care to drag the mouse pointer over one of the docking guides on the perimeter of the Visual Studio IDE, or a collection of four or more docking guides, called collectively a *guide diamond*.

   As you move the mouse over a docking guide, the Properties window snaps into place, and a blue-shaded rectangle indicates how your window will appear when you release the mouse button, as shown here. Note that there are several valid docking locations for tool windows in Visual Studio, so you might want to try two or three different spots until you find one that looks right to you. (A window should be located in a place that's handy and not in the way of other needed tools.)

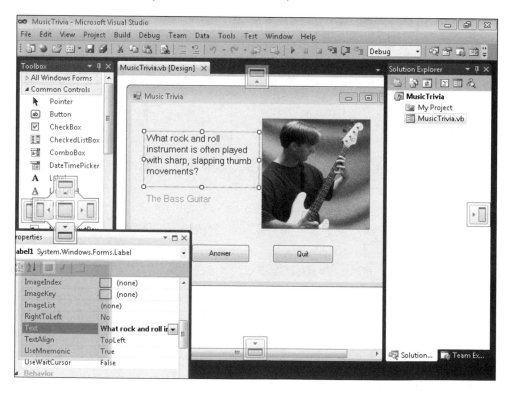

3. Release the mouse button to dock the Properties window.

   The window snaps into place in its new home.

> **Tip** To switch between dockable, tabbed documents, hidden windows, and floating windows, right-click the window's title bar (or tab, if it is a tabbed document), and then click the option you want. Although the Properties window works very well as a dockable window, you'll probably find that larger windows (the Visual Studio Start Page, for example) work best as tabbed document windows.

4. Try docking the Properties window several more times in different places to get the feel of how docking works.

   I guarantee that although a few of these window procedures seem confusing at first, after a while they'll become routine for you. In general, you want to create window spaces that have enough room for the information you need to see and use while you work on more important tasks in the Designer and in the Code Editor.

Hiding Tool Windows

To hide a tool window, click the Auto Hide pushpin button on the right side of the title bar to conceal the window beneath a tool tab on the edge of the IDE, and click it again to restore the window to its docked position. You can also use the Auto Hide command on the Window menu (or right-click a title bar and select Auto Hide) to auto hide a tool window. Give it a try now.

Use the Auto Hide feature

1. Locate the Auto Hide pushpin button on the title bar of the Properties window.

   The pushpin is currently in the "down," or "pushed in," position, meaning that the Properties window is "pinned" open and auto hide is disabled.

2. Click the Auto Hide button on the Properties window title bar.

   The Properties window slides off the screen and is replaced by a small tab named Properties. The benefit of enabling auto hide, of course, is that the process frees up additional work space in Visual Studio. But the hidden window is also quickly accessible.

3. Hold the mouse pointer over the Properties tab. (You can also click the Properties tab if you want.)

   The Properties window immediately reappears.

4. Move the mouse elsewhere within the IDE, and the window disappears again.

5. Finally, display the Properties window again, and then click the pushpin button on the Properties window title bar.

The Properties window returns to its familiar docked position, and you can use it without worrying about it sliding away.

Spend some time moving, resizing, docking, and auto hiding tool windows in Visual Studio now, to create your version of the perfect work environment. As you work through this book, you'll want to adjust your window settings periodically to adapt your work area to the new tools you're using.

 Tip Visual Studio lets you save your window and programming environment settings and copy them to a second computer or share them with members of your programming team. To experiment with this feature, click the Import And Export Settings command on the Tools menu and follow the wizard instructions to export (save) or import (load) settings from a file.

Switching Among Open Files and Tools by Using the IDE Navigator

Visual Studio has a feature that makes it even easier to switch among open files and programming tools in the development environment. This feature is called the IDE Navigator, and it lets you cycle through open files and tools by using key combinations, in much the same way that you cycle through open programs on the Windows taskbar. Give it a try now.

Use the IDE Navigator

1. Hold down the CTRL key and press TAB to open the IDE Navigator.

   The IDE Navigator opens and displays the active (open) files and tools in the IDE. Your screen will look similar to the following:

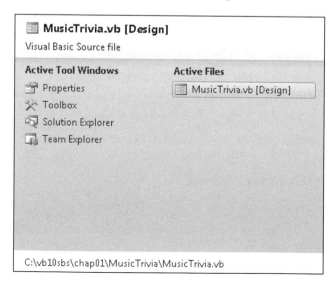

2. While holding down the CTRL key, press TAB repeatedly to cycle through the active files until the file you want is highlighted.

   To cycle through the files in the reverse direction, hold down CTRL+SHIFT and press TAB. (If you want this to look even more impressive, open another window or two so that the cycle order is more apparent.)

3. While holding down the CTRL key, press the arrow keys to cycle through both the active files and the active tools.

   You can also select an active file (or tool) by clicking its name.

4. When you're finished with the IDE Navigator, release the CTRL key.

   The last selected item in the IDE Navigator will become active.

 Tip To cycle through active tools without opening the IDE Navigator, you can also press ALT+F7. SHIFT+ALT+F7 lets you cycle through the tools in the reverse direction.

Opening a Web Browser Within Visual Studio

A handy feature in Visual Studio is the ability to open a simple Web browser within the development environment. The browser appears as a tabbed document window in the IDE, so it takes up little space but can be opened immediately when needed. You could open a stand-alone Web browser (such as Internet Explorer) and keep it nearby on the Windows taskbar, but running a Web browser *within* Visual Studio makes examining Web sites and copying data into Visual Studio even easier. Try using the Visual Studio Web browser now.

Open the Visual Studio Web browser

1. Click the Other Windows submenu on the View menu, and then click the Web Browser command.

   The Web Browser window appears, as shown on the next page.

   The browser is a tabbed document window by default, but you can change it into a floating window or a docked window by right-clicking the window title bar and then clicking the Float or Dock command.

 Tip You can change the default page that appears in the Web Browser window by changing the setting in the Options dialog box. Open the Options dialog box by clicking Options on the Tools menu. Select the Show All Settings check box, expand Environment, and then click Web Browser. Change the Home Page setting to a Uniform Resource Locator (URL) that you want for the default page.

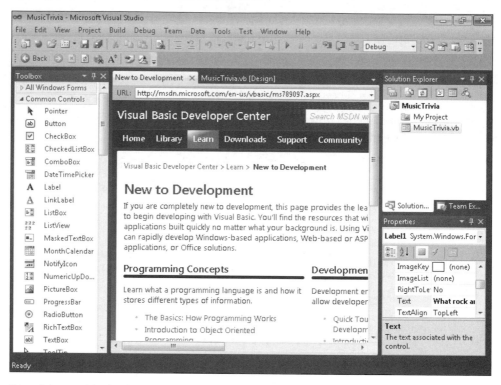

2. Experiment with the browser and how it functions within the IDE.

   Although the browser is more basic than Internet Explorer or another full-featured browser, you may find it a useful addition to the Visual Studio tool collection. You can also open and run Internet Explorer (or another browser) directly from the Windows taskbar.

3. When you're finished, click the Close button on the right side of the Web browser tab or title bar to close the window.

Getting Help

Visual Studio includes Help documentation that you can use to learn more about the Visual Studio IDE, the Visual Basic programming language, and the Microsoft .NET Framework. Take a moment to explore these Help resources now before moving on to Chapter 2, where you'll build your first program.

If you have used Visual Studio 2008, you will notice some differences in the Visual Studio 2010 Help documentation. Most significantly, Help is now hosted within your Web browser. Table 1-1 highlights the major differences that you should be aware of.

TABLE 1-1 Comparing Help Between Versions of Visual Studio

Visual Studio 2008 Help Documentation	Visual Studio 2010 Help Documentation
Local Help opened in a stand-alone application viewer named Microsoft Document Explorer.	Local Help is browser-based and opens in your Web browser.
Document Explorer was coupled with Visual Studio and could be updated only when Visual Studio was updated.	Because Help is browser-based and decoupled from Visual Studio, it can be updated more frequently.
Local Help was updated on a less frequent schedule.	Help can be updated on demand using the Help Library Manager.
F1 Help sometimes took a long time to open.	F1 Help is faster and search results are improved.
Help had a complete TOC tree of all topics.	Help has a simplified TOC tree that just displays the parent, peer, and child topics.
Local Help included an index.	Help no longer includes an index.
Local Help and online Help experiences are very different.	Local Help and online Help experiences are very similar.
Help documentation typically lists multiple languages, such as Visual Basic, C#, C++, and JScript, making it harder to read the documentation.	Help documentation displays the different languages in a tabbed view and displays just the language you are interested in.

Note Because Help is decoupled in Visual Studio 2010 and can be updated regularly, your experience might be different from the text and steps described in the next section.

Managing Help Settings

Visual Studio includes a Help Library Manager to manage your Help documentation and settings. Using the Help Library Manager, you can choose online or local Help, check for updates online, and find or remove content.

Help documentation for Visual Studio 2010 is delivered in two ways: local or online. Local Help is typically installed during Visual Studio 2010 setup. (You can also add it later by using the Help Library Manager.) Local Help is updated periodically, but you have to check the Help Library Manager for updates. Online Help is available at *http://msdn.microsoft.com/library/*. If you have an Internet connection, it is typically better to use online Help because you will always be using the latest version of the Help documentation.

Manage Help settings

1. On the Help menu, click Manage Help Settings. If you see a Set Local Content Location dialog box, click OK to accept the default location. The Help Library Manager appears, as shown here.

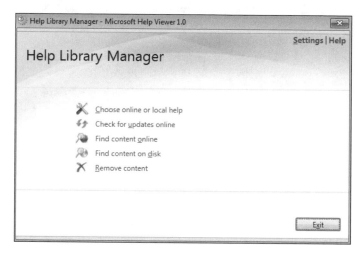

2. Click Choose Online Or Local Help.

   In the Settings box that opens, you can select the type of Help you plan to use.

3. If you have an Internet connection, make sure that the I Want To Use Online Help radio button is selected, and then click OK.

4. In the Help Library Manager window, click Install Content From Online.

5. Explore the Help content, which you can install locally if you choose.

6. Click Cancel.

7. Explore the other options in the Help Library Manager.

8. When you are finished, exit the Help Library Manager.

Using F1 Help

What is the fastest way to get help on what you are working on in Visual Studio? The quickest approach is usually to press the F1 key. Visual Studio has been designed to offer "context-sensitive help" related to the keyword or task that you are working with. Although F1 Help may not always display the exact information that you want, it usually puts you in the part of the Help documentation that will get you started. So when you need help, think of using the F1 key.

Use F1 Help

1. Click the *Label1* object on the form.

2. Press the F1 key. If a dialog box appears asking if you want to view Help content on the Internet, click Yes.

   The Label topic on MSDN should appear.

 Tip If you don't have an Internet connection but you do have local Help installed, you can try switching your Help settings to use local Help instead.

3. Switch back to Visual Studio.

4. Click the Answer button on the form.

5. Press the F1 key.

   The Button topic on MSDN should appear. Depending on your view, your screen looks something like this:

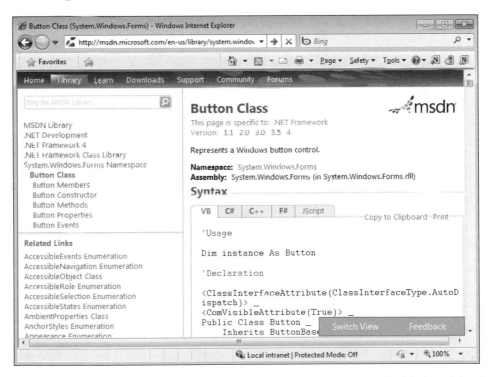

MSDN currently has different views. The view I'm showing you here is called *lightweight view*. You can select lightweight view by clicking the Lightweight View link or the Switch View link. The Switch View link is shown in the bottom right corner of the screen.

Inside MSDN Help

There are a couple of things to notice that will help you best utilize the Help documentation. First, version information is listed at the top of the content window. MSDN supports multiple versions of Visual Studio and the .NET Framework. As you'll learn later in the book, the current version of the .NET Framework is version 4.

In the Syntax section of the Help content, be sure that the VB tab is selected. When you select this tab, you will see only Visual Basic syntax and code snippets. The other languages will be hidden from view, making it easier to read the documentation. Your selection will be remembered the next time you open the documentation.

On the left side of the Help window is a simplified table of contents (TOC). The title of the topic currently being displayed is in bold and a different color. Above the current topic are the parent topics, and below it are the child topics. Beneath the TOC is the Related Links section. This section displays the peers of the current topic. You can click any links in the TOC area to navigate within the documentation. Above the TOC is a search box, which is another way to search the documentation.

Table 1-2 lists some useful tips about Help as you learn about the Visual Studio IDE, Visual Basic, and the .NET Framework.

TABLE 1-2 Help Topic Locations in Visual Studio 2010

To Get Help	Do This
Help documentation	Click View Help on the Help menu. or Open *http://msdn.microsoft.com/library/* in a browser to view online Help.
Visual Studio IDE	Select the item in Visual Studio and press the F1 key. or Search the Help documentation for "Visual Studio 2010."
A dialog box in Visual Studio	Click the Help button (the question mark) on the dialog box title bar.
Visual Basic	Search the Help documentation for "Getting Started with Visual Basic."
.NET Framework	Search the Help documentation for ".NET Framework 4."
Windows Forms	Search the Help documentation for "Getting Started with Windows Forms."
A keyword or program statement in the Code Editor	Select the keyword or program statement and press the F1 key.

Customizing IDE Settings to Match Step-by-Step Exercises

Like the tool windows and other environment settings within the IDE, the compiler settings within Visual Studio are highly customizable. It is important to review a few of these settings now so that your version of Visual Studio is configured in a way that is compatible with the step-by-step programming exercises that follow. You will also learn how to customize Visual Studio generally so that as you gain programming experience, you can set up Visual Studio in the way that is most productive for you.

Setting the IDE for Visual Basic Development

The first setting that you need to check was established when Visual Studio was first installed on your machine. During setup, you were asked how you wanted Visual Studio to configure your general development environment. Since Visual Studio is a multi-purpose programming tool, you had many options—Visual Basic development, Visual C++ development, Visual C# development, Web development, and so on. The selection you made configured not only the Code Editor and the development tools available to you, but also the menu and toolbar commands and the contents of several tool windows. For this reason, if you plan to use this book to learn Visual Basic programming but originally configured your software for a different language, a few of the menu commands and procedures described in this book will not exactly match your current software configuration.

Fortunately, you can fix this inconsistency and practice changing your environment settings by using the Import And Export Settings command on the Tools menu. The following steps show you how to change your environment setting to Visual Basic development, the recommended setting for this book.

Set the IDE for Visual Basic development

1. On the Tools menu, click Import And Export Settings.

     Tip If you are using Visual Basic 2010 Express, click the Tools menu, click Settings, and then click Import And Export Settings.

    You can use the wizard that appears to save your environment settings for use on another computer, load settings from another computer, or reset your settings.

2. Click Reset All Settings, and then click Next.

    Visual Studio asks you if you want to save your current settings in a file before you configure the IDE for a different type of programming. It is always a good idea to save your current settings as a backup, so that you can return to them if the new ones don't work out.

3. Verify that the Yes, Save My Current Settings radio button is selected, and note the file name and folder location in which Visual Studio plans to save the settings.

If you want to go back to these settings, you'll use this same wizard and the Import Selected Environmental Settings radio button to restore them.

4. Click Next to view the default list of settings that you can use for Visual Studio.

Depending on what Visual Studio components are installed, you will see a list of settings similar to those shown in the following screen shot:

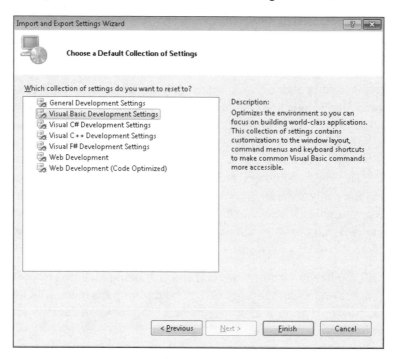

5. Click Visual Basic Development Settings (if it is not already selected), and click Finish.

 Tip If you are using Visual Basic 2010 Express, click Expert Settings, and click Finish.

The wizard switches your IDE settings, including menu commands, toolbars, and settings within a few dialog boxes, tool windows, and the Code Editor.

Feel free to repeat this customization process any time that you need to reset your settings (for example, if you make a customization mistake that you regret), or if you want to customize Visual Studio for another programming tool.

6. Click Close to close the wizard.

Checking Project and Compiler Settings

If you just reset your environment settings for Visual Basic development, you are now ready to begin the programming exercises. But if you didn't reset your settings—for example, if you were already configured for Visual Basic development and have been using Visual Studio 2010 for a while, or if your computer is a shared resource used by other programmers who might have modified the default settings (perhaps in a college computer lab)—complete the following steps to verify that your settings related to projects, solutions, and the Visual Basic compiler match those that I use in the book.

Check project and compiler settings

1. Click the Options command on the Tools menu to display the Options dialog box.

   The Options dialog box is your window to many of the customizable settings within Visual Studio. To see all the settings that you can adjust, click to select the Show All Settings check box in the lower-left corner of the dialog box.

2. Expand the Projects And Solutions category and then click the General item in the Options dialog box.

   This group of check boxes and options configures the Visual Studio project and solution settings.

3. So that your software matches the settings used in this book, adjust your settings to match those shown in the following dialog box:

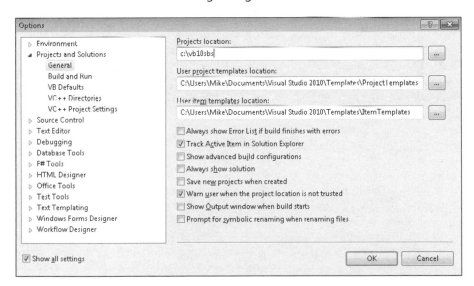

In particular, I recommend that you clear the Always Show Solution and Save New Projects When Created check boxes if they are selected. The first option shows additional solution commands in the IDE, which are not necessary for solutions that contain only one project (the situation for most programs in this book). The second option causes Visual Studio to postpone saving your project until you click the Save All command on the File menu and provide a location for saving the file. This "delayed save" feature allows you to create a test program, compile and debug the program, and even run it without actually saving the project on disk—a useful feature when you want to create a quick test program that you might want to discard instead of saving. (An equivalent situation in word-processing terms is when you open a new Word document, enter an address for a mailing label, print the address, and then exit Word without saving the file.) With this default setting, the exercises in this book prompt you to save your projects after you create them, although you can also save your projects in advance by selecting the Save New Projects When Created check box.

You'll also notice that I have typed "C:\Vb10sbs" in the Projects Location text box to indicate the default location for this book's sample files. Most of the projects that you create will be stored in this folder, and they will have a "My" prefix to distinguish them from the completed project I provide for you to examine. (Be sure to change this setting on your computer as well.)

After you have adjusted these settings, you're ready to check four Visual Basic compiler settings.

4. Click the VB Defaults item in the Options dialog box.

Visual Studio displays a list of four compiler settings: Option Explicit, Option Strict, Option Compare, and Option Infer. Your screen looks like this:

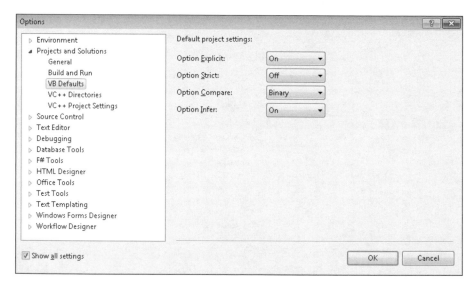

Although a detailed description of these settings is beyond the scope of this chapter, you'll want to verify that Option Explicit is set to On and Option Strict is set to Off—the default settings for Visual Basic programming within Visual Studio. Option Explicit On is a setting that requires you to declare a variable before using it in a program—a very good programming practice that I want to encourage. Option Strict Off allows variables and objects of different types to be converted in certain circumstances without generating a compiler error. (For example, a number can be assigned to a text box object without error.) Although this is a potentially worrisome programming practice, Option Strict Off is a useful setting for certain types of demonstration programs. If you don't keep this setting, a few projects will display error messages when you run them.

Option Compare determines the comparison method when different strings are compared and sorted. For more information about comparing strings and sorting text, see Chapter 13, "Exploring Text Files and String Processing."

Option Infer was a new setting in Visual Basic 2008. When you set Option Strict to Off and Option Infer to On, you can declare variables without explicitly stating a data type; or rather, if you make such a declaration, the Visual Basic compiler will infer (or take an educated guess) about the data type based on the initial assignment you made for the variable. The designers of Visual Basic created this setting to make writing code easier while still maintaining the benefits of type declaration. You'll learn more about the feature in Chapter 5, "Visual Basic Variables and Formulas, and the .NET Framework."

As a general rule, I recommend that you set Option Infer to Off to avoid unexpected results in how variables are used in your programs. I have set Option Infer to Off in most of the sample projects included on the companion CD.

5. Feel free to examine additional settings in the Options dialog box related to your programming environment and Visual Studio. When you're finished, click OK to close the Options dialog box.

You're ready to exit Visual Studio and start programming.

One Step Further: Exiting Visual Studio

Each chapter in this book concludes with a section titled "One Step Further" that enables you to practice an additional skill related to the topic at hand. After the "One Step Further" tutorial, I've compiled a Quick Reference table in each chapter that reprises the important concepts discussed in the chapter, so that if you need to refer to a concept quickly, you can have ready access to it.

When you're finished using Visual Studio for the day, save any projects that are open, and close the development environment. Give it a try.

Exit Visual Studio

1. Save any changes you've made to your program by clicking the Save All button on the Standard toolbar.

As you learned in the preceding section, the default behavior in Visual Studio 2010 is that you give your program a name when you begin a project or solution, but you don't specify a file location and save the project until you click the Save All button or the Save All command on the File menu. You've made a few changes to your project, so you should save your changes now.

2. On the File menu, click the Exit command.

The Visual Studio program closes. Time to move on to your first program in Chapter 2!

Chapter 1 Quick Reference

To	Do This
Start Visual Studio	Click Start on the taskbar, click All Programs, click the Microsoft Visual Studio 2010 folder, and then click the Microsoft Visual Studio 2010 program icon.
Open an existing project	Start Visual Studio. Click Open Project on the File menu. *or (if possible)* On the Start page, click the project in the Recent Projects pane.
Compile and run a program	Click the Start Debugging button on the Standard toolbar. *or* Press F5.
Set properties	Click the form object whose properties you want to set. In the Properties window, click the property name in the left column, and then change the corresponding property setting in the right column.
Resize a tool window	Display the tool as a floating window (if it is currently docked), and resize it by dragging its edges.
Move a tool window	Display the tool as a floating window (if it is in a docked state), and then drag its title bar.
Dock a tool window	With the mouse pointer, drag the window's title bar over a docking guide to preview how it will appear, and then release the mouse button to snap the tool into place.
Restore a floating tool window	Hold down the CTRL key and double-click the window's title bar.
Auto hide a docked tool window	Click the Auto Hide pushpin button on the right side of the title bar of the tool window. The window hides behind a small tab at the edge of the development environment until you hold the mouse over it.
Disable Auto Hide for a docked tool window	Click the tool tab, and then click the Auto Hide pushpin button.

To	Do This
Switch between active files	Hold down the CTRL key and press TAB to display the IDE Navigator. While holding down the CTRL key, press TAB to scroll through the list of active files. Use the arrow keys to scroll through both the list of active files and tools. You can also click a file or tool in the IDE Navigator to switch to it.
Switch between active tools	Press ALT+F7 to scroll in a forward direction through the active tools in the IDE. Press ALT+SHIFT+F7 to scroll in the reverse direction.
Get Help	Select the object or program statement in Visual Studio and then press the F1 key.
Manage Help Settings	Click Manage Help Settings on the Help menu to open the Help Library Manager.
Configure the Visual Studio environment for Visual Basic development	Click the Import And Export Settings command on the Tools menu, click Reset All Settings, and then click the Next button. Click Yes, Save My Current Settings, and then the Next button. Finally, click Visual Basic Development Settings and the Finish button, and then click Close.
Customize IDE settings	Click the Options command on the Tools menu, and then customize Visual Studio settings by category. To view and customize project settings, click the General item in the Projects And Solutions category. To view and customize compiler settings, click the VB Defaults item in the same category.
Exit Visual Studio	On the File menu, click Exit.

Chapter 2
Writing Your First Program

After completing this chapter, you will be able to:

- Create the user interface for a new program.
- Set the properties for each object in your user interface.
- Write program code.
- Save and run the program.
- Build an executable file.

As you learned in Chapter 1, "Exploring the Visual Studio Integrated Development Environment," the Microsoft Visual Studio 2010 Integrated Development Environment (IDE) contains several powerful tools to help you run and manage your programs. Visual Studio also contains everything you need to build your own applications for Windows and the Web from the ground up.

In this chapter, you'll learn how to create a simple but attractive user interface with the controls in the Visual Studio Toolbox. Next you'll learn how to customize the operation of these controls with property settings. Then you'll see how to identify just what your program should do by writing program code. Finally, you'll learn how to save and run your new program (a Las Vegas–style slot machine) and how to compile it as an executable file.

Lucky Seven: Your First Visual Basic Program

The Windows-based application you're going to construct is Lucky Seven, a game program that simulates a lucky number slot machine. Lucky Seven has a simple user interface and can be created and compiled in just a few minutes using Microsoft Visual Basic. Here's what your program will look like when it's finished:

Programming Steps

The Lucky Seven user interface contains two buttons, three lucky number boxes, a digital photo depicting your winnings, and the label "Lucky Seven." I produced these elements by creating seven objects on the Lucky Seven form and then changing several properties for each object. After I designed the interface, I added program code for the Spin and End buttons to process the user's button clicks and produce the random numbers. To re-create Lucky Seven, you'll follow three essential programming steps in Visual Basic: Create the user interface, set the properties, and write the program code. Table 2-1 shows the process for Lucky Seven.

TABLE 2-1 Building the Lucky Seven Program

Programming Step	Number of Items
1. Create the user interface.	7 objects
2. Set the properties.	13 properties
3. Write the program code.	2 objects

Creating the User Interface

In this exercise, you'll start building Lucky Seven by first creating a new project and then using controls in the Toolbox to construct the user interface.

Create a new project

1. Start Visual Studio 2010.

2. On the Visual Studio File menu, click New Project.

> **Tip** You can also start a new programming project by clicking the blue New Project link on the Start Page.

The New Project dialog box opens, as shown on the following page.

The New Project dialog box provides access to the major project types available for writing Windows and Web applications. If you indicated during setup that you are a Visual Basic programmer, Visual Basic is your primary development option (as shown here), but the other languages in Visual Studio (Visual C#, Visual C++, and Visual F#) are always available through this dialog box. Although you will select a basic Windows

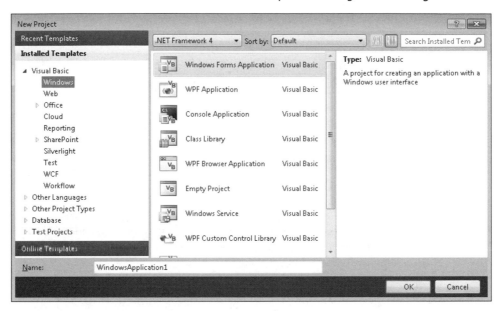

application project in this exercise, this dialog box is also the gateway to other types of development projects, such as a Web application, console application, Microsoft Office add-in, Windows Azure Cloud Service, Silverlight application, or Visual Studio deployment project.

Near the top of the New Project dialog box, you will notice a drop-down list box. This feature allows you to specify the version of the Microsoft .NET Framework that your application will target. This feature is sometimes called *multi-targeting*, meaning that through it, you can select the target environment that your program will run on. For example, if you retain the default selection of .NET Framework 4, any computer that your application will run on must have .NET Framework 4 installed. (Not to worry—the .NET Framework is usually installed as part of the operating system installation, or when you install a new Visual Basic program that you have written.) Unless you have a specific need, you can just leave this drop-down list at its default setting of .NET Framework 4. Visual Basic 2010 Express does not include this drop-down list. You'll learn more about the .NET Framework in Chapter 5, "Visual Basic Variables and Formulas, and the .NET Framework."

3. Click the Windows Forms Application icon in the central Templates area of the dialog box, if it is not already selected.

Visual Studio prepares the development environment for Visual Basic Windows application programming.

4. In the Name text box, type **MyLucky7**.

   Visual Studio assigns the name MyLucky7 to your project. (You'll specify a folder location for the project later.) I'm recommending the "My" prefix here so you don't confuse your new application with the Lucky7 project I've created for you on disk.

> **Tip** If your New Project dialog box contains Location and Solution Name text boxes, you need to specify a folder location and solution name for your new programming project now. The presence of these text boxes is controlled by a check box in the Project And Solutions category of the Options dialog box, but it is not the default setting. (You display this dialog box by clicking the Options command on the Tools menu.) Throughout this book, you will be instructed to save your projects (or discard them) *after* you have completed the programming exercise. For more information about this "delayed saving" feature and default settings, see the section entitled "Customizing IDE Settings to Match Step-by-Step Exercises" in Chapter 1.

5. Click OK to create the new project in Visual Studio.

   Visual Studio cleans the slate for a new programming project and displays the blank Windows form that you will use to build your user interface.

Now you'll enlarge the form and create the two buttons in the interface.

Create the user interface

1. Point to the lower-right corner of the form until the mouse pointer changes to a resizing pointer, and then drag to increase the size of the form to make room for the objects in your program.

   As you resize the form, scroll bars might appear in the Designer to give you access to the entire form you're creating. Depending on your screen resolution and the Visual Studio tools you have open, you might not be able to see the entire form at once. Don't worry about this—your form can be small, or it can fill the entire screen because the scroll bars give you access to the entire form.

   Size your form so that it is about the size of the form shown on the following page. If you want to match my example exactly, you can use the width and height dimensions (485 pixels × 278 pixels) shown in the lower-right corner of the screen.

   To see the entire form without obstruction, you can resize or close the other programming tools, as you learned in Chapter 1. (Return to Chapter 1 if you have questions about resizing windows or tools.)

   Now you'll practice adding a button object on the form.

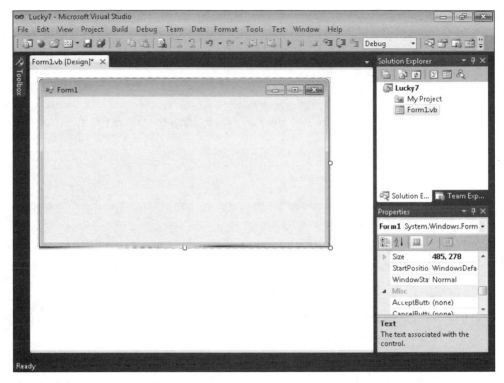

2. Click the Toolbox tab to display the Toolbox window in the IDE.

    The Toolbox contains all the controls that you'll use to build Visual Basic programs in this book. The controls suitable for creating a Windows application are visible now because you selected the Windows Application project type earlier. Controls are organized by type, and by default the Common Controls category is visible. (If the Toolbox is not visible now, click Toolbox on the View menu to display it.)

3. Double-click the *Button* control in the Toolbox, and then move the mouse pointer away from the Toolbox.

    Visual Studio creates a default-sized button object on the form and hides the Toolbox, as shown here:

The button is named *Button1* because it is the first button in the program. (You should make a mental note of this button name—you'll see it again when you write your program code.) The new button object is selected and enclosed by resize handles. When Visual Basic is in *design mode* (that is, whenever the Visual Studio IDE is active), you can move objects on the form by dragging them with the mouse, and you can resize them by using the resize handles. While a program is running, however, the user can't move user interface (UI) elements unless you've changed a property in the program to allow this. You'll practice moving and resizing the button now.

Move and resize a button

1. Point to the button so that the pointer changes to a four-headed arrow, and then drag the button down and to the right.

   The button moves across the surface of the form. If you move the object near the edge of the form or another object (if other objects are present), it automatically aligns itself to a hidden grid when it is an inch or so away. A little blue "snapline" also appears to help you gauge the distance of this object from the edge of the form or the other object. The grid is not displayed on the form by default, but you can use the snapline to judge distances with almost the same effect.

2. Position the mouse pointer on the lower-right corner of the button.

   When the mouse pointer rests on a resize handle of a selected object, it becomes a resizing pointer. You can use the resizing pointer to change the size of an object.

3. Enlarge the button by dragging the pointer down and to the right.

   When you release the mouse button, the button changes size and snaps to the grid.

4. Use the resizing pointer to return the button to its original size.

Now you'll add a second button to the form, below the first button.

Add a second button

1. Click the Toolbox tab to display the Toolbox.

2. Click the *Button* control in the Toolbox (single-click this time), and then move the mouse pointer over the form.

   The mouse pointer changes to crosshairs and a button icon. The crosshairs are designed to help you draw the rectangular shape of the button on the form, and you can use this method as an alternative to double-clicking to create a control of the default size.

3. Click and drag the pointer down and to the right. Release the mouse button to complete the button, and watch it snap to the form.

4. Resize the button object so that it is the same size as the first button, and then move it below the first button on the form. (Use the snapline feature to help you.)

 Tip At any time, you can delete an object and start over again by selecting the object on the form and then pressing DELETE. Feel free to create and delete objects to practice creating your user interface.

Now you'll add the labels used to display the numbers in the program. A *label* is a special user interface element designed to display text, numbers, or symbols when a program runs. When the user clicks the Lucky Seven program's Spin button, three random numbers appear in the label boxes. If one of the numbers is a 7, the user wins.

Add the number labels

1. Double-click the *Label* control in the Toolbox.

   Visual Studio creates a label object on the form. The label object is just large enough to hold the text contained in the object (it is rather small now), but it can be resized.

2. Drag the *Label1* object to the right of the two button objects.

   Your form looks something like this:

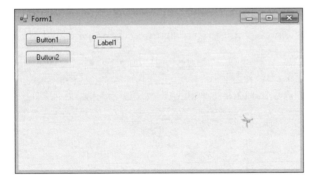

3. Double-click the *Label* control in the Toolbox to create a second label object.

   This label object will be named *Label2* in the program.

4. Double-click the *Label* control again to create a third label object.

5. Move the second and third label objects to the right of the first one on the form.

   Allow plenty of space between the three labels because you will use them to display large numbers when the program runs.

   Now you'll use the *Label* control to add a descriptive label to your form. This will be the fourth and final label in the program.

6. Double-click the *Label* control in the Toolbox.

7. Drag the *Label4* object below the two command buttons.

When you've finished, your four labels should look like those in the following screen shot. (You can move your label objects if they don't look quite right.)

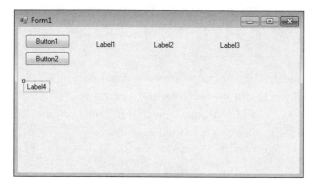

Now you'll add a picture box to the form to graphically display the payout you'll receive when you draw a 7 and hit the jackpot. A *picture box* is designed to display bitmaps, icons, digital photos, and other artwork in a program. One of the best uses for a picture box is to display a JPEG image file.

Add a picture

1. Click the *PictureBox* control in the Toolbox.

2. Using the control's drawing pointer, create a large rectangular box below the second and third labels on the form.

Leave a little space below the labels for their size to grow as I mentioned earlier. When you've finished, your picture box object looks similar to this:

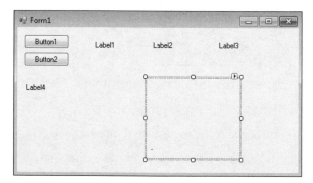

This object will be named *PictureBox1* in your program; you'll use this name later in the program code.

Now you're ready to customize your interface by setting a few properties.

Setting the Properties

As you discovered in Chapter 1, you can change properties by selecting objects on the form and changing their settings in the Properties window. You'll start by changing the property settings for the two buttons.

Set the button properties

1. Click the first button (*Button1*) on the form.

   The button is selected and is surrounded by resize handles.

2. Click the Properties window title bar.

   > **Tip** If the Properties window isn't visible, click the Properties Window command on the View menu, or press F4.

3. At the top of the Properties window, click the Categorized button.

   For information about categorized properties, see the section entitled "The Properties Window" in Chapter 1.

4. Resize the Properties window (if necessary) so that there is plenty of room to see the property names and their current settings.

   Once you get used to setting properties, you will probably use the Properties window without enlarging it, but making it bigger helps when you first try to use it. The Properties window in the following screen shot is a good size for setting properties:

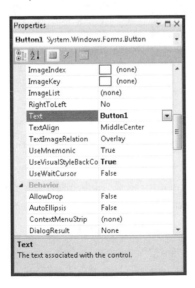

The Properties window lists the settings for the first button. These include settings for the background color, text, font height, and width of the button. Because there are so many properties, Visual Studio organizes them into categories and displays them in outline view. If you want to see the properties in a category, click the arrow sign (>) next to the category title.

5. If it is not already visible, scroll in the Properties window until you see the *Text* property located in the Appearance category.

6. Double-click the *Text* property in the first column of the Properties window.

The current *Text* setting ("Button1") is highlighted in the Properties window.

7. Type **Spin**, and then press ENTER.

The *Text* property changes to "Spin" in the Properties window and on the button on the form. Now you'll change the *Text* property of the second button to "End." (You'll select the second button in a new way this time.)

8. Open the Object list at the top of the Properties window.

A list of the interface objects in your program appears as follows:

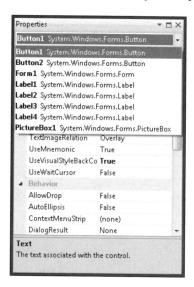

9. Click Button2 System.Windows.Forms.Button (the second button) in the list box.

The property settings for the second button appear in the Properties window, and Visual Studio highlights Button2 on the form.

10. Double-click the current *Text* property ("Button2"), type **End**, and then press ENTER.

The text of the second button changes to "End."

Tip Using the Object list is a handy way to switch between objects in your program. You can also switch between objects on the form by clicking each object.

Now you'll set the properties for the labels in the program. The first three labels will hold the random numbers generated by the program and will have identical property settings. (You'll set most of them as a group.) The descriptive label settings will be slightly different.

Set the number label properties

1. Click the first number label (*Label1*), hold down the SHIFT key, click the second and third number labels, and then release the SHIFT key. (If the Properties window is in the way, move it to a new place.)

   A selection rectangle and resize handles appear around each label you click. You'll change the *TextAlign*, *BorderStyle*, and *Font* properties now so that the numbers that will appear in the labels will be centered, boxed, and identical in font and font size. (All these properties are located in the Appearance category of the Properties window.) You'll also set the *AutoSize* property to False so that you can change the size of the labels according to your precise specifications. (The *AutoSize* property is located in the Layout category.)

Tip When more than one object is selected, only those properties that can be changed for the group are displayed in the Properties window.

2. Click the *AutoSize* property in the Properties window, and then click the arrow that appears in the second column.

3. Set the *AutoSize* property to False so that you can size the labels manually.

4. Click the *TextAlign* property, and then click the arrow that appears in the second column.

   A graphical assortment of alignment options appears in the list box; you can use these settings to align text anywhere within the borders of the label object.

5. Click the center option (MiddleCenter).

   The *TextAlign* property for each of the selected labels changes to MiddleCenter.

6. Click the *BorderStyle* property, and then click the arrow that appears in the second column.

   The valid property settings (None, FixedSingle, and Fixed3D) appear in the list box.

7. Click FixedSingle in the list box to add a thin border around each label.

8. Click the *Font* property, and then click the ellipsis button (the button with three dots that's located next to the current font setting).

   The Font dialog box opens.

9. Change the font to Times New Roman, the font style to Bold, and the font size to 24, and then click OK.

   The label text appears in the font, style, and size you specified.

   Now you'll set the text for the three labels to the number 0—a good "placeholder" for the numbers that will eventually fill these boxes in your game. (Because the program produces the actual numbers, you could also delete the text, but putting a placeholder here gives you something to base the size of the labels on.)

10. Click a blank area on the form to remove the selection from the three labels, and then click the first label.

11. Double-click the *Text* property, type **0**, and then press ENTER.

    The text of the *Label1* object is set to 0. You'll use program code to set this property to a random "slot machine" number later in this chapter.

12. Change the text in the second and third labels on the form to **0** also.

13. Move and resize the labels now so that they are appropriately spaced.

    Your form looks something like this:

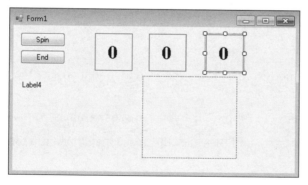

Now you'll change the *Text*, *Font*, and *ForeColor* properties of the fourth label.

Set the descriptive label properties

1. Click the fourth label object (*Label4*) on the form.

2. Change the *Text* property in the Properties window to **Lucky Seven**.

3. Click the *Font* property, and then click the ellipsis button.

4. Use the Font dialog box to change the font to Arial, the font style to Bold, and the font size to 18. Then click OK.

   The font in the *Label4* object is updated, and the label is resized automatically to hold the larger font size because the object's *AutoSize* property is set to True.

5. Click the *ForeColor* property in the Properties window, and then click the arrow in the second column.

Visual Studio displays a list box with Custom, Web, and System tabs for setting the foreground colors (the color of text) of the label object. The Custom tab offers many of the colors available in your system. The Web tab sets colors for Web pages and lets you pick colors using their common names. The System tab displays the current colors used for user interface elements in your system.

6. Click the purple color on the Custom tab.

The text in the label box changes to purple.

Now you're ready to set the properties for the last object.

The Picture Box Properties

When the person playing your game hits the jackpot (that is, when at least one 7 appears in the number labels on the form), the picture box object will contain a picture in JPEG format of a person dispensing money. (I am supplying you with this digitized image, but you can substitute your own if you like.) You need to set the *SizeMode* property to accurately size the picture and set the *Image* property to specify the name of the JPEG file that you will load into the picture box. You also need to set the *Visible* property, which specifies the picture state at the beginning of the program.

Set the picture box properties

1. Click the picture box object on the form.

2. Click the *SizeMode* property in the Properties window (listed in the Behavior category), click the arrow in the second column, and then click StretchImage.

Setting *SizeMode* to StretchImage before you open a graphic causes Visual Studio to resize the graphic to the exact dimensions of the picture box. (Typically, you set this property before you set the *Image* property.)

3. Click the *Image* property in the Properties window, and then click the ellipsis button in the second column.

The Select Resource dialog box opens.

4. Click the Local Resource radio button, and then click the Import button.

5. In the Open dialog box, navigate to the C:\Vb10sbs\Chap02 folder.

This folder contains the digital photo PayCoins.jpg.

6. Select PayCoins.jpg, and then click Open.

An screen shot of one person paying another appears in the Select Resource dialog box. (The letter "W" represents winning.)

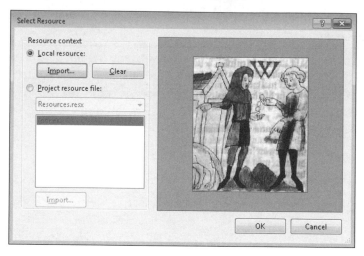

7. Click OK.

The PayCoins photo is loaded into the picture box. Because the photo is relatively small (24 KB), it opens quickly on the form.

8. Resize the picture box object now to fix any distortion problems that you see in the image.

I sized my picture box object to be 144 pixels wide by 146 pixels high. You can match this size by using the width and height dimensions located on the lower-right side of the Visual Studio IDE. (The dimensions of the selected object are given on the lower-right side, and the location on the form of the object's upper-left corner is given to the left of the dimensions.)

This particular image displays best when the picture box object retains a square shape.

> **Note** As you look at the picture box object, you might notice a tiny shortcut arrow called a *smart tag* near its upper-right corner. This smart tag is a button that you can click to quickly change a few common picture box settings and open the Select Resource dialog box. (You'll see the smart tag again in Chapter 4, "Working with Menus, Toolbars, and Dialog Boxes," when you use the *ToolStrip* control.)

Now you'll change the *Visible* property to False so that the image will be invisible when the program starts.

9. Click the *Visible* property in the Behavior category of the Properties window, and then click the arrow in the second column.

The valid settings for the *Visible* property appear in a list box.

10. Click False to make the picture invisible when the program starts.

Setting the *Visible* property to False affects the picture box when the program runs, but not now, while you're designing it. Your completed form looks similar to this:

Tip You can also double-click property names that have True and False settings (so-called Boolean properties), to toggle back and forth between True and False. Default Boolean properties are shown in regular type, and changed settings appear in bold.

11. You are finished setting properties for now, so if your Properties window is floating, hold down the CTRL key and double-click its title bar to return it to the docked position.

Reading Properties in Tables

In this chapter, you've set the properties for the Lucky Seven program step by step. In future chapters, the instructions to set properties will be presented in table format unless a setting is especially tricky. Table 2-2 lists the properties you've set so far in the Lucky Seven program, as they'd look later in the book. Settings you need to type in are shown in quotation marks. You shouldn't type the quotation marks.

TABLE 2-2 Lucky Seven Properties

Object	Property	Setting
Button1	*Text*	"Spin"
Button2	*Text*	"End"
Label1, Label2, Label3	*AutoSize*	False
	BorderStyle	FixedSingle
	Font	Times New Roman, Bold, 24-point
	Text	"0"
	TextAlign	MiddleCenter
Label4	*Text*	"Lucky Seven"
	Font	Arial, Bold, 18-point
	ForeColor	Purple
PictureBox1	*Image*	"C:\Vb10sbs\Chap02\Paycoins.jpg"
	SizeMode	StretchImage
	Visible	False

Writing the Code

Now you're ready to write the code for the Lucky Seven program. Because most of the objects you've created already "know" how to work when the program runs, they're ready to receive input from the user and process it. The inherent functionality of objects is one of the great strengths of Visual Studio and Visual Basic—after objects are placed on a form and their properties are set, they're ready to run without any additional programming. However, the "meat" of the Lucky Seven game—the code that actually calculates random numbers, displays them in boxes, and detects a jackpot—is still missing from the program. This computing logic can be built into the application only by using program statements—code that clearly spells out what the program should do at each step of the way. Because the Spin and End buttons drive the program, you'll associate the code for the game with those buttons. You enter and edit Visual Basic program statements in the Code Editor.

In the following steps, you'll enter the program code for Lucky Seven in the Code Editor.

Use the Code Editor

1. Double-click the End button on the form.

   The Code Editor appears as a tabbed document window in the center of the Visual Studio IDE, as shown here:

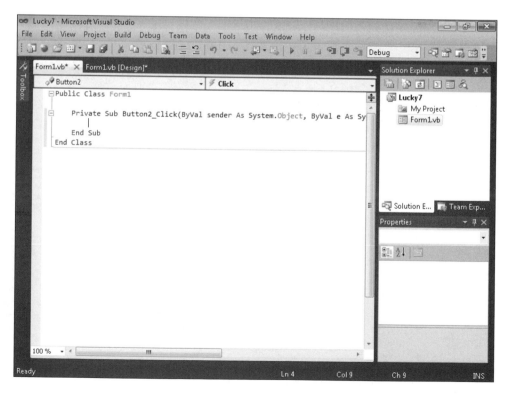

Inside the Code Editor are program statements associated with the current form. Program statements that are used together to perform some action are typically grouped in a programming construct called a *procedure*. A common type of procedure is a Sub procedure, sometimes called a *subroutine*. Sub procedures include a *Sub* keyword in the first line and end with *End Sub*. (I'll talk about the Public and Private keywords later.) Procedures are typically executed when certain events occur, such as when a button is clicked. When a procedure is associated with a particular object and an event, it is called an *event handler* or an *event procedure*.

When you double-clicked the End button (*Button2*), Visual Studio automatically added the first and last lines of the *Button2_Click* event procedure, as the following code shows. (The first line was wrapped to stay within the book margins.) You may notice other bits of code in the Code Editor (words like *Public* and *Class*), which Visual Studio has added to define important characteristics of the form, but I won't emphasize them here.

```
Private Sub Button2_Click(ByVal sender As System.Object, _
   ByVal e As System.EventArgs) Handles Button2.Click
End Sub
```

The body of a procedure fits between these lines and is executed whenever a user activates the interface element associated with the procedure. In this case, the event is a mouse click, but as you'll see later in the book, it could also be a different type of event.

2.   Type **End**, and then press the ENTER key.

When you type the statement, Visual Studio recognizes *End* as a unique reserved word or *keyword* and displays it in a list box with Common and All tabs. Microsoft calls this auto-extend feature IntelliSense because it tries to intelligently help you write code, and you can browse through various Visual Basic keywords and objects alphabetically. (In this way, the language is partially discoverable through the IDE itself.)

After you press the ENTER key, the letters in *End* turn blue and are indented, indicating that Visual Basic recognizes *End* as one of several hundred unique keywords within the Visual Basic language. You use the *End* keyword to stop your program and remove it from the screen. In this case, *End* is also a complete *program statement*, a self-contained instruction executed by the *Visual Basic compiler*, the part of Visual Studio that processes or *parses* each line of Visual Basic *source code*, combining the result with other resources to create an executable file. Program statements are a little like complete sentences in a human language—statements can be of varying lengths but must follow the grammatical "rules" of the compiler. In Visual Studio, program statements can be composed of keywords, properties, object names, variables, numbers, special symbols, and other values. You'll learn more about how program statements are constructed in Chapter 5.

As you enter program statements and make other edits, the Code Editor handles many of the formatting details for you, including adjusting indentation and spacing and adding any necessary parentheses. The exact spelling, order, and spacing of items within program statements is referred to as *statement syntax*. In the early days of compilers, programmers were almost totally responsible for getting the precise syntax for each program statement correct on their own, but now sophisticated development tools such as Visual Studio help immensely with the construction of accurate program statements.

When you pressed the ENTER key, the *End* statement was indented to set it apart from the *Private Sub* and *End Sub* statements. This indenting scheme is one of the programming conventions you'll see throughout this book to keep your programs clear and readable. The group of conventions regarding how code is organized in a program is often referred to as *program style*.

Now that you've written the code associated with the End button, you'll write code for the Spin button. These program statements will be a little more extensive and will give you a chance to learn more about statement syntax and program style. You'll study many of the program statements later in this book, so you don't need to know everything about them now. Just focus on the general structure of the code and on typing the program statements exactly as they are printed.

Write code for the Spin button

1. At the top of the Solution Explorer window, click the View Designer button in the Solution Explorer window to display your form again.

> **Note** When the Code Editor is visible, you won't be able to see the form you're working on. The View Designer button is one mechanism you can use to display it again. (If more than one form is loaded in Solution Explorer, click the form that you want to display first.) You can also click the Form1.vb [Design] tab at the top edge of the Code Editor. To display the Code Editor again, click the View Code button in Solution Explorer.

2. Double-click the Spin button.

   After a few moments, the Code Editor appears, and an event procedure associated with the *Button1* button appears near the *Button2* event procedure.

   Although you changed the text of this button to "Spin," its name in the program is still *Button1*. (The name and the text of an interface element can be different to suit the needs of the programmer.) Each object can have several procedures associated with it, one for each event it recognizes. The click event is the one you're interested in now because users will click the Spin and End buttons when they run the program.

3. Type the following program lines between the *Private Sub* and *End Sub* statements. Press ENTER after each line, press TAB to indent, and take care to type the program statements exactly as they appear here. (The Code Editor will scroll to the left as you enter the longer lines.) If you make a mistake (usually identified by a jagged underline), delete the incorrect statements and try again.

> **Tip** As you enter the program code, Visual Basic formats the text and displays different parts of the program in color to help you identify the various elements. When you begin to type a property, Visual Basic also displays the available properties for the object you're using in a list box, so you can double-click the property or keep typing to enter it yourself. If Visual Basic displays an error message, you might have misspelled a program statement. Check the line against the text in this book, make the necessary correction, and continue typing. (You can also delete a line and type it from scratch.) In addition, Visual Basic might add necessary code automatically. For example, when you type the following code, Visual Basic automatically adds the *End If* line. Readers of previous editions of this book have found this first typing exercise to be the toughest part of this chapter—"But Mr. Halvorson, I know I typed it just as you wrote it!"—so please give this program code your closest attention. I promise you, it works!

```
PictureBox1.Visible = False  ' hide picture
Label1.Text = CStr(Int(Rnd() * 10))  ' pick numbers
Label2.Text = CStr(Int(Rnd() * 10))
Label3.Text = CStr(Int(Rnd() * 10))
' if any number is 7 display picture and beep
If (Label1.Text = "7") Or (Label2.Text = "7") _
Or (Label3.Text = "7") Then
    PictureBox1.Visible = True
    Beep()
End If
```

When you've finished, the Code Editor looks as shown in the following screen shot:

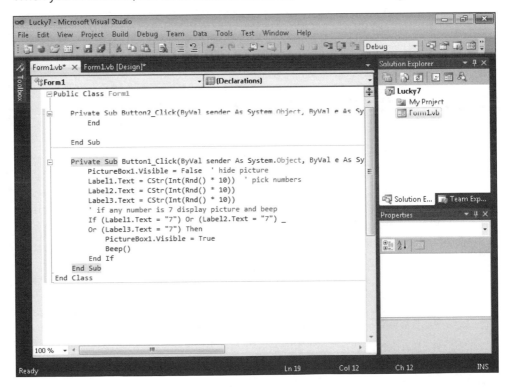

4. Click the Save All command on the File menu to save your additions to the program.

   The Save All command saves everything in your project—the project file, the form file, any code modules, and other related components in your application. Since this is the first time that you have saved your project, the Save Project dialog box opens, prompting you for the name and location of the project. (If your copy of Visual Studio is configured to prompt you for a location when you first create your project, you won't see the Save Project dialog box now—Visual Studio just saves your changes.)

5. Browse and select a location for your files.

   I recommend that you use the C:\Vb10sbs\Chap02 folder (the location of the book's sample files), but the location is up to you. Since you used the "My" prefix when you originally opened your project, this version won't overwrite the Lucky7 practice file that I built for you on disk.

6. Clear the Create Directory For Solution check box.

   When this check box is selected, it creates a second folder for your program's solution files, which is not necessary for solutions that contain only one project (the situation for most programs in this book).

7. Click Save to save your files.

 Note If you want to save just the item you are currently working on (the form, the code module, or something else), you can use the Save command on the File menu. If you want to save the current item with a different name, you can use the Save As command.

A Look at the *Button1_Click* Procedure

The *Button1_Click* procedure is executed when the user clicks the Spin button on the form. The procedure uses some pretty complicated statements, and because I haven't formally introduced them yet, it might look a little confusing. However, if you take a closer look, you'll probably see a few things that look familiar. Taking a peek at the contents of these procedures will give you a feel for the type of program code you'll be creating later in this book. (If you'd rather not stop for this preview, feel free to skip to the next section, "Running Visual Basic Applications.")

The *Button1_Click* procedure performs three tasks:

- It hides the digital photo.
- It creates three random numbers for the number labels.
- It displays the photo when the number 7 appears.

Let's look at each of these steps individually.

Hiding the photo is accomplished with the following line:

```
PictureBox1.Visible = False   ' hide picture
```

This line is made up of two parts: a program statement and a comment.

The *PictureBox1.Visible = False* program statement sets the *Visible* property of the picture box object (*PictureBox1*) to False (one of two possible settings). You might remember that you set this property to False once before by using the Properties window. You're doing it again now in the program code because the first task is a spin and you need to clear away a photo that might have been displayed in a previous game. Because the property will be changed at run time and not at design time, you must set the property by using program code. This is a handy feature of Visual Basic, and I'll talk about it more in Chapter 3, "Working with Toolbox Controls."

The second part of the first line (the part displayed in green type on your screen) is called a *comment*. Comments are explanatory notes included in program code following a single quotation mark ('). Programmers use comments to describe how important statements work in a program. These notes aren't processed by Visual Basic when the program runs; they exist only to document what the program does. You'll want to use comments often when you write Visual Basic programs to leave an easy-to-understand record of what you're doing.

The next three lines handle the random number computations. Does this concept sound strange? You can actually make Visual Basic generate unpredictable numbers within specific guidelines—in other words, you can create random numbers for lottery contests, dice games, or other statistical patterns. The *Rnd* function in each line creates a random number between 0 and 1 (a number with a decimal point and several decimal places), and the *Int* function returns the integer portion of the result of multiplying the random number by 10. This computation creates random numbers between 0 and 9 in the program—just what you need for this particular slot machine application.

```
Label1.Text = CStr(Int(Rnd() * 10))   ' pick numbers
```

You then need to jump through a little hoop in your code. You need to copy these random numbers into the three label boxes on the form, but first the numbers need to be converted to text with the *CStr* (convert to string) function. Notice how *CStr*, *Int*, and *Rnd* are all connected in the program statement—they work collectively to produce a result like a mathematical formula. After the computation and conversion, the values are assigned to the *Text* properties of the first three labels on the form, and the assignment causes the numbers to be displayed in bold, 24-point, Times New Roman font in the three number labels.

The last group of statements in the program checks whether any of the random numbers is 7. If one or more of them is, the program displays the graphical depiction of a payout, and a beep announces the winnings.

```
' if any number is 7 display picture and beep
If (Label1.Text = "7") Or (Label2.Text = "7") _
Or (Label3.Text = "7") Then
    PictureBox1.Visible = True
    Beep()
End If
```

Each time the user clicks the Spin button, the *Button1_Click* procedure is executed, or *called*, and the program statements in the procedure are run again.

Running Visual Basic Applications

Congratulations! You're ready to run your first real program. To run a Visual Basic program from the development environment, you can do any of the following:

- Click Start Debugging on the Debug menu.
- Click the Start Debugging button on the Standard toolbar.
- Press F5.

Try running your Lucky Seven program now. If Visual Basic displays an error message, you might have a typing mistake or two in your program code. Try to fix it by comparing the printed version in this book with the one you typed, or load Lucky7 from your hard disk and run it.

Run the Lucky Seven program

1. Click the Start Debugging button on the Standard toolbar.

   The Lucky Seven program compiles and runs in the IDE. After a few seconds, the user interface appears, just as you designed it.

2. Click the Spin button.

   The program picks three random numbers and displays them in the labels on the form, as follows:

Because a 7 appears in the first label box, the digital photo depicting the payoff appears, and the computer beeps. You win! (The sound you hear depends on your Default Beep setting in the Sound Control Panel. To make this game sound really cool, change the Default Beep sound to something more dynamic.)

3. Click the Spin button 15 or 16 more times, watching the results of the spins in the number boxes.

   About half the time you spin, you hit the jackpot—pretty easy odds. (The actual odds are about 2.8 times out of 10; you're just lucky at first.) Later on, you might want to make the game tougher by displaying the photo only when two or three 7s appear, or by creating a running total of winnings.

4. When you've finished experimenting with your new creation, click the End button.

   The program stops, and the development environment reappears on your screen.

> **Tip** If you run this program again, you might notice that Lucky Seven displays exactly the same sequence of random numbers. There is nothing wrong here—the Visual Basic *Rnd* function was designed to display a *repeating* sequence of numbers at first so that you can properly test your code using output that can be reproduced again and again. To create truly "random" numbers, use the *Randomize* function in your code, as shown in the exercise at the end of this chapter. The .NET Framework, which you'll learn to use later, also supplies random number functions.

Sample Projects on Disk

If you didn't build the MyLucky7 project from scratch (or if you did build the project and want to compare what you created to what I built for you as I wrote the chapter), take a moment to open and run the completed Lucky7 project, which is located in the C:\Vb10sbs\Chap02\Lucky7 folder on your hard disk (the default location for the practice files for this chapter). If you need a refresher course on opening projects, see the detailed instructions in Chapter 1. If you are asked if you want to save changes to the MyLucky7 project, be sure to click Save.

This book is a step-by-step tutorial, so you will benefit most from building the projects on your own and experimenting with them. But after you have completed the projects, it is often a good idea to compare what you have with the practice file "solution" that I provide, especially if you run into trouble. To make this easy, I will give you the name of the solution files on disk before you run the completed program in most of the step-by-step exercises.

After you have compared the MyLucky7 project to the Lucky7 solution files on disk, reopen MyLucky7 and prepare to compile it as an executable file. If you didn't create MyLucky7, use my solution file to complete the exercise.

Building an Executable File

Your last task in this chapter is to complete the development process and create an application for Windows, or an *executable file*. (Had you created a different project type, of course, such as a Web application, the result of your development efforts would have been a different type of file—but we'll discuss this later.) Windows applications created with Visual Studio have the file name extension .exe and can be run on any system that contains Windows and the necessary support files. (Visual Basic installs these support files—including the .NET Framework files—automatically.) If you plan to distribute your applications, see the section entitled "Deploying Your Application" later in the chapter.

At this point, you need to know that Visual Studio can create two types of executable files for your Windows application project: a debug build and a release build.

Debug builds are created automatically by Visual Studio when you create and test your program. They are stored in a folder called Bin\Debug within your project folder. The debug executable file contains debugging information that makes the program run slightly slower.

Release builds are optimized executable files stored in the Bin\Release folder within your project. To customize the settings for your release build, you click the [*ProjectName*] Properties command on the Project menu, and then click the Compile tab, where you see a list of compilation options that looks like this:

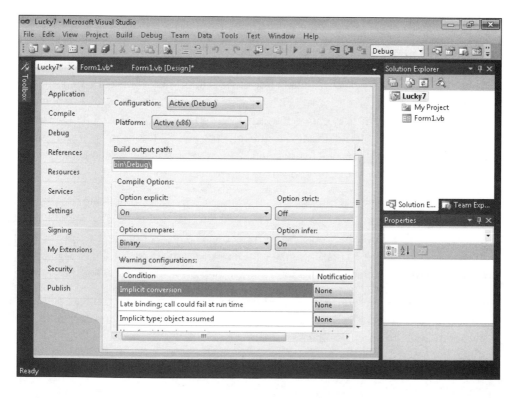

Try creating a release build named MyLucky7.exe now.

Create an executable file

1. On the Build menu, click the Build MyLucky7 command.

   The Build command creates a Bin\Release folder in which to store your project (if the folder doesn't already exist) and compiles the source code in your project. The result is an executable file of the Application type named MyLucky7.exe. To save you time, Visual Studio often creates temporary executable files while you develop your application; however, it's always a good idea to recompile your application manually with the Build or Rebuild command when you reach an important milestone.

   Try running this program outside the Visual Studio IDE now from the Windows Start menu.

2. On the Windows taskbar, click Start.

   The next command depends on the version of Windows you're using.

3. If you have Windows 7 or Windows Vista, type **run** in the Search text box and press ENTER to open the Run dialog box. If you have Windows XP or earlier, click the Run command to open the Run dialog box.

4. Click Browse and then navigate to the C:\Vb10sbs\Chap02\Mylucky7\Bin\Release folder.

5. Click the MyLucky7.exe application icon, click Open, and then click OK.

   The Lucky Seven program loads and runs in Windows. Because this is a simple test application and it does not possess a formal publisher certificate that emphasizes its reliability or authenticity, you may see the following message: "The publisher could not be verified. Are you sure you want to run this software?" If this happens to you, click Yes to run the program anyway. (Creating such certificates is beyond the scope of this chapter, but this program is quite safe.)

6. Click Spin a few times to verify the operation of the game, and then click End.

> **Tip** You can also run Windows applications, including compiled Visual Basic programs, by opening Windows Explorer and double-clicking the executable file. To create a shortcut icon for MyLucky7.exe on the Windows desktop, right-click the Windows desktop, point to New, and then click Shortcut. When you're prompted for the location of your application file, click Browse, and select the MyLucky7.exe executable file. Click the OK, Next, and Finish buttons. Windows places an icon on the desktop that you can double-click to run your program.

7. On the File menu, click Exit to close Visual Studio and the MyLucky7 project.

   The Visual Studio development environment closes.

Deploying Your Application

Visual Studio helps you distribute your Visual Basic applications by providing several options for *deployment*—that is, for installing the application on one or more computer systems. Since the release of Visual Studio in 2002, Visual Basic applications have been compiled as assemblies—deployment units consisting of one or more files necessary for the program to run. *Assemblies* contain four elements: Microsoft intermediate language (MSIL) code, metadata, a manifest, and supporting files and resources. Visual Studio 2010 continues to offer this same basic deployment architecture, with some noteworthy improvements for different platforms and application types.

How do assemblies actually work? First, assemblies are so comprehensive and self-describing that Visual Studio applications don't actually need to be formally registered with the operating system to run. This means that theoretically a Visual Basic 2010 application can be installed by simply copying the assembly for the program to a second computer that has the correct version of the .NET Framework installed—a process called *XCOPY installation*, after the MS-DOS XCOPY command that copies a complete directory (folder) structure from one location to another. In practice, however, it isn't practical to deploy Visual Basic applications by using a copy procedure such as XCOPY (via the command prompt) or Windows Explorer. For commercial applications, an installation program with a graphical user interface is usually preferred, and it's often desirable to register the program with the operating system so that it can be uninstalled later by using Control Panel. In addition, it is often useful to take advantage of the Web for an application's initial deployment and to have an application check the Web periodically for updates.

Although the advanced options related to deployment and security go beyond the scope of this book, you should be familiar with your deployment options. To manage the deployment process, Visual Studio 2010 supports two deployment technologies, *ClickOnce* and *Windows Installer*.

Essentially, ClickOnce is a robust Web-based publishing technology that allows you to control how applications are made available to users via the Internet, although ClickOnce installations can also be distributed via CD-ROM. With ClickOnce, you can create an installation service for Windows applications, Office solutions, or console applications that users can access on their own with minimal interaction. With ClickOnce, you can specify prerequisites, such as a particular version of the .NET Framework, and you can easily publish updates on a Web page or a network file share to make improvements to your program. You can get started with ClickOnce at any time by using the Publish command on the Build menu. And you can control how ClickOnce works by setting properties using the Properties command on the Project menu. (Click the Publish tab in the Project Designer for specific features.)

Windows Installer is a more classic installation process. In Visual Studio, you add a setup or a Windows Installer project to your solution, which automatically creates a setup program for the application. The installer package is distributed to your users, and individual users run the setup file and work through a wizard to install the application. The setup project can be customized to allow for different methods of installation, such as from CD-ROMs or Web servers. You can get started with Windows Installer by using the New Project command on the File menu to create a custom setup project. (Select the Setup And Deployment\Visual Studio Installer option under Other Project Types to see the list of available setup projects.)

Whether you choose ClickOnce or Windows Installer, you'll find that Visual Studio 2010 has brought many improvements to the installation process, and these technologies will directly benefit you and your customers. For additional information, see the online Help documentation related to the installation option that you want to use.

One Step Further: Adding to a Program

You can restart Visual Studio at any time and work on a programming project you've stored on disk. You'll restart Visual Studio now and add a *Randomize* statement to the Lucky Seven program.

Reload Lucky Seven

1. On the Windows taskbar, click Start, click All Programs, click Microsoft Visual Studio 2010, and then click the Microsoft Visual Studio 2010 program icon (or the Microsoft Visual Basic 2010 Express program icon, if you're using Visual Basic 2010 Express).

   A list of the projects that you've most recently worked on appears on the Visual Studio Start Page in the Recent Project pane. Because you just finished working with Lucky Seven, the MyLucky7 project should be first on the list.

2. Click the MyLucky7 link to open the Lucky Seven project.

   The Lucky Seven program opens, and the MyLucky7 form appears. (If you don't see the form, click Form1.vb in Solution Explorer, and then click the View Designer button.)

   Now you'll add the *Randomize* statement to the *Form_Load* procedure, a special procedure that is associated with the form and that is executed each time the program is started.

3. Double-click the form (not one of the objects) to display the *Form_Load* procedure.

   The *Form_Load* procedure appears in the Code Editor, as shown here:

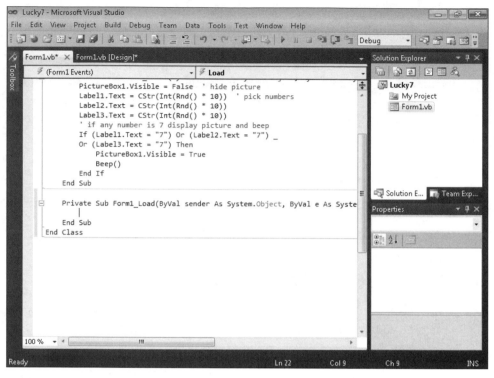

4. Type **Randomize**, and then press ENTER.

   The *Randomize* statement is added to the program and will be executed each time
   the program starts. *Randomize* uses the system clock to create a truly random
   starting point, or *seed*, for the *Rnd* statement used in the *Button1_Click* procedure.
   As I mentioned earlier, without the *Randomize* statement, the Lucky Seven program
   produces the same string of random spins every time you restart the program. With
   Randomize in place, the program spins randomly every time it runs, and the numbers
   don't follow a recognizable pattern.

5. Run the new version of Lucky Seven, and then save the project. If you plan to use the
   new version a lot, you might want to create a new .exe file, too.

6. When you're finished, click Close Project on the File menu.

   The files associated with the Lucky Seven program are closed.

Chapter 2 Quick Reference

To	Do This
Create a user interface	Use Toolbox controls to place objects on your form, and then set the necessary properties. Resize the form and the objects as appropriate.
Move an object	Point to the object, and when a four-headed arrow appears, drag the object.

To	Do This
Resize an object	Click the object to select it, and then drag the resize handle attached to the part of the object you want to resize.
Delete an object	Click the object, and then press DELETE.
Open the Code Editor	Double-click an object on the form (or the form itself). *or* Select a form or a module in Solution Explorer, and then click the View Code button.
Write program code	Type Visual Basic program statements associated with objects in the Code Editor.
Save a program	On the File menu, click the Save All command. *or* Click the Save All button on the Standard toolbar.
Save a form file	Make sure the form is open, and then, on the File menu, click the Save command. *or* Click the Save button on the Standard toolbar.
Create an .exe file	On the Build menu, click the Build or Rebuild command.
Deploy an application by using ClickOnce technology	Click the Publish command on the Build menu, and then use the Publish wizard to specify the location and settings for the application.
Reload a project	On the File menu, click the Open Project command. *or* On the File menu, point to Recent Projects and Solutions, and then click the desired project. *or* Click the project in the recent projects list on the Visual Studio Start Page.

Chapter 3
Working with Toolbox Controls

After completing this chapter, you will be able to:

- Use *TextBox* and *Button* controls to create a Hello World program.

- Use the *DateTimePicker* control to display your birth date.

- Use *CheckBox*, *RadioButton*, and *ListBox* controls to process user input.

- Use the *LinkLabel* control and the *Process.Start* method to display a Web page by using your system's default browser.

As you learned in earlier chapters, Microsoft Visual Studio 2010 controls are the graphical tools you use to build the user interface of a Microsoft Visual Basic program. Controls are located in the development environment's Toolbox, and you use them to create objects on a form with a simple series of mouse clicks and dragging motions.

Windows Forms controls are specifically designed for building Windows applications, and you'll find them organized on the All Windows Forms tab of the Toolbox, although many of the controls are also accessible on tabs such as Common Controls, Containers, and Printing. (You used a few of these controls in the previous chapter.) Among the Common Controls, there are few changes between Visual Basic 2008 and Visual Basic 2010, so if you're really experienced with the last version of Visual Basic, you may simply want to move on to the database and Web application chapters of this book (Part IV), or the detailed material about programming techniques in Parts II and III. However, for most casual Visual Basic users, there is a lot still to learn about the language's extensive collection of Windows Forms Toolbox controls, and we'll work with several of them here.

In this chapter, you'll learn how to display information in a text box; work with date and time information on your system; process user input with *CheckBox*, *RadioButton*, and *ListBox* controls; and display a Web page within a Visual Basic program. The exercises in this chapter will help you design your own Visual Basic applications and will teach you more about objects, properties, and program code. If you are new to Visual Studio and Visual Basic, this chapter will be especially useful.

The Basic Use of Controls: The Hello World Program

A great tradition in introductory programming books is the Hello World program, which demonstrates how the simplest utility can be built and run in a given programming language. In the days of character-based programming, Hello World was usually a two-line or three-line program typed in a program editor and assembled with a stand-alone compiler.

With the advent of complex operating systems and graphical programming tools, however, the typical Hello World has grown into a more sophisticated program containing dozens of lines and requiring several programming tools for its construction. Fortunately, creating a Hello World program is still quite simple with Visual Studio 2010 and Visual Basic. You can construct a complete user interface by creating two objects, setting two properties, and entering one line of code. Give it a try.

Create a Hello World program

1. Start Visual Studio 2010 if it isn't already open.

2. On the File menu, click New Project.

   Visual Studio displays the New Project dialog box, which prompts you for the name of your project and for the template that you want to use.

> **Note** Use the following instructions each time you want to create a new project on your hard disk.

3. Ensure that the Visual Basic Windows category is selected on the left side of the dialog box, and that Windows Forms Application template is also selected in the middle of the dialog box.

   These selections indicate that you'll be building a stand-alone Visual Basic application that will run under Windows.

4. Remove the default project name (WindowsApplication1) from the Name text box, and then type **MyHello**.

> **Note** Throughout this book, I ask you to create sample projects with the "My" prefix, to distinguish your own work from the practice files I include on the companion CD-ROM. However, I'll usually show projects in the Solution Explorer without the "My" prefix (because I've built the projects without it).

   The New Project dialog box now looks like the screen shot at the top of page 69. If you are using Visual Basic 2010 Express, you will just see a Visual Basic category on the left.

5. Click OK to create your new project.

   The new project is created, and a blank form appears in the Designer, as shown in the screen shot on the bottom of page 69. The two controls you'll use in this exercise, *Button* and *TextBox*, are visible in the Toolbox, which appears in the screen shot as a docked window. If your programming tools are configured differently, take a few moments to organize them, as shown in the screen shot. (Chapter 1, "Exploring the Visual Studio Integrated Development Environment," describes how to configure the IDE if you need a refresher course.)

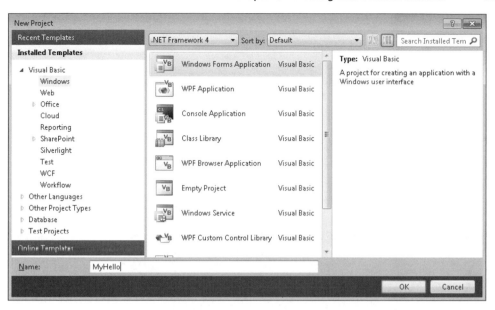

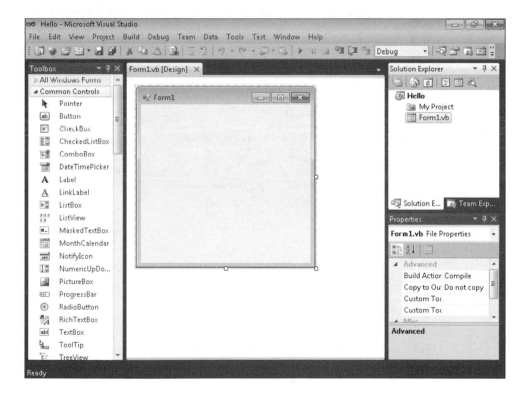

6. Click the *TextBox* control on the Common Controls tab of the Toolbox.

7. Draw a text box similar to this:

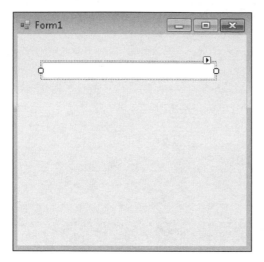

Text boxes are used to display text on a form or to get user input while a program is running. How a text box works depends on how you set its properties and how you reference the text box in the program code. In this program, a text box object will be used to display the message "Hello, world!" when you click a button object on the form.

You'll add a button to the form now.

8. Click the *Button* control in the Toolbox.

9. Draw a button below the text box on the form.

Your form looks something like this:

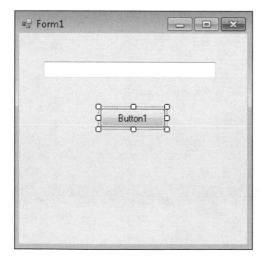

As you learned in Chapter 2, "Writing Your First Program," buttons are used to get the most basic input from a user. When a user clicks a button, he or she is requesting that the program perform a specific action immediately. In Visual Basic terms, the user is using the button to create an *event* that needs to be processed in the program. Typical buttons in a program are the OK button, which a user clicks to accept a list of options and to indicate that he or she is ready to proceed; the Cancel button, which a user clicks to discard a list of options; and the Quit button, which a user clicks to exit the program. In each case, you should use these buttons in the standard way so that they work as expected when the user clicks them. A button's characteristics (like those of all objects) can be modified with property settings and references to the object in program code.

10. Set the following property for the button object by using the Properties window:

Object	Property	Setting
Button1	Text	"OK"

For more information about setting properties and reading them in tables, see the section entitled "The Properties Window" in Chapter 1.

11. Double-click the OK button, and type the following program statement between the *Private Sub Button1_Click* and *End Sub* statements in the Code Editor:

```
TextBox1.Text = "Hello, world!"
```

> **Note** As you type statements, Visual Studio displays a list box containing all valid items that match your text. After you type the *TextBox1* object name and a period, Visual Studio displays a list box containing all the valid properties and methods for text box objects, to jog your memory if you've forgotten the complete list. This list box is called Microsoft IntelliSense and can be very helpful when you are writing code. If you click an item in the list box, you will typically get a tooltip that provides a short description of the selected item. You can add the property from the list to your code by double-clicking it or by using the arrow keys to select it and then pressing TAB. You can also continue typing to enter the property yourself. (I usually just keep typing, unless I'm exploring new features.)

The statement you've entered changes the *Text* property of the text box to "Hello, world!" when the user clicks the button at run time. (The equal sign (=) assigns everything between the quotation marks to the *Text* property of the *TextBox1* object.) This example changes a property at run time—one of the most common uses of program code in a Visual Basic program.

Now you're ready to run the Hello program.

Run the Hello program

 Tip The complete Hello program is located in the C:\Vb10sbs\Chap03\Hello folder.

1. Click the Start Debugging button on the Standard toolbar.

   The Hello program compiles and, after a few seconds, runs in the Visual Studio IDE.

2. Click OK.

   The program displays the greeting "Hello, world!" in the text box, as shown here:

   When you clicked the OK button, the program code changed the *Text* property of the empty *TextBox1* text box to "Hello, world!" and displayed this text in the box. If you didn't get this result, repeat the steps in the previous section, and build the program again. You might have set a property incorrectly or made a typing mistake in the program code. (Syntax errors appear with a jagged underline in the Code Editor.)

3. Click the Close button in the upper-right corner of the Hello World program window to stop the program.

 Note To stop a program running in Visual Studio, you can also click the Stop Debugging button on the Standard toolbar to close the program.

4. Click the Save All button on the Standard toolbar to save your new project to disk.

   Visual Studio now prompts you for a name and a location for the project.

5. Click the Browse button.

   The Project Location dialog box opens. You use this dialog box to specify the location of your project and to create new folders for your projects if necessary. Although you can save your projects in any location (the Documents\Visual Studio 2010\Projects folder is a common location), in this book I instruct you to save your projects in the C:\Vb10sbs folder, the default location for your *Step by Step* practice files. If you ever want to remove all the files associated with this programming course, you'll know just where the files are, and you'll be able to remove them easily by deleting the entire folder.

6. Browse to the C:\Vb10sbs\Chap03 folder.

7. Click the Select Folder or Open button to open the folder you specified.

8. Clear the check mark from the Create Directory For Solution check box if it is selected.

   Because this solution contains only one project (which is the case for most of the solutions in this book), you don't need to create a separate root folder to hold the solution files for the project. (However, you can create an extra folder if you want.)

9. Click Save to save the project and its files.

Congratulations—you've joined the ranks of programmers who've written a Hello World program. Now let's try another control.

Using the *DateTimePicker* Control

Some Visual Basic controls display information, and others gather information from the user or process data behind the scenes. In this exercise, you'll work with the *DateTimePicker* control, which prompts the user for a date or time by using a graphical calendar with scroll arrows. Although your use of the control will be rudimentary at this point, experimenting with *DateTimePicker* will give you an idea of how much Visual Basic controls can do for you automatically and how you process the information that comes from them.

The Birthday Program

The Birthday program uses a *DateTimePicker* control and a *Button* control to prompt the user for the date of his or her birthday. It then displays that information by using a message box. Give it a try now.

Build the Birthday program

1. On the File menu, click Close Project to close the MyHello project.

   The files associated with the Hello World program close.

2. On the File menu, click New Project.

   The New Project dialog box opens.

3. Create a new Visual Basic Windows Forms Application project named **MyBirthday**.

   The new project is created, and a blank form appears in the Designer.

4. Click the *DateTimePicker* control in the Toolbox.

5. Draw a date/time picker object near the top of the form, as shown in the following screen shot:

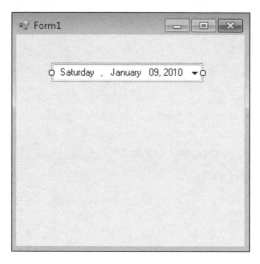

The date/time picker object by default displays the current date, but you can adjust the displayed date by changing the object's *Value* property. Displaying the date is a handy design guide—it lets you size the date/time picker object appropriately when you're creating it.

6. Click the *Button* control in the Toolbox, and then add a button object below the date/time picker.

You'll use this button to display your birth date and to verify that the date/time picker works correctly.

7. In the Properties window, change the *Text* property of the button object to **Show My Birthday**.

Now you'll add a few lines of program code to a procedure associated with the button object. This is an event procedure because it runs when an event, such as a mouse click, occurs, or *fires,* in the object.

8. Double-click the button object on the form to display its default event procedure, and then type the following program statements between the *Private Sub* and *End Sub* statements in the *Button1_Click* event procedure:

```
MsgBox("Your birth date was " & DateTimePicker1.Text)
MsgBox("Day of the year: " & _
  DateTimePicker1.Value.DayOfYear.ToString())
```

These program statements display two message boxes (small dialog boxes) with information from the date/time picker object. The first line uses the *Text* property of the date/time picker to display the birth date information that you select when using the object at run time. The *MsgBox* function displays the string value "Your birth date was" in addition to the textual value held in the date/time picker's *Text* property. These two pieces of information are joined together by the string concatenation operator (&). You'll learn more about the *MsgBox* function and the string concatenation operator in Chapter 5, "Visual Basic Variables and Formulas, and the .NET Framework."

The second and third lines collectively form one program statement and have been broken by the line continuation character (_) because the statement was a bit too long to print in this book.

Program lines can be more than 65,000 characters long in the Visual Studio Code Editor, but it's usually easiest to work with lines of 80 or fewer characters. You can divide long program statements among multiple lines by using a space and a line continuation character (_) at the end of each line in the statement except for the last line. (You cannot use a line continuation character to break a string that's in quotation marks, however.) I use the line continuation character in this exercise to break the second line of code into two parts.

> **Note** Starting in Visual Basic 2010, the line continuation character (_) is optional. There are a few instances where the line continuation character is needed, but they are rare. In this book, I still use line continuation characters to make it clear where there are long lines, but you don't have to include them.

The statement DateTimePicker1.Value.DayOfYear.ToString() uses the date/time picker object to calculate the day of the year in which you were born, counting from January 1. This is accomplished by the *DayOfYear* property and the *ToString* method, which converts the numeric result of the date calculation to a textual value that's more easily displayed by the *MsgBox* function.

Methods are special statements that perform an action or a service for a particular object, such as converting a number to a string or adding items to a list box. Methods differ from properties, which contain a value, and event procedures, which execute when a user manipulates an object. Methods can also be shared among objects, so when you learn how to use a particular method, you'll often be able to apply it to several circumstances. We'll discuss several important methods as you work through this book.

After you enter the code for the *Button1_Click* event procedure, the Code Editor looks similar to this:

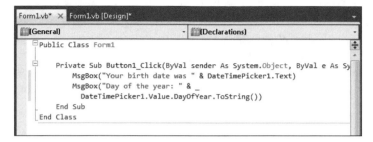

9. Click the Save All button to save your changes to disk, and specify C:\Vb10sbs\Chap03 as the folder location.

Now you're ready to run the Birthday program.

Run the Birthday program

 Tip The complete Birthday program is located in the C:\Vb10sbs\Chap03\Birthday folder.

1. Click the Start Debugging button on the Standard toolbar.

   The Birthday program starts to run in the IDE. The current date is displayed in the date/time picker.

2. Click the arrow in the date/time picker to display the object in Calendar view.

   Your form looks like the following screen shot, but with a different date.

3. Click the Left scroll arrow to look at previous months on the calendar.

Notice that the text box portion of the object also changes as you scroll the date. The "today" value at the bottom of the calendar doesn't change, however.

Although you can scroll all the way back to your exact birthday, you might not have the patience to scroll month by month. To move to your birth year faster, select the year value in the date/time picker text box and enter a new year.

4. Select the four-digit year in the date/time picker text box.

When you select the date, the date/time picker closes.

5. Type your birth year in place of the year that's currently selected, and then click the arrow again.

The calendar reappears in the year of your birth.

6. Click the scroll arrow again to locate the month in which you were born, and then click the exact day on which you were born.

If you didn't know the day of the week on which you were born, now you can find out!

When you select the final date, the date/time picker closes, and your birth date is displayed in the text box. You can click the button object to see how this information is made available to other objects on your form.

7. Click the Show My Birthday button.

Visual Basic executes your program code and displays a message box containing the day and date of your birth. Notice how the two dates shown in the two boxes match:

8. Click OK in the message box.

A second message box appears, indicating the day of the year on which you were born—everything seems to work! You'll find this control to be quite capable—not only does it remember the new date or time information that you enter, but it also keeps track of the current date and time, and it can display this date and time information in a variety of useful formats.

 Note To configure the date/time picker object to display times instead of dates, set the object's *Format* property to Time.

9. Click OK to close the message box, and then click the Close button on the form.

   You're finished using the *DateTimePicker* control for now.

Controls for Gathering Input

Visual Basic provides several mechanisms for gathering input in a program. *Text boxes* accept typed input, *menus* present commands that can be clicked or chosen with the keyboard, and *dialog boxes* offer a variety of elements that can be chosen individually or selected in a group. In the next few exercises, you'll learn how to use three important controls that help you gather input in several different situations. You'll learn about the *CheckBox*, *RadioButton*, *GroupBox*, *PictureBox*, *ListBox* controls. You'll explore each of these objects as you use a Visual Basic program called Input Controls, which is the user interface for a simple, graphics-based ordering system. As you run the program, you'll get some hands-on experience with the input objects. In the next chapter, I'll discuss how these objects can be used along with menus in a full-fledged program.

As a simple experiment, try using the *CheckBox* control now to see how user input is processed on a form and in program code.

Experiment with the *CheckBox* control

1. On the File menu, click Close Project to close the Birthday project.

2. On the File menu, click New Project.

   The New Project dialog box opens.

3. Create a new Visual Basic Windows Forms Application project named **MyCheckBox**.

   The new project is created, and a blank form appears in the Designer.

4. Click the *CheckBox* control in the Toolbox.

5. Draw two check box objects on the form, one above the other.

   Check boxes appear as objects on your form just as other objects do. You'll have to click the *CheckBox* control in the Toolbox a second time for the second check box.

6. Using the *PictureBox* control, draw two square picture box objects beneath the two check boxes.

7. Select the first *PictureBox* control named PictureBox1.

8. Click the *Image* property in the Properties window, and then click the ellipsis button in the second column.

   The Select Resource dialog box appears.

9. Click the Local Resource radio button, and then click the Import button.

10. In the Open dialog box, navigate to the C:\Vb10sbs\Chap03 folder.

11. Select Calcultr.bmp, and then click Open.

12. Click OK in the Select Resource dialog box.

    The calculator appears in the *PictureBox*.

13. Set the *SizeMode* property on the *PictureBox* to StretchImage.

14. Set the following properties for the check box and *PictureBox2* objects:

Object	Property	Setting
CheckBox1	Checked	True
	Text	"Calculator"
CheckBox2	Text	"Copy machine"
PictureBox2	SizeMode	StretchImage

In these steps, you'll use the check boxes to display and hide images of a calculator and a copy machine. The *Text* property of the check box object determines the contents of the check box label in the user interface. With the *Checked* property, you can set a default value for the check box. Setting *Checked* to True places a check mark in the box, and setting *Checked* to False (the default setting) removes the check mark. I use the *SizeMode* properties in the picture boxes to size the images so that they stretch to fit in the picture box.

Your form looks something like this:

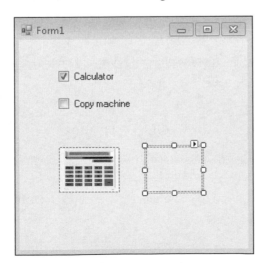

15. Double-click the first check box object to open the *CheckBox1_CheckedChanged* event procedure in the Code Editor, and then enter the following program code:

```
If CheckBox1.CheckState = 1 Then
    PictureBox1.Image = System.Drawing.Image.FromFile _
      ("c:\vb10sbs\chap03\calcultr.bmp")
    PictureBox1.Visible = True
Else
    PictureBox1.Visible = False
End If
```

The *CheckBox1_CheckedChanged* event procedure runs only if the user clicks in the first check box object. The event procedure uses an If … Then decision structure (described in Chapter 6, "Using Decision Structures") to confirm the current status, or *state*, of the first check box, and it displays a calculator picture from the C:\Vb10sbs\Chap03 folder if a check mark is in the box. The *CheckState* property holds a value of 1 if there's a check mark present and 0 if there's no check mark present. (You can also use the CheckState. Checked enumeration, which appears in IntelliSense when you type, as an alternative to setting the value to 1.) I use the *Visible* property to display the picture if a check mark is present or to hide the picture if a check mark isn't present. Notice that I wrapped the long line that loads the image into the picture box object by using the line continuation character (_).

16. Click the View Designer button in Solution Explorer to display the form again, double-click the second check box, and then add the following code to the *CheckBox2_CheckedChanged* event procedure:

```
If CheckBox2.CheckState = 1 Then
    PictureBox2.Image = System.Drawing.Image.FromFile _
      ("c:\vb10sbs\chap03\copymach.bmp")
    PictureBox2.Visible = True
Else
    PictureBox2.Visible = False
End If
```

This event procedure is almost identical to the one that you just entered; only the names of the image (Copymach.bmp), the check box object (*CheckBox2*), and the picture box object (*PictureBox2*) are different.

17. Click the Save All button on the Standard toolbar to save your changes, specifying the C:\Vb10sbs\Chap03 folder as the location.

Run the CheckBox program

Tip The complete CheckBox program is located in the C:\Vb10sbs\Chap03\Checkbox folder.

1. Click the Start Debugging button on the Standard toolbar.

   Visual Basic runs the program in the IDE. The calculator image appears in a picture box on the form, and the first check box contains a check mark.

2. Select the Copy Machine check box.

   Visual Basic displays the copy machine image, as shown here:

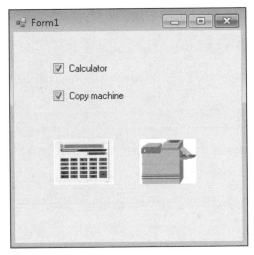

3. Experiment with different combinations of check boxes, selecting or clearing the boxes several times to test the program. The program logic you added with a few short lines of Visual Basic code manages the boxes perfectly. (You'll learn much more about program code in upcoming chapters.)

4. Click the Close button on the form to end the program.

Using Group Boxes and Radio Buttons

The *RadioButton* control is another tool that you can use to receive input in a program, and it is also located on the Common Controls tab of the Toolbox. Radio buttons get their name from the old push-button car radios of the 1950s and 1960s, when people pushed or "selected" one button on the car radio and the rest of the buttons clunked back to the unselected position. Only one button could be selected at a time, because (it was thought) the driver should listen to only one thing at a time. In Visual Studio, you can also offer mutually exclusive options for a user on a form, allowing them to pick one (and only one) option from a group. The procedure is to use the *GroupBox* control to create a frame on the form, and then to use the *RadioButton* control to place the desired number of radio buttons in the frame. (Because the *GroupBox* control is not used that often, it is located on the Containers tab of the Toolbox.) Note also that your form can have more than one group of radio buttons, each operating independently of one another. For each group that you want to construct, simply create a group box object first and then add radio buttons one by one to the group box.

In the following exercise, you'll create a simple program that uses *GroupBox*, *RadioButton*, and *PictureBox* controls to present three graphical ordering options to a user. Like the *CheckBox* control, the *RadioButton* control is programmed by using event procedures and program code, with which you'll also experiment. Give it a try now.

Gather input with the *GroupBox* and *RadioButton* controls

1. On the File menu, click Close Project to close the Check Box project.

2. On the File menu, click New Project.

   The New Project dialog box opens.

3. Create a new Visual Basic Windows Forms Application project named **MyRadioButton**.

   The new project is created, and a blank form appears in the Designer.

4. In the Toolbox, expand to the Containers tab and click the *GroupBox* control.

5. Create a medium-sized group box on the top half of the form.

6. Return to the Toolbox, scroll up to the Common Controls tab, and click the *RadioButton* control.

7. Create three radio button objects in the group box.

   It is handy to double-click the *RadioButton* control to create radio buttons. Notice that each radio button gets its own number, which you can use to set properties. Your form should look about like this:

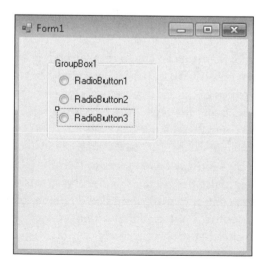

8. Using the *PictureBox* control, create one square picture box object beneath the group box on the form.

9. Set the following properties for the group box, radio button, and picture box objects:

Object	Property	Setting
GroupBox1	Text	"Select a Computer Type"
RadioButton1	Checked	True
	Text	"Desktop PC"
RadioButton2	Text	"Desktop Mac"
RadioButton3	Text	"Laptop"
PictureBox1	Image	C:\Vb10sbs\Chap03\Pcomputr.bmp
	SizeMode	StretchImage

The initial radio button state is controlled by the *Checked* property. Notice that the Desktop PC radio button now appears selected in the IDE. Now you'll add some program code to make the radio buttons operate while the program runs.

10. Double-click the *RadioButton1* object on the form to open the Code Editor.

The *CheckedChanged* event procedure for the *RadioButton1* object appears in the Code Editor. This procedure is run each time the user clicks the first radio button. Because you want to change the picture box image when this happens, you'll add a line of program code to accomplish that.

11. Type the following program code:

```
PictureBox1.Image = System.Drawing.Image.FromFile _
    ("c:\vb10sbs\chap03\pcomputr.bmp")
```

This program statement uses the *FromFile* method to load the picture of the PC from the hard disk into the picture box object. You'll use a similar statement for the second and third radio buttons.

12. Switch back to the Designer, double-click the *RadioButton2* object on the form, and type the following program code:

```
PictureBox1.Image = System.Drawing.Image.FromFile _
    ("c:\vb10sbs\chap03\computer.bmp")
```

13. Switch back to the Designer, double-click the *RadioButton3* object on the form, and type the following program code:

```
PictureBox1.Image = System.Drawing.Image.FromFile _
    ("c:\vb10sbs\chap03\laptop1.bmp")
```

14. Click the Save All button on the toolbar to save your changes, specifying the C:\Vb10sbs\Chap03 folder as the location.

Run the Radio Button program

> **Tip** The complete Radio Button program is located in the C:\Vb10sbs\Chap03\Radio Button folder.

1. Click the Start Debugging button on the Standard toolbar.

   Visual Basic runs the program in the IDE. The desktop PC image appears in a picture box on the form, and the first radio button is selected.

2. Click the second radio button (Desktop Mac).

   Visual Basic displays the image, as shown here:

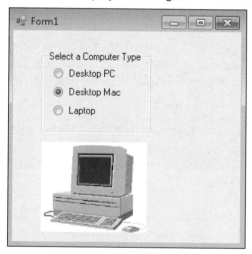

3. Click the third radio button (Laptop).

   The laptop image appears.

4. Click the first radio button (Desktop PC).

   The desktop PC image appears again. It appears that each of the three *CheckedChanged* event procedures is loading the images just fine. Nice work.

5. Click the Close button on the form to end the program.

   Perfect. You're finished working with radio buttons and group boxes for now. But can you imagine how you might use them on your own in a program?

Processing Input with List Boxes

As you well know from your own use of Windows, one of the key mechanisms for getting input from the user—in addition to check boxes and radio buttons—are basic *list boxes*, those rectangular containers used in dialog boxes or on forms that present a list of items and encourage the user to select one of them. List boxes are created in Visual Studio by using the *ListBox* control, and they are valuable because they can expand to include many items while the program is running. In addition, scroll bars can appear in list boxes if the number of items is larger than will fit in the box as you designed it on the form.

Unlike radio buttons, a list box doesn't require that the user be presented with a default selection. Another difference, from a programmatic standpoint, is that items in a list box can be rearranged while the program is running by adding items to a list, removing items, or sorting items. (You can also add a collection of items to a list box at design time by setting the *Items* property under the Data category with the Properties window.) However, if you prefer to see a list with check marks next to some of or all the items, you should use the *CheckedListBox* control in the Toolbox instead of *ListBox*. As a third option, you can use the handy *ComboBox* control to create a list box on a form that collapses to the size of a text box when not in use.

The key property of the *ListBox* control is *SelectedIndex*, which returns to the program the number of the item selected in the list box. Also important is the *Add* method, which allows you to add items to a list box in an event procedure. In the following exercise, you'll try out both of these features.

Create a list box to determine a user's preferences

1. On the File menu, click Close Project to close the Radio Button project.

2. On the File menu, click New Project, and create a new Windows Forms Application project named **MyListBox**.

    The new project is created, and a blank form appears in the Designer.

3. In the Toolbox, click the *ListBox* control in the Toolbox, and create a medium-sized list box object on the top half of the form.

    The list box object offers a *Text* property, which (like the *GroupBox* control) allows you to assign a title to your container.

4. Use the *PictureBox* control to create a square picture box object beneath the list box object on the form.

5. Set the following property for the picture box object:

Object	Property	Setting
PictureBox1	*SizeMode*	StretchImage

Your form now will look similar to this:

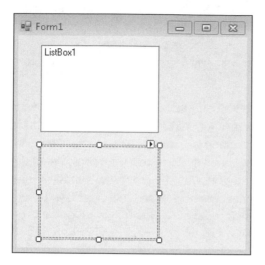

Now you'll add the necessary program code to fill the list box object with valid selections, and to pick from the selections while the program is running.

6. Double-click the *ListBox1* object on the form to open the Code Editor.

The *SelectedIndexChanged* event procedure for the *ListBox1* object appears in the Code Editor. This procedure runs each time the user clicks an item in the list box object. We need to update the image in the picture box object when this happens, so you'll add a line of program code to make it happen.

7. Type the following program code:

```
'The list box item selected (0-2) is held in the SelectedIndex property
Select Case ListBox1.SelectedIndex
    Case 0
        PictureBox1.Image = System.Drawing.Image.FromFile _
          ("c:\vb10sbs\chap03\harddisk.bmp")
    Case 1
        PictureBox1.Image = System.Drawing.Image.FromFile _
          ("c:\vb10sbs\chap03\printer.bmp")
    Case 2
        PictureBox1.Image = System.Drawing.Image.FromFile _
          ("c:\vb10sbs\chap03\satedish.bmp")
End Select
```

As you learned in Chapter 2, the first line of this event procedure is a comment. Comments, which are displayed in green type, are simply notes written by a programmer to describe what's important or interesting about a particular piece of program code. I wrote this comment to explain that the *SelectedIndex* property returns a number to the program corresponding to the placement of the item that the user selected in the list box. There will be three items in the list box in this program, and they will be numbered 0, 1, and 2 (from top to bottom). One interesting point here is that Visual Studio starts the count at 0, not 1, which is fairly typical among computer programs and something you'll see elsewhere in the book.

The entire block of code that you typed is actually called a *Select Case* decision structure, which explains to the compiler how to process the user's selection in the list box. The important keyword that begins this decision structure is *ListBox1 .SelectedIndex*, which is read as "the *SelectedIndex* property of the list box object named *ListBox1*." If item 0 is selected, the *Case 0* section of the structure, which uses the *FromFile* method to load a picture of an external hard disk into the picture box object, will be executed. If item 1 is selected, the *Case 1* section will be executed, and a printer will appear in the picture box object. If item 2 is selected, the *Case 2* section will be executed, and a satellite dish will appear. Don't worry too much if this is a little strange—you'll get a more fulsome introduction to decision structures in Chapter 6.

Now you need to enter some program code to add text to the list box object. To do this, we'll do something new—we'll put some program statements in the *Form1_Load* event procedure, which is run when the program first starts.

8. Switch back to the Designer and double-click the form (*Form1*) to display the *Form1_Load* event procedure in the Code Editor.

The *Form1_Load* event procedure appears. This program code is executed each time the List Box program is loaded into memory. Programmers put program statements in this special procedure when they want them executed every time a form loads. (Your program can display more than one form, or none at all, but the default behavior is that Visual Basic loads and runs the *Form1_Load* event procedure each time the user runs the program.) Often, as in the List Box program, these statements define an aspect of the user interface that couldn't be created easily by using the controls in the Toolbox or the Properties window.

9. Type the following program code:

```
'Add items to a list box like this:
ListBox1.Items.Add("Extra hard disk")
ListBox1.Items.Add("Printer")
ListBox1.Items.Add("Satellite dish")
```

The first line is simply a comment offering a reminder about what the code accomplishes. The next three lines add items to the list box (*ListBox1*) in the program. The words in quotes will appear in the list box when it appears on the form. The important keyword in these statements is *Add*, a handy method that adds items to list boxes or other items. Remember that in the *ListBox1_SelectedIndexChanged* event procedure, these items will be identified as 0, 1, and 2.

10. Click the Save All button on the toolbar to save your changes, specifying the C:\Vb10sbs\Chap03 folder as the location.

Run the List Box program

> **Tip** The complete List Box program is located in the C:\Vb10sbs\Chap03\List Box folder.

1. Click the Start Debugging button on the Standard toolbar.

   Visual Basic runs the program in the IDE. The three items appear in the list box, but because no item is currently selected, nothing appears yet in the picture box object.

2. Click the first item in the list box (Extra Hard Disk).

   Visual Basic displays the hard disk image, as shown here:

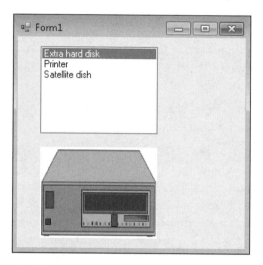

3. Click the second item in the list box (Printer).

   The printer image appears.

4. Click the third item in the list box (Satellite Dish).

   The satellite dish appears. Perfect—all of the list box code seems to be working correctly, although you should always continue to test these things (that is, check the various user input options) to make sure that nothing unexpected happens. As you'll learn later in the book, you always want to test your programs thoroughly, especially the UI elements that users have access to.

5. Click the Close button on the form to end the program.

   You're finished working with list boxes for now. If you like, you can continue to experiment with the *ComboBox* and *CheckedListBox* controls on your own—they operate similar to the tools you have been using in the last few exercises.

Tip Speaking of building robust programs, you should know that most of the images in this simple example were loaded by using an *absolute path name* in the program code. Absolute path names (that is, exact file location designations that include all the folder names and drive letters) work well enough so long as the item you are referencing actually exists at the specified path. However, in a commercial application, you can't always be sure that your user won't move around the application files, which could cause programs like this one to generate an error when the files they need are no longer located in the expected place. To make your applications more seaworthy, or *robust*, it is usually better to use relative paths when accessing images and other resources. You can also embed images and other resources within your application. For information about this handy technique, see the "How to: Create Embedded Resources" and "Accessing Application Resources" topics in the Visual Studio 2010 Help documentation.

A Word About Terminology

OK—now that this chapter is complete, let's do a quick terminology review. So far in this book, I've used several different terms to describe items in a Visual Basic program. Do you know what most these items are yet? It's worth listing several of them now to clear up any confusion. If they are still unclear to you, bookmark this section and review the chapters that you have just completed for more information. (A few new terms are also mentioned here for the sake of completeness, and I'll describe them more fully later in the book.)

- **Program statement**   A line of code in a Visual Basic program; a self-contained instruction executed by the Visual Basic compiler that performs useful work within the application. Program statements can vary in length (some contain only one Visual Basic keyword!), but all program statements must follow syntax rules defined and enforced by the Visual Basic compiler. In Visual Studio 2010, program statements can be composed of keywords, properties, object names, variables, numbers, special symbols, and other values. (See Chapters 2 and 5.)

- **Keyword**   A reserved word within the Visual Basic language that is recognized by the Visual Basic compiler and performs useful work. (For example, the *End* keyword stops program execution.) Keywords are one of the basic building blocks of program statements; they work with objects, properties, variables, and other values to form complete lines of code and (therefore) instructions for the compiler and operating system. Most keywords are shown in blue type in the Code Editor. (See Chapter 2.)

- **Variable**   A special container used to hold data temporarily in a program. The programmer creates variables by using the *Dim* statement and then uses these variables to store the results of a calculation, file names, input, and other items. Numbers, names, and property values can be stored in variables. (See Chapter 5.)

- **Control**   A tool that you use to create objects in a Visual Basic program (most commonly, on a form). You select controls from the Toolbox and use them to draw objects with the mouse on a form. You use most controls to create UI elements such as buttons, picture boxes, and list boxes. (See especially Chapters 2 through 4.)

- **Object**   An element that you create in a Visual Basic program with a control in the Toolbox. (In addition, objects are sometimes supplied by other system components, and many of these objects contain data.) In Visual Basic, the form itself is also an object. Technically speaking, objects are instances of a class that supports properties, methods, and events. In addition, objects have what is known as *inherent functionality*—they know how to operate and can respond to certain situations on their own. A list box "knows" how to scroll, for example. (See Chapters 1 through 4.)

- **Class**   A blueprint or template for one or more objects that defines what the object does. Accordingly, a class defines what an object can do, but it is not the object itself. In Visual Basic, you can use existing .NET Framework classes (like *System.Math* and *System.Windows.Forms.Form*), and you can build your own classes and inherit properties, methods, and events from them. (*Inheritance* allows one class to acquire the pre-existing interface and behavior characteristics of another class.) Although classes might sound esoteric at this point, they are a key feature of Visual Studio 2010. In this book, you will use them to build user interfaces rapidly and to extend the work that you do to other programming projects. (See Chapters 5 and 16.)

- **Namespace**   A hierarchical library of classes organized under a unique name, such as *System.Windows* or *System.Diagnostics*. To access the classes and underlying objects within a namespace, you place an *Imports* statement at the top of your program code. Every project in Visual Studio also has a root namespace, which is set using the project's Properties page. Namespaces are often referred to as *class libraries* in Visual Studio books and documentation. (See Chapter 5.)

- **Property**   A value or characteristic held by an object. For example, a button object has a *Text* property, to specify the text that appears on the button, and an *Image* property, to specify the path to an image file that should appear on the button face. In Visual Basic, properties can be set at design time by using the Properties window, or at run time by using statements in the program code. In code, the format for setting a property is

```
Object.Property = Value
```

where *Object* is the name of the object you're customizing, *Property* is the characteristic you want to change, and *Value* is the new property setting. For example,

```
Button1.Text = "Hello"
```

could be used in the program code to set the *Text* property of the *Button1* object to "Hello". (See Chapters 1 through 3.)

- **Event procedure**   A block of code that's executed when an object is manipulated in a program. For example, when the *Button1* object is clicked, the *Button1_Click* event procedure is executed. Event procedures typically evaluate and set properties and use other program statements to perform the work of the program. (See Chapters 1 through 3.)

- **Method**   A special statement that performs an action or a service for a particular object in a program. In program code. The notation for using a method is

```
Object.Method(Value)
```

where *Object* is the name of the object you want to work with, *Method* is the action you want to perform, and *Value* is zero or more arguments to be used by the method. For example, the statement

```
ListBox1.Items.Add("Check")
```

uses the *Add* method to put the word *Check* in the *ListBox1* list box. Methods and properties are often identified by their position in a collection or class library, so don't be surprised if you see long references such as *System.Drawing.Image.FromFile*, which would be read as "the *FromFile* method, which is a member of the *Image* class, which is a member of the *System.Drawing* namespace." (See Chapters 1 through 5.)

One Step Further: Using the *LinkLabel* Control

Providing access to the Web is now a standard feature of many Windows applications, and with Visual Studio, adding this functionality is easier than ever. You can create a Visual Basic program that runs from a Web server by creating a Web Forms project and using controls in the Toolbox optimized for the Web. Alternatively, you can use Visual Basic to create a Windows application that opens a Web browser within the application, providing access to the Web while remaining a Windows program running on a client computer. We'll postpone writing Web Forms projects for a little while longer in this book, but in the following exercise, you'll learn how to use the *LinkLabel* Toolbox control to create a Web link in a Windows program that provides access to the Internet through Windows Internet Explorer or the default Web browser on your system.

> **Note**   To learn more about writing Web-aware Visual Basic 2010 applications, read Chapter 20, "Creating Web Sites and Web Pages Using Visual Web Developer and ASP.NET."

Create the WebLink program

1. On the File menu, click Close Project to close the List Box project.

2. On the File menu, click New Project.

   The New Project dialog box opens.

3. Create a new Visual Basic Windows Forms Application project named **MyWebLink**.

The new project is created, and a blank form appears in the Designer.

4. Click the *LinkLabel* control in the Toolbox, and draw a rectangular link label object on your form.

Link label objects look like label objects except that all label text is displayed in blue underlined type on the form.

5. Set the *Text* property of the link label object to the Uniform Resource Locator (URL) for the Microsoft Press home page: *http://www.microsoft.com/learning/books/*.

Your form looks like this:

6. Click the form in the IDE to select it. (Click the form itself, not the link label object.)

This is the technique that you use to view the properties of the default form, Form1, in the Properties window. Like other objects in your project, the form also has properties that you can set.

7. Set the *Text* property of the form object to **Web Link Test**.

The *Text* property for a form specifies what appears on the form's title bar at design time and when the program runs. Although this customization isn't related exclusively to the Web, I thought you'd enjoy picking up that skill now, before we move on to other projects. (We'll customize the title bar in most of the programs we build.)

8. Double-click the link label object, and then type the following program code in the *LinkLabel1_LinkClicked* event procedure:

```
' Change the color of the link by setting LinkVisited to True.
LinkLabel1.LinkVisited = True
' Use the Process.Start method to open the default browser
' using the Microsoft Press URL:
```

```
System.Diagnostics.Process.Start _
  ("http://www.microsoft.com/learning/books/")
```

I've included more comments in the program code to give you some practice entering them. As soon as you enter the single quote character ('), Visual Studio changes the color of the line to green.

The two program statements that aren't comments control how the link works. Setting the *LinkVisited* property to True gives the link that dimmer color of purple, which indicates in many browsers that the Hypertext Markup Language (HTML) document associated with the link has already been viewed. Although setting this property isn't necessary to display a Web page, it's a good programming practice to provide the user with information in a way that's consistent with other applications.

The second program statement (which I have broken into two lines) runs the default Web browser (such as Internet Explorer) if the browser isn't already running. (If the browser is running, the URL just loads immediately.) The *Start* method in the *Process* class performs the important work, by starting a process or executable program session in memory for the browser. The *Process* class, which manages many other aspects of program execution, is a member of the *System.Diagnostics* namespace. By including an Internet address or a URL with the *Start* method, I'm letting Visual Basic know that I want to view a Web site, and Visual Basic is clever enough to know that the default system browser is the tool that would best display that URL, even though I didn't identify the browser by name.

An exciting feature of the *Process.Start* method is that it can be used to run other Windows applications, too. If I did want to identify a particular browser by name to open the URL, I could have specified one using the following syntax. (Here I'll request the Internet Explorer browser.)

```
System.Diagnostics.Process.Start("IExplore.exe", _
  "http://www.microsoft.com/learning/books/")
```

Here, two arguments are used with the *Start* method, separated by a comma. The exact location for the program named IExplore.exe on my system isn't specified, but Visual Basic will search the current system path for it when the program runs.

If I wanted to run a different application with the *Start* method—for example, if I wanted to run the Microsoft Office Word application and open the document C:\Myletter.doc— I could use the following syntax:

```
System.Diagnostics.Process.Start("Winword.exe", _
  "c:\myletter.doc")
```

As you can see, the *Start* method in the *Process* class is very useful.

Now that you've entered your code, you should save your project. (If you experimented with the *Start* syntax as I showed you, restore the original code shown at the beginning of step 8 first.)

9. Click the Save All button on the Standard toolbar to save your changes, and specify C:\Vb10sbs\Chap03 as the location.

   You can now run the program.

Run the WebLink program

> **Tip** The complete WebLink program is located in the C:\Vb10sbs\Chap03\Weblink folder.

1. Click the Start Debugging button on the Standard toolbar to run the WebLink program.

   The form opens and runs, showing its Web site link and handsome title bar text.

2. Click the link to open the Web site at *http://www.microsoft.com/learning/books/.*

   Recall that it's only a happy coincidence that the link label *Text* property contains the same URL as the site you named in the program code. (It is not necessary that these two items match.) You can enter any text you like in the link label. You can also use the *Image* property for a link label to specify a picture to display in the background of the link label. The following figure shows what the Microsoft Press Web page looks like (in English) when the WebLink program displays it using Internet Explorer.

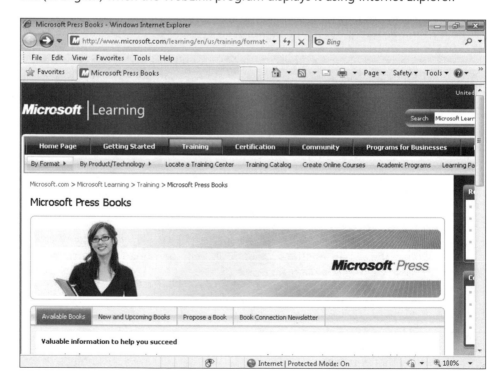

3. Display the form again. (Click the Web Link Test form icon on the Windows taskbar if the form isn't visible.)

Notice that the link now appears in a dimmed style. Like a standard Web link, your link label communicates that it's been used (but is still active) by the color and intensity that it appears in.

4. Click the Close button on the form to quit the test utility.

You're finished writing code in this chapter, and you're gaining valuable experience with some of the Toolbox controls available for creating Windows Forms applications. Let's keep going!

Chapter 3 Quick Reference

To	Do This
Create a text box	Click the *TextBox* control, and draw the box.
Create a button	Click the *Button* control, and draw the button.
Change a property at run time	Change the value of the property by using program code. For example: `Label1.Text = "Hello!"`
Create a radio button	Use the *RadioButton* control. To create multiple radio buttons, place more than one radio button object inside a box that you create by using the *GroupBox* control.
Create a check box	Click the *CheckBox* control, and draw a check box.
Create a list box	Click the *ListBox* control, and draw a list box.
Create a drop-down list box	Click the *ComboBox* control, and draw a drop-down list box.
Add items to a list box	Include statements with the *Add* method in the *Form1_Load* event procedure of your program. For example: `ListBox1.Items.Add("Printer")`
Use a comment in code	Type a single quotation mark (') in the Code Editor, and then type a descriptive comment that will be ignored by the compiler. For example: `' Use the Process.Start method to start IE`
Display a Web page	Create a link to the Web page by using the *LinkLabel* control, and then open the link in a browser by using the *Process.Start* method in program code.

Chapter 4
Working with Menus, Toolbars, and Dialog Boxes

After completing this chapter, you will be able to:

- Add menus to your programs by using the *MenuStrip* control.

- Process menu and toolbar selections by using event procedures and the Code Editor.

- Add toolbars and buttons by using the *ToolStrip* control.

- Use the *OpenFileDialog* and *ColorDialog* controls to create standard dialog boxes.

- Add access keys and shortcut keys to menus.

In Chapter 3, "Working with Toolbox Controls," you used several Microsoft Visual Studio 2010 controls to gather input from the user while he or she used a program. In this chapter, you'll learn how to present more choices to the user by creating professional-looking menus, toolbars, and dialog boxes.

A menu is located on the menu bar and contains a list of related commands; a toolbar contains buttons and other tools that perform useful work in a program. Most menu and toolbar commands are executed immediately after they're clicked; for example, when the user clicks the Copy command on the Edit menu, information is copied to the Clipboard immediately. If a menu command is followed by an ellipsis (…), however, clicking the command displays a dialog box requesting more information before the command is carried out, and many toolbar buttons also display dialog boxes.

In this chapter, you'll learn how to use the *MenuStrip* and *ToolStrip* controls to add a professional look to your application's user interface. You'll also learn how to process menu, toolbar, and dialog box commands.

Adding Menus by Using the *MenuStrip* Control

The *MenuStrip* control is a tool that adds menus to your programs, which you can customize with property settings in the Properties window. With *MenuStrip*, you can add new menus, modify and reorder existing menus, and delete old menus. You can also create a standard menu configuration automatically, and you can enhance your menus with special effects, such as access keys, check marks, and keyboard shortcuts. The menus look perfect—just like a professional Windows application—but *MenuStrip* creates only the *visible* part of your menus and commands. You still need to write event procedures that process the menu selections and make the commands perform useful work. In the following exercise, you'll take your first steps with this process by using the *MenuStrip* control to create a Clock menu containing commands that display the current date and time.

Create a menu

1. Start Visual Studio.

2. On the File menu, click New Project.

    The New Project dialog box opens.

3. Create a new Windows Forms Application project named **MyMenu**.

4. Click the *MenuStrip* control on the Menus & Toolbars tab of the Toolbox, and then draw a menu control on your form.

    Don't worry about the location—Visual Studio will move the control and resize it automatically. Your form looks like the one shown here:

The menu strip object doesn't appear on your form, but below it. Non-visible objects, such as menus and timers, are displayed in the Integrated Development Environment (IDE) in a separate pane named the *component tray*, and you can select them, set their properties, or delete them from this pane.

In addition to the menu strip object in the component tray, Visual Studio displays a visual representation of the menu that you created at the top of the form. The Type Here tag encourages you to click the tag and enter the title of your menu. After you enter the first menu title, you can enter submenu titles and other menu names by pressing the ARROW keys and typing additional names. Best of all, you can come back to this in-line Menu

Designer later and edit what you've done or add additional menu items—the menu strip object is fully customizable and with it you can create an exciting menu-driven user interface like the ones you've seen in the best Windows applications.

5. Click the Type Here tag, type **Clock**, and then press ENTER.

   The word *Clock* is entered as the name of your first menu, and two additional Type Here tags appear, with which you can create submenu items below the new Clock menu or additional menu titles. The submenu item is currently selected.

6. Type **Date** to create a Date command for the Clock menu, and then press ENTER.

   Visual Studio adds the Date command to the menu and selects the next submenu item.

7. Type **Time** to create a Time command for the menu, and then press ENTER.

   You now have a Clock menu with two menu commands, Date and Time. You could continue to create additional menus or commands, but what you've done is sufficient for this example program. Your form looks like the one shown here:

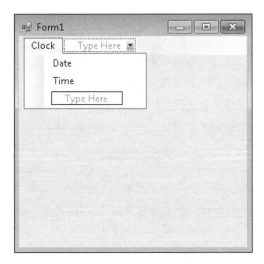

8. Click the form to close the Menu Designer.

   The Menu Designer closes, and your form opens in the IDE with a new Clock menu. You're ready to start customizing the menu now.

Adding Access Keys to Menu Commands

With most applications, you can access and execute menu commands by using the keyboard. In Visual Studio, for example, you can open the File menu by pressing the ALT key and then pressing the F key. Once the File menu is open, you can open a project by pressing the P key. The key that you press in addition to the ALT key and the key that you press to execute a command in an open menu are called *access keys*. You can identify the access key of a menu item because it's either underlined, or, in some Windows 7 applications, it appears in a small, handy box on the menu.

Visual Studio makes it easy to provide access key support. To add an access key to a menu item, activate the Menu Designer, and then type an ampersand (&) before the appropriate letter in the menu name. When you open the menu at run time (when the program is running), your program automatically supports the access key.

Menu Conventions

By convention, each menu title and menu command in a Windows application has an initial capital letter. File and Edit are often the first two menu names on the menu bar, and Help is usually the last. Other common menu names are View, Format, and Window. No matter what menus and commands you use in your applications, take care to be clear and consistent with them. Menus and commands should be easy to use and should have as much in common as possible with those in other Windows-based applications. As you create menu items, use the following guidelines:

- Use short, specific captions consisting of one or two words at most.

- Assign each menu item an access key. Use the first letter of the item if possible, or the access key that is commonly assigned (such as *x* for Exit).

- Menu items at the same level must have a unique access key.

- If a command is used as an on/off toggle, place a check mark to the left of the item when it's active. You can add a check mark by setting the *Checked* property of the menu command to True in the Properties window.

- Place an ellipsis (...) after a menu command that requires the user to enter more information before the command can be executed. The ellipsis indicates that you'll open a dialog box if the user selects this item.

 Note By default, most versions of Windows don't display the underline or small box for access keys in a program until you press the ALT key for the first time. In Windows XP, you can turn off this option by using the Effects button on the Appearance tab of the Display Properties control panel. In Windows Vista and Windows 7, you can turn off this option by clicking the Appearance And Personalization option in Control Panel, clicking Ease Of Access Center, clicking Make The Keyboard Easier To Use, and then selecting Underline Keyboard Shortcuts And Access Keys. Note, however, that in some applications running under Windows 7 (such as Visual Studio 2010 and Microsoft Office Word 2007), the access keys will not appear until you press the ALT key to activate them.

Try adding access keys to the Clock menu now.

Add access keys

1. Click the Clock menu name on the form, pause a moment, and then click it again.

   The menu name is highlighted, and a blinking I-beam (text-editing cursor) appears at the end of the selection. With the I-beam, you can edit your menu name or add the ampersand character (&) for an access key. (If you double-clicked the menu name, the Code Editor might have opened. If that happened, close the Code Editor and repeat step 1.)

2. Press the LEFT ARROW key five times to move the I-beam to just before the Clock menu name.

   The I-beam blinks before the letter *C* in *Clock*.

3. Type **&** to define the letter *C* as the access key for the Clock menu.

   An ampersand appears in the text box in front of the word *Clock*.

4. Click the Date command in the menu list, and then click Date a second time to display the I-beam.

5. Type **&** before the letter *D*.

   The letter *D* is now defined as the access key for the Date command.

6. Click the Time command in the menu list, and then click the command a second time to display the I-beam.

7. Type **&** before the letter *T*.

   The letter *T* is now defined as the access key for the Time command.

8. Press ENTER.

   Pressing ENTER locks in your text-editing changes. Your form looks like this:

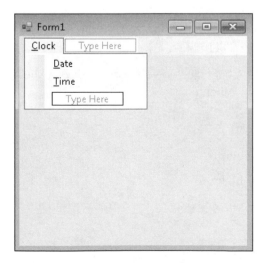

Now you'll practice using the Menu Designer to switch the order of the Date and Time commands on the Clock menu. Changing the order of menu items is an important skill because at times you'll think of a better way to define your menus.

Change the order of menu items

1. Click the Clock menu on the form to display its menu items.

   To change the order of a menu item, simply drag the item to a new location on the menu. Try it now.

2. Drag the Time menu on top of the Date menu, and then release the mouse button.

   Dragging one menu item on top of another menu item means that you want to place the first menu item ahead of the second menu item on the menu. As quickly as that, Visual Studio moved the Time menu item ahead of the Date item.

You've finished creating the user interface for the Clock menu. Now you'll use the menu event procedures to process the user's menu selections in the program.

Note To delete a menu item from a menu, click the unwanted item in the menu list, and then press the DELETE key. (If you try this now, remember that Visual Studio also has an Undo command, located on both the Edit menu and the Standard toolbar, so you can reverse the effects of the deletion.)

Processing Menu Choices

After menus and commands are configured by using the menu strip object, they also become new objects in your program. To make the menu objects do meaningful work, you need to write event procedures for them. Menu event procedures typically contain program statements that display or process information on the user interface (UI) form and modify one or more menu properties. If more information is needed from the user to process the selected command, you can write your event procedure so that it displays a dialog box and one or more of the input controls you used in Chapter 3.

In the following exercise, you'll add a label object to your form to display the output of the Time and Date commands on the Clock menu.

Add a label object to the form

1. Click the *Label* control in the Toolbox.

2. Create a label in the middle of the form.

   The label object appears on the form and displays the name *Label1* in the program code.

3. Set the following properties for the label:

Object	Property	Setting
Label1	AutoSize	False
	BorderStyle	FixedSingle
	Font	Microsoft Sans Serif, Bold, 24-point
	Text	(empty)
	TextAlign	MiddleCenter

4. Resize the label object so that it is much larger (it will be holding clock and date values), and position it in the center of the form. Your form should look similar to the following:

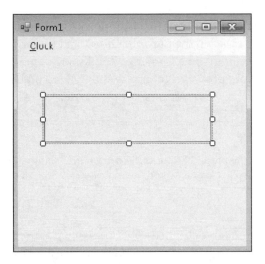

Now you'll add program statements to the Time and Date event procedures to process the menu commands.

> **Note** In the following exercises, you'll enter program code to process menu choices. It's OK if you're still a bit hazy on what program code does and how you use it—you'll learn much more about program statements in Chapters 5 through 7.

Edit the menu event procedures

1. Click the Clock menu on the form to display its commands.

2. Double-click the Time command in the menu to open an event procedure for the command in the Code Editor.

The *TimeToolStripMenuItem_Click* event procedure appears in the Code Editor. The name *TimeToolStripMenuItem_Click* includes the name "Time" that you gave this menu command. The words *ToolStripMenuItem* indicate that in its underlying technology, the

MenuStrip control is related to the *ToolStrip* control. (We'll see further examples of that later in this chapter.) The *_Click* syntax means that this is the event procedure that runs when a user clicks the menu item.

We'll keep this menu name for now, but if you wanted to create your own internal names for menu objects, you could select the object, open the Properties window, and change the *Name* property. Although I won't bother with that extra step in this chapter, later in the book you'll practice renaming objects in your program to conform more readily to professional programming practices.

3. Type the following program statement:

```
Label1.Text = TimeString
```

This program statement displays the current time (from the system clock) in the *Text* property of the *Label1* object, replacing the previous *Label1* text (if any). *TimeString* is a property that contains the current time formatted for display or printing. You can use *TimeString* at any time in your programs to display the time accurately down to the second. (*TimeString* is essentially a replacement for the older Microsoft Visual Basic *TIME$* statement.)

> **Note** The Visual Basic *TimeString* property returns the current system time. You can set the system time by using the Clock, Language, and Region category in the Control Panel in Windows Vista or Windows 7.

4. Press ENTER.

Visual Basic interprets the line and adjusts capitalization and spacing, if necessary. (Visual Basic checks each line for syntax errors as you enter it.)

> **Tip** You can enter a line by pressing ENTER or ESC. You can also press the UP ARROW or DOWN ARROW key to enter a line if you don't want the extra blank space (carriage return) in the Code Editor.

5. Click the View Designer button in Solution Explorer, and then double-click the Date command on the Clock menu.

The *DateToolStripMenuItem_Click* event procedure appears in the Code Editor. This event procedure is executed when the user clicks the Date command on the Clock menu.

6. Type the following program statement:

```
Label1.Text = DateString
```

This program statement displays the current date (from the system clock) in the *Text* property of the *Label1* object, replacing the previous *Label1* text. The *DateString* property is also available for general use in your programs. Assign *DateString* to the *Text* property of an object whenever you want to display the current date on a form.

> **Note** The Visual Basic *DateString* property returns the current system date. You can set the system date by using the Clock, Language, and Region category in the Control Panel of Windows Vista or Windows 7.

7. Press ENTER to enter the line.

Your screen looks similar to this:

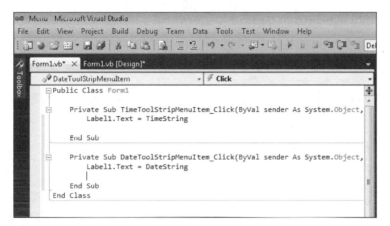

You've finished entering the menu demonstration program. Now you'll save your changes to the project and prepare to run it.

8. Click the Save All button on the Standard toolbar, and then specify the C:\Vb10sbs\Chap04 folder as the location.

Run the Menu program

> **Tip** The complete Menu program is located in the C:\Vb10sbs\Chap04\Menu folder.

1. Click the Start Debugging button on the Standard toolbar.

The Menu program runs in the IDE.

2. Click the Clock menu on the menu bar.

The contents of the Clock menu appear.

3. Click the Time command.

The current system time appears in the label box, as shown here:

Now you'll try displaying the current date by using the access keys on the menu.

4. Press and release the ALT key, and then press the C key.

The Clock menu opens, and the first item on it is highlighted.

5. Press the D key to display the current date.

The current date appears in the label box. However, if the box is not big enough, the date might be truncated. If this happens, stop the program, resize the label object, and try it again.

6. When you're finished experimenting, click the Close button on the program's title bar to stop the program.

Congratulations! You've created a working program that uses menus and access keys. In the next exercise, you'll learn how to use toolbars.

System Clock Properties and Methods

You can use various properties and methods to retrieve chronological values from the system clock. You can use these values to create custom calendars, clocks, and alarms in your programs. Table 4-1 lists the most useful system clock properties and methods. For more information, check the topics "Dates and Times Summary" and "DateAndTime Class" in the Visual Studio Help documentation.

TABLE 4-1 System Clock Properties and Methods

Property or Method	Description
TimeString	This property sets or returns the current time from the system clock.
DateString	This property sets or returns the current date from the system clock.
Now	This property returns an encoded value representing the current date and time. This property is most useful as an argument for other system clock functions.
Hour (date)	This method extracts the hour portion of the specified date/time value (0 through 23).
Minute (date)	This method extracts the minute portion of the specified date/time value (0 through 59).
Second (date)	This method extracts the second portion of the specified date/time value (0 through 59).
Month (date)	This method extracts a whole number representing the month (1 through 12).
Year (date)	This method extracts the year portion of the specified date/time value.
Weekday (date)	This method extracts a whole number representing the day of the week (1 is Sunday, 2 is Monday, and so on).

Adding Toolbars with the *ToolStrip* Control

Parallel to the *MenuStrip* control, you can use the Visual Studio *ToolStrip* control to quickly add toolbars to your program's user interface. The *ToolStrip* control is placed on a Visual Basic form but resides in the component tray in the IDE, just like the *MenuStrip* control. You can also add a variety of features to your toolbars, including labels, combo boxes, text boxes, and split buttons. Toolbars look especially exciting when you add them, but remember that as with menu commands, you must write an event procedure for each button that you want to use in your program. Still, compared with earlier versions of Visual Basic, it is amazing how much toolbar programming and configuring the IDE does for you. Practice creating a toolbar now.

Create a toolbar

1. Click the *ToolStrip* control on the Menus & Toolbars tab of the Toolbox, and then draw a toolbar control on your form.

   Don't worry about the location—Visual Studio will create a toolbar on your form automatically and extend it across the window. The tool strip object itself appears below the form in the component tray. On the form, the default toolbar contains one button. Now you'll use a special shortcut feature to populate the toolbar automatically.

2. Click the tiny smart tag in the upper-right corner of the new toolbar.

The smart tag points to the right and looks similar to the smart tag we saw in the *PictureBox* control in Chapter 2, "Writing Your First Program." When you click the tag, a ToolStrip Tasks window opens that includes a few of the most common toolbar tasks and properties, as shown here. You can configure the toolbar quickly with these commands.

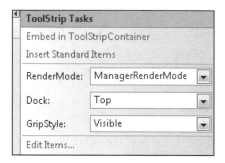

3. Click Insert Standard Items.

Visual Studio adds a collection of standard toolbar buttons to the toolbar, including New, Open, Save, Print, Cut, Copy, Paste, and Help. Your form looks similar to the following screen shot:

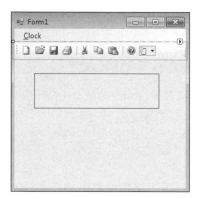

It is not necessary for you to start with a full toolbar of buttons as I have done here—I'm merely demonstrating one of the useful "automatic" features of Visual Studio 2010. You could also create the buttons on your toolbar one by one using the *ToolStrip* editing commands, as I'll demonstrate shortly. But for many applications, clicking Insert Standard Items is a time-saving feature. Remember, however, that although these toolbar buttons look professional, they are not functional yet. They need event procedures to make them work.

4. Click the Add ToolStripButton arrow on the right side of the new toolbar, and then click the Button item.

   Add ToolStripButton adds more items to your toolbar, such as buttons, labels, split buttons, text boxes, combo boxes, and other useful UI elements. You've now created a custom toolbar button; by default, it contains a picture of a mountain and a sun.

5. Widen the form window to ensure that you can see all the tool strip items.

6. Right-click the new button, point to DisplayStyle, and click ImageAndText.

   Your new button displays both text and a graphical image on the toolbar. Visual Studio names your new button *ToolStripButton1* in the program, and this name appears by default on the toolbar. If necessary, widen the form window to see the new button, because it contains the default text value ToolStripButton1.

7. Select the *ToolStripButton1* object.

8. In the Properties window, change the *ToolStripButton1* object's *Text* property to Color, which is the name of your button on the form, and then press ENTER.

   The Color button appears on the toolbar. You'll use this button later in the program to change the color of text on the form. Now insert a custom bitmap for your button.

9. Right-click the Color button, and then click the Set Image command.

   The Select Resource dialog box appears.

10. Click Local Resource (if it is not already selected), and then click the Import button.

11. Browse to the C:\Vb10sbs\Chap04 folder, click the ColorButton.bmp bitmap file that I created for you, click Open, and then click OK.

    Visual Studio loads the pink, blue, and yellow paint icon into the Color button, as shown in the following screen shot:

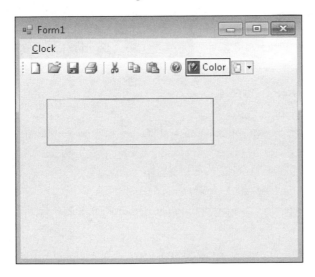

Your new button is complete, and you have learned how to add your own buttons to the toolbar, in addition to the default items supplied by Visual Studio. Now you'll learn how to delete and rearrange toolbar buttons.

Move and delete toolbar buttons

1. Drag the new Color button to the left side of the toolbar.

   Visual Studio lets you rearrange your toolbar buttons by using simple drag movements.

2. Right-click the second button in the toolbar (New), and then click the Delete command.

   The New button is removed from the toolbar. With the Delete command, you can delete unwanted buttons, which makes it easy to customize the standard toolbar buttons provided by the *ToolStrip* control.

3. Delete the Save and Print buttons, but be sure to keep the Color and Open buttons.

   You'll learn how to save and print in Chapter 13, "Exploring Text Files and String Processing," and Chapter 17, "Working with Printers," later in the book. Now, however, you'll learn to use dialog box controls and connect them to toolbar buttons.

Using Dialog Box Controls

Visual Studio contains eight standard dialog box controls on the Dialogs and Printing tabs of the Toolbox. These dialog boxes are ready-made, so you don't need to create your own custom dialog boxes for the most common tasks in Windows applications, such as opening, saving, and printing files. In many cases, you'll still need to write the event procedure code that connects these dialog boxes to your program, but the user interfaces are built for you and conform to the standards for common use among Windows applications.

The eight standard dialog box controls available to you are listed in Table 4-2. Note that the *PrintPreviewControl* control isn't listed here, but you'll find it useful if you use the *PrintPreviewDialog* control. (When you're ready to learn about adding printer support to your programs, see Chapter 17.)

TABLE 4-2 Standard Dialog Box Controls

Control	Purpose
OpenFileDialog	Gets the drive, folder name, and file name for an existing file
SaveFileDialog	Gets the drive, folder name, and file name for a new file
FontDialog	Lets the user choose a new font type and style
ColorDialog	Lets the user select a color from a palette
FolderBrowserDialog	Lets the user navigate through a computer's folder structure and select a folder

Control	Purpose
PrintDialog	Lets the user set printing options
PrintPreviewDialog	Displays a print preview dialog box as the Word program does
PageSetupDialog	Lets the user control page setup options, such as margins, paper size, and layout

In the following exercises, you'll practice using the *OpenFileDialog* and *ColorDialog* controls. The *OpenFileDialog* control lets your program open bitmap files, and the *ColorDialog* control enables your program to change the color of the clock output. You'll connect these dialog boxes to the toolbar that you just created, although you could just as easily connect them to menu commands.

Add *OpenFileDialog* and *ColorDialog* controls

1. Click the *OpenFileDialog* control on the Dialogs tab of the Toolbox, and then click the form.

   An open file dialog box object appears in the component tray.

2. Click the *ColorDialog* control on the Dialogs tab of the Toolbox, and then click the form again.

   The component tray now looks like this:

Just like the menu strip and tool strip objects, the open file dialog box and color dialog box objects appear in the component tray, and they can be customized with property settings.

Now you'll create a picture box object by using the *PictureBox* control. As you've seen, the picture box object displays artwork on a form. This time, you'll display artwork in the picture box by using the open file dialog box object.

Add a picture box object

1. Click the *PictureBox* control in the Toolbox.

2. Draw a large, square picture box object on the form, below the label.

3. Use the smart tag in the picture box object to set the *SizeMode* property of the picture box to StretchImage.

Now you'll create event procedures for the Color and Open buttons on the toolbar.

Event Procedures That Manage Common Dialog Boxes

After you create a dialog box object, you can use the dialog box in a program by doing the following:

- If necessary, set one or more dialog box properties by using program code before opening the dialog box.

- To open the dialog box, type the dialog box name with the *ShowDialog* method in an event procedure associated with a toolbar button or menu command.

- Use program code to respond to the user's dialog box selections after the dialog box has been manipulated and closed.

In the following exercise, you'll enter the program code for the *OpenToolStripButton_Click* event procedure, the routine that executes when the Open command is clicked. You'll set the *Filter* property in the *OpenFileDialog1* object to define the file type in the Open common dialog box. (You'll specify Windows bitmaps.) Then you'll use the *ShowDialog* method to display the Open dialog box. After the user has selected a file and closed this dialog box, you'll display the file he or she selected in a picture box by setting the *Image* property of the picture box object to the file name the user selected.

Edit the Open button event procedure

1. Double-click the Open button on your form's toolbar.

   The *OpenToolStripButton_Click* event procedure appears in the Code Editor.

2. Type the following program statements in the event procedure. Be sure to type each line exactly as it's printed here, and press the ENTER key after each line.

```
OpenFileDialog1.Filter = "Bitmaps (*.bmp)|*.bmp"
If OpenFileDialog1.ShowDialog() = DialogResult.OK Then
    PictureBox1.Image = System.Drawing.Image.FromFile _
      (OpenFileDialog1.FileName)
End If
```

The first three statements in the event procedure refer to three different properties of the open file dialog box object. The first statement uses the *Filter* property to define a list of valid files. (In this case, the list has only one item: *.bmp.) This is important for the Open dialog box because a picture box object can display a number of file types, including:

- Bitmaps (.bmp files)
- Windows metafiles (.wmf files)
- Icons (.ico files)

❑ Joint Photographic Experts Group (JPEG) format (.jpg and .jpeg files)

❑ Portable Network Graphics (PNG) format (.png files)

❑ Graphics Interchange Format (.gif files)

To add additional items to the *Filter* list, you can type a pipe symbol (|) between items. For example, this program statement

```
OpenFileDialog1.Filter = "Bitmaps (*.bmp)|*.bmp|Metafiles (*.wmf)|*.wmf"
```

allows both bitmaps and Windows metafiles to be chosen in the Open dialog box.

The second statement in the event procedure displays the Open dialog box in the program. The *ShowDialog* method returns a result named *DialogResult*, which indicates the button on the dialog box that the user clicked. To determine whether the user clicked the Open button, an *If ... Then* decision structure is used to check whether the returned result equals *DialogResult.OK*. It it does, a valid .bmp file path should be stored in the *FileName* property of the open file dialog box object. (You'll learn more about the syntax of *If ... Then* decision structures in Chapter 6, "Using Decision Structures.")

The third statement uses the file name selected in the dialog box by the user. When the user selects a drive, folder, and file name and then clicks Open, the complete path is passed to the program through the *OpenFileDialog1.FileName* property. The *System. Drawing.Image.FromFile* method, which loads electronic artwork, is then used to copy the specified Windows bitmap into the picture box object. (I wrapped this statement with the line continuation character (_) because it was rather long.)

Now you'll write an event procedure for the Color button that you added to the toolbar.

Write the Color button event procedure

1. Display the form again, and then double-click the Color button on the toolbar that you added to the form.

    An event procedure named *ToolStripButton1_Click* appears in the Code Editor. The object name includes *Button1* because it was the first nonstandard button that you added to the toolbar. (You can change the name of this object to something more intuitive, such as *ColorToolStripButton*, by clicking the button on the form and changing the *Name* property in the Properties window.)

2. Type the following program statements in the event procedure:

    ```
    ColorDialog1.ShowDialog()
    Label1.ForeColor = ColorDialog1.Color
    ```

    The first program statement uses the *ShowDialog* method to open the color dialog box. As you learned earlier in this chapter, *ShowDialog* is the method you use to open any form as a dialog box, including a form created by one of the standard dialog box controls that Visual Studio provides. The second statement in the event procedure assigns the color that the user selected in the dialog box to the *ForeColor* property of the *Label1* object. You might remember *Label1* from earlier in this chapter—it's the label box you used to display the current time and date on the form. You'll use the color returned from the color dialog box to set the color of the text in the label.

Note that the color dialog box can be used to set the color of any UI element that supports color. Other possibilities include the background color of the form, the colors of shapes on the form, and the foreground and background colors of objects.

3. Click the Save All button on the Standard toolbar to save your changes.

Controlling Color Choices by Setting Color Dialog Box Properties

If you want to further customize the color dialog box, you can control what color choices the dialog box presents to the user when the dialog box opens. You can adjust these color settings by selecting the *ColorDialog1* object and using the Properties window, or by setting properties by using program code before you display the dialog box with the *ShowDialog* method. Table 4-3 describes the most useful properties of the *ColorDialog* control. Each property should be set with a value of True to enable the option or False to disable the option.

TABLE 4-3 *ColorDialog* Control Properties

Property	Meaning
AllowFullOpen	Set to True to enable the Define Custom Colors button in the dialog box.
AnyColor	Set to True if the user can select any color shown in the dialog box.
FullOpen	Set to True if you want to display the Custom Colors area when the dialog box first opens.
ShowHelp	Set to True if you want to enable the Help button in the dialog box.
SolidColorOnly	Set to True if you want the user to select only solid colors (dithered colors—those that are made up of pixels of different colors—are disabled).

Now you'll run the Menu program and experiment with the menus and dialog boxes you've created.

Run the Menu program

 Tip The complete Menu program is located in the C:\Vb10sbs\Chap04\Menu folder.

1. Click the Start Debugging button on the Standard toolbar.

   The program runs, and the Clock menu and the toolbar appear at the top of the screen.

2. On the form's toolbar, click Open.

   The Open dialog box opens. It looks great, doesn't it? (In other words, it looks just like a regular Windows application.) Notice the Bitmaps (*.bmp) entry in the dialog box. You defined this entry with the statement

   ```
   OpenFileDialog1.Filter = "Bitmaps (*.bmp)|*.bmp"
   ```

   in the *OpenToolStripButton_Click* event procedure. The first part of the text in quotes— Bitmaps (*.bmp)—specifies which items are listed in the Files Of Type box. The second part—*.bmp—specifies the file name extension of the files that are to be listed in the dialog box.

3. Open a folder on your system that contains bitmap Images. I'm using the color toolbar button I've used in this chapter (located in C:\Vb10sbs\Chap04), but you can display any .bmp file on your system.

4. Select the bitmap file in the Open dialog box, and then click the Open button.

   A picture of the bitmap appears in the picture box. My form looks like this:

   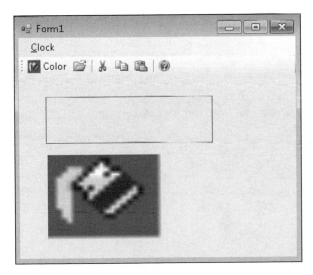

   Now you'll practice using the Clock menu.

5. On the Clock menu, click the Time command.

   The current time appears in the label box.

6. Click the Color button on the toolbar.

The Color dialog box opens, as shown here:

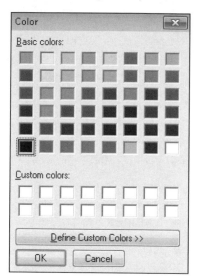

The Color dialog box contains elements that you can use to change the color of the clock text in your program. The current color setting, black, is selected.

7. Click one of the blue color boxes, and then click OK.

The Color dialog box closes, and the color of the text in the clock label changes to blue. (That's not visible in this book, alas, but you'll see it on the screen.)

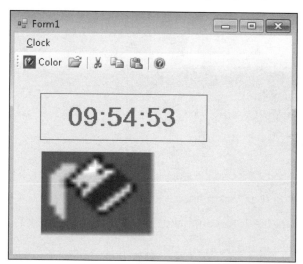

8. On the Clock menu, click the Date command.

The current date is displayed in blue type. Now that the text color has been set in the label, it remains blue until the color is changed again or the program closes.

9. Close the program.

    The application terminates, and the Visual Studio IDE appears.

That's it! You've learned several important commands and techniques for creating menus, toolbars, and dialog boxes in your programs. After you learn more about program code, you'll be able to create very sophisticated user interfaces in your own programs.

Adding Nonstandard Dialog Boxes to Programs

OK, you've gotten this far—but what if you need to add a dialog box to your program that *isn't* provided by one of the eight dialog box controls in Visual Studio? Unique dialog boxes pop up all the time in programs, right? No problem—but you'll need to spend a little time building the custom dialog box in the Visual Studio IDE. As you'll learn in future chapters, a Visual Basic program can use more than one form to receive and display information. To create nonstandard dialog boxes, you need to add new forms to your program, add input and output objects, and process the dialog box clicks in your program code. (These techniques will be discussed in Chapter 14, "Managing Windows Forms and Controls at Run Time.") In Chapter 5, "Visual Basic Variables and Formulas, and the .NET Framework," you'll learn how to use two handy dialog boxes that are specifically designed for receiving text input (*InputBox*) and displaying text output (*MsgBox*). These dialog boxes help bridge the gap between the dialog box controls and the dialog boxes that you need to create on your own.

One Step Further: Assigning Shortcut Keys to Menus

The *MenuStrip* control lets you assign shortcut keys to your menus. *Shortcut keys* are key combinations that a user can press to activate a command without using the menu bar. For example, on a typical Edit menu in a Windows application, such as Word, you can copy selected text to the Clipboard by pressing CTRL+C. With the *MenuStrip* control's *ShortcutKeys* property, you can customize this setting. Try assigning two shortcut keys to the Clock menu in the Menu program now.

Assign shortcut keys to the Clock menu

1. Make sure that your program has stopped running and is in design mode.

    You can modify a program only when it isn't running. (For an exception to this rule, see Chapter 8: "Debugging Visual Basic Programs.")

2. Click the Clock menu, and then click the Time command to highlight it.

    Before you set the shortcut key for a menu command, you must select it. You assign a shortcut key by setting the *ShortcutKeys* property for the command by using the Properties window. The menu strip object provides an easy way for you to do this.

3. Open the Properties window, click the *ShortcutKeys* property in the Misc category, and then click the arrow in the second column.

A pop-up menu appears that helps you assign the shortcut key.

4. Select the Ctrl check box, click the Key list box, and select the letter *T* in the alphabetical list.

The Properties window looks like this:

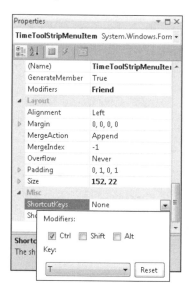

Tip Visual Basic normally displays the shortcut key combination in the menu when you run the program, to give users a hint about which keys to press. To hide shortcut key combinations from the user (if you're running out of space), set the *ShowShortcutKeys* property to False. The shortcut key still works, but users won't see a visual reminder for it. You can also set what will be displayed within the program as a shortcut key by setting the *ShortcutKeyDisplayString* property.

5. Click the Date command, and then change its *ShortcutKeys* property setting to Ctrl+D.

Now you'll run the program and try the shortcut keys.

6. Click the form to close the Clock menu.

7. Click the Start Debugging button on the Standard toolbar.

8. Press CTRL+D to run the Date command.

The current date appears in the program.

9. Press CTRL+T to run the Time command.

The current time appears in the program.

10. Click the Clock menu.

The shortcut keys are listed beside the Time and Date commands, as shown in the following screen shot. Visual Basic adds these key combinations when you define the shortcuts by using the *ShortcutKeys* property.

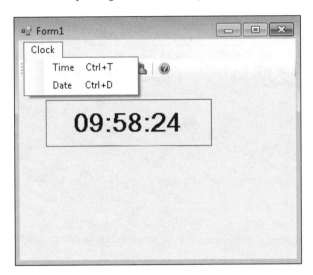

11. Close the program.

The Menu program closes, and the development environment appears.

Nice work! You're ready to move deeper into writing programs now, in the part of the book I call "Programming Fundamentals."

Chapter 4 Quick Reference

To	Do This
Create a menu item	Click the *MenuStrip* control, and draw a menu on your form. Click the Type Here tag on your form, and type the name of the menus and commands that you want to create.
Add an access key to a menu item	Click the menu item twice to display the I-beam, and then type an ampersand (**&**) followed by the letter you want to use as an access key.
Assign a shortcut key to a menu item	Set the *ShortcutKeys* property of the menu item by using the Properties window. A list of common shortcut keys is provided.
Change the order of menu items	Drag the menu item you want to move to a new location.
Add a toolbar to your program	Click the *ToolStrip* control, and then draw a toolbar on your form. Right-click buttons to customize them. Double-click buttons and write event procedures to configure them.

To	Do This
Use a standard dialog box in your program	Add one of the eight standard dialog box controls to your form, and then customize it with property settings and program code. Dialog box controls are located on the Dialogs and Printing Toolbox tabs.
Display an Open dialog box	Add the *OpenFileDialog* control to your form. Display the dialog box with the *ShowDialog* method. The *FileName* property contains the name of the file selected.
Display a Color dialog box	Add the *ColorDialog* control to your form. Display the dialog box with the *ShowDialog* method. The *Color* property contains the color the user selected.

Part II
Programming Fundamentals

In Part I, "Getting Started with Visual Basic 2010," you learned how to create the user interface of a Microsoft Visual Basic 2010 program and how to build and run a program in the Microsoft Visual Studio 2010 development environment. In the nine chapters in Part II, "Programming Fundamentals," you'll learn more about Visual Basic program code—the statements and keywords that form the core of a Visual Basic program. You'll learn how to manage information within programs and control how your code is executed, and you'll learn how to use decision structures, loops, timers, arrays, collections, and text files. You'll also learn how to debug your programs and handle run-time errors if they occur. After you complete Part II, you'll be ready for more advanced topics, such as customizing the user interface, database programming, and Web programming.

Chapter 5
Visual Basic Variables and Formulas, and the .NET Framework

After completing this chapter, you will be able to:

- Use variables to store data in your programs.

- Get input by using the *InputBox* function.

- Display messages by using the *MsgBox* function.

- Work with different data types.

- Use variables and operators to manipulate data.

- Use methods in the .NET Framework.

- Use arithmetic operators and functions in formulas.

In this chapter, you'll learn how to use variables and constants to store data temporarily in your program, and how to use the *InputBox* and *MsgBox* functions to gather and present information by using dialog boxes. You'll also learn how to use functions and formulas to perform calculations, and how to use arithmetic operators to perform tasks such as multiplication and string concatenation. Finally, you'll learn how to tap into the powerful classes and methods of Microsoft .NET Framework 4 to perform mathematical calculations and other useful work.

The Anatomy of a Visual Basic Program Statement

As you learned in Chapter 2, "Writing Your First Program," a line of code in a Microsoft Visual Basic program is called a *program statement*. A program statement is any combination of Visual Basic keywords, properties, object names, variables, numbers, special symbols, and other values that collectively create a valid instruction recognized by the Visual Basic compiler. A complete program statement can be a simple keyword, such as

```
End
```

which halts the execution of a Visual Basic program, or it can be a combination of elements, such as the following statement, which uses the *TimeString* property to assign the current system time to the *Text* property of the *Label1* object:

```
Label1.Text = TimeString
```

The rules of construction that must be used when you build a programming statement are called *statement syntax*. Visual Basic shares many of its syntax rules with the other development products in Visual Studio, as well as earlier versions of the BASIC programming language. The trick to writing good program statements is learning the syntax of the most useful elements in a programming language and then using those elements correctly to process the data in your program. Fortunately, Visual Basic does a lot of the toughest work for you, so the time you spend writing program code is relatively short, and you can reuse the results in future programs. The Visual Studio IDE also points out potential syntax errors and suggests corrections, much as the AutoCorrect feature of Microsoft Office Word does.

In this chapter and the following chapters, you'll learn the most important Visual Basic keywords and program statements, as well as many of the objects, properties, and methods provided by Visual Studio controls and the .NET Framework. You'll find that these keywords and objects complement nicely the programming skills you've already learned and will help you write powerful programs in the future. The first topics—variables and data types—are critical features of nearly every program.

Using Variables to Store Information

A *variable* is a temporary storage location for data in your program. You can use one or many variables in your code, and they can contain words, numbers, dates, properties, or other values. By using variables, you can assign a short and easy-to-remember name to each piece of data you plan to work with. Variables can hold information entered by the user at run time, the result of a specific calculation, or a piece of data you want to display on your form. In short, variables are handy containers that you can use to store and track almost any type of information.

Using variables in a Visual Basic program requires some planning. Before you can use a variable, you must set aside memory in the computer for the variable's use. This process is a little like reserving a seat at a theater or a baseball game. I'll cover the process of making reservations for, or *declaring*, a variable in the next section.

Setting Aside Space for Variables: The *Dim* Statement

Since the release of Visual Basic in 2002, it has been necessary for Visual Basic programmers to explicitly declare variables before using them. This was a change from Visual Basic 6 and earlier versions of Visual Basic, where (under certain circumstances) you could declare variables implicitly—in other words, simply by using them and without having to include a *Dim* statement. The earlier practice was flexible but rather risky—it created the potential for variable confusion and misspelled variable names, which introduced potential bugs into the code that might or might not be discovered later.

In Visual Basic 2008, a bit of the past returned in the area of variable declaration: It became possible once again to declare a variable implicitly. I don't recommend this for most uses, however, so I won't discuss this feature until you learn the recommended programming practice, which experienced programmers far and wide will praise you for adopting.

To declare a variable in Visual Basic 2010, type the variable name after the *Dim* statement. (Dim stands for *dimension*.) This declaration reserves room in memory for the variable when the program runs and lets Visual Basic know what type of data it should expect to see later. Although this declaration can be done at any place in the program code (as long as the declaration happens before the variable is used), most programmers declare variables in one place at the top of their event procedures or code modules.

For example, the following statement creates space for a variable named *LastName* that will hold a textual, or *string*, value:

```
Dim LastName As String
```

Note that in addition to identifying the variable by name, I've used the *As* keyword to give the variable a particular type, and I've identified the type by using the keyword *String*. (You'll learn about other data types later in this chapter.) A string variable contains textual information: words, letters, symbols—even numbers. I find myself using string variables a lot; they hold names, places, lines from a poem, the contents of a file, and many other "wordy" data.

Why do you need to declare variables? Visual Basic wants you to identify the name and the type of your variables in advance so that the compiler can set aside the memory the program will need to store and process the information held in the variables. Memory management might not seem like a big deal to you (after all, modern personal computers have lots of RAM and gigabytes of free hard disk space), but in some programs, memory can be consumed quickly, and it's a good practice to take memory allocation seriously even as you take your first steps as a programmer. As you'll soon see, different types of variables have different space requirements and size limitations.

Note In some earlier versions of Visual Basic, specific variable types (such as *String* or *Integer*) aren't required—information is simply held by using a generic (and memory hungry) data type called *Variant*, which can hold data of any size or format. Variants are not supported in Visual Basic 2010, however. Although they are handy for beginning programmers, their design makes them slow and inefficient, and they allow variables to be converted from one type to another too easily—sometimes causing unexpected results. As you'll learn later, however, you can still store information in generic containers called *Object*, which are likewise general-purpose in function but rather inefficient in size.

After you declare a variable, you're free to assign information to it in your code by using the assignment operator (=). For example, the following program statement assigns the last name "Jefferson" to the *LastName* variable:

```
LastName = "Jefferson"
```

Note that I was careful to assign a textual value to the *LastName* variable because its data type is *String*. I can also assign values with spaces, symbols, or numbers to the variable, such as

```
LastName = "1313 Mockingbird Lane"
```

but the variable is still considered a string value. The number portion could be used in a mathematical formula only if it were first converted to an integer or a floating-point value by using one of a handful of conversion functions that I'll discuss in Chapter 13, "Exploring Text Files and String Processsing."

After the *LastName* variable is assigned a value, it can be used in place of the name "Jefferson" in your code. For example, the assignment statement

```
Label1.Text = LastName
```

displays "Jefferson" in the label named *Label1* on a form.

Implicit Variable Declaration

If you really want to declare variables "the old way" in Visual Basic 2010—that is, without explicitly declaring them by using the *Dim* statement—you can place the *Option Explicit Off* statement at the very top of your form's or module's program code (before any event procedures), and it will turn off the Visual Basic default requirement that variables be declared before they're used. As I mentioned earlier, I don't recommend this statement as a permanent addition to your code, but you might find it useful temporarily as you convert older Visual Basic programs to Visual Basic 2010.

Another possibility is to use the *Option Infer* statement, which was added to Visual Basic 2008. If *Option Infer* is set to On, Visual Basic will deduce or *infer* the type of a variable by examining the initial assignment you make. This allows you to declare variables without specifically identifying the type used, and allowing Visual Basic to make the determination. For example, the expression

```
Dim attendance = 100
```

will declare the variable named *attendance* as an *Integer*, because 100 is an integer expression. In other words, with *Option Infer* set to On, it is the same as typing

```
Dim attendance As Integer = 100
```

Likewise, the expression

```
Dim address = "1012 Daisy Lane"
```

will declare the variable address as type *String*, because its initial assignment was of type *String*. If you set *Option Infer* to Off, however, Visual Basic will declare the variable as type *Object*—a general (though somewhat bulky and inefficient) container for any type of data.

If you plan to use *Option Infer* to allow this type of inferred variable declaration (a flexible approach, but one that could potentially lead to unexpected results), place the following two statements at the top of your code module (above the *Class Form* statement):

```
Option Explicit Off
Option Infer On
```

Option Explicit Off allows variables to be declared as they are used, and *Option Infer On* allows Visual Basic to determine the type automatically. You can also set these options using the Options command on the Tools menu, as discussed in Chapter 1, "Exploring the Visual Studio Integrated Development Environment."

Using Variables in a Program

Variables can maintain the same value throughout a program, or they can change values several times, depending on your needs. The following exercise demonstrates how a variable named *LastName* can contain different text values and how the variable can be assigned to object properties.

Change the value of a variable

1. Start Visual Studio.

2. On the File menu, click Open Project.

   The Open Project dialog box opens.

3. Open the Variable Test project in the C:\Vb10sbs\Chap05\Variable Test folder.

4. If the project's form isn't visible, click Form1.vb in Solution Explorer, and then click the View Designer button.

   The Variable Test form opens in the Designer. Variable Test is a *skeleton program*—it contains a form with labels and buttons for displaying output, but little program code. (I create these skeleton programs now and then to save you time, although you can also create the project from scratch.) You'll add code in this exercise.

   The Variable Test form looks like this:

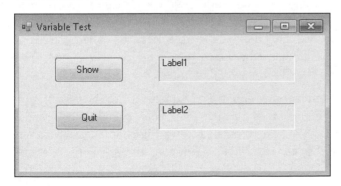

The form contains two labels and two buttons. You'll use variables to display information in each of the labels.

> **Note** The label objects look like boxes because I set their *BorderStyle* properties to Fixed3D.

5. Double-click the Show button.

    The *Button1_Click* event procedure appears in the Code Editor.

6. Type the following program statements to declare and use the *LastName* variable:

```
Dim LastName As String

LastName = "Luther"
Label1.Text = LastName

LastName = "Bodenstein von Karlstadt"
Label2.Text = LastName
```

The program statements are arranged in three groups. The first statement declares the *LastName* variable by using the *Dim* statement and the *String* type. After you type this line, Visual Studio places a green jagged line under the *LastName* variable, because it has been declared but not used in the program. There is nothing wrong here—Visual Studio is just reminding you that a new variable has been created and is waiting to be used.

> **Tip** If the variable name still has a jagged underline when you finish writing your program, it could be a sign that you misspelled a variable name somewhere within your code.

The second and third lines assign the name "Luther" to the *LastName* variable and then display this name in the first label on the form. This example demonstrates one of the most common uses of variables in a program—transferring information to a property. As you have seen before, all string values assigned to variables are displayed in red type.

The fourth line assigns the name "Bodenstein von Karlstadt" to the *LastName* variable (in other words, it changes the contents of the variable). Notice that the second string is longer than the first and contains a few blank spaces. When you assign text strings to variables, or use them in other places, you need to enclose the text within quotation marks. (You don't need to do this with numbers.)

Finally, keep in mind another important characteristic of the variables being declared in this event procedure—they maintain their *scope*, or hold their value, only within the event procedure you're using them in. Later in this chapter, you'll learn how to declare variables so that they can be used in any of your form's event procedures.

7. Click the Form1.vb [Design] tab to display the form again.

8. Double-click the Quit button.

The *Button2_Click* event procedure appears in the Code Editor.

9. Type the following program statement to stop the program:

End

Your screen looks like this:

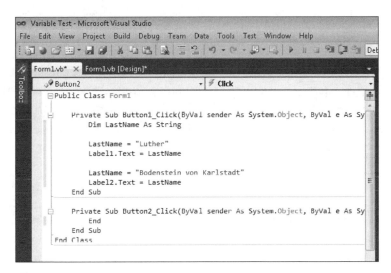

10. Click the Save All button on the Standard toolbar to save your changes.

11. Click the Start Debugging button on the Standard toolbar to run the program.

The program runs in the IDE.

12. Click the Show button.

The program declares the variable, assigns two values to it, and copies each value to the appropriate label on the form. The program produces the output shown in the following screen shot.

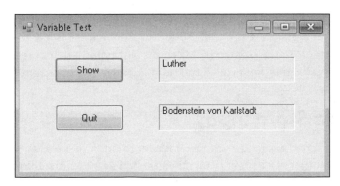

13. Click the Quit button to stop the program.

The program stops, and the development environment returns.

Variable Naming Conventions

Naming variables can be a little tricky because you need to use names that are short but intuitive and easy to remember. To avoid confusion, use the following conventions when naming variables:

- Begin each variable name with a letter or underscore. This is a Visual Basic requirement. Variable names can contain only letters, underscores, and numbers.

- Although variable names can be virtually any length, try to keep them under 33 characters to make them easier to read. (Variable names were limited to 255 characters in Visual Basic 6, but that's no longer a constraint.)

- Make your variable names descriptive by combining one or more words when it makes sense to do so. For example, the variable name *SalesTaxRate* is much clearer than *Tax* or *Rate*.

- Use a combination of uppercase and lowercase characters and numbers. An accepted convention is to capitalize the first letter of each word in a variable; for example, *DateOfBirth*. However, some programmers prefer to use so-called camel casing (making the first letter of a variable name lowercase) to distinguish variable names from functions and module names, which usually begin with uppercase letters. Examples of camel casing include *dateOfBirth*, *employeeName*, and counter.

- Don't use Visual Basic keywords, objects, or properties as variable names. If you do, you'll get an error when you try to run your program.

- Optionally, you can begin each variable name with a two-character or three-character abbreviation corresponding to the type of data that's stored in the variable. For example, use strName to show that the Name variable contains string data. Although you don't need to worry too much about this detail now, you should make a note of this convention for later—you'll see it in parts of the Visual Studio Help documentation and in some of the advanced books about Visual Basic programming. (This convention and abbreviation scheme was originally created by Microsoft Distinguished Engineer Charles Simonyi and is sometimes called the Hungarian Naming Convention.)

Using a Variable to Store Input

One practical use for a variable is to temporarily hold information that was entered by the user. Although you can often use an object such as a list box or a text box to gather this information, at times you might want to deal directly with the user and save the input in a variable rather than in a property. One way to gather input is to use the *InputBox* function to display a dialog box on the screen and then use a variable to store the text the user types. You'll try this approach in the following example.

Get input by using the *InputBox* function

1. On the File menu, click Open Project.

   The Open Project dialog box opens.

2. Open the Input Box project in the C:\Vb10sbs\Chap05\Input Box folder.

   The Input Box project opens in the IDE. Input Box is a skeleton program.

3. If the project's form isn't visible, click Form1.vb in Solution Explorer, and then click the View Designer button.

   The form contains one label and two buttons. You'll use the *InputBox* function to get input from the user, and then you'll display the input in the label on the form.

4. Double-click the Input Box button.

   The *Button1_Click* event procedure appears in the Code Editor.

5. Type the following program statements to declare two variables and call the *InputBox* function:

```
Dim Prompt, FullName As String
Prompt = "Please enter your name."

FullName = InputBox(Prompt)
Label1.Text = FullName
```

This time, you're declaring two variables by using the *Dim* statement: *Prompt* and *FullName*. Both variables are declared using the *String* type. (You can declare as many variables as you want on the same line, so long as they are of the same type.) Note that in Visual Basic 6, this same syntax would have produced different results. *Dim* would create the *Prompt* variable using the *Variant* type (because no type was specified) and the *FullName* variable using the *String* type. But this logical inconsistency has been fixed in Visual Basic versions 2002 and later.

The second line in the event procedure assigns a text string to the *Prompt* variable. This message is used as a text argument for the *InputBox* function. (An *argument* is a value or an expression passed to a procedure or a function.) The next line calls the *InputBox* function and assigns the result of the call (the text string the user enters) to the *FullName* variable. *InputBox* is a special Visual Basic function that displays a dialog box on the screen and prompts the user for input. In addition to a prompt string, the *InputBox* function supports other arguments you might want to use occasionally. Consult the Visual Studio Help documentation for details.

After *InputBox* has returned a text string to the program, the fourth statement in the procedure places the user's name in the *Text* property of the *Label1* object, which displays it on the form.

6. Save your changes.

7. Click the Start Debugging button on the Standard toolbar to run the program.

The program runs in the IDE.

8. Click the Input Box button.

Visual Basic executes the *Button1_Click* event procedure, and the Input Box dialog box opens on your screen, as shown here:

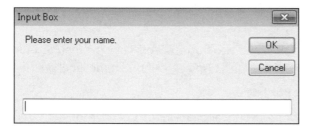

9. Type your full name, and then click OK.

The *InputBox* function returns your name to the program and places it in the *FullName* variable. The program then uses the variable to display your name on the form, as shown here:

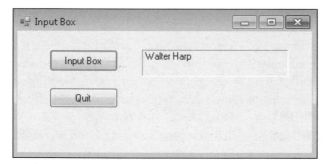

Use the *InputBox* function in your programs anytime you want to prompt the user for information. You can use this function in combination with the other input controls to regulate the flow of data into and out of a program. In the next exercise, you'll learn how to use a similar function to display text in a dialog box.

10. Click the Quit button on the form to stop the program.

The program stops, and the development environment reappears.

What Is a Function?

InputBox is a special Visual Basic keyword known as a *function*. A function is a statement that performs meaningful work (such as prompting the user for information or calculating an equation) and then returns a result to the program. The value returned by a function can be assigned to a variable, as it was in the Input Box program, or it can be assigned to a property or another statement or function. Visual Basic functions often use one or more arguments to define their activities. For example, the *InputBox* function you just executed used the *Prompt* variable to display dialog box instructions for the user. When a function uses more than one argument, commas separate the arguments, and the whole group of arguments is enclosed in parentheses. The following statement shows a function call that has two arguments:

```
FullName = InputBox(Prompt, Title)
```

Notice that I'm using italic in this syntax description to indicate that certain items are placeholders for information you specify. This is a style you'll find throughout the book and in the Visual Studio Help documentation.

Using a Variable for Output

You can display the contents of a variable by assigning the variable to a property (such as the *Text* property of a label object) or by passing the variable as an argument to a dialog box function. One useful dialog box function for displaying output is the *MsgBox* function. When you call the *MsgBox* function, it displays a dialog box, sometimes called a *message box*, with various options that you can specify. Like *InputBox*, it takes one or more arguments as input, and the results of the function call can be assigned to a variable. The syntax for the *MsgBox* function is

```
ButtonClicked = MsgBox(Prompt, Buttons, Title)
```

where *Prompt* is the text to be displayed in the message box; *Buttons* is a number that specifies the buttons, icons, and other options to display for the message box; and *Title* is the text displayed in the message box title bar. The variable *ButtonClicked* is assigned the result returned by the function, which indicates which button the user clicked in the dialog box.

If you're just displaying a message using the *MsgBox* function, the *ButtonClicked* variable, the assignment operator (=), the *Buttons* argument, and the *Title* argument are optional. You'll be using the *Title* argument, but you won't be using the others in the following exercise; for more information about them (including the different buttons you can include in *MsgBox* and a few more options), search for the topic "MsgBox Method" in the Visual Studio Help documentation. As the article notes, the *MsgBox* function is sometimes also referred to as a *method,* reflecting the internal organization of the *Microsoft.VisualBasic* namespace.

> **Note** Visual Studio provides both the *MsgBox* function and the *MessageBox* class for displaying text in a message box. The *MessageBox* class is part of the *System.Windows.Forms* namespace; it takes arguments much like *MsgBox*, and it is displayed by using the *Show* method. I'll use both *MsgBox* and *MessageBox* in this book.

Now you'll add a *MsgBox* function to the Input Box program to display the name that the user enters in the Input Box dialog box.

Display a message by using the *MsgBox* function

1. If the Code Editor isn't visible, double-click the Input Box button on the Input Box form.

   The *Button1_Click* event procedure appears in the Code Editor. (This is the code you entered in the last exercise.)

2. Select the following statement in the event procedure (the last line):

   ```
   Label1.Text = FullName
   ```

   This is the statement that displays the contents of the *FullName* variable in the label.

3. Press the DELETE key to delete the line.

   The statement is removed from the Code Editor.

4. Type the following line into the event procedure as a replacement:

   ```
   MsgBox(FullName, , "Input Results")
   ```

   This new statement will call the *MsgBox* function, display the contents of the *FullName* variable in the dialog box, and place the words *Input Results* in the title bar. (The optional *Buttons* argument and the *ButtonClicked* variable are irrelevant here and have been omitted.) Your event procedure looks like this in the Code Editor:

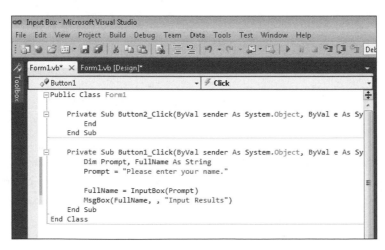

5. Click the Start Debugging button on the Standard toolbar.

6. Click the Input Box button, type your name in the input box, and then click OK.

   Visual Basic stores the input in the program in the *FullName* variable and then displays it in a message box. After typing the name *Walter Harp* in the input box, I received this message box:

7. Click OK to close the message box. Then click Quit to close the program.

   The program closes, and the development environment returns.

Working with Specific Data Types

The *String* data type is useful for managing text in your programs, but what about numbers, dates, and other types of information? To allow for the efficient memory management of all types of data, Visual Basic provides several additional data types that you can use for your variables. Many of these are familiar data types from earlier versions of BASIC or Visual Basic, and some of the data types were introduced in Visual Studio 2005 to allow for the efficient processing of data in newer 64-bit computers.

Table 5-1 lists the fundamental (or elementary) data types in Visual Basic. Types preceded by an *S* are designed for *signed numbers,* meaning that they can hold both positive and negative values. Types preceded by a *U* are *unsigned data types,* meaning that they cannot hold negative values. If your program needs to perform a lot of calculations, you might gain a performance advantage in your programs if you choose the right data type for your variables—a size that's neither too big nor too small. In the next exercise, you'll see how several of these data types work.

Note Variable storage size is measured in bits. The amount of space required to store one standard (ASCII) keyboard character in memory is 8 bits, which equals 1 byte.

TABLE 5-1 Fundamental Data Types in Visual Basic

Data Type	Size	Range	Sample Usage
Short	16-bit	−32,768 through 32,767	`Dim Birds As Short` `Birds = 12500`
UShort	16-bit	0 through 65,535	`Dim Days As UShort` `Days = 55000`
Integer	32-bit	−2,147,483,648 through 2,147,483,647	`Dim Insects As Integer` `Insects = 37500000`
UInteger	32-bit	0 through 4,294,967,295	`Dim Joys As UInteger` `Joys = 3000000000`
Long	64-bit	−9,223,372,036,854,775,808 to 9,223,372,036,854,775,807	`Dim WorldPop As Long` `WorldPop = 4800000004`

ULong	64-bit	0 through 18,446,744,073,709,551,615	`Dim Stars As ULong`
			`Stars = _`
			`    1800000000000000000`

Single	32-bit floating point	−3.4028235E38 through 3.4028235E38	`Dim Price As Single` `Price = 899.99`
Double	64-bit floating point	−1.79769313486231E308 through 1.79769313486231E308	`Dim Pi As Double` `Pi = 3.1415926535`
Decimal	128-bit	0 through +/−79,228,162,514,264, 337,593,543,950,335 (+/−7.9…E+28) with no decimal point; 0 through +/− 7.9228162514264337593543950335 with 28 places to the right of the decimal. Append "D" if you want to force Visual Basic to initialize a *Decimal*.	`Dim Debt As Decimal` `Debt = 7600300.5D`
Byte	8-bit	0 through 255 (no negative numbers)	`Dim RetKey As Byte` `RetKey = 13`
SByte	8-bit	−128 through 127	`Dim NegVal As SByte` `NegVal = −20`
Char	16-bit	Any Unicode symbol in the range 0–65,535. Append "c" when initializing a *Char*.	`Dim UnicodeChar As Char` `UnicodeChar = "Ä"c`
String	Usually 16-bits per character	0 to approximately 2 billion 16-bit Unicode characters	`Dim Dog As String` `Dog = "pointer"`
Boolean	16-bit	True or False. (During conversions, 0 is converted to False, other values to True.)	`Dim Flag as Boolean` `Flag = True`
Date	64-bit	January 1, 0001, through December 31, 9999	`Dim Birthday as Date` `Birthday = #3/1/1963#`

Object	32-bit	Any type can be stored in a variable of type *Object*.	`Dim MyApp As Object`
			`MyApp = CreateObject _`
			`    ("Word.Application")`

Use fundamental data types in code

1. On the File menu, click Open Project.

   The Open Project dialog box opens.

2. Open the Data Types project from the C:\Vb10sbs\Chap05\Data Types folder.

3. If the project's form isn't visible, click Form1.vb in Solution Explorer, and then click the View Designer button.

   Data Types is a complete Visual Basic program that I created to demonstrate how the fundamental data types work. You'll run the program to see what the data types look like, and then you'll look at how the variables are declared and used in the program code. You'll also learn where to place variable declarations so that they're available to all the event procedures in your program.

4. Click the Start Debugging button on the Standard toolbar.

   The following application window opens:

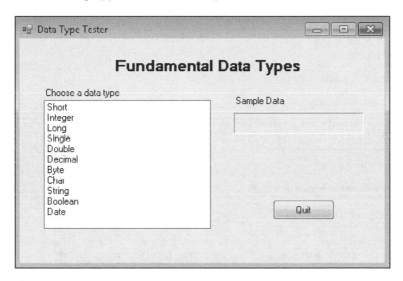

   The Data Types program lets you experiment with 11 data types, including integer, single-precision floating point, and date. The program displays an example of each type when you click its name in the list box.

5. Click the *Integer* type in the list box.

   The number 37500000 appears in the Sample Data box.

> **Note**   With the *Short*, *Integer*, and *Long* data types, you can't insert or display commas. To display commas, you'll need to use the *Format* function.

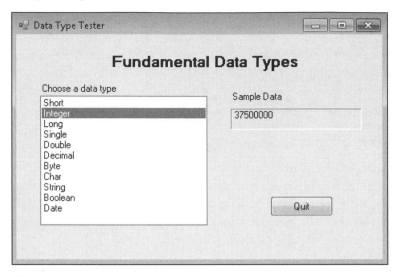

6. Click the *Date* type in the list box.

   The date 3/1/1963 appears in the Sample Data box.

7. Click each data type in the list box to see how Visual Basic displays it in the Sample Data box.

8. Click the Quit button to stop the program.

   Now you'll examine how the fundamental data types are declared at the top of the form and how they're used in the *ListBox1_SelectedIndexChanged* event procedure.

9. Double-click the form itself (not any objects on the form), and enlarge the Code Editor to see more of the program code.

   The Code Editor looks like this:

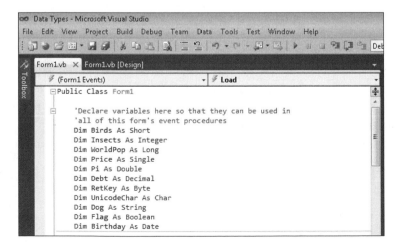

Scroll to the top of the Code Editor to see the dozen or so program statements I added to declare 11 variables in your program—one for each of the fundamental data types in Visual Basic. (I didn't create an example for the *SByte*, *UShort*, *UInteger*, and *ULong* types, because they closely resemble their signed or unsigned counterparts.) By placing each *Dim* statement here, at the top of the form's code initialization area, I'm ensuring that the variables will be valid, or will have *scope*, for all of the form's event procedures. That way, I can set the value of a variable in one event procedure and read it in another. Normally, variables are valid only in the event procedure in which they're declared. To make them valid across the form, you need to declare variables at the top of your form's code.

> **Note** I've given each variable the same name as I did in the data types table earlier in the chapter so that you can see the examples I showed you in actual program code.

10. Scroll down in the Code Editor, and examine the *Form1_Load* event procedure.

    You'll see the following statements, which add items to the list box object in the program. (You might remember this syntax from Chapter 3, "Working with Toolbox Controls"—I used some similar statements there.)

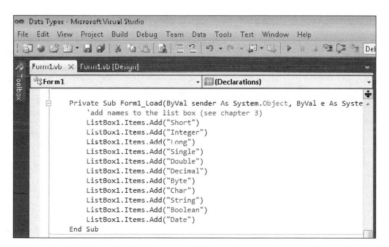

11. Scroll up and examine the *ListBox1_SelectedIndexChanged* event procedure.

The *ListBox1_SelectedIndexChanged* event procedure processes the selections you make in the list box and looks like this:

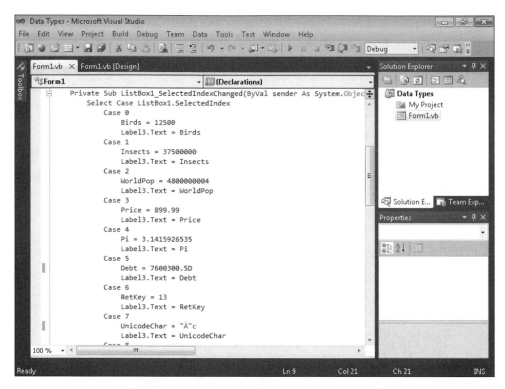

The heart of the event procedure is a *Select Case* decision structure. In the next chapter, we'll discuss how this group of program statements selects one choice from many. For now, notice how each section of the *Select Case* block assigns a sample value to one of the fundamental data type variables and then assigns the variable to the *Text* property of the *Label4* object on the form. I used code like this in Chapter 3 to process list box choices, and you can use these techniques to work with list boxes and data types in your own programs.

> **Note** If you have more than one form in your project, you need to declare variables in a slightly different way (and place) to give them scope throughout your program (that is, in each form that your project contains). The type of variable that you'll declare is a public, or global, variable, and it's declared in a module, a special file that contains declarations and procedures not associated with a particular form. For information about creating public variables in modules, see Chapter 10, "Creating Modules and Procedures."

12. Scroll through the *ListBox1_SelectedIndexChanged* event procedure, and examine each of the variable assignments closely.

Try changing the data in a few of the variable assignment statements and running the program again to see what the data looks like. In particular, you might try assigning values to variables that are outside their accepted range, as shown in the data types table presented earlier. If you make such an error, Visual Basic adds a jagged line below the incorrect value in the Code Editor, and the program won't run until you change it. To learn more about your mistake, you can point to the jagged underlined value and read a short tooltip error message about the problem.

> **Tip** By default, a green jagged line indicates a warning, a red jagged line indicates a syntax error, a blue jagged line indicates a compiler error, and a purple jagged line indicates some other error.

13. If you made any changes you want to save to disk, click the Save All button on the Standard toolbar.

User-Defined Data Types

Visual Basic also lets you create your own data types. This feature is most useful when you're dealing with a group of data items that naturally fit together but fall into different data categories. You create a *user-defined type* (UDT) by using the *Structure* statement, and you declare variables associated with the new type by using the *Dim* statement. Be aware that the *Structure* statement cannot be located in an event procedure—it must be located at the top of the form along with other variable declarations, or in a code module.

For example, the following declaration creates a user-defined data type named *Employee* that can store the name, date of birth, and hire date associated with a worker:

```
Structure Employee
    Dim Name As String
    Dim DateOfBirth As Date
    Dim HireDate As Date
End Structure
```

After you create a data type, you can use it in the program code for the form's or module's event procedures. The following statements use the new *Employee* type. The first statement creates a variable named *ProductManager*, of the *Employee* type, and the second statement assigns the name "Erin M. Hagens" to the *Name* component of the variable:

```
Dim ProductManager As Employee
ProductManager.Name = "Erin M. Hagens"
```

This looks a little similar to setting a property, doesn't it? Visual Basic uses the same notation for the relationship between objects and properties as it uses for the relationship between user-defined data types and component variables.

Constants: Variables That Don't Change

If a variable in your program contains a value that never changes (such as π, a fixed mathematical entity), you might consider storing the value as a constant instead of as a variable. A *constant* is a meaningful name that takes the place of a number or a text string that doesn't change. Constants are useful because they increase the readability of program code, they can reduce programming mistakes, and they make global changes easier to accomplish later. Constants operate a lot like variables, but you can't modify their values at run time. They are declared with the *Const* keyword, as shown in the following example:

```
Const Pi As Double = 3.14159265
```

This statement creates a constant named *Pi* that can be used in place of the value of π in the program code. To make a constant available to all the objects and event procedures in your form, place the statement at the top of your form along with other variable and structure declarations that will have scope in all of the form's event procedures. To make the constant available to all the forms and modules in a program (not just *Form1*), create the constant in a code module, with the *Public* keyword in front of it. For example:

```
Public Const Pi As Double = 3.14159265
```

The following exercise demonstrates how you can use a constant in an event procedure.

Use a constant in an event procedure

1. On the File menu, click Open Project.

   The Open Project dialog box opens.

2. Open the Constant Tester project in the C:\Vb10sbs\Chap05\Constant Tester folder.

3. If the project's form isn't visible, click Form1.vb in Solution Explorer, and then click the View Designer button.

   The Constant Tester form opens in the Designer. Constant Tester is a skeleton program. The user interface is finished, but you need to type in the program code.

4. Double-click the Show Constant button on the form.

   The *Button1_Click* event procedure appears in the Code Editor.

5. Type the following statements in the *Button1_Click* event procedure:

```
Const Pi As Double = 3.14159265
Label1.Text = Pi
```

> **Tip** The location you choose for your declarations should be based on how you plan to use the constants or the variables. Programmers typically keep the scope for declarations as small as possible, while still making them available for code that needs to use them. For example, if a constant is needed only in a single event procedure, you should put the constant declaration within that event procedure. However, you could also place the declaration at the top of the form's code, which would give all the event procedures in your form access to it.

6. Click the Start Debugging button on the Standard toolbar to run the program.

7. Click the Show Constant button.

The *Pi* constant appears in the label box, as shown here:

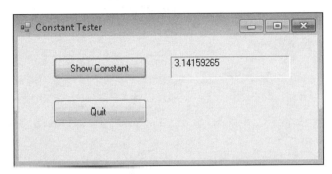

8. Click the Quit button to stop the program.

Constants are useful in program code, especially in involved mathematical formulas, such as Area = πr². The next section describes how you can use operators and variables to write similar formulas.

Working with Visual Basic Operators

A *formula* is a statement that combines numbers, variables, operators, and keywords to create a new value. Visual Basic contains several language elements designed for use in formulas. In this section, you'll practice working with arithmetic (or mathematical) *operators*, the symbols used to tie together the parts of a formula. With a few exceptions, the arithmetic symbols you'll use are the ones you use in everyday life, and their operations are fairly intuitive. You'll see each operator demonstrated in the following exercises.

Visual Basic includes the arithmetic operators listed in Table 5-2.

TABLE 5-2 Arithmetic Operators

Operator	Description
+	Addition
–	Subtraction
*	Multiplication
/	Division
\	Integer (whole number) division
Mod	Remainder division
^	Exponentiation (raising to a power)
&	String concatenation (combination)

Basic Math: The +, −, *, and / Operators

The operators for addition, subtraction, multiplication, and division are pretty straightforward and can be used in any formula where numbers or numeric variables are used. The following exercise demonstrates how you can use them in a program.

Work with basic operators

1. On the File menu, click Open Project.

2. Open the Basic Math project in the C:\Vb10sbs\Chap05\Basic Math folder.

3. If the project's form isn't visible, click Form1.vb in Solution Explorer, and then click the View Designer button.

   The Basic Math form opens in the Designer. The Basic Math program demonstrates how the addition, subtraction, multiplication, and division operators work with numbers you type. It also demonstrates how you can use text box, radio button, and button objects to process user input in a program.

4. Click the Start Debugging button on the Standard toolbar.

   The Basic Math program runs in the IDE. The program displays two text boxes in which you enter numeric values, a group of operator radio buttons, a box that displays results, and two button objects (Calculate and Quit).

5. Type **100** in the Variable 1 text box, and then press TAB.

   The insertion point, or *focus*, moves to the second text box.

6. Type **17** in the Variable 2 text box.

   You can now apply any of the mathematical operators to the values in the text boxes.

7. Click the Addition radio button, and then click the Calculate button.

   The operator is applied to the two values, and the number 117 appears in the Result box, as shown in the following screen shot.

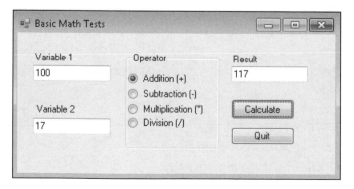

8. Practice using the subtraction, multiplication, and division operators with the two numbers in the variable boxes. (Click Calculate to calculate each formula.)

   The results appear in the Result box. Feel free to experiment with different numbers in the variable text boxes. (Try a few numbers with decimal points if you like.) I used the *Double* data type to declare the variables, so you can use very large numbers.

   Now try the following test to see what happens:

9. Type **100** in the Variable 1 text box, type **0** in the Variable 2 text box, click the Division radio button, and then click Calculate.

   Dividing by zero is not allowed in mathematical calculations, because it produces an infinite result. Visual Basic is able to handle this calculation and displays a value of Infinity in the Result text box. Being able to handle some divide-by-zero conditions is a feature that Visual Basic 2010 automatically provides.

10. When you've finished contemplating this and other tests, click the Quit button.

    The program stops, and the development environment returns.

Now take a look at the program code to see how the results were calculated. Basic Math uses a few of the standard input controls you experimented with in Chapter 3 and an event procedure that uses variables and operators to process the simple mathematical formulas. The program declares its variables at the top of the form so that they can be used in all the *Form1* event procedures.

Examine the Basic Math program code

1. Double-click the Calculate button on the form.

   The Code Editor displays the *Button1_Click* event procedure. At the top of the form's code, you'll see the following statement, which declares two variables of type *Double*:

   ```
   'Declare FirstNum and SecondNum variables
   Dim FirstNum, SecondNum As Double
   ```

   I used the *Double* type because I wanted a large, general-purpose variable type that could handle many different numbers—integers, numbers with decimal points, very big numbers, small numbers, and so on. The variables are declared on the same line by using the shortcut notation. Both *FirstNum* and *SecondNum* are of type *Double*, and are used to hold the values input in the first and second text boxes, respectively.

2. Scroll down in the Code Editor to see the contents of the *Button1_Click* event procedure.

Your screen looks similar to this:

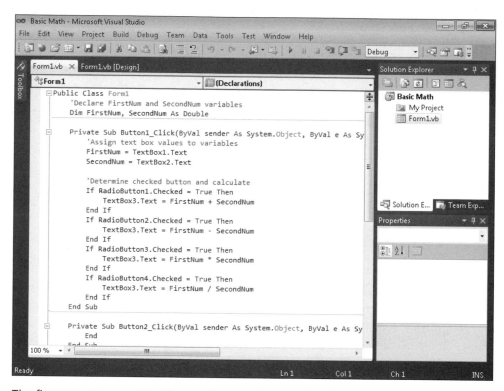

The first two statements in the event procedure transfer data entered in the text box objects into the *FirstNum* and *SecondNum* variables.

```
'Assign text box values to variables
FirstNum = TextBox1.Text
SecondNum = TextBox2.Text
```

The *TextBox* control handles the transfer with the *Text* property—a property that accepts text entered by the user and makes it available for use in the program. I'll make frequent use of the *TextBox* control in this book. When it's set to multiline and resized, it can display many lines of text—even a whole file!

After the text box values are assigned to the variables, the event procedure determines which radio button has been selected, calculates the mathematical formula, and displays the result in a third text box. The first radio button test looks like this:

```
'Determine checked button and calculate
If RadioButton1.Checked = True Then
    TextBox3.Text = FirstNum + SecondNum
End If
```

Remember from Chapter 3 that only one radio button object in a group box object can be selected at any given time. You can tell whether a radio button has been selected by evaluating the *Checked* property. If it's True, the button has been selected. If the *Checked* property is False, the button has not been selected. After this simple test, you're ready to compute the result and display it in the third text box object. That's all there is to using basic arithmetic operators. (You'll learn more about the syntax of *If … Then* tests in Chapter 6, "Using Decision Structures.")

You're done using the Basic Math program.

Shortcut Operators

An interesting feature of Visual Basic is that you can use shortcut operators for mathematical and string operations that involve changing the value of an existing variable. For example, if you combine the + symbol with the = symbol, you can add to a variable without repeating the variable name twice in the formula. Thus, you can write the formula X = X + 6 by using the syntax X += 6. Table 5-3 shows examples of these shortcut operators.

TABLE 5-3 Shortcut Operators

Operation	Long-Form Syntax	Shortcut Syntax
Addition (+)	X = X + 6	X += 6
Subtraction (–)	X = X – 6	X -= 6
Multiplication (*)	X = X * 6	X *= 6
Division (/)	X = X / 6	X /= 6
Integer division (\)	X = X \ 6	X \= 6
Exponentiation (^)	X = X ^ 6	X ^= 6
String concatenation (&)	X = X & "ABC"	X &= "ABC"

Using Advanced Operators: \, *Mod,* ^, and &

In addition to the four basic arithmetic operators, Visual Basic includes four advanced operators, which perform integer division (\), remainder division (*Mod*), exponentiation (^), and string concatenation (&). These operators are useful in special-purpose mathematical formulas and text processing applications. The following utility (a slight modification of the Basic Math program) shows how you can use each of these operators in a program.

Work with advanced operators

1. On the File menu, click Open Project.

   The Open Project dialog box opens.

2. Open the Advanced Math project in the C:\Vb10sbs\Chap05\Advanced Math folder.

3. If the project's form isn't visible, click Form1.vb in Solution Explorer, and then click the View Designer button.

The Advanced Math form opens in the Designer. The Advanced Math program is identical to the Basic Math program, with the exception of the operators shown in the radio buttons and in the program.

4. Click the Start Debugging button on the Standard toolbar.

    The program displays two text boxes in which you enter numeric values, a group of operator radio buttons, a text box that displays results, and two buttons.

5. Type **9** in the Variable 1 text box, and then press TAB.

6. Type **2** in the Variable 2 text box.

    You can now apply any of the advanced operators to the values in the text boxes.

7. Click the Integer Division radio button, and then click the Calculate button.

    The operator is applied to the two values, and the number 4 appears in the Result box, as shown here:

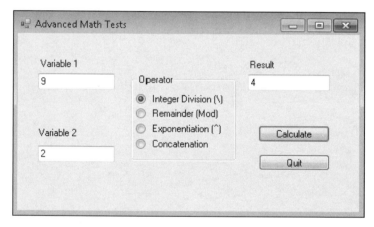

Integer division produces only the whole number result of the division operation. Although 9 divided by 2 equals 4.5, the integer division operation returns only the first part, an integer (the whole number 4). You might find this result useful if you're working with quantities that can't easily be divided into fractional components, such as the number of adults who can fit in a car.

8. Click the Remainder radio button, and then click the Calculate button.

    The number 1 appears in the Result box. Remainder division (modulus arithmetic) returns the remainder (the part left over) after two numbers are divided. Because 9 divided by 2 equals 4 with a remainder of 1 (2 * 4 + 1 = 9), the result produced by the *Mod* operator is 1. In addition to adding an early-1970s vibe to your code, the *Mod* operator can help you track "leftovers" in your calculations, such as the amount of money left over after a financial transaction.

9. Click the Exponentiation radio button, and then click the Calculate button.

The number 81 appears in the Result box. The exponentiation operator (^) raises a number to a specified power. For example, 9 ^ 2 equals 9^2, or 81. In a Visual Basic formula, 9^2 is written 9 ^ 2.

10. Click the Concatenation radio button, and then click the Calculate button.

The number 92 appears in the Result box. The string concatenation operator (&) combines two strings in a formula, but not through addition. The result is a combination of the "9" character and the "2" character. String concatenation can be performed on numeric variables—for example, if you're displaying the inning-by-inning score of a baseball game as they do in old-time score boxes—but concatenation is more commonly performed on string values or variables.

Because I declared the *FirstNum* and *SecondNum* variables as type *Double*, you can't combine words or letters by using the program code as written. As an example, try the following test, which causes an error and ends the program.

11. Type **birth** in the Variable 1 text box, type **day** in the Variable 2 text box, verify that Concatenation is selected, and then click Calculate.

Visual Basic is unable to process the text values you entered, so the program stops running, and an error message appears on the screen.

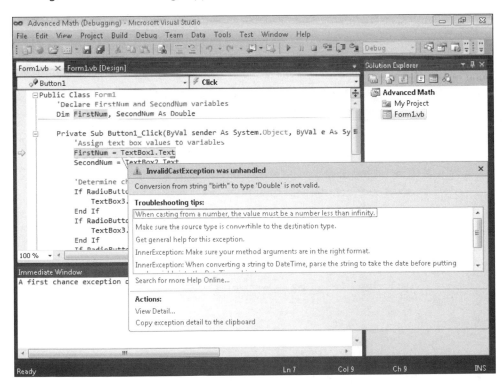

This type of error is called a *run-time error*—an error that surfaces not during the design and compilation of the program but later, when the program is running and encounters a condition that it doesn't know how to process. If this seems odd, you might imagine that Visual Basic is simply offering you a modern rendition of the robot plea "Does not compute!" from the best science-fiction films of the 1950s. The computer-speak message "Conversion from string 'birth' to type 'Double' is not valid" means that the words you entered in the text boxes ("birth" and "day") could not be converted, or *cast*, by Visual Basic to variables of the type *Double*. *Double* types can contain only numbers—period.

As we shall explore in more detail later, Visual Studio doesn't leave you hanging with such a problem, but provides a dialog box with different types of information to help you resolve the run-time error. For now, you have learned another important lesson about data types and when not to mix them.

12. Click the Stop Debugging button on the Standard toolbar to end the program.

    Your program ends and returns you to the development environment.

> **Note** In Chapter 8, "Debugging Visual Basic Programs," you'll learn about debugging mode, which allows you to track down the defects, or *bugs*, in your program code.

Now take a look at the program code to see how variables were declared and how the advanced operators were used.

13. Scroll to the code at the top of the Code Editor, if it is not currently visible.

    You see the following comment and program statement:

    ```
    'Declare FirstNum and SecondNum variables
    Dim FirstNum, SecondNum As Double
    ```

    As you might recall from the previous exercise, *FirstNum* and *SecondNum* are the variables that hold numbers coming in from the *TextBox1* and *TextBox2* objects.

14. Change the data type from *Double* to *String* so that you can properly test how the string concatenation (&) operator works.

15. Scroll down in the Code Editor to see how the advanced operators are used in the program code.

    You see the following code:

    ```
    'Assign text box values to variables
    FirstNum = TextBox1.Text
    SecondNum = TextBox2.Text

    'Determine checked button and calculate
    If RadioButton1.Checked = True Then
        TextBox3.Text = FirstNum \ SecondNum
    End If
    ```

```
If RadioButton2.Checked = True Then
    TextBox3.Text = FirstNum Mod SecondNum
End If
If RadioButton3.Checked = True Then
    TextBox3.Text = FirstNum ^ SecondNum
End If
If RadioButton4.Checked = True Then
    TextBox3.Text = FirstNum & SecondNum
End If
```

Like the Basic Math program, this program loads data from the text boxes and places it in the *FirstNum* and *SecondNum* variables. The program then checks to see which radio button the user checked and computes the requested formula. In this event procedure, the integer division (\), remainder (*Mod*), exponentiation (^), and string concatenation (&) operators are used. Now that you've changed the data type of the variables to *String*, run the program again to see how the & operator works on text.

16. Click the Start Debugging button.

17. Type **birth** in the Variable 1 text box, type **day** in the Variable 2 text box, click Concatenation, and then click Calculate.

The program now concatenates the string values and doesn't produce a run-time error, as shown here:

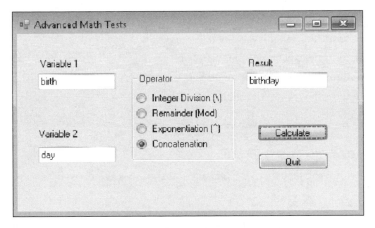

18. Click the Quit button to close the program.

As you can see, the *String* data type has fixed the concatenation problem. However, it is not a total solution because variables of type *String* will not function correctly if you try the Integer Division, Remainder, or Exponentiation operations with them. So, if you really wanted to have your program process numbers *and* text strings interchangeably, you'd need to add some additional program logic to your code. For now, however, you're finished working with the Advanced Math program.

Tip Run-time errors are difficult to avoid completely—even the most sophisticated application programs, such as Word or Microsoft Office Excel, sometimes run into error conditions that they can't handle, producing run-time errors, or *crashes*. Designing your programs to handle many different data types and operating conditions helps you produce solid, or *robust*, applications. In Chapter 9, "Trapping Errors by Using Structured Error Handling," you'll learn about another helpful tool for preventing run-time error crashes—the structured error handler.

Working with Math Methods in the .NET Framework

Now and then you'll want to do a little extra number crunching in your programs. You might need to round a number, calculate a complex mathematical expression, or introduce randomness into your programs. The math methods shown in Table 5-4 can help you work with numbers in your formulas. These methods are provided by the *System.Math* class of the .NET Framework, a class library that lets you tap into the power of the Windows operating system and accomplish many of the common programming tasks that you need to create your projects. The argument *n* in the table represents the number, variable, or expression that you want the method to evaluate.

TABLE 5-4 Useful Math Methods

Method	Purpose
Abs(n)	Returns the absolute value of *n*.
Atan(n)	Returns the arctangent, in radians, of *n*.
Cos(n)	Returns the cosine of the angle *n*. The angle *n* is expressed in radians.
Exp(n)	Returns the constant *e* raised to the power *n*.
Sign(n)	Returns −1 if *n* is less than 0, 0 if *n* equals 0, and +1 if *n* is greater than 0.
Sin(n)	Returns the sine of the angle *n*. The angle *n* is expressed in radians.
Sqrt(n)	Returns the square root of *n*.
Tan(n)	Returns the tangent of the angle *n*. The angle *n* is expressed in radians.

Note This is only a partial listing of the methods in the *System.Math* class; there are many more classes in the .NET Framework that Windows applications can use.

To use one or more of these methods, put the statement

```
Imports System.Math
```

at the top of your form's code in the Code Editor. This statement references the *System.Math* class so that you can use its methods in your program.

What is the purpose of the .NET Framework, anyway? The .NET Framework is a major feature of Visual Studio that is shared by Visual Basic, Microsoft Visual C++, Microsoft Visual C#, Microsoft F#, and other tools in Visual Studio. It's an underlying interface that becomes part of the Windows operating system itself, and it is installed on each computer that runs Visual Studio programs. The key components in the .NET Framework are the common language runtime (CLR) and the .NET Framework class library, which includes ADO.NET, ASP.NET, Windows Forms, and Windows Presentation Foundation (WPF). With each version of Visual Studio, the .NET Framework is extended to provide additional functionality. In Visual Studio 2010, the .NET Framework 4 library is being introduced, which offers an update to the .NET Framework 3.5 library and offers more deployment options, support for parallel computing (multithreaded and asynchronous code), improved security, networking enhancements, and new Web services supplied through ASP.NET.

Many of the improvements in the .NET Framework will come to you automatically as you use Visual Basic 2010, and some will become useful as you explore advanced programming techniques. Starting now and continuing throughout this book, I'll teach you how to use several methods in the .NET Framework to enhance your Visual Basic programs. After you finish with this book, you may want to seek out additional books and resources about the .NET Framework because it offers an important extension to what you can do with Visual Basic and the other languages in Visual Studio.

Give the math methods in the .NET Framework a try now by completing the following exercise.

Use the *System.Math* class to compute square roots

1. On the File menu, click New Project.

   The New Project dialog box opens.

2. Create a new Visual Basic Windows Forms Application project named **My Framework Math**.

   The new project is created, and a blank form opens in the Designer.

3. Click the *Button* control on the Windows Forms tab of the Toolbox, and then create a button object at the top of your form.

4. Click the *TextBox* control in the Toolbox, and then draw a text box below the button object.

5. Set the *Text* property of the button object to Square Root.

6. Double-click the button object to display the Code Editor.

7. At the very top of the Code Editor, above the *Public Class Form1* statement, type the following program statement:

```
Imports System.Math
```

The *System.Math* class is a collection of methods provided by the .NET Framework for arithmetic operations. The .NET Framework is organized in a hierarchical fashion and can be very deep. The *Imports* statement makes it easier to reference classes, properties, and methods in your project. For example, if you didn't include the previous *Imports* statement, to call the *Sqrt* method you would have to type *System.Math.Sqrt* instead of just *Sqrt*. The *Imports* statement must be the first statement in your program—it must come even before the variables that you declare for the form and the *Public Class Form1* statement that Visual Basic automatically provides.

8. Move down in the Code Editor, and then add the following code to the *Button1_Click* event procedure between the *Private Sub* and *End Sub* statements:

```
Dim Result As Double
Result = Sqrt(625)
TextBox1.Text = Result
```

These three statements declare a variable of the double type named *Result*, use the *Sqrt* method to compute the square root of 625, and assign the *Result* variable to the *Text* property of the text box object so that the answer is displayed.

9. Click the Save All button on the Standard toolbar to save your changes. Specify the C:\Vb10sbs\Chap05 folder as the location.

10. Click the Start Debugging button on the Standard toolbar.

The Framework Math program runs in the IDE.

11. Click the Square Root button.

Visual Basic calculates the square root of 625 and displays the result (25) in the text box. As you can see here, the *Sqrt* method works!

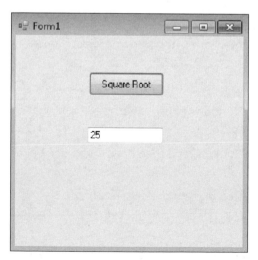

12. Click the Close button on the form to end the program.

To make it easier to reference classes, properties, and methods in the .NET Framework, include the *Imports* statement and specify the appropriate namespace or class. You can use this technique to use any class in the .NET Framework, and you'll see many more examples of this technique as you work through this book.

One Step Further: Establishing Order of Precedence

In the previous few exercises, you experimented with several arithmetic operators and one string operator. Visual Basic lets you mix as many arithmetic operators as you like in a formula, so long as each numeric variable and expression is separated from another by one operator. For example, this is an acceptable Visual Basic formula:

```
Total = 10 + 15 * 2 / 4 ^ 2
```

The formula processes several values and assigns the result to a variable named *Total*. But how is such an expression evaluated by Visual Basic? In other words, what sequence does Visual Basic follow when solving the formula? You might not have noticed, but the order of evaluation matters a great deal in this example.

Visual Basic solves this dilemma by establishing a specific *order of precedence* for mathematical operations. This list of rules tells Visual Basic which operator to use first, second, and so on when evaluating an expression that contains more than one operator.

Table 5-5 lists the operators from first to last in the order in which they are evaluated. (Operators on the same level in this table are evaluated from left to right as they appear in an expression.)

TABLE 5-5 Order of Precedence of Operators

Operator	Order of Precedence
( )	Values within parentheses are always evaluated first.
^	Exponentiation (raising a number to a power) is second.
–	Negation (creating a negative number) is third.
* /	Multiplication and division are fourth.
\	Integer division is fifth.
Mod	Remainder division is sixth.
+ –	Addition and subtraction are last.

Given the order of precedence in this table, the expression

```
Total = 10 + 15 * 2 / 4 ^ 2
```

is evaluated by Visual Basic in the following steps. (Shading is used to show each step in the order of evaluation.)

```
Total = 10 + 15 * 2 / 4 ^ 2
Total = 10 + 15 * 2 / 16
Total = 10 + 30 / 16
Total = 10 + 1.875
Total = 11.875
```

Using Parentheses in a Formula

You can use one or more pairs of parentheses in a formula to clarify the order of precedence or impose your own order of precedence over the standard one. For example, Visual Basic calculates the formula

```
Number = (8 − 5 * 3) ^ 2
```

by determining the value within the parentheses (–7) before doing the exponentiation—even though exponentiation is higher in order of precedence than subtraction and multiplication, according to the preceding table. You can further refine the calculation by placing nested parentheses in the formula. For example,

```
Number = ((8 − 5) * 3) ^ 2
```

directs Visual Basic to calculate the difference in the inner set of parentheses first, perform the operation in the outer parentheses next, and then determine the exponentiation. The result produced by the two formulas is different: the first formula evaluates to 49 and the second to 81. Parentheses can change the result of a mathematical operation, as well as make it easier to read.

Chapter 5 Quick Reference

To	Do This
Declare a variable	Type **Dim** followed by the variable name, the **As** keyword, and the variable data type in the program code. To make the variable valid in all a form's event procedures, place this statement at the top of the code for the form, before any event procedures. For example: `Dim Country As String`
Change the value of a variable	Assign a new value with the assignment operator (=). For example: `Country = "Japan"`
Get input by using a dialog box	Use the *InputBox* function and assign the result to a variable. For example: `UserName = InputBox("What is your name?")`

To	Do This
Display output in a dialog box	Use the *MsgBox* function. (The string to be displayed in the dialog box can be stored in a variable.) For example: ``` Forecast = "Rain, mainly on the plain." MsgBox(Forecast, , "Spain Weather Report") ```
Create a constant	Type the *Const* keyword followed by the constant name, the assignment operator (=), the constant data type, and the fixed value. For example: ``` Const JackBennysAge As Short = 39 ```
Create a formula	Link together numeric variables or values with one of the seven arithmetic operators, and then assign the result to a variable or a property. For example: ``` Result = 1 ^ 2 * 3 \ 4 'this equals 0 ```
Combine text strings	Use the string concatenation operator (&). For example: ``` Msg = "Hello" & "," & " world!" ```
Make it easier to reference a class library from the .NET Framework	Place an *Imports* statement at the very top of the form's code that identifies the class library. For example: ``` Imports System.Math ```
Make a call to a method from an included class library	Use the method name, and include any necessary arguments so that it can be used in a formula or a program statement. For example, to make a call to the *Sqrt* method in the *System.Math* class: ``` Hypotenuse = Sqrt(x ^ 2 + y ^ 2) ```
Control the evaluation order in a formula	Use parentheses in the formula. For example: ``` Result = 1 + 2 ^ 3 \ 4 'this equals 3 Result = (1 + 2) ^ (3 \ 4) 'this equals 1 ```

Chapter 6
Using Decision Structures

After completing this chapter, you will be able to:

- Write conditional expressions.

- Use an *If … Then* statement to branch to a set of program statements based on a varying condition.

- Use the *MaskedTextBox* control to receive user input in a specific format.

- Short-circuit an *If … Then* statement.

- Use a *Select Case* statement to select one choice from many options in program code.

- Use the *Name* property to rename objects within a program.

- Manage mouse events and write a *MouseHover* event handler.

In the past few chapters, you used several features of Microsoft Visual Basic 2010 to process user input. You used menus, toolbars, dialog boxes, and other Toolbox controls to display choices for the user, and you processed input by using property settings, variables, operators, formulas, and the Microsoft .NET Framework.

In this chapter, you'll learn how to branch conditionally to a specific area in your program based on input you receive from the user. You'll also learn how to evaluate one or more properties or variables by using conditional expressions, and then execute one or more program statements based on the results. In short, you'll increase your programming vocabulary by creating code blocks called *decision structures* that control how your program executes, or *flows*, internally.

Event-Driven Programming

The programs you've written so far in this book have displayed Toolbox controls, menus, toolbars, and dialog boxes on the screen, and with these programs, users could manipulate the screen elements in whatever order they saw fit. The programs put the user in charge, waited patiently for a response, and then processed the input predictably. In programming circles, this methodology is known as *event-driven programming*. You build a program by creating a group of "intelligent" objects that know how to respond to input, and then the program processes the input by using event procedures associated with the objects.

Where does this input come from? Fundamentally, of course, most input comes from the user of your program, who is opening menus, clicking the mouse, typing in text boxes, and so on. However, program input can also come from the computer system itself. For example, your program might be notified when a piece of e-mail arrives or when a specified period of time has elapsed on the system clock. In these situations, the computer, not the user, triggers the important events. But regardless of how an event is triggered, Visual Basic reacts by calling the event procedure associated with the object that recognized the event and executes the program code in the event procedure. So far, you've dealt primarily with the *Click*, *CheckedChanged*, and *SelectedIndexChanged* events. However, Visual Basic objects also can respond to many other types of events.

The event-driven nature of Visual Basic means that most of the computing done in your programs is accomplished by event procedures. These event-specific blocks of code process input, calculate new values, display output, and handle other tasks.

In this chapter, you'll learn how to use decision structures to compare variables, properties, and values, and how to execute one or more statements based on the results. In Chapter 7, "Using Loops and Timers," you'll use loops to execute a group of statements over and over until a condition is met or while a specific condition is true. Together, these powerful flow-control structures will help you build your event procedures so that they can respond to almost any situation.

Events Supported by Visual Basic Objects

Each object in Visual Basic has a predefined set of events to which it can respond. These events are listed when you select an object name in the Class Name list box at the top of the Code Editor and then click the Method Name arrow. (Events are visually identified in Microsoft Visual Studio by a lightning bolt icon.) You can write an event procedure for any of these events, and if that event occurs in the program, Visual Basic will execute the event procedure that's associated with it. For example, a list box object supports more than 60 events, including *Click*, *DoubleClick*, *DragDrop*, *DragOver*, *GotFocus*, *KeyDown*, *KeyPress*, *KeyUp*, *LostFocus*, *MouseDown*, *MouseMove*, *MouseUp*, *MouseHover*, *SelectedIndexChanged*, *TextChanged*, and *Validated*. You probably won't need to write code for more than three or four of these events in your applications, but it's nice to know that you have so many choices when you create elements in your interface. The following screen shot shows a partial listing of the events for a list box object in the Code Editor:

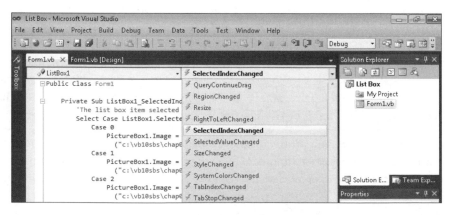

Using Conditional Expressions

One of the most useful tools for processing information in an event procedure is a conditional expression. A *conditional expression* is a part of a complete program statement that asks a True-or-False question about a property, a variable, or another piece of data in the program code. For example, the conditional expression

```
Price < 100
```

evaluates to True if the *Price* variable contains a value that is less than 100, and it evaluates to False if *Price* contains a value that is greater than or equal to 100.

You can use the following comparison operators shown in Table 6-1 within a conditional expression.

TABLE 6-1 Visual Basic Comparison Operators

Comparison Operator	Meaning
=	Equal to
< >	Not equal to
>	Greater than
<	Less than
>=	Greater than or equal to
<=	Less than or equal to

Table 6-2 shows some conditional expressions and their results. You'll work with conditional expressions several times in this chapter.

TABLE 6-2 Using Conditional Expressions

Conditional Expression	Result
10 <> 20	True (10 is not equal to 20)
Score < 20	True if *Score* is less than 20; otherwise False
Score = Label1.Text	True if the *Text* property of the *Label1* object contains the same value as the *Score* variable; otherwise False
TextBox1.Text = "Bill"	True if the word "Bill" is in the *TextBox1* object; otherwise False

If ... Then Decision Structures

When a conditional expression is used in a special block of statements called a *decision structure*, it controls whether other statements in your program are executed and in what order they're executed. You can use an *If ... Then* decision structure to evaluate a condition in the program and take a course of action based on the result. In its simplest form, an *If … Then* decision structure is written on a single line:

```
If condition Then statement
```

where *condition* is a conditional expression, and *statement* is a valid Visual Basic program statement. For example:

```
If Score >= 20 Then Label1.Text = "You win!"
```

is an *If … Then* decision structure that uses the conditional expression:

```
Score >= 20
```

to determine whether the program should set the *Text* property of the *Label1* object to "You win!" If the *Score* variable contains a value that's greater than or equal to 20, Visual Basic sets the *Text* property; otherwise, it skips the assignment statement and executes the next line in the event procedure. This sort of comparison always results in a True or False value. A conditional expression never results in a value of maybe.

Testing Several Conditions in an *If … Then* Decision Structure

Visual Basic also supports an *If … Then* decision structure that you can use to include several conditional expressions. This block of statements can be several lines long and contains the important keywords *ElseIf*, *Else*, and *End If*:

```
If condition1 Then
    statements executed if condition1 is True
ElseIf condition2 Then
    statements executed if condition2 is True
[Additional ElseIf conditions and statements can be placed here]
Else
    statements executed if none of the conditions is True
End If
```

In this structure, *condition1* is evaluated first. If this conditional expression is True, the block of statements below it is executed, one statement at a time. (You can include one or more program statements.) If the first condition isn't True, the second conditional expression (*condition2*) is evaluated. If the second condition is True, the second block of statements is executed. (You can add additional *ElseIf* conditions and statements if you have more conditions to evaluate.) If none of the conditional expressions is True, the statements below the *Else* keyword are executed. Finally, the whole structure is closed by the *End If* keywords.

The following code shows how a multiple-line *If … Then* structure could be used to determine the amount of tax due in a hypothetical progressive tax return. (The income and percentage numbers are from the projected U.S. Internal Revenue Service 2010 Tax Rate Schedule for single filing status.)

```
Dim AdjustedIncome, TaxDue As Double
AdjustedIncome = 50000
If AdjustedIncome <= 8375 Then            '10% tax bracket
    TaxDue = AdjustedIncome * 0.1
ElseIf AdjustedIncome <= 34000 Then       '15% tax bracket
    TaxDue = 837.5 + ((AdjustedIncome - 8375) * 0.15)
ElseIf AdjustedIncome <= 82400 Then       '25% tax bracket
    TaxDue = 4681.25 + ((AdjustedIncome - 34000) * 0.25)
ElseIf AdjustedIncome <= 171850 Then      '28% tax bracket
    TaxDue = 16781.25 + ((AdjustedIncome - 82400) * 0.28)
ElseIf AdjustedIncome <= 373650 Then      '33% tax bracket
    TaxDue = 41827.25 + ((AdjustedIncome - 171850) * 0.33)
Else                                      '35% tax bracket
    TaxDue = 108421.25 + ((AdjustedIncome - 373650) * 0.35)
End If
```

Important The order of the conditional expressions in your *If ... Then* and *ElseIf* statements is critical. What happens if you reverse the order of the conditional expressions in the tax computation example and list the rates in the structure from highest to lowest? Taxpayers in the 10 percent, 15 percent, 25 percent, 28 percent, and 33 percent tax brackets are all placed in the 35 percent tax bracket because they all have an income that's less than or equal to $373,650. (This occurs because Visual Basic stops at the first conditional expression that is True, even if others are also True.) All the conditional expressions in this example test the same variable, so they need to be listed in ascending order to get the taxpayers to be placed in the right groups. Moral: When you use more than one conditional expression, consider the order carefully.

This useful decision structure tests the double-precision variable *AdjustedIncome* at the first income level and subsequent income levels until one of the conditional expressions evaluates to True, and then determines the taxpayer's income tax accordingly. With some simple modifications, it could be used to compute the tax owed by any taxpayer in a progressive tax system, such as the one in the United States. Provided that the tax rates are complete and up to date and that the value in the *AdjustedIncome* variable is correct, the program as written will give the correct tax owed for single U.S. taxpayers for 2010. If the tax rates change, it's a simple matter to update the conditional expressions. With an additional decision structure to determine taxpayers' filing status, the program readily extends itself to include all U.S. taxpayers.

Tip Expressions that can be evaluated as True or False are also known as *Boolean expressions*, and the True or False result can be assigned to a Boolean variable or property. You can assign Boolean values to certain object properties or Boolean variables that have been created by using the *Dim* statement and the *As Boolean* keywords.

In the next exercise, you'll use an *If ... Then* decision structure that recognizes users as they enter a program—a simple way to get started with writing your own decision structures. You'll also learn how to use the *MaskedTextBox* control to receive input from the user in a specific format.

Validate users by using *If ... Then*

1. Start Visual Studio, and create a new Windows Forms Application project named **My User Validation**.

   The new project is created, and a blank form opens in the Designer.

2. Click the form, and then set the form's *Text* property to "User Validation."

3. Use the *Label* control to create a label on your form, and use the Properties window to set the *Text* property to "Enter Your Social Security Number."

4. Use the *Button* control to create a button on your form, and set the button's *Text* property to "Sign In."

5. Click the *MaskedTextBox* control on the Common Controls tab in the Toolbox, and then create a masked text box object on your form below the label.

   The *MaskedTextBox* control is similar to the *TextBox* control that you have been using, but by using *MaskedTextBox*, you can control the format of the information entered by the user into your program. You control the format by setting the *Mask* property; you can use a predefined format supplied by the control or choose your own format. You'll use the *MaskedTextBox* control in this program to require that users enter a Social Security number in the standard nine-digit format used by the U.S. Internal Revenue Service.

6. With the *MaskedTextBox1* object selected, click the *Mask* property in the Properties window, and then click the ellipses button in the second column.

   The Input Mask dialog box opens, showing a list of your predefined formatting patterns, or *masks*.

7. Click Social Security Number in the list.

   The Input Mask dialog box looks like this:

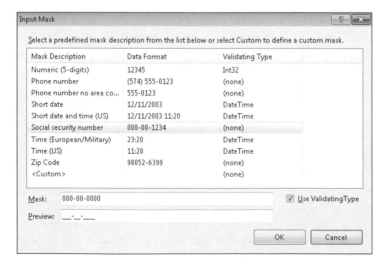

Although you won't use it now, take a moment to note the <Custom> option, which you can use later to create your own input masks using numbers and placeholder characters such as a hyphen (-).

8. Click OK to accept Social Security Number as your input mask.

Visual Studio displays your input mask in the *MaskedTextBox1* object, as shown in the following screen shot:

9. Double-click the Sign In button.

The *Button1_Click* event procedure appears in the Code Editor.

10. Type the following program statements in the event procedure:

```
If MaskedTextBox1.Text = "555-55-1212" Then
    MsgBox("Welcome to the system!")
Else
    MsgBox("I don't recognize this number")
End If
```

This simple *If … Then* decision structure checks the value of the *MaskedTextBox1* object's *Text* property, and if it equals "555-55-1212," the structure displays the message "Welcome to the system!" If the number entered by the user is some other value, the structure displays the message "I don't recognize this number." The beauty in this program, however, is how the *MaskedTextBox1* object automatically filters input to ensure that it is in the correct format.

11. Click the Save All button on the Standard toolbar to save your changes. Specify the C:\Vb10sbs\Chap06 folder as the location for your project.

12. Click the Start Debugging button on the Standard toolbar.

The program runs in the IDE. The form prompts the user to enter a Social Security number (SSN) in the appropriate format, and displays underlines and hyphens to offer the user a hint of the format required.

13. Type **abcd** to test the input mask.

Visual Basic prevents the letters from being displayed because letters do not fit the requested format. A nine-digit SSN is required.

14. Type **1234567890** to test the input mask.

Visual Basic displays the number 123-45-6789 in the masked text box, ignoring the 10th digit that you typed. Again, Visual Basic has forced the user's input into the proper format. Your form looks like this:

15. Click the Sign In button.

Visual Basic displays the message "I don't recognize this number" because the SSN does not match the number the *If . . . Then* decision structure is looking for.

16. Click OK, delete the SSN from the masked text box, enter **555-55-1212** as the number, and then click Sign In again.

This time the decision structure recognizes the number and displays a welcome message. You see the following message box:

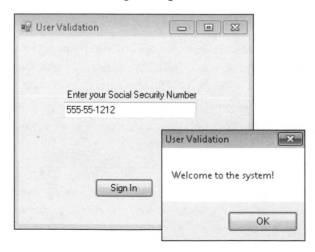

Your code has prevented an unauthorized user from using the program, and you've learned a useful skill related to controlling input from the user.

17. Exit the program.

Using Logical Operators in Conditional Expressions

You can test more than one conditional expression in *If … Then* and *ElseIf* clauses if you want to include more than one selection criterion in your decision structure. The extra conditions are linked by using one or more of the logical operators listed in Table 6-3.

TABLE 6-3 Visual Basic Logical Operators

Logical Operator	Meaning
And	If both conditional expressions are True, then the result is True.
Or	If either conditional expression is True, then the result is True.
Not	If the conditional expression is False, then the result is True. If the conditional expression is True, then the result is False.
Xor	If one and only one of the conditional expressions is True, then the result is True. If both are True or both are False, then the result is False. (*Xor* stands for exclusive *Or*.)

> **Tip** When your program evaluates a complex expression that mixes different operator types, it evaluates mathematical operators first, comparison operators second, and logical operators third.

Table 6-4 lists some examples of the logical operators at work. In the expressions, it is assumed that the *Vehicle* string variable contains the value "Bike," and the integer variable *Price* contains the value 200.

TABLE 6-4 Using Logical Expressions

Logical Expression	Result
`Vehicle = "Bike" And Price < 300`	True (both conditions are True)
`Vehicle = "Car" Or Price < 500`	True (one condition is True)
`Not Price < 100`	True (condition is False)
`Vehicle = "Bike" Xor Price < 300`	False (both conditions are True)

In the following exercise, you'll modify the My User Validation program to prompt the user for a personal identification number (PIN) during the validation process. To do this, you will add a second text box to get the PIN from the user, and then modify the *If … Then* clause in the decision structure so that it uses the *And* operator to verify the PIN.

Add password protection by using the *And* operator

1. Display the User Validation form, and then add a second *Label* control to the form below the first masked text box.

2. Set the new label's *Text* property to "PIN."

3. Add a second *MaskedTextBox* control to the form below the first masked text box and the new label.

4. Click the smart tag on the *MaskedTextBox2* object to open the MaskedTextBox Tasks list, and then click the Set Mask command to display the Input Mask dialog box.

5. Click the Numeric (5-digits) input mask, and then click OK.

   Like many PINs found online, this PIN will be five digits long. Again, if the user types a password of a different length or format, it will be rejected.

6. Double-click the Sign In button to display the *Button1_Click* event procedure in the Code Editor.

7. Modify the event procedure so that it contains the following code:

   ```
   If MaskedTextBox1.Text = "555-55-1212" _
   And MaskedTextBox2.Text = "54321" Then
       MsgBox("Welcome to the system!")
   Else
       MsgBox("I don't recognize this number")
   End If
   ```

   The statement now includes the *And* logical operator, which requires that the user's PIN correspond with his or her SSN before the user is admitted to the system. (In this case, the valid PIN is 54321; in a real-world program, this value would be extracted along with the SSN from a secure database.) I modified the earlier program by adding a line continuation character (_) to the end of the first line, and by adding the second line beginning with *And*.

8. Click the Start Debugging button on the Standard toolbar.

   The program runs in the IDE.

9. Type **555-55-1212** in the Social Security Number masked text box.

10. Type **54321** in the PIN masked text box.

11. Click the Sign In button.

    The user is welcomed to the program, as shown in the screen shot on the following page.

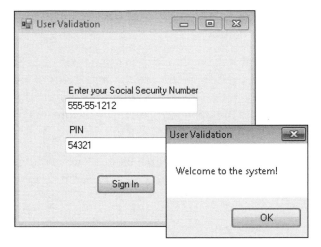

12. Click OK to close the message box.

13. Experiment with other values for the SSN and PIN.

    Test the program carefully to be sure that the welcome message is not displayed when other PINs or SSNs are entered.

14. Click the Close button on the form when you're finished.

    The program ends, and the development environment returns.

> **Tip** You can further customize this program by using the *PasswordChar* property in masked text box objects. The *PasswordChar* property can be used to display a placeholder character, such as an asterisk (*), when the user types. (You specify the character by using the Properties window.) Using a password character gives users additional secrecy as they enter their protected password—a standard feature of such operations.

Short-Circuiting by Using *AndAlso* and *OrElse*

Visual Basic offers two logical operators that you can use in your conditional statements, *AndAlso* and *OrElse*. These operators work the same as *And* and *Or* respectively, but offer an important subtlety in the way they're evaluated that is worth a few moments of thoughtful consideration. However, they are also somewhat advanced, so if you would like to skip this section (offered here for completeness sake) feel free to do so.

Consider an *If* statement that has two conditions that are connected by an *AndAlso* operator. For the statements of the *If* structure to be executed, both conditions must evaluate to True. If the first condition evaluates to False, Visual Basic skips to the next line or the *Else* statement immediately, without testing the second condition. This partial, or *short-circuiting*, evaluation of an *If* statement makes logical sense—why should Visual Basic continue to evaluate the *If* statement if both conditions cannot be True?

The *OrElse* operator works in a similar fashion. Consider an *If* statement that has two conditions that are connected by an *OrElse* operator. For the statements of the *If* structure to be executed, at least one condition must evaluate to True. If the first condition evaluates to True, Visual Basic begins to execute the statements in the *If* structure immediately, without testing the second condition.

Here's an example of the short-circuit situation in Visual Basic, a simple routine that uses an *If* statement and an *AndAlso* operator to test two conditions and display the message "Inside If" if both conditions are True:

```
Dim Number As Integer = 0
If Number = 1 AndAlso MsgBox("Second condition test") Then
    MsgBox("Inside If")
Else
    MsgBox("Inside Else")
End If
```

The *MsgBox* function itself is used as the second conditional test, which is somewhat unusual, but the strange syntax is completely valid and gives us a perfect opportunity to see how short-circuiting works up close. The text "Second condition test" appears in a message box only if the *Number* variable is set to 1; otherwise, the *AndAlso* operator short-circuits the *If* statement, and the second condition isn't evaluated. If you actually try this code, remember that it's for demonstration purposes only—you wouldn't want to use *MsgBox* with this syntax as a test because it doesn't really test anything. But by changing the *Number* variable from 0 to 1 and back, you can get a good idea of how the *AndAlso* statement and short-circuiting work.

Here's a second example of how short-circuiting functions in Visual Basic when two conditions are evaluated using the *AndAlso* operator. This time, a more complex conditional test (7 / HumanAge <= 1) is used after the *AndAlso* operator to determine what some people call the "dog age" of a person:

```
Dim HumanAge As Integer
HumanAge = 7
'One year for a dog is seven years for a human
If HumanAge <> 0 AndAlso 7 / HumanAge <= 1 Then
    MsgBox("You are at least one dog year old")
Else
    MsgBox("You are less than one dog year old")
End If
```

As part of a larger program that determines the so-called dog age of a person by dividing his or her current age by 7, this bare-bones routine tries to determine whether the value in the *HumanAge* integer variable is at least 7. (If you haven't heard the concept of "dog age" before, bear with me—following this logic, a 28-year-old person would be four dog years old. This has been suggested as an interesting way of relating to dogs, since dogs have a lifespan of roughly one-seventh that of humans.) The code uses two *If* statement conditions and can be used in a variety of different contexts—I used it in the *Click* event procedure for a button object. The first condition checks to see whether a non-zero number has been placed in the *HumanAge* variable—I've assumed momentarily that the user has enough sense to place a positive age into *HumanAge* because a negative number would produce incorrect results. The second condition tests whether the person is at least seven years old. If both conditions evaluate to True, the message "You are at least one dog year old" is displayed in a message box. If the person is less than seven, the message "You are less than one dog year old" is displayed.

Now imagine that I've changed the value of the *HumanAge* variable from 7 to 0. What happens? The first *If* statement condition is evaluated as False by the Visual Basic compiler, and that evaluation prevents the second condition from being evaluated, thus halting, or short-circuiting, the *If* statement and saving us from a nasty "divide by zero" error that could result if we divided 7 by 0 (the new value of the *HumanAge* variable). And recall that if you divide by zero in a Visual Basic program and don't catch the problem somehow, the result will be an error because division by zero isn't permitted.

In summary, the *AndAlso* and *OrElse* operators in Visual Basic open up a few new possibilities for Visual Basic programmers, including the potential to prevent run-time errors and other unexpected results. It's also possible to improve performance by placing conditions that are time-consuming to calculate at the end of the condition statement because Visual Basic doesn't perform these expensive condition calculations unless it's necessary. However, you need to think carefully about all the possible conditions that your *If* statements might encounter as variable states change during program execution.

Select Case Decision Structures

With Visual Basic, you can also control the execution of statements in your programs by using *Select Case* decision structures. You used *Select Case* structures in Chapters 3 and 5 of this book when you wrote event procedures to process list box and combo box choices. A *Select Case* structure is similar to an *If … Then … ElseIf* structure, but it's more efficient when the branching depends on one key variable, or *test case*. You can also use *Select Case* structures to make your program code more readable.

The syntax for a *Select Case* structure looks like this:

```
Select Case variable
    Case value1
        statements executed if value1 matches variable
    Case value2
        statements executed if value2 matches variable
    Case value3
```

```
            statements executed if value3 matches variable
    ...
    Case Else
        statements executed if no match is found
End Select
```

A *Select Case* structure begins with the *Select Case* keywords and ends with the *End Select* keywords. You replace *variable* with the variable, property, or other expression that is to be the key value, or test case, for the structure. You replace *value1*, *value2*, and *value3* with numbers, strings, or other values related to the test case being considered. If one of the values matches the variable, the statements below the *Case* clause are executed, and then Visual Basic jumps to the line after the *End Select* statement and picks up execution there. You can include any number of *Case* clauses in a *Select Case* structure, and you can include more than one value in a *Case* clause. If you list multiple values after a case, separate them with commas.

The following example shows how a *Select Case* structure could be used to print an appropriate message about a person's age and cultural milestones in a program. Since the *Age* variable contains a value of 18, the string "You can vote now!" is assigned to the *Text* property of the label object. (You'll notice that the "milestones" have a U.S. slant to them; please customize freely to match your cultural setting.)

```
Dim Age As Integer
Age = 18

Select Case Age
    Case 16
        Label1.Text = "You can drive now!"
    Case 18
        Label1.Text = "You can vote now!"
    Case 21
        Label1.Text = "You can drink wine with your meals."
    Case 65
        Label1.Text = "Time to retire and have fun!"
End Select
```

A *Select Case* structure also supports a *Case Else* clause that you can use to display a message if none of the preceding cases matches the *Age* variable. Here's how *Case Else* would work in the following example—note that I've changed the value of *Age* to 25 to trigger the *Case Else* clause:

```
Dim Age As Integer
Age = 25

Select Case Age
    Case 16
        Label1.Text = "You can drive now!"
    Case 18
        Label1.Text = "You can vote now!"
    Case 21
        Label1.Text = "You can drink wine with your meals."
```

```
    Case 65
        Label1.Text = "Time to retire and have fun!"
    Case Else
        Label1.Text = "You're a great age! Enjoy it!"
End Select
```

Using Comparison Operators with a Select Case Structure

You can use comparison operators to include a range of test values in a *Select Case* structure. The Visual Basic comparison operators that can be used are =, <>, >, <, >=, and <=. To use the comparison operators, you need to include the *Is* keyword or the *To* keyword in the expression to identify the comparison you're making. The *Is* keyword instructs the compiler to compare the test variable to the expression listed after the *Is* keyword. The *To* keyword identifies a range of values. The following structure uses *Is*, *To*, and several comparison operators to test the *Age* variable and to display one of five messages:

```
Select Case Age
    Case Is < 13
        Label1.Text = "Enjoy your youth!"
    Case 13 To 19
        Label1.Text = "Enjoy your teens!"
    Case 21
        Label1.Text = "You can drink wine with your meals."
    Case Is > 100
        Label1.Text = "Looking good!"
    Case Else
        Label1.Text = "That's a nice age to be."
End Select
```

If the value of the *Age* variable is less than 13, the message "Enjoy your youth!" is displayed. For the ages 13 through 19, the message "Enjoy your teens!" is displayed, and so on.

A *Select Case* decision structure is usually much clearer than an *If… Then* structure and is more efficient when you're making three or more branching decisions based on one variable or property. However, when you're making two or fewer comparisons, or when you're working with several different values, you'll probably want to use an *If… Then* decision structure.

In the following exercise, you'll see how you can use a *Select Case* structure to process input from a list box. You'll use the *ListBox.Text* and *ListBox.SelectedIndex* properties to collect the input, and then you'll use a *Select Case* structure to display a greeting in one of four languages.

Use a *Select Case* structure to process input from a list box

1. On the File menu, click New Project.

   The New Project dialog box opens.

2. Create a new Windows Forms Application project named **My Select Case**.

   A blank form opens in the Designer.

3. Click the *Label* control in the Toolbox, and then draw a label near the top of the form to display a title for the program.

4. Use the *Label* control to create a second label object below the first.

   You'll use this label as a title for the list box.

5. Click the *ListBox* control in the Toolbox, and then create a list box below the second label.

6. Use the *Label* control to draw two more labels below the list box to display program output.

7. Use the *Button* control to create a small button on the bottom of the form.

8. Open the Properties window, and then set the properties as shown in the following table, for the objects that you have just created.

Object	Property	Setting
Form1	Text	"Case Greeting"
Label1	Font	Times New Roman, Bold, 12 point
	Name	lblTitle
	Text	"International Welcome Program"
Label2	Name	lblTextBoxLabel
	Text	"Choose a country"
Label3	Font	Microsoft Sans Serif 10 point
	Name	lblCountry
	Text	(empty)
Label4	AutoSize	False
	BorderStyle	Fixed3D
	ForeColor	Red
	Name	lblGreeting
	Text	(empty)
ListBox1	Name	lstCountryBox
Button1	Name	btnQuit
	Text	"Quit"

Since there are so many objects, you'll also assign *Name* properties to help you easily identify the control on the form and within your program code. (When the properties in the Properties window are sorted alphabetically, you'll find *Name* listed in parentheses near the top of the Properties window. When the properties in the Properties window are sorted by category, you'll find *Name* listed in parentheses in the Design category.) I recommend that you use the *Name* property whenever you have more than four or five objects in a program. In this example, I've given the objects names that feature a three-character prefix to identify the object type, such as btn (for button), lbl (for label), and lst (for list box).

When you've finished setting properties, your form looks similar to this:

Now you'll enter the program code to initialize the list box.

9. Double-click the form.

   The *Form1_Load* event procedure appears in the Code Editor.

10. Type the following program code to initialize the list box:

```
lstCountryBox.Items.Add("England")
lstCountryBox.Items.Add("Germany")
lstCountryBox.Items.Add("Mexico")
lstCountryBox.Items.Add("Italy")
```

These lines use the *Add* method of the list box object to add entries to the list box on your form.

11. Click the Form1.vb [Design] tab at the top of the Code Editor to switch back to the Designer, and then double-click the list box object on your form to edit its event procedure.

   The *lstCountryBox_SelectedIndexChanged* event procedure appears in the Code Editor.

12. Type the following lines to process the list box selection made by the user:

```
lblCountry.Text = lstCountryBox.Text
Select Case lstCountryBox.SelectedIndex
    Case 0
        lblGreeting.Text = "Hello, programmer"
    Case 1
        lblGreeting.Text = "Hallo, programmierer"
    Case 2
        lblGreeting.Text = "Hola, programador"
    Case 3
        lblGreeting.Text = "Ciao, programmatore"
End Select
```

The first line copies the name of the selected list box item to the *Text* property of the third label on the form (which you renamed *lblCountry*). The most important property used in the statement is *lstCountryBox.Text*, which contains the exact text of the item selected in the list box. The remaining statements are part of the *Select Case* decision structure. The structure uses the *lstCountryBox.SelectedIndex* property as a test case variable and compares it to several values. The *SelectedIndex* property always contains the number of the item selected in the list box; the item at the top is 0 (zero), the second item is 1, the next item is 2, and so on. By using *SelectedIndex*, the *Select Case* structure can quickly identify the user's choice and display the correct greeting on the form.

13. Display the form again, and then double-click the Quit button (*btnQuit*).

    The *btnQuit_Click* event procedure appears in the Code Editor.

14. Type **End** in the event procedure.

15. Click the Save All button on the Standard toolbar to save your changes. Specify the C:\Vb10sbs\Chap06 folder as the location.

    Now run the program, and see how the *Select Case* statement works.

> **Tip** The complete Select Case project is located in the C:\Vb10sbs\Chap06\Select Case folder.

16. Click the Start Debugging button on the Standard toolbar to run the program.

17. Click each of the country names in the Choose A Country list box.

    The program displays a greeting for each of the countries listed. The following screen shot shows the greeting for Italy:

18. Click the Quit button to stop the program.

The program stops, and the development environment returns.

You've finished working with *If… Then* and *Select Case* decision structures in this chapter. You'll have several additional opportunities to work with them in this book, however. *If… Then* and *Select Case* are two of the crucial decision-making mechanisms in the Visual Basic programming language, and you'll find that you use them in almost every program that you write.

One Step Further: Detecting Mouse Events

I began this chapter by discussing a few of the events that Visual Basic programs can respond to, and as the chapter progressed, you learned how to manage different types of events by using the *If… Then* and *Select Case* decision structures. In this section, you'll add an event handler to the Select Case program that detects when the pointer "hovers" over the Country list box for a moment or two. You'll write the special routine, or *event handler*, by building a list box event procedure for the *MouseHover* event, one of several mouse-related activities that Visual Basic can monitor and process. This event procedure will display the message "Please click the country name" if the user points to the country list box for a moment or two but doesn't make a selection, perhaps because he or she doesn't know how to make a selection or has become engrossed in another task.

Add a mouse event handler

1. Open the Code Editor if it isn't already open.

2. At the top of the Code Editor just below the Form1.vb tab, click the Class Name arrow, and then click the *lstCountryBox* object.

3. Click the Method Name arrow, and then click the *MouseHover* event.

Visual Basic adds the *lstCountryBox_MouseHover* event procedure in the Code Editor, as shown here:

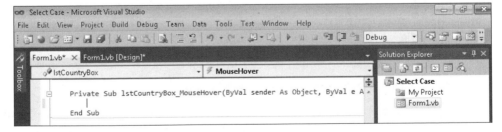

Each object on the form has one event procedure that is added automatically when you double-click the object on the form. When you need to add other event procedures for an object, you can use the Method Name list box.

4. Type the following program statements in the *lstCountryBox_MouseHover* event procedure:

```
If lstCountryBox.SelectedIndex < 0 Then
    lblGreeting.Text = "Please click the country name"
End If
```

This *If* statement evaluates the *SelectedIndex* property of the list box object by using a conditional statement. The event handler assumes that if the *SelectedIndex* property is zero or greater, the user doesn't need help picking the country name (because he or she has already selected a country). But if the *SelectedIndex* property is less than zero, the event handler displays the message "Please click the country name" in the greeting label at the bottom of the form. This Help message appears when the user holds the pointer over the list box and disappears when a country name is selected.

5. Click the Start Debugging button to run the program.

6. Hold the pointer over the country list box, and wait a few moments.

The message "Please click the country name" appears in red text in the label, as shown here:

7. Click a country name in the list box.

The translated greeting appears in the label, and the Help message disappears.

8. Click the Quit button to stop the program.

You've learned how to process mouse events in a program, and you've also learned that writing event handlers is quite simple. Try writing additional event handlers on your own as you continue reading this book—it will help you learn more about the events available to Visual Studio objects, and it will give you more practice with *If … Then* and *Select Case* decision structures.

Chapter 6 Quick Reference

To	Do This
Write a conditional expression	Use one of the following comparison operators between two values: =, < >, >, <, >=, or <=.

Use an *If … Then* decision structure	Use the following syntax:
	
	```If condition1 Then```
	``` statements executed if condition1 True```
	```ElseIf condition2 Then```
	``` statements executed if condition2 True```
	```Else```
	``` statements executed if none are True```
	```End If```

Receive input from the user in a specific format	Add a *MaskedTextBox* control to your form, and specify the input format by configuring the *Mask* property.

Use a *Select Case* decision structure	Use the following syntax:
	
	```Select Case variable```
	```Case value1```
	``` statements executed if value1 matches```
	```Case value2```
	``` statements executed if value2 matches```
	```Case Else```
	``` statements executed if none match```
	```End Select```

Rename an object in a program	Select the object that you want to rename, and then modify the object's *(Name)* property by using the Properties window. If you give the object a three-character prefix that identifies its object type (btn, lbl, lst, etc.), the object is easier to spot in program code.
Make two comparisons in a conditional expression	Use a logical operator between comparisons (*And*, *Or*, *Not*, or *Xor*).
Short-circuit an *If … Then* statement	*If … Then* statements can be short-circuited when the *AndAlso* and *OrElse* operators are used and two or more conditional expressions are given. Depending on the result of the first condition, Visual Basic might not evaluate the additional conditions, and the statement is short-circuited.
Write an event handler	In the Code Editor, click an object name in the Class Name list box, and then click an event name in the Method Name list box. Add program statements to the event procedure (called an *event handler*) that respond to the event you are customizing.

Chapter 7
Using Loops and Timers

After completing this chapter, you will be able to:

- Use a *For ... Next* loop to execute statements a set number of times.

- Display output in a multiline text box by using string concatenation.

- Use a *Do* loop to execute statements until a specific condition is met.

- Use the *Timer* control to execute code at specific times.

- Create your own digital clock and timed password utility.

- Use the Insert Snippet command to insert ready-made code templates or snippets into the Code Editor.

In Chapter 6, "Using Decision Structures," you learned how to use the *If ... Then* and *Select Case* decision structures to choose which statements to execute in a program. You also learned how to process user input and evaluate different conditions in a program and how to determine which block of program statements to execute based on changing conditions. Now you'll continue learning about program execution and *flow control* by using *loops* to execute a block of statements over and over again. You'll also create a digital clock and other interesting utilities that perform actions at set times or in relation to intervals on your computer's system clock.

In this chapter, you'll use a *For ... Next* loop to execute statements a set number of times, and you'll use a *Do* loop to execute statements until a conditional expression is met. You'll also learn how to display more than one line of text in a text box object by using the string concatenation (&) operator, and you'll learn how to use the Microsoft Visual Studio *Timer* control to execute code at specific intervals in your program. Finally, you'll learn how to use the Insert Snippet command to insert code templates into your programs—a time-saving feature within the Visual Studio Integrated Design Environment (IDE).

Writing *For ... Next* Loops

With a *For ... Next* loop, you can execute a specific group of program statements a set number of times in an event procedure or a code module. This approach can be useful if you're performing several related calculations, working with elements on the screen, or processing several pieces of user input. A *For ... Next* loop is really just a shorthand way of writing out a long list of program statements. Because each group of statements in such a list does essentially the same thing, you can define just one group of statements and request that it be executed as many times as you want.

The syntax for a *For … Next* loop looks like this:

```
For variable = start To end
    statements to be repeated
Next [variable]
```

In this syntax statement, *For, To,* and *Next* are required keywords, as is the equal to operator (=). You replace *variable* with the name of a numeric variable that keeps track of the current loop count (the variable after *Next* is optional), and you replace *start* and *end* with numeric values representing the starting and stopping points for the loop. (Note that you must declare *variable* before it's used in the *For … Next* statement and that you don't type in the brackets, which I include to indicate an optional item.) The line or lines between the *For* and *Next* statements are the instructions that are repeated each time the loop is executed.

For example, the following *For … Next* loop sounds four beeps in rapid succession from the computer's speaker (although the result might be difficult to hear):

```
Dim i As Integer
For i = 1 To 4
    Beep()
Next i
```

This loop is the functional equivalent of writing the *Beep* statement four times in a procedure. The compiler treats it the same as:

```
Beep()
Beep()
Beep()
Beep()
```

The variable used in the loop is *i*, a single letter that, by convention, stands for the first integer counter in a *For … Next* loop and is declared as an *Integer* type. Each time the loop is executed, the counter variable is incremented by 1. (The first time through the loop, the variable contains a value of 1, the value of *start*; the last time through, it contains a value of 4, the value of *end*.) As you'll see in the following examples, you can use this counter variable to great advantage in your loops.

> **Tip** In loops that use counter variables, the usual practice is to use the *Integer* type for the variable declaration, as I did previously. However, you will get similar performance in Visual Basic 2010 if you declare the counter variable as type *Long* or *Decimal*.

Using a Counter Variable in a Multiline *TextBox* Control

A counter variable is just like any other variable in an event procedure. It can be assigned to properties, used in calculations, or displayed in a program. One of the practical uses for a counter variable is to display output in a *TextBox* control. You used the *TextBox* control earlier in this book to display a single line of output, but in this chapter, you'll display many lines of text by using a *TextBox* control. The trick to displaying more than one line is simply to set the *Multiline* property of the *TextBox* control to True and to set the *ScrollBars* property to Vertical. Using these simple settings, the one-line text box object becomes a multiline text box object with scroll bars for easy access.

Display information by using a *For ... Next* loop

1. Start Visual Studio, and create a new Microsoft Visual Basic Windows Forms Application project named **My For Loop**.

   A blank form opens in the Designer. Your first programming step is to add a *Button* control to the form, but this time you'll do it in a new way.

2. Double-click the *Button* control in the Toolbox.

   Visual Studio places a button object in the upper-left corner of the form. With the *Button* control and many others, double-clicking is a quick way to create a standard-sized object on the form. Now you can drag the button object where you want it and customize it with property settings.

3. Drag the button object to the right, and center it near the top of the form.

4. Open the Properties window, and then set the *Text* property of the button to "Loop."

5. Double-click the *TextBox* control in the Toolbox.

   Visual Studio creates a small text box object on the form.

6. Set the *Multiline* property of the text box object to True, and then set the *ScrollBars* property of the text box object to Vertical.

> **Note** The *TextBox1* object contains a smart tag, which you can use to set the *Multiline* property to True. Collectively, the *Multiline* and *ScrollBars* properties prepare the text box for displaying more than one line of text.

7. Move the text box below the button, and enlarge it so that it takes up two-thirds of the form.

8. Double-click the Loop button on the form.

   The *Button1_Click* event procedure appears in the Code Editor.

9. Type the following program statements in the procedure:

```
Dim i As Integer
Dim Wrap As String
Wrap = Chr(13) & Chr(10)
For i = 1 To 10
    TextBox1.Text = TextBox1.Text & "Line " & i & Wrap
Next i
```

This event procedure declares two variables, one of type *Integer* (*i*) and one of type *String* (*Wrap*). It then assigns a string value representing the carriage return character to the second variable.

> **Tip** In programmer terms, a carriage return character is the equivalent of pressing the ENTER key on the keyboard. I created a special variable for this character in the program code, which is made up of return and linefeed elements, to make coding a carriage return less cumbersome. The return element, Chr(13) moves the I-beam to the beginning of the line. The linefeed element, Chr(10), reminiscent of an older style typewriter, moves the I-beam to the next line.

After the variable declaration and assignment, I use a *For … Next* loop to display Line *X* 10 times in the text box object, where *X* is the current value of the counter variable (in other words, Line 1 through Line 10). The string concatenation characters (&) join together the component parts of each line in the text box. First, the entire value of the text box, which is stored in the *Text* property, is added to the object so that previous lines aren't discarded when new ones are added. Next, the *Line* string, the current line number, and the carriage return character (*Wrap*) are combined to display a new line and move the I-beam to the left margin and down one line. The *Next* statement completes the loop.

Note that Visual Studio automatically adds the *Next* statement to the bottom of the loop when you type *For* to begin the loop. In this case, I edited the *Next* statement to include the *i* variable name—this is an optional syntax clarification that I like to use. (The variable name makes it clear which variable is being updated, especially in nested *For … Next* loops.)

10. Click the Save All button on the Standard toolbar to save your changes, and specify the C:\Vb10sbs\Chap07 folder as the location.

Now you're ready to run the program.

> **Tip** The complete For Loop program is available in the C:\Vb10sbs\Chap07\For Loop folder.

11. Click the Start Debugging button on the Standard toolbar.

12. Click the Loop button.

The *For…Next* loop displays 10 lines in the text box, as shown here:

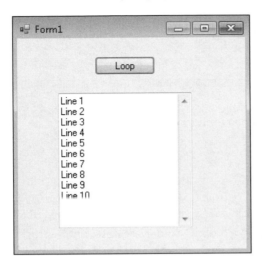

13. Click the Loop button again.

The *For…Next* loop displays another 10 lines on the form. (You can see any nonvisible lines by using the vertical scroll bar to scroll down.) Each time the loop is repeated, it adds 10 more lines to the text box object.

> **Tip** Worried about running out of room in the text box object? It will take a while if you're displaying only simple text lines. The maximum number of characters is specified in the *MaxLength* property for a text box. By default, *MaxLength* is set to 32,767 characters. If you need more characters, you can increase this value. If you want more formatting options, you can use the *RichTextBox* control in the Toolbox—a similar but even more capable control for displaying and manipulating text.

14. Click the Close button on the form to stop the program.

As you can see, a *For…Next* loop can considerably simplify your code and reduce the total number of statements that you need to type. In the previous example, a loop three lines long processed the equivalent of 10 program statements each time you clicked the Loop button.

Creating Complex *For…Next* Loops

The counter variable in a *For…Next* loop can be a powerful tool in your programs. With a little imagination, you can use it to create several useful sequences of numbers in your loops. To create a loop with a counter pattern other than 1, 2, 3, 4, and so on, you can specify a different value for *start* in the loop and then use the *Step* keyword to increment the counter at different intervals. For example, the code:

```
Dim i As Integer
Dim Wrap As String
Wrap = Chr(13) & Chr(10)

For i = 5 To 25 Step 5
    TextBox1.Text = TextBox1.Text & "Line " & i & Wrap
Next i
```

displays the following sequence of line numbers in a text box:

```
Line 5
Line 10
Line 15
Line 20
Line 25
```

You can also specify decimal values in a loop if you declare *i* as a single-precision or double-precision type. For example, the *For ... Next* loop:

```
Dim i As Single
Dim Wrap As String
Wrap = Chr(13) & Chr(10)

For i = 1 To 2.5 Step 0.5
    TextBox1.Text = TextBox1.Text & "Line " & i & Wrap
Next i
```

displays the following line numbers in a text box:

```
Line 1
Line 1.5
Line 2
Line 2.5
```

In addition to displaying the counter variable, you can use the counter to set properties, calculate values, or process files. The following exercise shows how you can use the counter to open Visual Basic icons that are stored on your hard disk in files that have numbers in their names. You'll find many icons, bitmaps, and animation files in the C:\Program Files\Microsoft Visual Studio 10.0\Common7\Vs2010imagelibrary folder. These files are contained in a compressed .zip file, so you will need to extract the files. These files are not included in Visual Basic 2010 Express. Also note that Microsoft changes the location for these types of files on occasion.

Open files by using a *For ... Next* loop

1. On the File menu, click the New Project command.

   The New Project dialog box opens.

2. Create a new Windows Forms Application project named **My For Loop Icons**.

   Your new project starts, and a blank form opens in the Designer.

> **Note** If you're opening the project from the practice files I provided, you'll see slightly different code than what is shown in Step 7 of this exercise because we modify the For Loop Icons project in the next exercise.

3. Click the *PictureBox* control in the Toolbox, and then draw a medium-sized square picture box object centered on the top half of the form.

4. Click the *Button* control, and then draw a very wide button below the picture box. (You'll put a longer-than-usual label on the button.)

5. Set the following properties for the two objects:

Object	Property	Setting
PictureBox1	BorderStyle	Fixed3D
	SizeMode	StretchImage
Button1	Text	"Display Four Faces"

6. Double-click the Display Four Faces button on the form to display the event procedure for the button object.

   The *Button1_Click* event procedure appears in the Code Editor.

7. Type the following *For … Next* loop:

```
Dim i As Integer
For i = 1 To 4
    PictureBox1.Image = System.Drawing.Image.FromFile _
        ("c:\vb10sbs\chap07\face0" & i & ".ico")
    MsgBox("Click here for next face.")
Next
```

> **Tip** The *FromFile* method in this event procedure is too long to fit on one line in this book, so I broke it into two lines by using a space and the line continuation character (_). You can use this character anywhere in your program code except within a string expression. Starting in Visual Basic 2010, including the line continuation character (_) is optional in most cases.

The loop uses the *FromFile* method to load four icon files from the C:\Vb10sbs\Chap07 folder on your hard disk. The file name is created by using the counter variable and the concatenation operator you used earlier in this chapter. The code:

```
PictureBox1.Image = System.Drawing.Image.FromFile _
  ("c:\vb10sbs\chap07\face0" & i & ".ico")
```

combines a path, a file name, and the .ico extension to create four valid file names of icons on your hard disk. In this example, you're loading Face01.ico, Face02.ico, Face03. ico, and Face04.ico into the picture box. This statement works because several files in the C:\Vb10sbs\Chap07 folder have the file name pattern Face*xx*.ico. By recognizing the pattern, you can build a *For ... Next* loop around the file names.

> **Note** The message box function (*MsgBox*) is used primarily to slow the action down so that you can see what's happening in the *For ... Next* loop. In a normal application, you probably wouldn't use such a function (but you're welcome to).

8. Click the Save All button on the Standard toolbar to save your changes. Specify the C:\Vb10sbs\Chap07 folder as the location.

9. Click the Start Debugging button to run the program, and then click the Display Four Faces button.

   The *For ... Next* loop loads the first face into the picture box and then displays this message box:

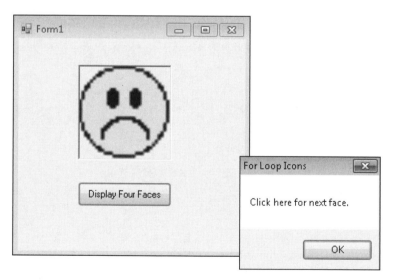

> **Note** If Visual Basic displays an error message, ensure that your program code has no typos and then verify that the icon files are in the path you specified in the program. If you installed the *Step by Step* practice files in a folder other than the default folder, or if you moved your icon files after installation, the path in the event procedure might not be correct.

10. Click OK to display the next face.

Your screen looks something like this:

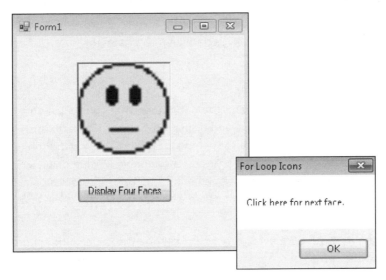

11. Click OK three more times to see the entire face collection.

You can repeat the sequence if you want.

12. When you're finished, click the Close button on the form.

The program stops, and the development environment returns.

Using a Counter That Has Greater Scope

Are there times when using a *For ... Next* loop isn't that efficient or elegant? Sure. In fact, the preceding example, although useful as a demonstration, was a little hampered by the intrusive behavior of the message box, which opened four times in the *For ... Next* loop and distracted the user from the form, where we want his or her attention to be. Is there a way we can do away with that intrusive message box?

One solution is to remove both the *MsgBox* function and the *For ... Next* loop, and substitute in their place a counter variable that has greater scope throughout the form. As you learned in Chapter 5, "Visual Basic Variables and Formulas, and the .NET Framework," you can declare a variable that has scope (or maintains its value) throughout the entire form by placing a *Dim* statement for the variable at the top of the form in the Code Editor—a special location above the event procedures. In the following exercise, you'll use an *Integer* variable named *Counter* that maintains its value between calls to the *Button1_Click* event procedure, and you'll use that variable to open the same icon files without using the *MsgBox* function to pause the action.

Use a global counter

1. Open the Code Editor for the My For Loop Icons project.

2. Move the insertion point above the *Button1_Click* event procedure, and directly below the *Public Class Form1* statement, declare an *Integer* variable named *Counter* by using this syntax:

```
Dim Counter As Integer = 1
```

Notice that Visual Studio separates the declaration that you've just entered from the event procedure with a solid line and displays the word "(Declarations)" in the Method Name list box. You've also done something unusual here—in addition to declaring the *Counter* variable, you've also assigned the variable a value of 1. Declaring and assigning at the same time has been a handy feature of Visual Basic since version 2002. In Chapter 5, I used this syntax to declare a constant, but this is the first time that I've used it for variable declarations.

3. Within the *Button1_Click* event procedure, change the code so that it precisely matches the following group of program statements. (Delete any statements that aren't here.)

```
PictureBox1.Image = System.Drawing.Image.FromFile _
   ("c:\vb10sbs\chap07\face0" & Counter & ".ico")
Counter += 1
If Counter = 5 Then Counter = 1
```

As you can see, I've deleted the declaration for the *i* integer, the *For* and *Next* statements, and the *MsgBox* function, and I've changed the way the *FromFile* method works. (I've replaced the *i* variable with the *Counter* variable.) I've also added two new statements that use the *Counter* variable. The first statement adds 1 to *Counter* (*Counter += 1*), and the second statement resets the *Counter* variable if the value has been incremented to 5. (Resetting the variable in this way allows the list of icon files to cycle indefinitely.) The *Counter += 1* syntax is a shortcut feature in Visual Basic 2010—the functional equivalent of the following statement:

```
Counter = Counter + 1
```

Now you'll run the program.

 Tip The modified For Loop Icons program is available in the C:\Vb10sbs\Chap07\For Loop Icons folder.

4. Click the Start Debugging button on the Standard toolbar to run the program.

The program runs in the development environment.

5. Click the Display Four Faces button several times. (Notice how the mood of the faces develops from glum to cheery, as shown here.)

6. When you're finished, click the Close button on the form to stop the program.

As you can see, this solution is a little more elegant than the previous example because the user can click just one button, not a form button *and* a message box button. The shortcoming of the interface in the first program wasn't the fault of the *For ... Next* loop, however, but rather the limitation I imposed that the *Button1_Click* event procedure use only local variables (in other words, variables that were declared within the event procedure itself). Between button clicks, these local variables lost their value, and the only way I could increment the counter was to build a loop. By using an *Integer* variable with a greater scope, I can preserve the value of the *Counter* variable between clicks and use that numeric information to display files within the *Button1_Click* event procedure.

The *Exit For* Statement

Most *For ... Next* loops run to completion without incident, but now and then you'll find it useful to end the computation of a *For ... Next* loop if a particular "exit condition" occurs. Visual Basic allows for this possibility by providing the *Exit For* statement, which you can use to terminate the execution of a *For ... Next* loop early and move execution to the first statement after the loop.

For example, the following *For ... Next* loop prompts the user for 10 names and displays them one by one in a text box unless the user enters the word "Done":

```
Dim i As Integer
Dim InpName As String
For i = 1 To 10
    InpName = InputBox("Enter your name or type Done to quit.")
    If InpName = "Done" Then Exit For
    TextBox1.Text = InpName
Next i
```

If the user does enter "Done," the *Exit For* statement terminates the loop, and execution picks up with the statement after *Next*.

Writing *Do* Loops

As an alternative to a *For…Next* loop, you can write a *Do* loop that executes a group of statements until a certain condition is True. *Do* loops are valuable because often you can't know in advance how many times a loop should repeat. For example, you might want to let the user enter names in a database until the user types the word *Done* in an input box. In that case, you can use a *Do* loop to cycle indefinitely until the *Done* text string is entered.

A *Do* loop has several formats, depending on where and how the loop condition is evaluated. The most common syntax is:

```
Do While condition
    block of statements to be executed
Loop
```

For example, the following *Do* loop prompts the user for input and displays that input in a text box until the word *Done* is typed in the input box:

```
Dim InpName As String
Do While InpName <> "Done"
    InpName = InputBox("Enter your name or type Done to quit.")
    If InpName <> "Done" Then TextBox1.Text = InpName
Loop
```

The conditional statement in this loop is InpName <> "Done", which the Visual Basic compiler translates to mean "loop so long as the *InpName* variable doesn't contain the exact word 'Done'." This brings up an interesting fact about *Do* loops: If the condition at the top of the loop isn't True when the *Do* statement is first evaluated, the *Do* loop is never executed. Here, if the *InpName* string variable did contain the "Done" value before the loop started (perhaps from an earlier assignment in the event procedure), Visual Basic would skip the loop altogether and continue with the line below the *Loop* keyword.

If you always want the loop to run at least once in a program, put the conditional test at the bottom of the loop. For example, the loop:

```
Dim InpName As String
Do
    InpName = InputBox("Enter your name or type Done to quit.")
    If InpName <> "Done" Then TextBox1.Text = InpName
Loop While InpName <> "Done"
```

is essentially the same as the previous *Do* loop, but here the loop condition is tested after a name is received from the *InputBox* function. This has the advantage of updating the *InpName* variable before the conditional test in the loop so that a preexisting *Done* value won't cause the loop to be skipped. Testing the loop condition at the bottom ensures that your loop is executed at least once, but often it forces you to add a few extra statements to process the data.

Note The previous code samples asked the user to type *Done* to quit. Note that the test of the entered text is case-sensitive, which means that typing *done* or *DONE* doesn't end the program. You can make the test case-insensitive by using the *StrComp* function, which I'll discuss in Chapter 13, "Exploring Text Files and String Processing."

Avoiding an Endless Loop

Because of the relentless nature of *Do* loops, it's very important to design your test conditions so that each loop has a true exit point. If a loop test never evaluates to False, the loop executes endlessly, and your program might not respond to input. Consider the following example:

```
Dim Number as Double
Do
    Number = InputBox("Enter a number to square. Type -1 to quit.")
    Number = Number * Number
    TextBox1.Text = Number
Loop While Number >= 0
```

In this loop, the user enters number after number, and the program squares each number and displays it in the text box. Unfortunately, when the user has had enough, he or she can't quit because the advertised exit condition doesn't work. When the user enters –1, the program squares it, and the *Number* variable is assigned the value 1. (The problem can be fixed by setting a different exit condition. The next example demonstrates how to check if the user clicked the Cancel button and exited the loop.) Watching for endless loops is essential when you're writing *Do* loops. Fortunately, they're pretty easy to spot if you test your programs thoroughly.

Important Be sure that each loop has a legitimate exit condition.

The following exercise shows how you can use a *Do* loop to convert Fahrenheit temperatures to Celsius temperatures. The simple program prompts the user for input by using the *InputBox* function, converts the temperature, and displays the output in a message box.

Convert temperatures by using a *Do* loop

1. On the File menu, click New Project.

   The New Project dialog box opens.

2. Create a new Visual Basic Windows Forms Application project named **My Celsius Conversion**.

The new project is created, and a blank form opens in the Designer. This time, you'll place all the code for your program in the *Form1_Load* event procedure so that Visual Basic immediately prompts you for the Fahrenheit temperature when you start the application. You'll use an *InputBox* function to request the Fahrenheit data, and you'll use a *MsgBox* function to display the converted value.

3. Double-click the form.

The *Form1_Load* event procedure appears in the Code Editor.

4. Type the following program statements in the *Form1_Load* event procedure:

```
Dim FTemp, Celsius As Single
Dim strFTemp As String
Dim Prompt As String = "Enter a Fahrenheit temperature."
Do
    strFTemp = InputBox(Prompt, "Fahrenheit to Celsius")
    If strFTemp <> "" Then
        FTemp = CSng(strFTemp)
        Celsius = Int((FTemp + 40) * 5 / 9 - 40)
        MsgBox(Celsius, , "Temperature in Celsius")
    End If
Loop While strFTemp <> ""
End
```

> **Tip** Be sure to include the *End* statement at the bottom of the *Form1_Load* event procedure. When the user has had his or her fill of converting temperatures, this is how the program terminates.

This code handles the calculations for the project. The first line declares two single-precision variables, *FTemp* and *Celsius*, to hold the Fahrenheit and Celsius temperatures, respectively. The second line declares a string variable named *strFTemp* that holds a string version of the Fahrenheit temperature. The third line declares a string variable named *Prompt*, which will be used in the *InputBox* function, and assigns it an initial value. The *Do* loop repeatedly prompts the user for a Fahrenheit temperature, converts the number to Celsius, and then displays it on the screen by using the *MsgBox* function.

The value that the user enters in the input box is stored in the *strFTemp* variable. The *InputBox* function always returns a value of type *String*, even if the user enters numbers. Because we want to perform mathematical calculations on the entered value, *strFTemp* must be converted to a number. The *CSng* function is used to convert a string into the *Single* data type. *CSng* is one of many conversion functions you can use to convert a string to a different data type. The converted single value is then stored in the *FTemp* variable.

The loop executes until the user clicks the Cancel button or until the user presses ENTER or clicks OK with no value in the input box. Clicking the Cancel button or entering no value returns an empty string (""). The loop checks for the empty string by using a *While* conditional test at the bottom of the loop. The program statement:

```
Celsius = Int((FTemp + 40) * 5 / 9 - 40)
```

handles the conversion from Fahrenheit to Celsius in the program. This statement employs a standard conversion formula, but it uses the *Int* function to return a value that contains no decimal places to the Celsius variable. (Everything to the right of the decimal point is discarded.) This cutting sacrifices accuracy, but it helps you avoid long, unsightly numbers such as 21.11111, the Celsius value for 70 degrees Fahrenheit.

5. Click the Save All button on the Standard toolbar to save your changes. Specify the C:\Vb10sbs\Chap07 folder as the location.

   Now you'll try running the program.

> **Tip** The complete Celsius Conversion program is available in the C:\Vb10sbs\Chap07\ Celsius Conversion folder.

6. Click the Start Debugging button on the Standard toolbar.

   The program starts, and the *InputBox* function prompts you for a Fahrenheit temperature.

7. Type **212**.

   Your screen looks like this:

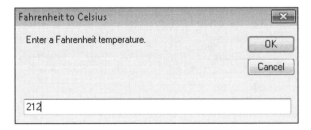

8. Click OK.

   The temperature 212 degrees Fahrenheit is converted to 100 degrees Celsius, as shown in this message box:

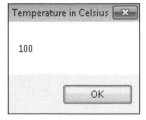

9.   Click OK. Then type **72** in the input box, and click OK again.

The temperature 72 degrees Fahrenheit is converted to 22 degrees Celsius.

10.   Click OK, and then click Cancel in the input box.

The program closes, and the development environment returns.

Using the *Until* Keyword in *Do* Loops

The *Do* loops you've worked with so far have used the *While* keyword to execute a group of statements so long as the loop condition remains True. With Visual Basic, you can also use the *Until* keyword in *Do* loops to cycle *until* a certain condition is True. Use the *Until* keyword at the top or bottom of a *Do* loop to test a condition, just like the *While* keyword. For example, the following *Do* loop uses the *Until* keyword to loop repeatedly until the user enters the word *Done* in the input box:

```
Dim InpName As String
Do
    InpName = InputBox("Enter your name or type Done to quit.")
    If InpName <> "Done" Then TextBox1.Text = InpName
Loop Until InpName = "Done"
```

As you can see, a loop that uses the *Until* keyword is similar to a loop that uses the *While* keyword, except that the test condition usually contains the opposite operator—in this case, the = (equal to) operator versus the <> (not equal to) operator. If using the *Until* keyword makes sense to you, feel free to use it with test conditions in your *Do* loops.

The *Timer* Control

As we wrap up our consideration of flow control tools and techniques in this chapter, you should also consider the benefits of using the Visual Studio *Timer* control, which you can use to execute a group of statements for a specific period of *time* or at specific *intervals*. The *Timer* control is essentially an invisible stopwatch that gives you access to the system clock in your programs. The *Timer* control can be used like an egg timer to count down from a preset time, to cause a delay in a program, or to repeat an action at prescribed intervals.

Although timer objects aren't visible at run time, each timer is associated with an event procedure that runs every time the timer's preset interval has elapsed. You set a timer's interval by using the *Interval* property, and you activate a timer by setting the timer's *Enabled* property to True. Once a timer is enabled, it runs constantly—executing its event procedure at the prescribed interval—until the user stops the program or the timer object is disabled. Your job as a programmer is to conceive of how to use time in your programs creatively. In other words, what events in a program (or in life) happen at regular intervals? Can you predict or envision the passage of time so that it can be integrated into your code?

Creating a Digital Clock by Using a *Timer* Control

One of the most straightforward uses for a *Timer* control is creating a custom digital clock. In the following exercise, you'll create a simple digital clock that keeps track of the current time down to the second. In the example, you'll set the *Interval* property for the timer to 1000, directing Visual Studio to update the clock time every 1000 milliseconds, or once a second. Because the Windows operating system is a multitasking environment and other programs also require processing time, Visual Studio might not update the clock *precisely* every second, but it will always catch up if it falls a bit behind. To keep track of the time at other intervals, such as once every tenth of a second, you simply adjust the number in the *Interval* property.

Create the Digital Clock program

1. On the File menu, click the New Project command, and create a new Windows Forms Application project named **My Digital Clock**.

   The new project is created and a blank form opens in the Designer.

2. Resize the form to a small rectangular window (one that's wider than it is tall).

   You don't want the clock to take up much room.

3. Double-click the *Timer* control on the Components tab of the Toolbox.

   This is the first time that you have used the Components tab and the *Timer* control in this book. (The Components tab provides a number of interesting controls that work "behind the scenes" in your programs.) Visual Studio creates a small timer object in the component tray beneath your form, as shown here:

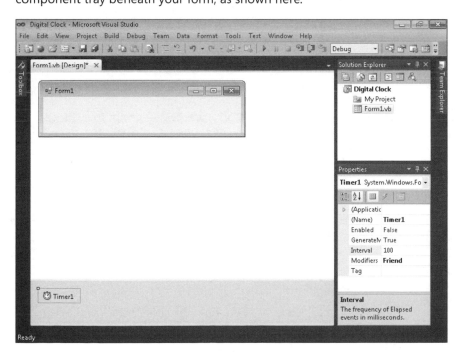

Recall from Chapter 4, "Working with Menus, Toolbars, and Dialog Boxes," that certain Visual Studio controls don't have a visual representation on the form, and when objects for these controls are created, they appear in the component tray beneath the form. (This was the case for the *MenuStrip* and *ToolStrip* controls that you used in Chapter 4.) However, you can still select controls in this special pane and set properties for them, as you'll do for the timer object in this exercise.

4. Click the *Label* control in the Toolbox, and then draw a very large label object on the form—a label that's almost the size of the entire form itself.

   You'll use the label to display the time in the clock, and you want to create a very big label to hold the 24-point type you'll be using.

> **Note** When you first create the label object, it resizes automatically to hold the text *Label1* in the default size. But when you set the *AutoSize* property to False in the next step, the label object is restored to the size you originally created.

5. Open the Properties window, and set the following properties for the form and the two objects in your program:

Object	Property	Setting
Label1	AutoSize	False
	Font	Times New Roman, Bold, 24-point
	Text	(empty)
	TextAlign	MiddleCenter
Timer1	Enabled	True
	Interval	1000
Form1	Text	"Digital Clock"

> **Tip** If you'd like to put some artwork in the background of your clock, set the *BackgroundImage* property of the *Form1* object to the path of a graphics file.

Now you'll write the program code for the timer.

6. Double-click the timer object in the component tray.

   The *Timer1_Tick* event procedure appears in the Code Editor. This is the event procedure that runs each time that the timer clock ticks.

7. Type the following statement:

```
Label1.Text = TimeString
```

This statement gets the current time from the system clock and assigns it to the *Text* property of the *Label1* object. (If you'd like to have the date displayed in the clock as well as the time, use the *System.DateTime.Now* property instead of the *TimeString* property.) Only one statement is required in this program because you set the *Interval* property for the timer by using the Properties window. The timer object handles the rest.

8. Click the Save All button on the Standard toolbar to save your changes. Specify C:\Vb10sbs\Chap07 as the folder location.

 Tip The complete Digital Clock program is available in the C:\Vb10sbs\Chap07\Digital Clock folder.

9. Click the Start Debugging button on the Standard toolbar to run the clock.

   The clock appears, as shown in the following screen shot. (Your time will be different, of course.)

   If you used the *System.DateTime.Now* property, you'll also see the date in the clock, as shown here:

   I needed to enlarge the label object and the form a little here to get the date and time to appear on one line. If your system clock information appears wrapped, close the program and resize your label and form.

10. Watch the clock for a few moments.

    Visual Basic updates the time every second.

11. Click the Close button in the title bar to stop the clock.

The Digital Clock program is so handy that you might want to compile it into an executable file and use it now and then on your computer. Feel free to customize it by using your own artwork, text, and colors.

Using a Timer Object to Set a Time Limit

Another interesting use of a timer object is to set it to wait a given period of time before either permitting or prohibiting an action. You can also use this timer technique to display a welcome message or a copyright message on the screen or to repeat an event at a set interval, such as saving a file every 10 minutes or backing up important files each night at 2:00 A.M. Again, this is a little like setting an egg timer in your program. You set the *Interval* property with the delay you want, and then you start the clock ticking by setting the *Enabled* property to True. So long as the program is still running, your timer object will be active.

The following exercise shows how you can use this approach to set a time limit for entering a password. (The password for this program is "secret.") The program uses a timer to close its own program if a valid password isn't entered in 15 seconds. (Normally, a program like this would be one of the initial forms in a larger application.)

Set a password time limit

1. On the File menu, click the New Project command, and create a new Windows Forms Application project named **My Timed Password**.

   The new project is created, and a blank form opens in the Designer.

2. Resize the form to a small rectangular window about the size of an input box.

3. Click the *TextBox* control in the Toolbox, and then draw a text box for the password in the middle of the form.

4. Click the *Label* control in the Toolbox, and then draw a long label above the text box.

5. Click the *Button* control in the Toolbox, and then draw a button below the text box.

6. Double-click the *Timer* control on the Components tab of the Toolbox.

   Visual Studio adds a timer object to the component tray below the form.

7. Set the properties for the program in the following table:

Object	Property	Setting
Label1	Text	"Enter your password within 15 seconds"
TextBox1	PasswordChar	"*"
Button1	Text	"Try Password"
Timer1	Enabled	True
	Interval	15000
Form1	Text	"Password"

The *PasswordChar* setting displays asterisk (*) characters in the text box as the user enters a password. Setting the timer *Interval* property to 15000 gives the user 15 seconds to enter a password and click the Try Password button. Setting the *Enabled* property to

True starts the timer running when the program starts. (If the timer wasn't needed until later in the program, you could disable this property and then enable it in an event procedure.)

Your form looks like this:

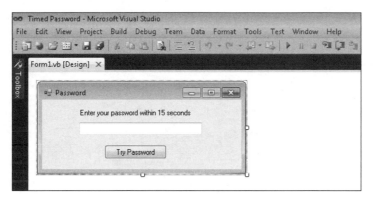

8. Double-click the timer object in the component tray, and then type the following statements in the *Timer1_Tick* event procedure:

```
MsgBox("Sorry, your time is up.")
End
```

The first statement displays a message indicating that the time has expired, and the second statement stops the program. Visual Basic executes this event procedure if the timer interval reaches 15 seconds and a valid password hasn't been entered.

9. Display the form, double-click the button object, and then type the following statements in the *Button1_Click* event procedure:

```
If TextBox1.Text = "secret" Then
    Timer1.Enabled = False
    MsgBox("Welcome to the system!")
    End
Else
    MsgBox("Sorry, friend, I don't know you.")
End If
```

This program code tests whether the password entered in the text box is "secret." If it is, the timer is disabled, a welcome message is displayed, and the program ends. (A more useful program would continue working rather than ending here.) If the password entered isn't a match, the user is notified with a message box and is given another chance to enter the password. But the user has only 15 seconds to do so!

10. Click the Save All button on the Standard toolbar to save your changes. Specify the C:\Vb10sbs\Chap07 folder as the location.

Test the Timed Password program

 Tip The complete Timed Password program is available in the C:\Vb10sbs\Chap07\Timed Password folder.

1. Click the Start Debugging button to run the program.

   The program starts, and the 15-second clock starts ticking.

2. Type **open** in the text box.

   The asterisk characters hide your input, as shown here:

3. Click the Try Password button.

   The following message box opens on the screen, noting your incorrect response:

4. Click OK, and then wait patiently until the sign-on period expires.

   The program displays the time-up message shown in this message box:

5. Click OK to end the program.

6. Run the program again, type **secret** (the correct password) in the text box, and then click Try Password.

The program displays this message:

7. Click OK to end the program.

The Visual Basic development environment appears.

As you can imagine, there are many practical uses for timer objects. As with *For … Next* loops and *Do* loops, you can use timer objects to repeat commands and procedures as many times as you need in a program. Combined with what you learned about the *If … Then* and *Select Case* decision structures in Chapter 6, you now have several statements, controls, and techniques that can help you organize your programs and make them respond to user input and data processing tasks in innovative ways. Learning to pick the best tool for the flow-control situation at hand takes some practice, of course, but you'll have ample opportunity to try these tools and techniques as you continue working in the upcoming chapters, and as you construct interesting applications on your own. In fact, you might take the opportunity right now to create a simple project or two from scratch before you tackle the next chapter, which discusses debugging. How about creating a digital clock that displays a different piece of art in a picture box object every 30 seconds?

One Step Further: Inserting Code Snippets

If you enjoyed using the system clock and other Windows resources in this chapter, you might appreciate one additional example that uses the *Computer.Info* object to display useful information about the operating system you're currently using. This example also demonstrates an interesting feature of Visual Studio called the Insert Snippet command, which lets you insert ready-made code templates or *snippets* into the Code Editor from a list of common programming tasks. Visual Studio comes automatically configured with a library of useful code snippets, and you can add additional snippets from your own programs or from online resources such as MSDN. The following exercise shows you how to use this helpful feature.

Insert the Current Windows Version Snippet

1. On the File menu, click the New Project command, and create a new Windows Forms Application project named **My Windows Version Snippet**.

The new project is created, and a blank form opens in the Designer.

2. Create a new button object in the middle of the form, and set the *Text* property of the button to "Display Windows Version."

3. Double-click the button object to display the *Button1_Click* event procedure.

Now you'll use the Insert Snippet command to insert a code template that automatically returns information about the version of Windows installed on your computer. Note that this particular snippet is just one example from a list of dozens of useful code templates.

4. Click the Edit menu, point to the IntelliSense submenu, and then click the Insert Snippet command.

The Insert Snippet list box appears in the Code Editor, as shown in the following screen shot. Depending on what components of Visual Studio you have installed, your snippet list will have some differences.

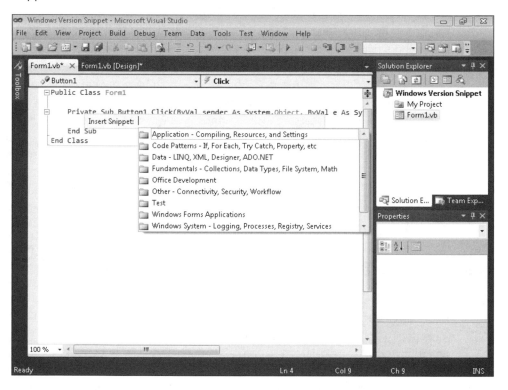

Tip You can also open the snippet list by right-clicking in the Designer and selecting Insert Snippet.

The Insert Snippet list box is a navigation tool that you can use to explore the snippet library and insert snippets into your program at the insertion point. To open a folder in the list box, double-click the folder name. To return to the previous folder in the folder hierarchy, press the BACKSPACE key.

5. Scroll down in the list box, and then double-click the Windows System - Logging, Processes, Registry, Services folder.

In this folder, you'll find snippets related to querying and setting operating system settings.

> **Tip** If you are using Visual Basic 2010 Express, you might not see the Windows System - Logging, Processes, Registry, Services folder. If you do not see this folder, you can just type the code listed in Step 7.

6. Double-click the Windows - System Information folder.

A list of system information snippets appears. Now you'll select the snippet that returns information about the current version of Windows.

7. Double-click the snippet entitled "Determine the Current Windows Version."

Visual Studio inserts the following line of code into the *Button1_Click* event procedure at the insertion point:

```
Dim osVersion = My.Computer.Info.OSVersion
```

These statements declare the string variable *osVersion* to hold version information about the operating system, and then use the *Computer.Info* object to fill the variable with current information. The snippet also uses the *My* namespace to gather information about your computer. The *My* namespace is a "speed-dial" feature of Visual Basic designed to reduce the time it takes to code common tasks, and I will introduce it more fully in Chapter 13.

This code snippet is called a template because it supplies the majority of the code that you need to insert for a particular task, but the code is not fully integrated into your project yet. In this case, we should add a second variable to hold the name of the operating system (because there are different Windows versions), and we'll add a *MsgBox* function to display the results for the user. (In other cases, you might need to add controls to your form, create new variables or data structures, or write additional program statements that use the snippet.)

8. Press the ENTER key twice to add a blank line below the snippet.

9. Type the following program statements:

```
Dim osName = My.Computer.Info.OSFullName
MsgBox(osName & vbCr & osVersion)
```

These statements declare a second string variable named *osName* that will hold the Windows version retrieved by the *OSFullName* property of the *Computer.Info* object. There is also a *MsgBox* function that displays the two returned values: the operating system name (*osName*) and the operating system version number (*osVersion*). As you probably know, the operating system version number has now become quite detailed in Windows because

Windows has the ability to be updated automatically over the Web each time a new security update or improvement is released. Examining the version number is therefore a handy way to see whether your system is up-to-date and safe.

You'll also notice that I used *vbCr*. This is a constant that represents a carriage return. This can be used as an alternative to the *Chr(13)* statement that was used earlier in the chapter. There are several of these constants that can be helpful. When you type *vb* in the Code Editor, you'll see a list of all these constants. Your screen looks like this:

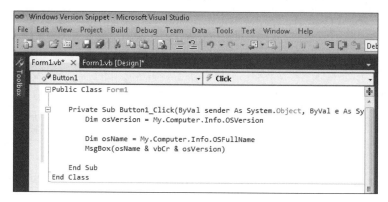

10. Click the Save All button to save your changes, and specify the C:\Vb10sbs\Chap07 folder as the location.

11. Click the Start Debugging button to run the program.

    Visual Studio runs the program in the IDE.

12. Click the Display Windows Version button to display the version information returned by the snippet.

    Your dialog box looks similar to the following:

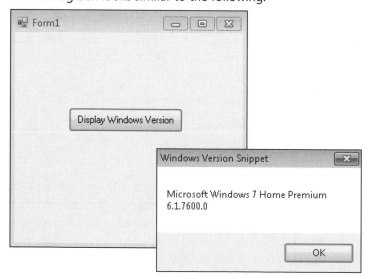

13. Click OK to close the dialog box, and then click the Close button to end the program.

You've learned a handy skill that will allow you to insert a variety of useful code templates into your own programs.

> **Tip** To insert new snippets or reorganize the snippets you have, click the Code Snippets Manager command on the Tools menu. The Code Snippets Manager dialog box gives you complete control over the contents of the Insert Snippet list box and also contains a mechanism for gathering new snippets online.

Chapter 7 Quick Reference

To	Do This
Execute a group of program statements a specific number of times	Insert the statements between *For* and *Next* statements in a loop. For example: ```Dim i As Integer For i = 1 To 10 MsgBox("Press OK already!") Next```
Use a specific sequence of numbers with statements	Insert the statements in a *For … Next* loop, and use the *To* and *Step* keywords to define the sequence of numbers. For example: ```Dim i As Integer For i = 2 To 8 Step 2 TextBox1.Text = TextBox1.Text & i Next```
Avoid an endless *Do* loop	Be sure the loop has a test condition that can evaluate to False.
Declare a variable and assign a value to it at the same time	Use *Dim* to declare the variable, and then assign a value with the equal to (=) operator. For example: ```Dim Counter As Integer = 1```

Exit a *For … Next* loop prematurely	Use the *Exit For* statement. For example:
	
	``Dim InpName As String
	Dim i As Integer
	For i = 1 To 10
	    InpName = InputBox("Name?")
	    If InpName = "Trotsky" Then Exit For
	    TextBox1.Text = InpName
	Next```

Execute a group of program statements until a specific condition is met	Insert the statements between the *Do* and *Loop* statements. For example:
	
	``Dim Query As String = ""
	Do While Query <> "Yes"
	    Query = InputBox("Trotsky?")
	    If Query = "Yes" Then MsgBox("Hi")
	Loop```

To	Do This
Loop until a specific condition is True	Use a *Do* loop with the *Until* keyword. For example: ```\nDim GiveIn As String\nDo\n GiveIn = InputBox("Say 'Uncle'")\nLoop Until GiveIn = "Uncle"\n```
Loop for a specific period of time in your program	Use the *Timer* control.
Insert a code snippet into your program	In the Code Editor, position the insertion point (I-beam) at the location where you want to insert the snippet. On the Edit menu, click IntelliSense, and then click Insert Snippet. Browse to the snippet that you want to use, and then double-click the snippet name.
Add or reorganize snippets in the Insert Snippet list box	Click the Code Snippet Manager command on the Tools menu.

Chapter 8
Debugging Visual Basic Programs

After completing this chapter, you will be able to:

- Identify different types of errors in your programs.

- Use Visual Studio debugging tools to set breakpoints and correct mistakes.

- Use the Autos and Watch windows to examine variables during program execution.

- Use a visualizer to examine string data types and complex data types within the IDE.

- Use the Immediate and Command windows to change the value of variables and execute commands in Visual Studio.

- Remove breakpoints.

In the past few chapters, you've had plenty of opportunity to make programming mistakes in your code. Unlike human conversation, which usually works well despite occasional grammatical mistakes and mispronunciations, communication between a software developer and the Microsoft Visual Basic compiler is successful only when the precise rules and regulations of the Visual Basic programming language are followed.

In this chapter, you'll learn more about the software defects, or *bugs*, that stop Visual Basic programs from running. You'll learn about the different types of errors that turn up in programs and how to use the Microsoft Visual Studio debugging tools to detect and correct these defects. What you learn will be useful as you experiment with the programs in this book and when you write longer programs in the future.

Why focus on debugging now? Some programming books skip this topic altogether or place it near the end of the book (*after* you've learned all the language features of a particular product). There is a certain logic to postponing the discussion, but I think it makes the most sense to master debugging techniques *while* you learn to program so that detecting and correcting errors becomes part of your standard approach to writing programs and solving problems. At this point in this book, you know just enough about objects, decision structures, and statement syntax to create interesting programs—but also enough to get yourself into a little bit of trouble! As you'll soon see, however, Visual Studio 2010 makes it easy to uncover your mistakes and get back on the straight and narrow.

Finding and Correcting Errors

The defects you've encountered in your programs so far have probably been simple typing mistakes or syntax errors. But what if you discover a nastier problem in your program—one you can't find and correct by a simple review of the objects, properties, and statements you've used? The Visual Studio Integrated Development Environment (IDE) contains several tools that help you track down and fix errors in your programs. These tools won't stop you from making mistakes, but they often ease the pain when you encounter one.

Three Types of Errors

Three types of errors can occur in a Visual Basic program: syntax errors, run-time errors, and logic errors, as follows:

- A *syntax error* (or *compiler error*) is a mistake (such as a misspelled property or keyword) that violates the programming rules of Visual Basic. Visual Basic will point out several types of syntax errors in your programs while you enter program statements, and it won't let you run a program until you fix each syntax error.

- A *run-time error* is a mistake that causes a program to stop unexpectedly during execution. Run-time errors occur when an outside event or an undiscovered syntax error forces a program to stop while it's running. For instance, if you misspell a file name when you use the *System.Drawing.Image.FromFile* method, or if you try to read a disk drive and it doesn't contain a CD or DVD, your code will generate a run-time error.

- A *logic error* is a human error—a mistake that causes the program code to produce the wrong results. Most debugging efforts are focused on tracking down logic errors introduced by the programmer.

If you encounter a syntax error, you often can solve the problem by using the Visual Studio Help documentation to learn more about the error message, and you can fix the mistake by paying close attention to the exact syntax of the functions, objects, methods, and properties that you have used. In the Code Editor, incorrect statements are underlined with a jagged line, and you can learn more about the error by holding the mouse pointer over the statement. The following screen shot shows the error message that appears in Visual Studio when I type the keyword *Case* incorrectly as "Csae" and then hold the mouse pointer over the error. This error message appears as a ScreenTip.

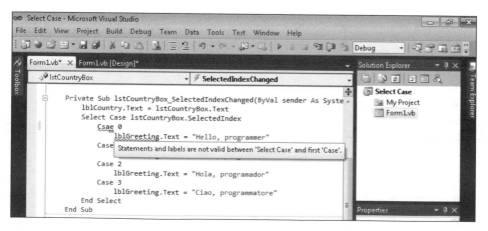

> **Tip** By default, a green jagged line indicates a warning, a red jagged line indicates a syntax error, a blue jagged line indicates a compiler error, and a purple jagged line indicates some other error. The color of these items and most of the features in the user interface can be adjusted by selecting the Options command on the Tools menu, clicking the Fonts And Colors option under Environment, and adjusting the default values under Display Items.

If you encounter a run-time error, you often can address the problem by correcting your typing. For example, if a bitmap loads incorrectly into a picture box object, the problem might simply be a misspelled path. However, many run-time errors require a more thorough solution. You can add a *structured error handler*—a special block of program code that recognizes a run-time error when it happens, suppresses any error messages, and adjusts program conditions to handle the problem—to your programs. I discuss the new syntax for structured error handlers in Chapter 9, "Trapping Errors by Using Structured Error Handling."

Identifying Logic Errors

Logic errors in your programs are often the most difficult to fix. They're the result of faulty reasoning and planning, not a misunderstanding about Visual Basic syntax. Consider the following *If … Then* decision structure, which evaluates two conditional expressions and then displays one of two messages based on the result.

```
If Age > 13 And Age < 20 Then
    TextBox2.Text = "You're a teenager"
Else
    TextBox2.Text = "You're not a teenager"
End If
```

Can you spot the problem with this decision structure? A teenager is a person who is between 13 and 19 years old, inclusive, but the structure fails to identify the person who's exactly 13. (For this age, the structure erroneously displays the message "You're not a teenager.") This type of mistake isn't a syntax error (because the statements follow the rules of Visual Basic); it's a mental mistake or logic error. The correct decision structure contains a greater than or equal to operator (>=) in the first comparison after the *If … Then* statement, as shown here:

```
If Age >= 13 And Age < 20 Then
```

Believe it or not, this type of mistake is the most common problem in a Visual Basic program. Code that produces the expected results most of the time—but not all the time—is the hardest to identify and to fix.

Debugging 101: Using Debugging Mode

One way to identify a logic error is to execute your program code one line at a time and examine the content of one or more variables or properties as they change. To do this, you can enter *debugging mode* (or break mode) while your program is running and then view your code in the Code Editor. Debugging mode gives you a close-up look at your program while the Visual Basic compiler is executing it. It's kind of like pulling up a chair behind the pilot and copilot and watching them fly the airplane. But in this case, you can touch the controls.

While you're debugging your application, you'll use buttons on the Standard toolbar and the Debug toolbar, as well as commands on the Debug menu and special buttons and windows in the IDE. The following screen shot shows the debugging buttons on the Standard and Debug toolbars, which you can open by pointing to the Toolbars command on the View menu and then clicking Standard or Debug. In this chapter, you'll use the Immediate, Locals, Start Debugging, Stop Debugging, and Step Into commands.

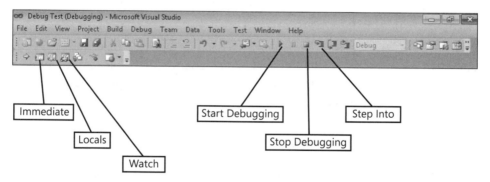

In the following exercise, you'll set a breakpoint—a place in a program where execution stops. You'll then use debugging mode to find and correct the logic error you discovered earlier in the *If ... Then* structure. (The error is part of an actual program.) To isolate the problem, you'll use the Step Into button on the Standard toolbar to execute program instructions one at a time, and you'll use the Autos window to examine the value of key program variables and properties. Pay close attention to this debugging strategy. You can use it to correct many types of glitches in your own programs.

Debug the Debug Test program

1. Start Visual Studio.

2. On the File menu, click Open Project.

   The Open Project dialog box opens.

3. Open the Debug Test project in the C:\Vb10sbs\Chap08\Debug Test folder.

   The project opens in the development environment.

4. If the form isn't visible, display it now.

   The Debug Test program prompts the user for his or her age. When the user clicks the Test button, the program informs the user whether he or she is a teenager. The program still has the problem with 13-year-olds that we identified earlier in the chapter, however. You'll open the Debug toolbar now and set a breakpoint to find the problem.

5. If the Debug toolbar isn't visible, click the View menu, point to Toolbars, and then click Debug.

   The Debug toolbar appears below or to the right of the Standard toolbar.

6. Click the Start Debugging button on the Standard toolbar.

   The program runs and the Debug Test form opens.

7. Remove the 0 from the Age text box, type **14**, and then click the Test button.

   The program displays the message "You're a teenager." So far, the program displays the correct result.

8. Type **13** in the Age text box, and then click the Test button again.

   The program displays the message "You're not a teenager," as shown in the following screen shot:

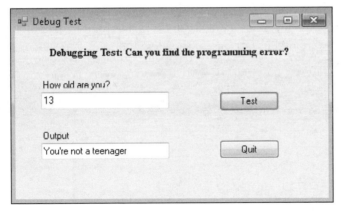

   This answer is incorrect, and you need to look at the program code to fix the problem.

9. Click the Quit button on the form, and then open the Code Editor.

10. Move the mouse pointer to the Margin Indicator bar (the gray bar just beyond the left margin of the Code Editor window), next to the statement *Age = TextBox1.Text* in the *Button1_Click* event procedure, and then click the bar to set a breakpoint.

The breakpoint immediately appears in red. See the following screen shot for the breakpoint's location and shape:

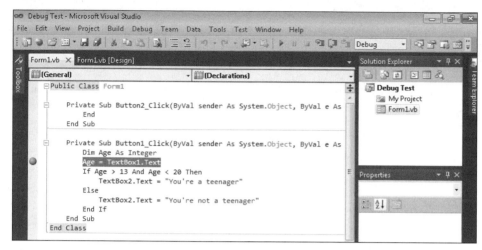

11. Click the Start Debugging button to run the program again.

The form opens just as before, and you can continue your tests.

12. Type **13** in the Age text box, and then click Test.

Visual Basic opens the Code Editor again and displays the *Button1_Click* event procedure—the program code currently being executed by the compiler. The statement that you selected as a breakpoint is highlighted in yellow, and an arrow appears in the Margin Indicator bar, as shown in the following screen shot:

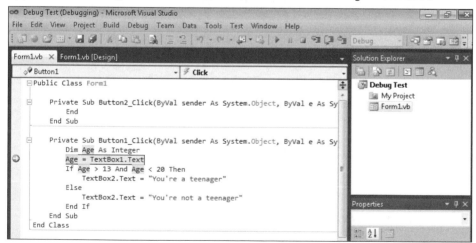

You can tell that Visual Studio is now in debugging mode because the word "Debugging" appears in its title bar. In debugging mode, you have an opportunity to see how the logic in your program is evaluated.

> **Note** You can also enter debugging mode in a Visual Basic program by placing the *Stop* statement in your program code where you'd like to pause execution. This is an older, but still reliable, method for entering debugging mode in a Visual Basic program.

13. Place the pointer over the *Age* variable in the Code Editor.

Visual Studio displays the message "Age | 0" and a tiny pin icon appears next to the value. While you're in debugging mode, you can display the value of variables or properties by simply holding the mouse pointer over the value in the program code. *Age* currently holds a value of 0 because it hasn't yet been filled by the *TextBox1* text box—that statement is the next statement the compiler will evaluate.

The pin icon is a new feature of Visual Studio 2010 that lets you pin the value of an expression somewhere in the IDE while you are debugging. The pinned expression is called a *DataTip*, and there are four commands on the Debug menu that are related to this feature. Try using a DataTip now to watch the value of the *Age* variable.

14. Click the pin icon to create a DataTip for the *Age* variable in the IDE.

15. Hold the mouse over the DataTip that appears until three small buttons are displayed next to the *Age* variable.

Your screen will look like the following:

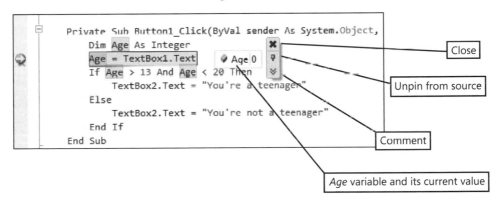

Until you remove this DataTip, it will display the value of the *Age* variable in the IDE. If you click the Unpin From Source button, the *Age* variable will remain in its current position in the IDE, even if you scroll the Code Editor window up or down. The Comment button lets you add a descriptive comment to the *Age* variable, and the Close button lets you remove the DataTip from the IDE.

16. Click the Close button next to the DataTip to remove the *Age* variable and its value of 0 for now.

As you can see, this is a handy way to watch variables change in a program as it runs, and you should feel free to use DataTips whenever you debug your code. Before you use them exclusively, however, experiment with some additional techniques in the following steps.

>
> **Note** If you add more than a few DataTips to your program code, be sure to use the Clear All DataTips, Import DataTips, and Export DataTips commands on the Debug menu. These features are especially useful in large development projects where you have numerous variables and expressions and many DataTips active. In particular, the Import and Export commands will allow you to transfer DataTips from one project to the next.

17. Continue by clicking the Step Into button on the Standard toolbar.

The Step Into button executes the next program statement in the event procedure (the line that's currently highlighted). By clicking the Step Into button, you can see how the program state changes when just one more program statement is evaluated. If you hold the pointer over the *Age* variable now, you'll see that it contains a value of 13.

18. On the Debug menu, point to Windows, and then click Autos.

> **Tip** If you are using Visual Basic 2010 Express, the Autos window is not available. Alternatively, you can open the Locals window to see the value of the Age variable. The Locals window displays a different set of variables.

The Windows submenu provides access to the entire set of debugging windows in Visual Studio. The Autos window shows the state of variables and properties currently being used (not only the properties you are currently setting, but others as well). As you can see in the following screen shot, the *Age* variable holds a value of 13 and the *TextBox1.Text* property holds a string of "13".

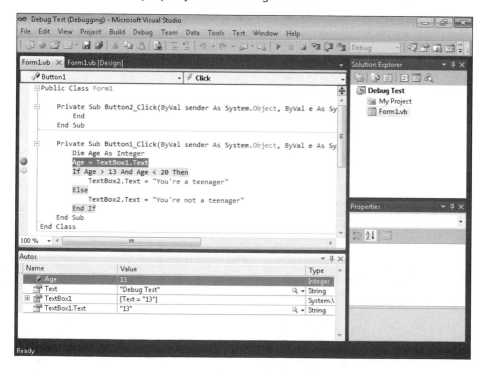

19. Click the Step Into button twice more.

The *If* statement evaluates the conditional expression to False, and the compiler moves to the *Else* statement in the decision structure. Here's our bug—the decision structure logic is incorrect because a 13-year-old *is* a teenager. Do you recognize the problem? The first comparison needs the greater than or equal to (>=) operator to specifically test for this boundary case of 13. You'll stop debugging now so that you can fix this logic error.

20. Click the Stop Debugging button on the Standard toolbar.

21. In the Code Editor, add the equal to sign (=) to the first condition in the *If* statement so that it reads:

```
If Age >= 13 And Age < 20 Then
```

22. Run the program again and test your solution, paying particular attention to the numbers 12, 13, 19, and 20—the boundary, or "tringe," cases that are likely to cause problems.

Remember that you still have a breakpoint set, so you'll enter debugging mode when you run the program again. Use the Step Into button to watch the program flow around the crucial *If* statement, and use the Autos window to track the value of your variables as you complete the tests. When the form opens, enter a new value and try the test again. (You'll learn how to remove the breakpoint later in the chapter.)

23. When you're finished experimenting with debugging mode, click the Stop Debugging button on the Standard toolbar to end the program.

Congratulations! You've successfully used debugging mode to find and correct a logic error in a program.

Tracking Variables by Using a Watch Window

The Autos window is useful for examining the state of certain variables and properties as they're evaluated by the compiler, but items in the Autos window *persist*, or maintain their values, only for the current statement (the statement highlighted in the debugger) and the previous statement (the statement just executed). When your program goes on to execute code that doesn't use the variables, they disappear from the Autos window.

To view the contents of variables and properties *throughout* the execution of a program, you need to use a Watch window, a special Visual Studio tool that tracks important values for you so long as you're working in debugging mode. In Visual Studio, you can open up to four Watch windows, numbered Watch 1, Watch 2, Watch 3, and Watch 4. If you are using Visual Basic 2010 Express, only one Watch window is available. When you are in debugging mode, you can open these windows by pointing to the Windows command on the Debug menu, pointing to Watch, and then clicking the window you want on the Watch submenu. You can also add expressions, such as *Age >= 13*, to a Watch window.

Open a Watch window

> **Tip** The Debug Test project is located in the C:\Vb10sbs\Chap08\Debug Test folder.

1. Click the Start Debugging button on the Standard toolbar to run the Debug Test program again.

   I'm assuming that the breakpoint you set on the line *Age = TextBox1.Text* in the previous exercise is still present. If that breakpoint isn't set, stop the program now, and set the breakpoint by clicking in the Margin Indicator bar next to the statement, as shown in Step 10 of the previous exercise, and then start the program again.

2. Type **20** in the Age text box, and then click Test.

   The program stops at the breakpoint and Visual Studio enters debugging mode, which is where you need to be if you want to add variables, properties, or expressions to a Watch window. One way to add an item is to select its value in the Code Editor, right-click the selection, and then click the Add Watch command.

3. Select the *Age* variable, right-click it, and then click the Add Watch command.

   Visual Studio opens the Watch 1 window and adds the *Age* variable to it. The value for the variable is currently 0, and the Type column in the window identifies the *Age* variable as an *Integer* type.

   Another way to add an item is to drag the item from the Code Editor into the Watch window.

4. Select the *TextBox2.Text* property, and then drag it to the empty row in the Watch 1 window.

   When you release the mouse button, Visual Studio adds the property and displays its value. (Right now, the property is an empty string.)

5. Select the expression *Age < 20*, and then add it to the Watch window.

Age < 20 is a conditional expression, and you can use the Watch window to display its logical, or Boolean, value. Your Watch window looks like this:

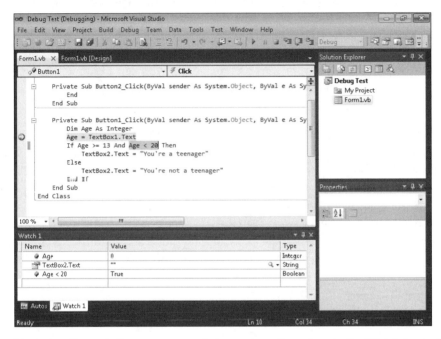

Now step through the program code to see how the values in the Watch 1 window change.

6. Click the Step Into button on the Standard toolbar.

> **Tip** Instead of clicking the Step Into button on the Standard toolbar, you can press the F8 key on the keyboard.

The *Age* variable is set to 20, and the *Age < 20* condition evaluates to False. These values are displayed in red type in the Watch window because they've just been updated.

7. Click the Step Into button three more times.

The *Else* clause is executed in the decision structure, and the value of the *TextBox2.Text* property in the Watch window changes to "You're not a teenager." This conditional test is operating correctly. Because you're satisfied with this condition, you can remove the test from the Watch window.

8. Click the Age < 20 row in the Watch window, and then press the DELETE key.

Visual Studio removes the value from the Watch window. As you can see, adding and removing values from the Watch window is a speedy process.

Leave Visual Studio running in debugging mode for now. You'll continue using the Watch window in the next section.

Visualizers: Debugging Tools That Display Data

Although you can use the DataTip, Watch, Autos, and Locals windows to examine simple data types such as *Integer* and *String* in the IDE, you'll eventually be faced with more complex data in your programs. For example, you might be examining a variable or property containing structured information from a database (a dataset) or a string containing Hypertext Markup Language (HTML) or Extensible Markup Language (XML) formatting information from a Web page. So that you can examine this type of item more closely in a debugging session, Visual Studio offers a set of tools in the IDE called *visualizers*. The icon for a visualizer is a small magnifying glass.

The Visual Studio 2010 IDE offers a number of standard visualizers, such as the text, HTML, and XML visualizers (which work on string objects), and the dataset visualizer (which works for *DataSet*, *DataView*, and *DataTable* objects). Microsoft has implied that it will offer additional visualizers as downloads at some point in the future, and they have designed Visual Studio so that third-party developers can write their own visualizers and install them into the Visual Studio debugger. In the following exercise, you'll see how the text visualizer works. (For this exercise, I assume that you are still in debugging mode and that the Watch window is open with a few expressions in it from the Debug Test program.)

Open a text visualizer in the debugger

1. Look on the right side of the Watch window for a small magnifying glass icon.

    A magnifying glass icon indicates that a visualizer is available for the variable or property that you are examining in a Watch window, an Autos window, or a Locals window. If you completed the previous exercise, the *TextBox2.Text* property shows a visualizer now.

2. Click the visualizer arrow.

    When the property you are examining is a text (string) property, Visual Studio offers three visualizers: a simple text visualizer that displays the selected string expression as readable text, an HTML visualizer that converts HTML code to a Web page, and an XML visualizer that converts XML code to a viewable document. The Watch window looks like this:

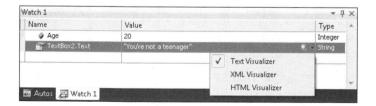

3. Select the Text Visualizer option.

Visual Studio opens a dialog box and displays the contents of the *TextBox2.Text* property. Your screen looks like this:

Although this particular result offers little more than the Watch window did, the benefits of the visualizer tool become immediately obvious when the *Text* property of a multiline text box object is displayed, or when you examine variables or properties containing database information or Web documents. You'll experiment with these more sophisticated data types later in the book.

4. Click Close to close the Text Visualizer dialog box.

Leave Visual Studio running in debugging mode. You'll continue using the Watch window in the next section, too.

 Tip In debugging mode, visualizers also sometimes appear in the Code Editor next to interesting variables or properties. If a visualizer appears, feel free to click it to get more information about the underlying data, as you did in the previous exercise.

Using the Immediate and Command Windows

So far, you've used the Visual Studio debugging tools that allow you to enter debugging mode; execute code one statement at a time; and examine the value of important variables, properties, and expressions in your program. Now you'll learn how to change the value of a variable by using the Immediate window, and you'll learn how to run commands, such as Save All or Print, within the Visual Studio IDE by using the Command window. The windows contain scroll bars, so you can execute more than one command and view the results by using the arrow keys.

The following exercises demonstrate how the Immediate and Command windows work. I discuss these windows together because, with the following special commands, you can switch between them:

- In the Immediate window, the >*cmd* command switches to the Command window.

- In the Command window, the *immed* command switches to the Immediate window.

The exercises assume that you're debugging the Debug Test program in debugging mode.

Use the Immediate window to modify a variable

1. Click the Immediate button on the Standard or Debug toolbar. (Alternatively, you can click the Debug menu, point to Windows, and then click Immediate.)

    When you select the command, Visual Studio opens the Immediate window and prepares the compiler to receive commands from you *while the Debug Test program is running*. This is a very handy feature because you can test program conditions on the fly, without stopping the program and inserting program statements in the Code Editor.

2. In the Immediate window, type **Age = 17**, and then press ENTER.

    You've just used the Immediate window to change the value of a variable. The value of the *Age* variable in the Watch window immediately changes to 17, and the next time the *If* statement is executed, the value in the *TextBox2.Text* property will change to "You're a teenager." Your Immediate window looks like this:

3. Type the following statement in the Immediate window, and then press ENTER:

    ```
    TextBox2.Text = "You're a great age!"
    ```

    The *Text* property of the *TextBox2* object is immediately changed to "You're a great age!" In the Immediate window, you can change the value of properties, as well as variables.

4. Display the Watch 1 window if it is not currently visible. (Click the Watch 1 tab in the Visual Studio IDE to do this.)

The Watch window looks like this:

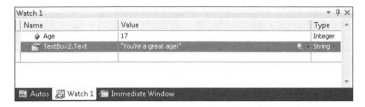

As you can see, both items now contain new values, and this gives you the opportunity to test the program further.

5. Click the Step Into button two times to display the Debug Test form again.

Notice that the *Text* property of the *TextBox2* object has been changed, as you directed, but the *Text* property of the *TextBox1* object still holds a value of 20 (not 17). This is because you changed the *Age* variable in the program, not the property that assigned a value to *Age*. Your screen looks like the following screen shot:

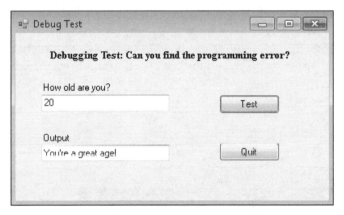

The Immediate window has many uses—it provides an excellent companion to the Watch window, and it can help you experiment with specific test cases that might otherwise be very difficult to enter into your program.

Switching to the Command Window

The text-based Command window offers a complement to the Visual Studio Immediate window. Reminiscent of the UNIX or MS-DOS command prompt, it can be used to run interface commands in the Visual Studio IDE. For example, entering the *File.SaveAll* command in the Command window saves all the files in the current project. (This command is the equivalent of the Save All command on the File menu.) If you already have the Immediate window open, you can switch between the Immediate and the Command windows by entering the >*cmd* and *immed* commands, respectively. You can also click the View menu, point to Other Windows, and then click Command Window to open the Command window. You'll practice using the Command window in the following exercise.

> **Tip** Visual Basic 2010 Express does not include the Command window. (If you're using the Express version you will not be able to complete this exercise.)

Run the *File.SaveAll* command

1. Click the Immediate Window tab to display the Immediate window.

2. Type **>cmd**, and then press ENTER to switch to the Command window.

    The Command window opens, and the Immediate or Watch window might now be partially (or totally) hidden. (You can return to the Immediate window by clicking its tab or typing **immed** in the Command window.) The > prompt appears, a visual clue that you are now working in the Command window.

3. Type **File.SaveAll** in the Command window, and then press ENTER.

    As you begin typing **File,** all the Visual Studio commands associate with the File menu and file operations appear in a pop-up list box. This Microsoft IntelliSense feature offers a useful way to learn about the many commands that can be executed within the Command window. After you type **File.SaveAll** and press ENTER, Visual Studio saves the current project, and the command prompt returns, as shown in the following screen shot:

4. Experiment with other commands now if you like. (Begin your commands with menu names to discover the different commands available.) When you're finished, click the Close button in both the Command and Immediate windows. You're finished with them for now.

One Step Further: Removing Breakpoints

If you've been following the instructions in this chapter carefully, the Debug Test program is still running and has a breakpoint in it. Follow these steps to remove the breakpoint and end the program. You're finished debugging the Debug Test program.

> **Tip** Visual Basic 2010 Express does not include the Delete All Breakpoints command mentioned below, so to remove breakpoints you need to delete them one by one.

Remove a breakpoint

1. In the Code Editor, click the red circle associated with the breakpoint in the Margin Indicator bar.

    The breakpoint disappears. That's all there is to it! But note that if you have more than one breakpoint in a program, you can remove them all by clicking the Delete All Breakpoints command on the Debug menu. Visual Studio saves breakpoints with your project, so it's important to know how to remove them; otherwise, they'll still be in your program, even if you close Visual Studio and restart it!

2. Click the Stop Debugging button on the Standard toolbar.

    The Debug Test program ends.

3. On the View menu, point to Toolbars, and then click Debug.

    The Debug toolbar closes.

You've learned the fundamental techniques of debugging Visual Basic programs with Visual Studio. Place a bookmark in this chapter so that you can return to it as you encounter problems later in the book. In the next chapter, you'll learn how to handle run-time errors by using structured error handling techniques.

Chapter 8 Quick Reference

To	Do This
Display the Debug toolbar	On the View menu, point to Toolbars, and then click Debug.
Set a breakpoint	In the Code Editor, click in the Margin Indicator bar next to the statement where you want to stop program execution. When the compiler reaches the breakpoint, it will enter debugging mode. *or* Place a *Stop* statement in the program code where you want to enter debugging mode.
Execute one line of code in the Code Editor	Click the Step Into button on the Standard toolbar.
Examine a variable, a property, or an expression in the Code Editor	In debugging mode, select the value in the Code Editor, and then hold the pointer over it.
Use the Autos window to examine a variable on the current or previous line	In debugging mode, click the Debug menu, point to Windows, and then click Autos.
Add a variable, a property, or an expression to a Watch window	In debugging mode, select the value in the Code Editor, right-click the value, and then click Add Watch.

To	Do This
Display a Watch window	In debugging mode, click the Debug menu, point to Windows, point to Watch, and then click the window.
Display HTML, XML, or dataset information during a debugging session	Click the visualizer icon in an Autos window, a Watch window, a Locals window, or a DataTip window during a debugging session.
Open the Immediate window	Click the Debug menu, point to Windows, and then click Immediate.
Run a command in the Visual Studio IDE from the Command window	At the > prompt, type the name of the command, and then press ENTER. For example, to save the current project, type **File.SaveAll**, and then press ENTER.
Switch to the Command window from the Immediate window	Type **>cmd**, and then press ENTER. To switch back to the Immediate window, type **immed,** and then press ENTER.
Remove one or more breakpoints	Click the breakpoint in the Margin Indicator bar of the Code Editor. *or* Click the Delete All Breakpoints command on the Debug menu.
Stop debugging	Click the Stop Debugging button on the Standard toolbar.

Chapter 9
Trapping Errors by Using Structured Error Handling

After completing this chapter, you will be able to:

- Manage run-time errors by using the *Try … Catch* error handler.
- Create a disc drive error handler that tests specific error conditions by using the *Catch* statement.
- Write complex error handlers that use the *Exception* object and the *Message* property.
- Build nested *Try … Catch* statements.
- Use error handlers in combination with defensive programming techniques.
- Leave error handlers prematurely by using the *Exit Try* statement.

In Chapter 8, "Debugging Visual Basic Programs," you learned how to recognize run-time errors in a Microsoft Visual Basic program and how to locate logic errors and other defects in your program code by using the Microsoft Visual Studio 2010 debugging tools. In this chapter, you'll learn how to build blocks of code that handle run-time errors, also referred to as *exceptions*, which occur as a result of normal operating conditions—for example, errors due to a CD or DVD not being in an optical drive, a broken Internet connection, or an offline printer. These routines are called *structured error handlers* (or *structured exception handlers*), and you can use them to recognize run-time errors, suppress unwanted error messages, and adjust program conditions so that your application can regain control and run again.

Fortunately, Visual Basic offers the powerful *Try … Catch* code block for handling errors. In this chapter, you'll learn how to trap run-time errors by using *Try … Catch* code blocks, and you'll learn how to use the *Exception* object to identify specific run-time errors. You'll also learn how to use multiple *Catch* statements to write more flexible error handlers, build nested *Try … Catch* code blocks, and use the *Exit Try* statement to exit a *Try … Catch* code block prematurely. The programming techniques you'll learn are similar to the structured error handlers provided by the most advanced programming languages, such as Java and C++. The most reliable, or *robust*, Visual Basic programs use several error handlers to manage unforeseen circumstances and provide users with consistent and trouble-free computing experiences.

Processing Errors by Using the *Try … Catch* Statement

A *program crash* is an unexpected problem from which a program can't recover. You might have experienced your first program crash when Visual Basic couldn't load artwork from a file, or when you intentionally introduced errors into your program code during debugging in Chapter 8. It's not that Visual Basic isn't smart enough to handle the glitch; it's just that the program hasn't been "told" what to do when something goes wrong.

Fortunately, you don't have to live with occasional errors that cause your programs to crash. You can write special Visual Basic routines, called *structured error handlers*, to manage and respond to run-time errors before they force the Visual Basic compiler to terminate your program. An error handler handles a run-time error by telling the program how to continue when one of its statements doesn't work. Error handlers can be placed in each event procedure where there is potential for trouble, or in generic functions or subprograms that receive control after an error has occurred and handle the problem systematically. (You'll learn more about writing functions and subprograms in Chapter 10, "Creating Modules and Procedures.")

Error handlers handle, or *trap*, a problem by using a *Try ... Catch* code block and a special error-handling object named *Exception*. The *Exception* object has a *Message* property that you can use to display a description of the error. For example, if the run-time error is associated with loading a file from a CD or DVD drive, your error handler might display a custom error message that identifies the problem and prompts the user to insert a CD or DVD, rather than allowing the failed operation to crash the program.

When to Use Error Handlers

You can use error handlers in any situation where an action (either expected or unexpected) has the potential to produce an error that stops program execution. Typically, error handlers are used to manage external events that influence a program—for example, events caused by a failed network or Internet connection, a CD, DVD, or diskette not being inserted correctly in the drive, or an offline printer or scanner. Table 9-1 lists potential problems that can be addressed by error handlers.

TABLE 9-1 Potential Problems for Error Handlers

Problem	Description
Network/Internet problems	Network servers, Internet connections, and other resources that fail, or *go down*, unexpectedly.
Database problems	Unable to make a database connection, a query can't be processed or times out, a database returns an error, and so on.
Disc drive problems	Unformatted or incorrectly formatted CDs, DVDs, diskettes, or media that aren't properly inserted; bad sectors, CDs, DVDs, or diskettes that are full; problems with a CD or DVD drive; and so on.
Path problems	A path to a necessary file that is missing or incorrect.
Printer problems	Printers that are offline, out of paper, out of memory, or otherwise unavailable.
Software not installed	A file or component that your application relies on but that is not installed on the user's computer, or an operating system incompatibility.
Security problems	An application or process that attempts to modify operating system files, use the Internet inappropriately, or modify other programs or files.

Problem	Description
Permissions problems	User permissions that are not appropriate for performing a task.
Overflow errors	An activity that exceeds the allocated storage space.
Out-of-memory errors	Insufficient application or resource space available in the Microsoft Windows memory management scheme.
Clipboard problems	Problems with data transfer or the Windows Clipboard.
Logic errors	Syntax or logic errors undetected by the compiler and previous tests (such as an incorrectly spelled file name).

Setting the Trap: The *Try ... Catch* Code Block

The code block used to handle a run-time error is called *Try ... Catch*. You place the *Try* statement in an event procedure right before the statement you're worried about, and the *Catch* statement follows immediately with a list of the statements that you want to run if a run-time error actually occurs. A number of optional statements, such as *Finally*, *Exit Try*, and nested *Try ... Catch* code blocks can also be included, as the examples in this chapter will demonstrate. However, the basic syntax for a *Try ... Catch* exception handler is simply the following:

```
Try
    Statements that might produce a run-time error
Catch
    Statements to run if a run-time error occurs
Finally
    Optional statements to run whether an error occurs or not
End Try
```

The *Try* statement identifies the beginning of an error handler in which *Try*, *Catch*, and *End Try* are required keywords, and *Finally* and the statements that follow are optional. Note that programmers sometimes call the statements between the *Try* and *Catch* keywords *protected code* because any run-time errors resulting from these statements won't cause the program to crash. (Instead, Visual Basic executes the error-handling statements in the *Catch* code block.)

Path and Disc Drive Errors

The following example demonstrates a common run-time error situation—a problem with a path, disc drive, or attached peripheral device. To complete this exercise, you'll load a sample Visual Basic project that I created to show how artwork files are opened in a picture box object on a Windows form.

To prepare for the exercise, insert a blank CD or DVD into drive D (or equivalent), and use Windows Explorer or your CD or DVD creation software to copy or *burn* the Fileopen.bmp file to it. Alternatively, you can copy the .bmp file to a diskette in drive A or another type of removable storage media, such as an attached digital camera, memory stick, MP3 player, or USB flash drive.

> **Tip** You'll find the Fileopen.bmp file, along with the Disc Drive Error project, in the C:\Vb10sbs\Chap09 folder.

To complete the exercise, you'll need to be able to remove the CD or DVD, or connect and disconnect your external storage device, as test conditions dictate, and you'll need to modify the program code with the drive letter you're using. You'll use the CD or DVD (or equivalent media) throughout the chapter to force run-time errors and recover from them.

Experiment with disc drive errors

1. Insert a blank CD or DVD in drive D (or the drive in which you create CDs or DVDs), and copy the Fileopen.bmp file to it.

    Use Windows Explorer or a third-party CD or DVD creation program to copy the file and burn the disc. If you're using a different external storage device, connect the device or insert a blank disc, copy Fileopen.bmp to it, and make a note of the drive letter that Windows assigns to the device.

2. Start Visual Studio, and then open the Disc Drive Error project, which is located in the C:\Vb10sbs\Chap09\Disc Drive Error folder.

    The Disc Drive Error project opens in the IDE.

3. If the project's form isn't visible, display it now.

    The Disc Drive Error project is a skeleton program that displays the Fileopen.bmp file in a picture box when the user clicks the Check Drive button. I designed the project as a convenient way to create and trap run-time errors, and you can use it throughout this chapter to build error handlers by using the *Try … Catch* code block.

4. Double-click the Check Drive button on the form to display the *Button1_Click* event procedure.

    You'll see the following line of program code between the *Private Sub* and *End Sub* statements:

    ```
    PictureBox1.Image = _
        System.Drawing.Bitmap.FromFile("d:\fileopen.bmp")
    ```

    As you've learned in earlier chapters, the *FromFile* method opens the specified file. This particular use of *FromFile* opens the Fileopen.bmp file on drive D and displays it in a picture box. However, if the CD or DVD is missing, the CD or DVD tray is open, the file is not on the CD or DVD, or there is another problem with the path or drive letter specified in the code, the statement produces a "File Not Found" error in Visual Basic. This is the run-time error we want to trap.

5. If your CD or DVD drive or attached peripheral device is using a drive letter other than "D" now, change the drive letter in this program statement to match the letter you're using.

For example, a floppy disc drive typically requires the letter "A." USB flash drives, digital cameras, and other detachable media typically use "E," "F," or higher letters for the drive.

6. With your CD or DVD still in drive D (or equivalent), click the Start Debugging button on the Standard toolbar to run the program.

The form for the project opens, as shown here:

7. Click the Check Drive button on the form.

The program loads the Fileopen.bmp file from the CD or DVD and displays it in the picture box, as shown in the following screen shot:

The *SizeMode* property of the picture box object is set to StretchImage, so the file fills the entire picture box object. Now see what happens when the CD or DVD isn't in the drive when the program attempts to load the file.

8. Remove the CD or DVD from the drive.

    If you are using a different media type, remove it now. If you are testing with a removable storage device, follow your usual procedure to safely remove or turn it off, and remove the media containing Fileopen.bmp.

9. Click the Check Drive button again on the form.

    The program can't find the file, and Visual Basic issues a run-time error, or *unhandled exception*, which causes the program to crash. Visual Studio enters debugging mode, highlighting the problem statement.

    Your screen will look like this:

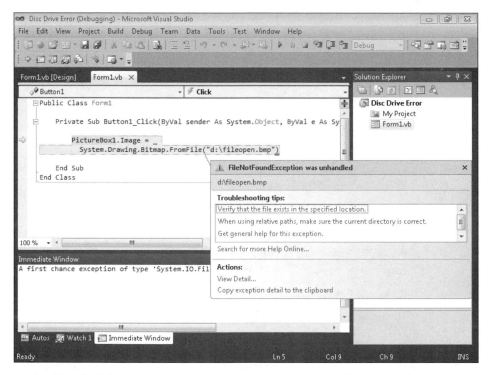

Notice how helpful Visual Studio is trying to be here, by offering troubleshooting tips to assist you in locating the source of the unhandled exception that has stopped the program. The Actions list allows you to learn even more about the specific error message that is displayed at the top of the dialog box.

10. Click the Stop Debugging button on the Standard toolbar to close the program.

    The development environment returns.

Now you'll modify the code to handle this plausible error scenario in the future.

Writing a Disc Drive Error Handler

The problem with the Disc Drive Error program isn't that it somehow defies the inherent capabilities of Visual Basic to process errors. We just haven't specified what Visual Basic should do when it encounters an exception that it doesn't know how to handle. The solution to this problem is to write a *Try … Catch* code block that recognizes the error and tells Visual Basic what to do about it. You'll add this error handler now.

Use *Try … Catch* to trap the error

1. Display the *Button1_Click* event procedure if it isn't visible in the Code Editor.

    You need to add an error handler to the event procedure that's causing the problems. As you'll see in this example, you actually build the *Try … Catch* code block around the code that's the potential source of trouble, protecting the rest of the program from the run-time errors that it might produce.

2. Modify the event procedure so that the existing *FromFile* statement fits between *Try* and *Catch* statements, as shown in the following code block:

```
Try
    PictureBox1.Image = _
      System.Drawing.Bitmap.FromFile("d:\fileopen.bmp")
Catch
    MsgBox("Please insert the disc in drive D!")
End Try
```

    You don't need to retype the *FromFile* statement—just type the *Try*, *Catch*, *MsgBox*, and *End Try* statements above and below it. If Visual Studio adds *Catch*, variable declaration, or *End Try* statements in the wrong place, simply delete the statements and retype them as shown in the book. (The Code Editor tries to be helpful, but its Auto Complete feature sometimes gets in the way.)

    This program code demonstrates the most basic use of a *Try … Catch* code block. It places the problematic *FromFile* statement in a *Try* code block so that if the program code produces an error, the statements in the *Catch* code block are executed. The *Catch* code block simply displays a message box asking the user to insert the required disc in drive D so that the program can continue. This *Try … Catch* code block contains no *Finally* statement, so the error handler ends with the keywords *End Try*.

    Again, if you are using a removable storage device or media associated with a different drive letter, you would make those changes in the statements that you just typed.

Test the error handler

1. Remove the CD or DVD from drive D, and then click the Start Debugging button to run the program.

2. Click the Check Drive button.

   Instead of stopping program execution, Visual Basic invokes the *Catch* statement, which displays the following message box:

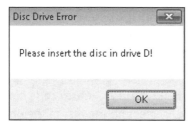

3. Click OK, and then click the Check Drive button again.

   The program displays the message box again, asking you to insert the disc in drive D. Each time there's a problem loading the file, this message box appears.

4. Insert the disc in drive D, wait a moment for the system to recognize the CD or DVD (close any windows that appear when you insert the disc), click OK, and then click the Check Drive button again.

   The bitmap graphic appears in the picture box, as expected. The error handler has completed its work effectively—rather than the program crashing inadvertently, it's told you how to correct your mistake, and you can now continue working with the application.

5. Click the Close button on the form to stop the program.

It's time to learn some of the variations of the *Try … Catch* error handler.

Using the *Finally* Clause to Perform Cleanup Tasks

As with the syntax description for *Try … Catch* noted earlier in the chapter, you can use the optional *Finally* clause with *Try … Catch* to execute a block of statements regardless of how the compiler executes the *Try* or *Catch* blocks. In other words, whether or not the *Try* statements produced a run-time error, there might be some code that you need to run each time an error handler is finished. For example, you might want to update variables or properties, display the results of a computation, close database connections, or perform "cleanup" operations by clearing variables or disabling unneeded objects on a form.

The following exercise demonstrates how the *Finally* clause works, by displaying a second message box whether or not the *FromFile* method produces a run-time error.

Use *Finally* to display a message box

1. Display the *Button1_Click* event procedure, and then edit the *Try … Catch* code block so that it contains two additional lines of code above the *End Try* statement. The complete error handler should look like this:

```
Try
    PictureBox1.Image = _
      System.Drawing.Bitmap.FromFile("d:\fileopen.bmp")
Catch
    MsgBox("Please insert the disc in drive D!")
Finally
    MsgBox("Error handler complete")
End Try
```

The *Finally* statement indicates to the compiler that a final block of code should be executed whether or not a run-time error is processed. To help you learn exactly how this feature works, I've inserted a *MsgBox* function to display a test message after the *Finally* statement. Although this simple use of the *Finally* statement is helpful for testing purposes, in a real program you'll probably want to use the *Finally* code block to update important variables or properties, display data, or perform other cleanup operations.

2. Remove the CD or DVD from drive D, and then click the Start Debugging button to run the program.

3. Click the Check Drive button.

   The error handler displays a dialog box asking you to insert the disc in drive D.

4. Click OK.

   The program executes the *Finally* clause in the error handler, and the following message box appears:

5. Click OK, insert the disc in drive D, and then click the Check Drive button again.

   The file appears in the picture box as expected. In addition, the *Finally* clause is executed, and the "Error handler complete" message box appears again. As I noted earlier, *Finally* statements are executed at the end of a *Try … Catch* block whether or not there's an error.

6. Click OK, and then click the Close button on the form to stop the program.

More Complex *Try ... Catch* Error Handlers

As your programs become more sophisticated, you might find it useful to write more complex *Try ... Catch* error handlers that manage a variety of run-time errors and unusual error-handling situations. *Try ... Catch* provides for this complexity by:

- Permitting multiple lines of code in each *Try*, *Catch*, or *Finally* code block.

- Using the *Catch* statement with particular *Exception* objects, which tests specific error conditions.

- Allowing nested *Try ... Catch* code blocks, which can be used to build sophisticated and robust error handlers.

In addition, by using a special error-handling object named *Exception*, you can identify and process specific run-time errors and conditions in your program. You'll investigate each of these error-handling features in the following section.

The *Exception* Object

The Microsoft .NET Framework provides the *Exception* object to help you learn about the errors that occur in your programs. *Exception* provides you with information about the exception that occurred so that you can respond to it programmatically. The most useful *Exception* property is the *Message* property, which contains a short message about the error.

There are several different types of *Exception* objects. Table 9-2 lists the most important *Exception* objects and what they mean.

TABLE 9-2 Important *Exception* Objects

Exception	Description
ArgumentException	Occurs when an argument passed to a method is not valid.
ArgumentOutOfRangeException	Occurs when an argument is passed to a method that is outside the allowable range.
ArithmeticException	Occurs when there is an arithmetic-related error.
DataException	Occurs when there is an error when accessing data using ADO.NET.
DirectoryNotFoundException	Occurs when a folder can't be found.
DivideByZeroException	Occurs when an attempt is made to divide by zero.
EndOfStreamException	Occurs when an attempt is made to read past the end of a stream.
Exception	Occurs for any exception that is thrown. Other exceptions inherit from this object.
FileNotFoundException	Occurs when a file can't be found.
IndexOutOfRangeException	Occurs when an index is used that is outside the allowable range of an array.

Exception	Description
IOException	Occurs when there is an input/output error.
OutOfMemoryException	Occurs when there isn't enough memory.
OverflowException	Occurs when an arithmetic-related operation results in an overflow.
SecurityException	Occurs when there is a security-related error.
SqlException	Occurs when there is an error when accessing data in Microsoft SQL Server.
UnauthorizedAccessException	Occurs when the operation denies access.

So how do you know which exception types to use? That depends on your code. For example, in the exercise that we are working on you have been using the *System.Drawing .Bitmap.FromFile* method. If you open the Visual Studio Help documentation for *FromFile*, you will see an "Exceptions" section.

> **Tip** To quickly open up the Help documentation for *FromFile*, put your cursor in the *FromFile* text in Visual Studio and then press the F1 key. From here, you can open the Image.FromFile Method (String) topic.

The "Exceptions" section in the Image.FromFile Method (String) topic lists the following exceptions:

- *ArgumentException*
- *FileNotFoundException*
- *OutOfMemoryException*

With this information in hand, you can write code to handle common exceptions that take place when a programmer uses *FromFile*. As you write more code, you will discover additional *Exception* objects, and you can also learn about them by using the Help documentation. Even though there are many different *Exception* objects, you will use them in the same way described here and demonstrated below. The following exercise uses two of the *Exception* objects above in a *Try ... Catch* error handler to test for more than one run-time error condition.

Test for multiple run-time error conditions

1. In the *Button1_Click* event procedure, edit the *Try ... Catch* error handler so that it looks like the following code block. (The original *FromFile* statement is the same as the code you used in the previous exercises, but the *Catch* statements are all new.)

```
Try
    PictureBox1.Image = _
        System.Drawing.Bitmap.FromFile("d:\fileopen.bmp")
```

```
Catch ex As System.IO.FileNotFoundException 'if File Not Found error
    MsgBox("Check pathname and disc drive")
Catch ex As OutOfMemoryException  'if Out Of Memory error
    MsgBox("Is this really a bitmap?", , ex.Message)
Catch ex As Exception
    MsgBox("Problem loading file", , ex.Message)
End Try
```

This code has three *Catch* statements. If the *FileNotFoundException* occurs during the file open procedure, the message "Check pathname and disc drive" is displayed in a message box. If the *OutOfMemoryException* occurs—probably the result of loading a file that doesn't actually contain artwork—the message "Is this really a bitmap?" is displayed. (I get this error if I accidentally try to open a Microsoft Word document in a picture box object by using the *FromFile* method.)

The final *Catch* statement handles all other run-time errors that could potentially occur during a file-opening process—it's a general "catch-all" code block that prints a general error message inside a message box and a specific error message from the *Message* property in the title bar of the message box.

2. Click the Start Debugging button to run the program.

3. Remove the CD or DVD from drive D.

4. Click the Check Drive button.

   The error handler displays the error message "Check pathname and disc drive" in a message box. The first *Catch* statement works.

5. Click OK, and then click the Close button on the form to end the program.

6. Insert the CD or DVD again, and then use Windows Explorer or another tool to copy a second file to the CD or DVD that isn't an artwork file. For example, copy a Word document or a Microsoft Excel spreadsheet to the CD or DVD.

   You won't open this file in Word or Excel, but you will try to open it (unsuccessfully, we hope) in your program's picture box object. (If your CD or DVD software or drive doesn't allow you to add additional files to a CD or DVD after you have burned it, you might need to create a second CD or DVD with the two files.)

7. In the Code Editor, change the name of the Fileopen.bmp file in the *FromFile* program statement to the name of the file (Word, Excel, or other) you copied to the CD or DVD in drive D.

   Using a file with a different format gives you an opportunity to test a second type of run-time error—an Out of Memory exception, which occurs when Visual Basic attempts to load a file that isn't a graphic or has too much information for a picture box.

8. Run the program again, and then click the Check Drive button.

The error handler displays the following error message:

Notice that I have used the *Message* property to display a short description of the problem ("Out of memory.") in the message box title bar. Using this property in your error handler can give the user a clearer idea of what has happened.

9. Click OK, and then click the Close button on the form to stop the program.

10. Change the file name back to Fileopen.bmp in the *FromFile* method. (You'll use it in the next exercise.)

The *Catch* statement is very powerful. By using *Catch* in combination with the *Exception* object and *Message* property, you can write sophisticated error handlers that recognize and respond to several types of exceptions.

Raising Your Own Errors

For testing purposes and other specialized uses, you can artificially generate your own run-time errors in a program with a technique called *throwing*, or *raising*, exceptions. To accomplish this, you use the *Throw* statement. For example, the following syntax uses the *Throw* statement to produce an exception and then handles the exception by using a *Catch* statement:

```
Try
    Throw New Exception("There was a problem")
Catch ex As Exception
    MsgBox(ex.Message)
End Try
```

When you learn how to write your own procedures, you can generate your own errors by using this technique and return them to the calling routine.

Specifying a Retry Period

Another strategy that you can use in an error handler is to try an operation a few times and then disable it if the problem isn't resolved. For example, in the following exercise, a *Try ... Catch* block employs a counter variable named *Retries* to track the number of times the message "Please insert the disc in drive D!" is displayed, and after the second time, the error handler disables the Check Drive button. The trick to this technique is declaring the

Retries variable at the top of the form's program code so that it has scope throughout all the form's event procedures. The *Retries* variable is then incremented and tested in the *Catch* code block. The number of retries can be modified by simply changing the "2" in the statement, as shown here:

```
If Retries <= 2
```

Use a variable to track run-time errors

1. In the Code Editor, scroll to the top of the form's program code, and directly below the *Public Class Form1* statement, type the following variable declaration:

   ```
   Dim Retries As Short = 0
   ```

   Retries is declared as a *Short* integer variable because it won't contain very big numbers. It's assigned an initial value of 0 so that it resets properly each time the program runs.

2. In the *Button1_Click* event procedure, edit the *Try … Catch* error handler so that it looks like the following code block:

   ```
   Try
       PictureBox1.Image = _
         System.Drawing.Bitmap.FromFile("d:\fileopen.bmp")
   Catch
       Retries += 1
       If Retries <= 2 Then
           MsgBox("Please insert the disc in drive D!")
       Else
           MsgBox("File Load feature disabled")
           Button1.Enabled = False
       End If
   End Try
   ```

   The *Try* block tests the same file-opening procedure, but this time, if an error occurs, the *Catch* block increments the *Retries* variable and tests the variable to be sure that it's less than or equal to 2. The number 2 can be changed to allow any number of retries—currently it allows only two run-time errors. After two errors, the *Else* clause is executed, and a message box appears indicating that the file-loading feature has been disabled. The Check Drive button is then disabled—in other words, dimmed and rendered unusable for the remainder of the program.

> **Tip** This revised version of the error handler that you have been building has been renamed Disc Drive Handler and is stored in the C:\Vb10sbs\Chap09\Disc Drive Handler folder. You may notice the new project title in the title bar of your message boxes, but otherwise the project is the same as what you have been experimenting with thus far. (I've simply saved the revised version so that you can open it later if you want.)

3. Click the Start Debugging button to run the program.

4. Remove the CD or DVD from drive D.

5. Click the Check Drive button.

The error handler displays the error message "Please insert the disc in drive D!" in a message box, as shown here. Behind the scenes, the *Retries* variable is also incremented to 1.

6. Click OK, and then click the Check Drive button again.

The *Retries* variable is set to 2, and the message "Please insert the disc in drive D!" appears again.

7. Click OK, and then click the Check Drive button a third time.

The *Retries* variable is incremented to 3, and the *Else* clause is executed. The message "File Load feature disabled" appears, as shown here:

8. Click OK in the message box.

The Check Drive button is disabled on the form, as shown here:

The error handler has responded to the disc drive problem by allowing the user a few tries to fix the problem, and then it has disabled the problematic button. (In other words, the user can no longer click the button.) This disabling action stops future run-time errors, although the program might no longer function exactly as it was originally designed.

9. Click the Close button on the form to stop the program.

Using Nested *Try ... Catch* Blocks

You can also use nested *Try ... Catch* code blocks in your error handlers. For example, the following disc drive error handler uses a second *Try ... Catch* block to retry the file open operation a single time if the first attempt fails and generates a run-time error:

```
Try
    PictureBox1.Image = _
        System.Drawing.Bitmap.FromFile("d:\fileopen.bmp")
Catch
    MsgBox("Insert the disc in drive D, then click OK!")
    Try
        PictureBox1.Image = _
            System.Drawing.Bitmap.FromFile("d:\fileopen.bmp")
    Catch
        MsgBox("File Load feature disabled")
        Button1.Enabled = False
    End Try
End Try
```

If the user inserts the disc in the drive as a result of the message prompt, the second *Try* block opens the file without error. However, if a file-related run-time error still appears, the second *Catch* block displays a message saying that the file load feature is being disabled, and the button is disabled.

In general, nested *Try ... Catch* error handlers work well so long as you don't have too many tests or retries to manage. If you do need to retry a problematic operation many times, use a variable to track your retries, or develop a function containing an error handler that can be called repeatedly from your event procedures. (For more information about creating functions, see Chapter 10.)

Comparing Error Handlers with Defensive Programming Techniques

Error handlers aren't the only mechanism for protecting a program against run-time errors. For example, the following program code uses the *File.Exists* method in the *System.IO* namespace of the .NET Framework class library to check whether a file exists on CD or DVD before it's opened:

```
If File.Exists("d:\fileopen.bmp") Then
    PictureBox1.Image = _
```

```
        System.Drawing.Bitmap.FromFile("d:\fileopen.bmp")
Else
    MsgBox("Cannot find fileopen.bmp on drive D.")
End If
```

This *If ... Then* statement isn't an actual error handler because it doesn't prevent a run-time error from halting a program. Instead, it's a validation technique that some programmers call *defensive programming*. It uses a handy method in the .NET Framework class library to verify the intended file operation *before* it's actually attempted in the program code. And in this particular case, testing to see whether the file exists with the .NET Framework method is actually faster than waiting for Visual Basic to issue an exception and recover from a run-time error using an error handler.

> **Note** To get this particular program logic to work, the following statement must be included in the declarations section at the very top of the form's program code to make reference to the .NET Framework class library that's being invoked:
>
> ```
> Imports System.IO
> ```
>
> For more information about utilizing the *Imports* statement to use the objects, properties, and methods in the .NET Framework class libraries, see Chapter 5, "Visual Basic Variables and Formulas, and the .NET Framework."

When should you use defensive programming techniques, and when should you use structured error handlers? The answer is really that you should use a combination of defensive programming and structured error-handling techniques in your code. Defensive programming logic is usually the most efficient way to manage potential problems. As I mentioned earlier when discussing the *If ... Then* code block, the *File.Exists* method is actually faster than using a *Try ... Catch* error handler, so it also makes sense to use a defensive programming technique if performance issues are involved. You should use defensive programming logic for errors that you expect to occur frequently in your program. Use structured error handlers for errors that you don't expect to occur very often. Structured error handlers are essential if you have more than one condition to test and if you want to provide the user with numerous options for responding to the error. Structured error handlers also allow you to gracefully handle errors that you aren't even aware of.

One Step Further: The *Exit Try* Statement

You've learned a lot about error handlers in this chapter; now you're ready to put them to work in your own programs. But before you move on to the next chapter, here's one more syntax option for *Try ... Catch* code blocks that you might find useful: the *Exit Try* statement. *Exit Try* is a quick and slightly abrupt technique for exiting a *Try ... Catch* code block prematurely. If you've written Visual Basic programs before, you might notice its similarity to the *Exit For* and *Exit Sub* statements, which you can use to leave a structured routine early.

Using the *Exit Try* syntax, you can jump completely out of the current *Try* or *Catch* code block. If there's a *Finally* code block, this code will be executed, but *Exit Try* lets you jump over any remaining *Try* or *Catch* statements you don't want to execute.

The following sample routine shows how the *Exit Try* statement works. It first checks to see whether the *Enabled* property of the *PictureBox1* object is set to False, a flag that might indicate that the picture box isn't ready to receive input. If the picture box isn't yet enabled, the *Exit Try* statement skips to the end of the *Catch* code block, and the file load operation isn't attempted.

```
Try
    If PictureBox1.Enabled = False Then Exit Try
    PictureBox1.Image = _
      System.Drawing.Bitmap.FromFile("d:\fileopen.bmp")
Catch
    Retries += 1
    If Retries <= 2 Then
        MsgBox("Please insert the disc in drive D!")
    Else
        MsgBox("File Load feature disabled")
        Button1.Enabled = False
    End If
End Try
```

The example builds on the last error handler that you experimented with in this chapter (the Disc Drive Handler project). If you'd like to test the *Exit Try* statement in the context of that program, open the Disc Drive Handler project and enter the *If* statement that contains the *Exit Try* in the Code Editor. You'll also need to use the Properties window to disable the picture box object on the form (in other words, to set its *Enabled* property to False).

Congratulations! You've learned a number of important fundamental programming techniques in Visual Basic, including how to write error handlers. Now you're ready to increase your programming efficiency by learning to write Visual Basic modules and procedures.

Chapter 9 Quick Reference

To	Do this
Detect and process run-time errors	Build an error handler by using one or more *Try … Catch* code blocks. For example, the following error handler code tests for path or disc drive problems: ```Try PictureBox1.Image = _ System.Drawing.Bitmap.FromFile("d:\fileopen.bmp")Catch MsgBox("Check path or insert disc")Finally MsgBox("Error handler complete")End Try```

To	Do this

Test for specific error conditions in an event handler	Use the *Catch* statement and the appropriate *Exception* object. For example:
	
	``
	Try
	    PictureBox1.Image = _
	        System.Drawing.Bitmap.FromFile("d:\fileopen.bmp")
	Catch ex As System.IO.FileNotFoundException 'if File Not Found
	    MsgBox("Check pathname and disc drive")
	Catch ex As OutOfMemoryException 'if Out Of Memory
	    MsgBox("Is this really a bitmap?", , ex.Message)
	Catch ex As Exception
	    MsgBox("Problem loading file", , ex.Message)
	End Try
	``

Create your own errors in a program	Use the *Throw* statement. For example, the following code generates an exception and handles it:
	
	``
	Try
	    Throw New Exception("There was a problem")
	Catch ex As Exception
	    MsgBox(ex.Message)
	End Try
	``

Write nested *Try … Catch* error handlers	Place one *Try … Catch* code block within another. For example:
	
	``
	Try
	    PictureBox1.Image = _
	        System.Drawing.Bitmap.FromFile("d:\fileopen.bmp")
	Catch
	    MsgBox("Insert the disc in drive D!, then click OK!")
	    Try
	        PictureBox1.Image = _
	            System.Drawing.Bitmap.FromFile("d:\fileopen.bmp")
	    Catch
	        MsgBox("File Load feature disabled")
	        Button1.Enabled = False
	    End Try
	End Try
	``

Exit the current *Try* or *Catch* code block	Use the *Exit Try* statement in the *Try* or the *Catch* code block. For example: ``` If PictureBox1.Enabled = False Then Exit Try ```

Chapter 10
Creating Modules and Procedures

After completing this chapter, you will be able to:

- Employ structured programming techniques and create modules containing public variables and procedure definitions.

- Practice using public variables that have a global scope.

- Increase programming efficiency by creating user-defined Sub and Function procedures.

- Master the syntax for calling and using user-defined procedures.

- Pass arguments to procedures by value and by reference.

In the first nine chapters of this book, you have used event procedures such *as Button1_Click*, *Timer1_Tick*, and *Form1_Load* to manage events and organize the flow of your programs. In Microsoft Visual Basic programming, all executable statements must be placed inside some procedure; only general declarations and instructions to the compiler can be placed outside a procedure's scope. In this chapter, you'll continue to organize your programs by breaking computing tasks into discrete logical units.

You'll start by learning how to create *modules*, which are separate areas within a program that contain global, or *public*, variables and Function and Sub procedures. You'll learn how to declare and use public variables, and you'll learn how to build general-purpose procedures that save coding time and can be used in more than one project. The skills you'll learn will be especially applicable to larger programming projects and team development efforts.

Working with Modules

As you write longer programs, you're likely to have several forms and event procedures that use some of the same variables and routines. By default, variables are *local* to an event procedure—they can be read or changed only within the event procedure in which they were created. You can also declare variables at the top of a form's program code and give the variables a greater scope throughout the form. However, if you create multiple forms in a project, the variables declared at the top of a form are valid only in the form in which they were declared. Likewise, event procedures are by default declared as private and are only local to the form in which they are created. For example, you can't call the *Button1_Click* event procedure from a second form named Form2 if the event procedure is declared to be private to Form1. (You'll learn how to add additional forms to your project in Chapter 14, "Managing Windows Forms and Controls at Run Time.")

To share variables and procedures among all the forms and event procedures in a project, you can declare them in one or more modules included in the project. A module is a special file that has a .vb file name extension and contains variable declarations and procedures that can be used anywhere in the program.

Like forms, modules are listed separately in Solution Explorer. Unlike forms, modules contain only code and don't have a user interface. And although modules have some similarities with classes, they are unlike classes in that they are not object-oriented, do not define the structure and characteristics of objects, and cannot be inherited. (You'll learn more about creating classes in Chapter 16, "Inheriting Forms and Creating Base Classes.")

Creating a Module

To create a new module in a program, you click the Add New Item button on the Standard toolbar or click the Add New Item command on the Project menu. (You can also click the Add Module command on the Project menu.) A dialog box opens, in which you select the Module template and specify the name of the module. A new, blank module then appears in the Code Editor. The first module in a program is named Module1.vb by default, but you can change the name by right-clicking the module in Solution Explorer, selecting Rename, and typing a new name. You can also rename a module by changing the *File Name* property in the Properties window. Try creating an empty module in a project now.

Create and save a module

1. Start Microsoft Visual Studio 2010, and then create a new Visual Basic Windows Forms Application project named **My Module Test**.

   The new project is created, and a blank form opens in the Designer.

2. Click the Add New Item command on the Project menu.

   The Add New Item dialog box opens.

3. Scroll down the list of common templates in the central pane, and then select the Module template.

   The default name, Module1.vb, appears in the Name text box, as shown on the following page:

> **Tip** The Add New Item dialog box offers several templates that you can use in your projects. Each template has different characteristics and includes starter code to help you use them. Visual Studio includes many useful Windows Forms templates, including Explorer Form, Splash Screen, and Login Form, plus numerous class-related templates. You'll use these templates after you read the introductory material about object-oriented programming in Chapter 16.

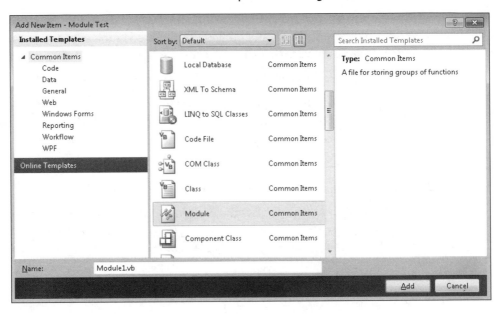

4. Click the Add button.

Visual Basic adds Module1 to your project. The module appears in the Code Editor, as shown here:

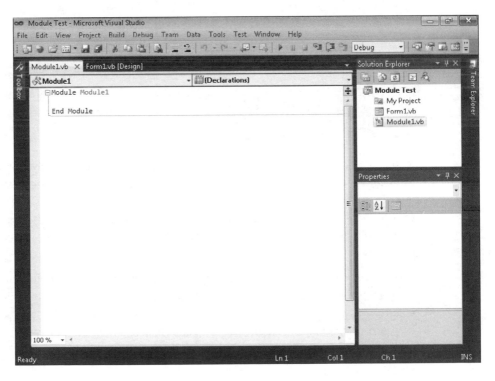

The Method Name list box indicates that the general declarations section of the module is open. Variables and procedures declared in this section are available to the entire project. (You'll try declaring variables and procedures later.)

5. Double-click the Solution Explorer title bar to undock the Solution Explorer window.

As shown previously, Solution Explorer lists the module you added to the program in the list of components for the project. The name Module1 identifies the default file name of the module. You'll change this file name in the following steps.

6. Select Module1.vb in the Solution Explorer.

7. Double-click the Properties window title bar to undock it.

The Properties window displays the properties for Module1.vb, as shown here:

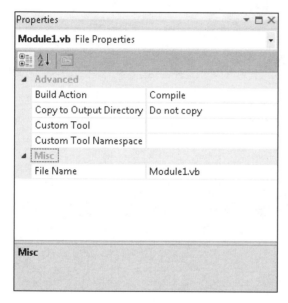

Because a module contains only code, it has only a few properties. By using the most significant property, *File Name*, you can create a custom file name for the module to describe its purpose. Give this identifying label some thought because later you might want to incorporate your module into another solution. The remaining properties for the module are useful for more sophisticated projects—you don't need to worry about them now.

8. Change the *File Name* property to **Math Functions.vb** or another file name that sounds impressive, and then press ENTER. (I'm granting you considerable leeway here because this project is simply for testing purposes—you won't actually create math functions or any other "content" for the module, and later you'll discard it.)

The file name for your module is updated in the Properties window, Solution Explorer, and the Code Editor.

9. Return the Properties window and Solution Explorer to their regular docked positions by pressing the CTRL key and double-clicking their title bars.

As you can see, working with modules in a project is a lot like working with forms. In the next exercise, you'll add a public variable to a module.

> **Tip** To remove a module from a project, click the module in Solution Explorer, and then click the Exclude From Project command on the Project menu. (Visual Basic 2010 Express does not include the Exclude From Project command.) Exclude From Project doesn't delete the module from your hard disk, but it does remove the link between the specified module and the current project. You can reverse the effects of this command by clicking the Add Existing Item command on the Project menu, selecting the file that you want to add to the project, and then clicking Add.

Working with Public Variables

Declaring a global, or public, variable in a module is simple—you type the keyword *Public* followed by the variable name and a type declaration. After you declare the variable, you can read it, change it, or display it in any procedure in your program. For example, the program statement:

```
Public RunningTotal As Integer
```

declares a public variable named *RunningTotal* of type *Integer*.

The following exercises demonstrate how you can use a public variable named *Wins* in a module. You'll revisit Lucky Seven, the first program you created in this book, and you'll use the *Wins* variable to record how many spins you win as the slot machine runs.

> **Note** Lucky Seven is the slot machine program from Chapter 2, "Writing Your First Program."

Revisit the Lucky Seven project

1. Click the Close Project command on the File menu to close the Module Test project.

   Because you have named (but not saved) the project yet, you see the following dialog box:

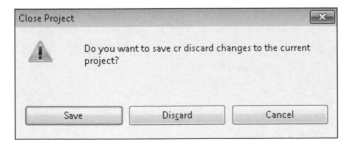

You don't need to keep this project on your hard disk; it was only for testing purposes. To demonstrate the "close without saving" feature in Visual Studio, you'll discard the project now.

2. Click the Discard button.

Visual Studio discards the entire project, removing any temporary files associated with the module from your computer's memory and hard disk. It seems like a rather obvious feature, but I wanted to demonstrate that the ability to close a project without saving it is just the thing for this type of test. (Just be careful with it, OK?) Now you'll open a more substantial project and modify it.

3. Open the Track Wins project in the C:\Vb10sbs\Chap10\Track Wins folder.

The project opens in the Integrated Development Environment (IDE).

4. If the form isn't visible, display it now.

You see the following user interface:

The Track Wins project is the same slot machine program that you created in Chapter 2. With this program, the user can click a spin button to display random numbers in three number boxes, and if the number 7 appears in one of the boxes, the computer beeps and displays a bitmap showing an eclectic cash payout. I've simply renamed the Lucky7 solution in this chapter so that you won't confuse this new version with the original.

5. Click the Start Debugging button on the Standard toolbar to run the program.

6. Click the Spin button six or seven times, and then click the End button.

As you might recall, the program uses the *Rnd* function to generate three random numbers each time you click the Spin button. If one of the numbers is a 7, the event procedure for the Spin button (*Button1_Click*) displays a cash payout picture and beeps.

Now you'll edit the form and add a module to enhance the program.

Add a module

1. Click the *Label* control in the Toolbox, and then create a new rectangular label on the form below the Lucky Seven label.

2. Set the properties shown in the following table for the new label. To help identify the new label in the program code, you'll change the new label object's name to lblWins.

Object	Property	Setting
Label5	Font	Arial, Bold Italic, 12-point
	ForeColor	Green (on Custom tab)
	Name	lblWins
	Text	"Wins: 0"
	TextAlign	MiddleCenter

When you've finished, your form looks similar to this:

Now you'll add a new module to the project.

3. Click the Add New Item command on the Project menu, select the Module template, and then click Add.

A module named Module1.vb appears in the Code Editor.

4. Move the insertion point to the blank line between the *Module Module1* and *End Module* statements, type **Public Wins As Short**, and then press ENTER.

This program statement declares a public variable of the *Short* integer type in your program. It's identical to a normal variable declaration that you might make in your program code, except the *Public* keyword has been substituted for the *Dim* keyword. When your program runs, each event procedure in the program will have access to this variable. Your module looks like this:

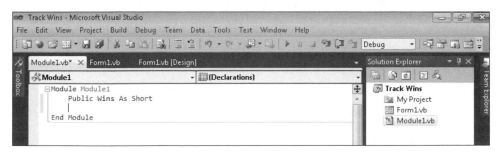

5. In Solution Explorer, click Form1.vb, click the View Designer button, and then double-click the Spin button.

The *Button1_Click* event procedure for the Spin button appears in the Code Editor.

6. Type the following statements below the *Beep()* statement in the event procedure:

```
Wins = Wins + 1
lblWins.Text = "Wins: " & Wins
```

This part of the program code increments the *Wins* public variable if a 7 appears during a spin. The second statement uses the concatenation operator (&) to assign a string to the *lblWins* object in the format *Wins: X*, in which *X* is the number of wins. The completed event procedure looks like this:

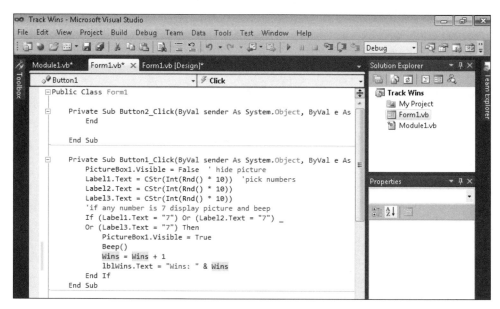

7. Click the Save All button on the Standard toolbar to save all your changes to disk.

Save All saves your module changes as well as the changes on your form and in your event procedures.

8. Click the Start Debugging button to run the program.

9. Click the Spin button until you have won a few times.

The Wins label keeps track of your jackpots. Each time you win, it increments the total by 1. After eight spins, I had the output shown on the following page:

> **Note** The exact number of wins will be different each time you run the program due to the *Randomize* statement in the *Form1_Load* event procedure.

10. Click End to exit the program.

The public variable *Wins* was useful in the previous procedure because it maintained its value through several calls to the *Button1_Click* event procedure. If you had declared *Wins* locally in the *Button1_Click* event procedure, the variable would have reset each time, just as the trip odometer in your car does when you reset it. By using a public variable in a module, you can avoid "hitting the reset button."

Public Variables vs. Form Variables

In the preceding exercise, you used a public variable to track the number of wins in the slot machine program. Alternatively, you could have declared the *Wins* variable at the top of the form's program code. Both techniques produce the same result because both a public variable and a variable declared in the general declarations area of a form have scope throughout the entire form. Public variables are unique, however, because they maintain their values in *all* the forms and modules you use in a project—in other words, in all the components that share the same project namespace. The project namespace keyword is set automatically when you first save your project. You can view or change the namespace name by selecting the project in Solution Explorer, clicking the Track Wins Properties command on the Project menu, and then examining or changing the text in the Root Namespace text box on the Application tab.

Creating Procedures

Procedures provide a way to group a set of related statements to perform a task. Visual Basic includes two primary types of procedures:

- *Function procedures* are called by name from event procedures or other procedures. Often used for calculations, function procedures can receive arguments and always return a value in the function name.

- *Sub procedures* are called by name from event procedures or other procedures. They can receive arguments and also pass back modified values in an argument list. Unlike functions, however, Sub procedures don't return values associated with their particular Sub procedure names. Sub procedures are typically used to receive or process input, display output, or set properties.

Function procedures and Sub procedures can be defined in a form's program code, but for many users, creating procedures in a module is more useful because then the procedures have scope throughout the entire project. This is especially true for procedures that might be called *general-purpose procedures*—blocks of code that are flexible and useful enough to serve in a variety of programming contexts.

For example, imagine a program that has three mechanisms for printing a bitmap on different forms: a menu command named Print, a Print toolbar button, and a drag-and-drop printer icon. You could place the same printing statements in each of the three event procedures, or you could handle printing requests from all three sources by using one procedure in a module.

Advantages of General-Purpose Procedures

General-purpose procedures provide the following benefits:

- They enable you to associate a frequently used group of program statements with a familiar name.

- They eliminate repeated lines. You can define a procedure once and have your program execute it any number of times.

- They make programs easier to read. A program divided into a collection of small parts is easier to take apart and understand than a program made up of one large part.

- They simplify program development. Programs separated into logical units are easier to design, write, and debug. Plus, if you're writing a program in a group setting, you can exchange procedures and modules instead of entire programs.

- They can be reused in other projects and solutions. You can easily incorporate standard-module procedures into other programming projects.

- They extend the Visual Basic language. Procedures often can perform tasks that can't be accomplished by individual Visual Basic keywords or Microsoft .NET Framework methods.

Writing Function Procedures

A Function procedure is a group of statements located between a *Function* statement and an *End Function* statement. The statements in the function do the meaningful work—typically processing text, handling input, or calculating a numeric value. You execute, or *call*, a function in a program by placing the function name in a program statement along with any required arguments.

Arguments are the data used to make functions work, and they must be included between parentheses and be separated by commas. Basically, using a Function procedure is exactly like using a built-in function or method such as *Int*, *Rnd*, or *FromFile*.

> **Tip** Functions declared in modules are public by default. As a result, you can use them in any event procedure within the project.

Function Syntax

The basic syntax of a function is as follows:

```
Function FunctionName([arguments]) As Type
    function statements
    [Return value]
End Function
```

The following syntax items are important:

- *FunctionName* is the name of the function you're creating.

- As *Type* is a pair of keywords that specifies the function return type. It is strongly recommended that you specify a specific data type. If you don't provide a type, the return type defaults to *Object*.

- *arguments* is a list of optional arguments (separated by commas) to be used in the function. Each argument should also be declared as a specific type. (By default, Visual Basic adds the *ByVal* keyword to each argument, indicating that a copy of the data is passed to the function through this argument but that any changes to the arguments won't be returned to the calling routine.)

- *function statements* is a block of statements that accomplishes the work of the function. The first statements in a function typically declare local variables that will be used in the function, and the remaining statements perform the work of the function.

- *Return* allows you to return a value to the calling procedure and specify that value. The type of the return value must be the same type as specified in the As *Type* keywords. When a *Return* statement is executed, the function is exited, so if there are any function statements after the *Return* statement, these won't be executed. (Alternatively, you can return a value to the calling routine by assigning the value to *FunctionName*.)

- Brackets ([]) enclose optional syntax items. Visual Basic requires that those syntax items are not enclosed by brackets.

Functions always return a value to the calling procedure in the function's name (*FunctionName*). For this reason, the last statement in a function is often an assignment statement that places the final calculation of the function in *FunctionName*. For example, the Function procedure *TotalTax* computes the state and city taxes for an item and then assigns the result to the *TotalTax* name, as shown here:

```
Function TotalTax(ByVal Cost as Single) As Single
    Dim StateTax, CityTax As Single
    StateTax = Cost * 0.05   'State tax is 5%
    CityTax = Cost * 0.015   'City tax is 1.5%
    TotalTax = StateTax + CityTax
End Function
```

Alternatively, you can return a value to the calling procedure by using the *Return* statement, as shown in the following function declaration:

```
Function TotalTax(ByVal Cost as Single) As Single
    Dim StateTax, CityTax As Single
    StateTax = Cost * 0.05   'State tax is 5%
    CityTax = Cost * 0.015   'City tax is 1.5%
    Return StateTax + CityTax
End Function
```

I'll use the *Return* syntax most often in this book, but you can use either mechanism for returning data from a function.

Calling a Function Procedure

To call the *TotalTax* function in an event procedure, you use a statement similar to the following:

```
lblTaxes.Text = TotalTax(500)
```

This statement computes the total taxes required for a $500 item and then assigns the result to the *Text* property of the *lblTaxes* object. The *TotalTax* function can also take a variable as an argument, as shown in the following statements:

```
Dim TotalCost, SalesPrice As Single
SalesPrice = 500
TotalCost = SalesPrice + TotalTax(SalesPrice)
```

The last statement uses the *TotalTax* function to determine the taxes for the number in the *SalesPrice* variable and then adds the computed tax to *SalesPrice* to get the total cost of an item. See how much clearer the code is when a function is used?

Using a Function to Perform a Calculation

In the following exercise, you'll add a function to the Track Wins program to calculate the win rate in the game—in other words, the percentage of spins in which one or more 7s appear. To perform the calculation, you'll add a function named *HitRate* and a public variable named

Spins to the module. Then you'll call the *HitRate* function every time the Spin button is clicked. You'll display the results in a new label that you'll create on the form.

Create a win rate function

1. Display the form for the Track Wins program that you've been modifying.

   The user interface for the slot machine game appears.

2. Use the *Label* control to create a new label below the Wins label. Set the following properties for the label:

Object	Property	Setting
Label5	Font	Arial, Bold Italic, 12-point
	ForeColor	Red (on Custom tab)
	Name	lblRate
	Text	"0.0%"
	TextAlign	MiddleCenter

   Your form looks similar to the following graphic:

   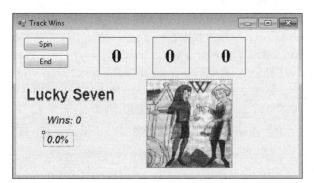

3. In Solution Explorer, click the Module1.vb module, and then click the View Code button.

   The Module1 module appears in the Code Editor.

4. Type the following public variable declaration below the *Public Wins As Short* statement:

   ```
   Public Spins As Short
   ```

   The module now includes two public variables, *Wins* and *Spins*, which will be available to all the procedures in the project. You'll use *Spins* as a counter to keep track of the number of spins you make.

5. Insert a blank line in the module, and then type the following function declaration:

   ```
   Function HitRate(ByVal Hits As Short, ByVal Tries As Short) As String
       Dim Percent As Single
   ```

```
    Percent = Hits / Tries
    Return Format(Percent, "0.0%")
End Function
```

After you type the first line of the function code, Visual Basic automatically adds an *End Function* statement. After you type the remainder of the function's code, your screen looks like this:

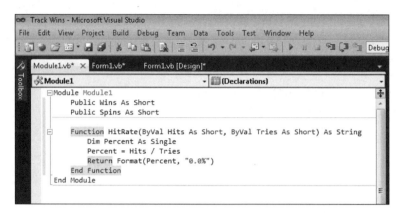

The *HitRate* function determines the percentage of wins by dividing the *Hits* argument by the *Tries* argument and then adjusts the appearance of the result by using the *Format* function. The *HitRate* function is declared as a string because the *Format* function returns a string value. The *Hits* and the *Tries* arguments are placeholders for the two short integer variables that will be passed to the function during the function call. The *HitRate* function is general-purpose enough to be used with any shorter integer numbers or variables, not only with *Wins* and *Spins*.

6. Display the form again, and then double-click the Spin button on the Form1.vb form to bring up the *Button1_Click* event procedure.

7. Below the fourth line of the event procedure (*Label3.Text = CStr(Int(Rnd() * 10))*), type the following statement:

```
Spins = Spins + 1
```

This statement increments the *Spins* variable each time the user clicks Spin, and new numbers are placed in the spin windows.

8. Scroll down in the Code Editor, and then, between the *End If* and the *End Sub* statements, type the following statement as the last line in the *Button1_Click* event procedure:

```
lblRate.Text = HitRate(Wins, Spins)
```

As you type the *HitRate* function, notice how Visual Studio automatically displays the names and types of the arguments for the *HitRate* function you just built (a nice touch).

The purpose of this statement is to call the *HitRate* function by using the *Wins* and the *Spins* variables as arguments. The result returned is a percentage in string format, and this value is assigned to the *Text* property of the *lblRate* label on the form after each spin. Now remove the *Randomize* function from the *Form1_Load* event procedure, so that while you test the project, your results will follow a familiar pattern.

9. Scroll down in the Code Editor to the *Form1_Load* event procedure, and remove or "comment out" (place a comment character (') before) the *Randomize* function.

   Now, each time that you run this program, the random numbers generated will follow a predictable pattern. This helps you test your code, but when you're finished testing, you'll want to add the function back again so that your results are truly random.

Now you'll run the program.

Run the Track Wins program

1. Click the Start Debugging button to run the modified Track Wins program.

2. Click the Spin button 10 times.

   The first five times you click Spin, the win rate stays at 100.0%. You're hitting the jackpot every time. As you continue to click, however, the win rate adjusts to 83.3%, 71.4%, 75.0% (another win), 66.7%, and 60.0% (a total of 6 for 10). After 10 spins, your screen looks like this:

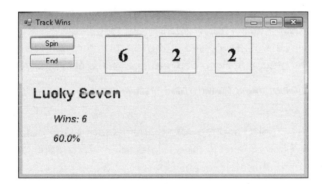

   If you continue to spin, you'll notice that the win rate drops to about 28%. The *HitRate* function shows that you were really pretty lucky when you started spinning, but after a while reality sets in.

3. When you're finished with the program, click the End button.

   The program stops, and the development environment returns. You can add the *Randomize* function to the *Form1_Load* event procedure again to see how the program works with "true" randomness. After about 100 spins (enough iterations for statistical variation to even out a little), you should be close to the 28% win rate each time that you run the program. If you like numbers, it is an interesting experiment.

4. Click the Save All button on the Standard toolbar to save your changes.

Writing Sub Procedures

A Sub procedure is similar to a Function procedure, except that a Sub procedure doesn't return a value associated with its name. Sub procedures are typically used to get input from the user, display or print information, or manipulate several properties associated with a condition. Sub procedures can also be used to process and update variables received in an argument list during a procedure call and pass back one or more of these values to the calling program.

Sub Procedure Syntax

The basic syntax for a Sub procedure is:

```
Sub ProcedureName([arguments])
    procedure statements
End Sub
```

The following syntax items are important:

- *ProcedureName* is the name of the Sub procedure you're creating.

- *arguments* is a list of optional arguments (separated by commas if there's more than one) to be used in the Sub procedure. Each argument should also be declared as a specific type. (Visual Studio adds the *ByVal* keyword by default to each argument, indicating that a copy of the data is passed to the function through this argument but that any changes to the arguments won't be returned to the calling routine.)

- *procedure statements* is a block of statements that accomplishes the work of the procedure.

In the Sub procedure call, the number and type of arguments sent to the procedure must match the number and type of arguments in the Sub procedure declaration, and the entire group must be enclosed in parentheses. If variables passed to a Sub procedure are modified during the procedure, the updated variables aren't passed back to the program unless the procedure defined the arguments by using the *ByRef* keyword. Sub procedures declared in a module are public by default, so they can be called by any event procedure in a project.

> **Important** All calls to a Sub procedure must include parentheses after the procedure name. A set of empty parentheses is required even if no arguments are being passed to the procedure.

For example, the following Sub procedure receives a string argument representing a person's name and uses a text box to wish that person happy birthday. If this Sub procedure is declared in a module, it can be called from any event procedure in the program.

```
Sub BirthdayGreeting (ByVal Person As String)
    Dim Msg As String
    If Person <> "" Then
        Msg = "Happy birthday " & Person & "!"
    Else
        Msg = "Name not specified."
    End If
    MsgBox(Msg, , "Best Wishes")
End Sub
```

The *BirthdayGreeting* procedure receives the name to be greeted by using the *Person* argument, a string variable received by value during the procedure call. If the value of *Person* isn't empty, or *null*, the specified name is used to build a message string that will be displayed with a *MsgBox* function. If the argument is null, the procedure displays the message "Name not specified."

Calling a Sub Procedure

To call a Sub procedure in a program, you specify the name of the procedure, and then list the arguments required by the Sub procedure. For example, to call the *BirthdayGreeting* procedure, you could type the following statement:

```
BirthdayGreeting("Robert")
```

In this example, the *BirthdayGreeting* procedure would insert the name "Robert" into a message string, and the routine would display the following message box:

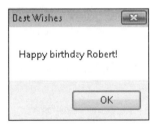

The space-saving advantages of a procedure become clear when you call the procedure many times using a variable, as shown in the example below:

```
Dim NewName As String
Do
    NewName = InputBox("Enter a name for greeting.", "Birthday List")
    BirthdayGreeting(NewName)
Loop Until NewName = ""
```

Here the user can enter as many names for birthday greetings as he or she likes. The next exercise gives you a chance to practice using a Sub procedure to handle another type of input in a program.

Using a Sub Procedure to Manage Input

Sub procedures are often used to handle input in a program when information comes from two or more sources and needs to be in the same format. In the following exercise, you'll create a Sub procedure named *AddName* that prompts the user for input and formats the text so that it can be displayed on multiple lines in a text box. The procedure will save you programming time because you'll use it in two event procedures, each associated with a different text box. Because the procedure will be declared in a module, you'll need to type it in only one place. If you add additional forms to the project, the procedure will be available to them as well.

Create a text box Sub procedure

1. On the File menu, click the Close Project command.

   Visual Studio closes the current project (the Track Wins slot machine).

2. Create a new Windows Forms Application project named **My Text Box Sub**.

   The new project is created, and a blank form opens in the Designer.

3. Use the *TextBox* control to create two text boxes, side by side, in the middle of the form.

   Today you'll make some personnel decisions, and you'll use these text boxes to hold the names of employees you'll be assigning to two departments.

4. Use the *Label* control to create two labels above the text boxes.

   These labels will hold the names of the departments.

5. Use the *Button* control to create three buttons: one under each text box and one at the bottom of the form.

   You'll use the first two buttons to assign employees to their departments and the last button to quit the program.

6. Set the properties shown in the following table for the objects on the form.

   Because the text boxes will contain more than one line, you'll set their *Multiline* properties to True and their *ScrollBars* properties to Vertical. These settings are typically used when multiple lines are displayed in text boxes. You'll also set their *TabStop* properties to False and their *ReadOnly* properties to True so that the information can't be modified.

Object	Property	Setting
TextBox1	Multiline	True
	Name	txtSales
	ReadOnly	True
	ScrollBars	Vertical
	TabStop	False

Object	Property	Setting
TextBox2	Multiline	True
	Name	txtMkt
	ReadOnly	True
	ScrollBars	Vertical
	TabStop	False
Label1	Font	Bold
	Name	lblSales
	Text	"Sales"
Label2	Font	Bold
	Name	lblMkt
	Text	"Marketing"
Button1	Name	btnSales
	Text	"Add Name"
Button2	Name	btnMkt
	Text	"Add Name"
Button3	Name	btnQuit
	Text	"Quit"
Form1	Text	"Assign Department Teams"

7. Resize and position the objects so that your form looks similar to this:

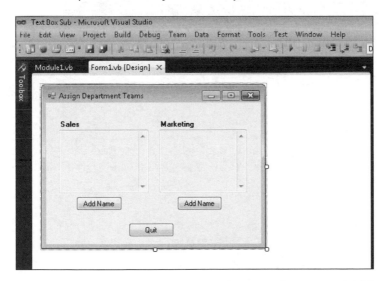

Now you'll add a module and create the general-purpose *AddName* Sub procedure.

8. On the Project menu, click the Add New Item command, select the Module template, and then click Add.

A new module appears in the Code Editor.

9. Type the following *AddName* procedure between the *Module Module1* and *End Module* statements:

```
Sub AddName(ByVal Team As String, ByRef ReturnString As String)
    Dim Prompt, Nm, WrapCharacter As String
    Prompt = "Enter a " & Team & " employee."
    Nm = InputBox(Prompt, "Input Box")
    WrapCharacter = Chr(13) + Chr(10)
    ReturnString = Nm & WrapCharacter
End Sub
```

This general-purpose Sub procedure uses the *InputBox* function to prompt the user for an employee name. It receives two arguments during the procedure call: *Team*, a string containing the department name; and *ReturnString*, an empty string variable that will contain the formatted employee name. *ReturnString* is declared with the *ByRef* keyword so that any changes made to this argument in the procedure will be passed back to the calling routine through the argument.

Before the employee name is returned, carriage return and linefeed characters are appended to the string so that each name in the text box will appear on its own line. You can use this general technique in any string to create a new line.

Your Code Editor looks like this:

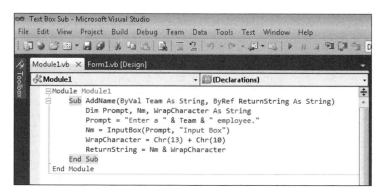

10. Display the form again, and then double-click the first Add Name button on the form (the button below the Sales text box). Type the following statements in the *btnSales_Click* event procedure:

```
Dim SalesPosition As String = ""
AddName("Sales", SalesPosition)
txtSales.Text = txtSales.Text & SalesPosition
```

The call to the *AddName* Sub procedure includes one argument passed by value (*"Sales"*) and one argument passed by reference (*SalesPosition*). The last line uses the argument passed by reference to add text to the *txtSales* text box. The concatenation operator (&) adds the new name to the end of the text in the text box.

11. In the Code Editor, just below the Form1.vb tab name, click the Class Name arrow, and then click the *btnMkt* object in the list. Then click the Method Name arrow, and click the *Click* event.

    The *btnMkt_Click* event procedure appears in the Code Editor. Using the Class Name and Method Name list boxes is another way to practice adding event procedures.

12. Type the following statements in the event procedure:

    ```
    Dim MktPosition As String = ""
    AddName("Marketing", MktPosition)
    txtMkt.Text = txtMkt.Text & MktPosition
    ```

    This event procedure is identical to *btnSales_Click*, except that it sends *"Marketing"* to the *AddName* procedure and updates the *txtMkt* text box. (The name of the local return variable *MktPosition* was renamed to make it more intuitive.)

13. Click the Class Name arrow, and then click the *btnQuit* object in the list. Then click the Method Name arrow, and click the *Click* event.

    The *btnQuit_Click* event procedure appears in the Code Editor.

14. Type **End** in the *btnQuit_Click* event procedure.

15. Click the Save All button on the Standard toolbar, and then specify the C:\Vb10sbs\Chap10 folder as the location.

That's it! Now you'll run the Text Box Sub program.

Run the Text Box Sub program

 Tip The complete Text Box Sub program is located in the C:\Vb10sbs\Chap10\Text Box Sub folder.

1. Click the Start Debugging button on the Standard toolbar to run the program.

2. Click the Add Name button under the Sales text box, and then type **Manuel Oliveira** in the input box. (Feel free to type a different name.)

    Your input box looks like this:

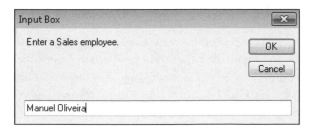

3. Click the OK button to add the name to the Sales text box.

The name appears in the first text box.

4. Click the Add Name button under the Marketing text box, type **Raymond Fong** in the Marketing input box, and then press ENTER.

The name appears in the Marketing text box. Your screen looks like this:

5. Enter a few more names in each of the text boxes. This is your chance to create your own dream office staffing configurations.

Each name appears on its own line in the text boxes. The text boxes don't scroll automatically, so you won't see every name you've entered if you enter more names than can fit in a text box. You can use the scroll bars to access names that aren't visible.

6. When you've finished, click the Quit button to stop the program.

You've demonstrated that one Sub procedure can manage input tasks from two or more event procedures. Using this basic concept as a starting point, you can now create more sophisticated programs that use Sub and Function procedures as organizing tools and that place common tasks in logical units that can be called over and over again.

One Step Further: Passing Arguments by Value and by Reference

In the discussion of Sub and Function procedures, you learned that arguments are passed to procedures by value or by reference. Using the *ByVal* keyword indicates that variables should be passed to a procedure by value (the default). Any changes made to a variable passed in by value aren't passed back to the calling procedure. However, as you learned in the Text Box Sub program, using the *ByRef* keyword indicates that variables should be passed to a procedure by reference, meaning that any changes made to the variable in the procedure are passed back to the calling routine. Passing by reference can have significant advantages, so long as you're careful not to change a variable unintentionally in a procedure. For example, consider the following Sub procedure declaration and call:

```
Sub CostPlusInterest(ByRef Cost As Single, ByRef Total As Single)
    Cost = Cost * 1.05  'add 5% to cost...
    Total = Int(Cost)    'then make integer and return
End Sub
.
.
.
Dim Price, TotalPrice As Single
Price = 100
TotalPrice = 0
CostPlusInterest(Price, TotalPrice)
MsgBox(Price & " at 5% interest is " & TotalPrice)
```

In this example, the programmer passes two single-precision variables by reference to the CostPlusInterest procedure: *Price* and *TotalPrice*. The programmer plans to use the updated *TotalPrice* variable in the subsequent *MsgBox* call but has unfortunately forgotten that the *Price* variable was also updated in an intermediate step in the CostPlusInterest procedure. (Because *Price* was passed by reference, changes to *Cost* automatically result in the same changes to *Price*.) This produces the following erroneous result when the program is run:

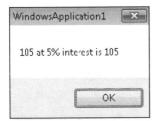

However, the programmer probably wanted to show the following message:

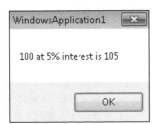

So how should the CostPlusInterest procedure be fixed to produce the desired result? The easiest way is to declare the *Cost* argument by using the *ByVal* keyword, as shown in the following program statement:

```
Sub CostPlusInterest(ByVal Cost As Single, ByRef Total As Single)
```

By declaring *Cost* using *ByVal*, you can safely modify *Cost* in the CostPlusInterest procedure without sending the changes back to the calling procedure. By keeping *Total* declared using *ByRef*, you can modify the variable that's being passed, and only those changes will be passed back to the calling procedure. In general, if you use *ByRef* only when it's needed, your programs will be freer of defects.

Here are some guidelines on when to use *ByVal* and when to use *ByRef*:

- Use *ByVal* when you don't want a procedure to modify a variable that's passed to the procedure through an argument.

- Use *ByRef* when you want to allow a procedure to modify a variable that's passed to the procedure through an argument.

- When in doubt, use the *ByVal* keyword.

Chapter 10 Quick Reference

To	Do This
Create a new module	Click the Add New Item button on the Standard toolbar, and then select the Module template; *or* Click the Add New Item command on the Project menu, and then select the Module template.
Rename a module	Select the module in Solution Explorer. In the Properties window, specify a new name in the *File Name* property; *or* Right-click the module in Solution Explorer, select Rename, and then specify a new name.
Remove a module from a program	Select the module in Solution Explorer, and then click the Exclude From Project command on the Project menu.
Add an existing module to a project	On the Project menu, click the Add Existing Item command.
Create a public variable	Declare the variable by using the *Public* keyword between the *Module* and *End Module* keywords in a module. For example: `Public TotalSales As Integer`

Create a public function	Place the function statements between the *Function* and *End Function* keywords in a module. Functions are public by default. For example:
	
	`Function HitRate(ByVal Hits As Short, ByVal _`
	`  Tries As Short) As String`
	`    Dim Percent As Single`
	`    Percent = Hits / Tries`
	`    Return Format(Percent, "0.0%")`
	`End Function`

To	Do This
Call a Function procedure	Type the function name and any necessary arguments in a program statement, and assign it to a variable or property of the appropriate return type. For example: `lblRate.Text = HitRate(Wins, Spins)`

Create a public Sub procedure	Place the procedure statements between the *Sub* and *End Sub* keywords in a module. Sub procedures are public by default. For example:
	`Sub CostPlusInterest(ByVal Cost As Single, _`
	`   ByRef Total As Single)`
	`      Cost = Cost * 1.05`
	`      Total = Int(Cost)`
	`End Sub`

Call a Sub procedure	Type the procedure name and any necessary arguments in a program statement. For example: `CostPlusInterest(Price, TotalPrice)`
Pass an argument by value	Use the *ByVal* keyword in the procedure declaration. For example: `Sub GreetPerson(ByVal Name As String)`
Pass an argument by reference	Use the *ByRef* keyword in the procedure declaration. For example: `Sub GreetPerson(ByRef Name As String)`

Chapter 11
Using Arrays to Manage Numeric and String Data

After completing this chapter, you will be able to:

- Organize information in fixed-size and dynamic arrays.

- Preserve array data when you redimension arrays.

- Use arrays in your code to manage large amounts of data.

- Use the *Sort* and *Reverse* methods in the *Array* class to reorder arrays.

- Use the *ProgressBar* control in your programs to show how long a task is taking.

Managing information in a Microsoft Visual Basic application is an important task, and as your programs become more substantial, you'll need additional tools to store and process data. A quick-and-dirty approach to data management in programs is to store and retrieve information in auxiliary text files, as you'll see in Chapter 13, "Exploring Text Files and String Processing." However, the most comprehensive approach is storing and retrieving information by using databases, and you'll start learning how to integrate Visual Basic programs with databases in Chapter 18, "Getting Started with ADO.NET."

In this chapter, you'll learn how to organize variables and other information into useful containers called *arrays*. You'll learn how to streamline data-management tasks with fixed-size and dynamic arrays and how to use arrays in your code to manage large amounts of data. You'll learn how to redimension arrays and preserve the data in arrays when you decide to change an array's size. To demonstrate how large arrays can be processed, you'll use the *Sort* and *Reverse* methods in the Microsoft .NET Framework *Array* class to reorder an array containing random six-digit integer values. Finally, you'll learn to use the *ProgressBar* control to give your users an indication of how long a process (array-related or otherwise) is taking. The techniques you'll learn provide a solid introduction to the database programming techniques that you'll explore later in the book.

Working with Arrays of Variables

In this section, you'll learn about arrays, a useful method for storing almost any amount of data during program execution. Arrays are a powerful and time-tested mechanism for storing logically related values in a program. The developers of BASIC, Pascal, C, and other popular programming languages incorporated arrays into the earliest versions of these products to refer to a group of values by using one name and to process those values individually or collectively.

Arrays can help you track a small set of values in ways that are impractical using traditional variables. For example, imagine creating a nine-inning baseball scoreboard in a program. To save and recall the scores for each inning of the game, you might be tempted to create two groups of 9 variables (a total of 18 variables) in the program. You'd probably name them something like *Inning1HomeTeam*, *Inning1VisitingTeam*, and so on, to keep them straight. Working with these variables individually would take considerable time and space in your program. Fortunately, with Visual Basic you can organize groups of similar variables into an array that has one common name and an easy-to-use index. For example, you can create a two-dimensional array (two units high by nine units wide) named *Scoreboard* to contain the scores for the baseball game. Let's see how this works.

Creating an Array

You create, or *declare*, arrays in program code just as you declare simple variables. As usual, the place in which you declare the array determines where it can be used, or its *scope*, as follows:

- If you declare an array locally in a procedure, you can use it only in that procedure.

- If you declare an array at the top of a form, you can use it throughout the form.

- If you declare an array publicly in a module, you can use it anywhere in the project.

When you declare an array, you typically include the information shown in Table 11-1 in your declaration statement.

TABLE 11-1 Syntax Elements for an Array Declaration

Syntax Elements in Array Declaration	Description
Array name	The name you'll use to represent your array in the program. In general, array names follow the same rules as variable names. (See Chapter 5, "Visual Basic Variables and Formulas, and the .NET Framework," for more information about variables.)
Data type	The type of data you'll store in the array. In most cases, all the variables in an array are the same type. You can specify one of the fundamental data types, or if you're not yet sure which type of data will be stored in the array or whether you'll store more than one type, you can specify the *Object* type.
Number of dimensions	The number of dimensions that your array will contain. Most arrays are one-dimensional (a list of values) or two-dimensional (a table of values), but you can specify additional dimensions if you're working with a complex mathematical model, such as a three-dimensional shape. The number of dimensions in an array is sometimes called the array's *rank*.
Number of elements	The number of elements that your array will contain. The elements in your array correspond directly to the array index. The first array index is always 0 (zero).

Tip Arrays that contain a set number of elements are called *fixed-size arrays*. Arrays that contain a variable number of elements (arrays that can expand during the execution of the program) are called *dynamic arrays*.

Declaring a Fixed-Size Array

The basic syntax for a public fixed-size array is

```
Dim ArrayName(Dim1Index, Dim2Index, ...) As DataType
```

The following arguments are important:

- *Dim* is the keyword that declares the array. Use *Public* instead if you place the array in a module.

- *ArrayName* is the variable name of the array.

- *Dim1Index* is the upper bound of the first dimension of the array, which is the number of elements minus 1.

- *Dim2Index* is the upper bound of the second dimension of the array, which is the number of elements minus 1. (Additional dimensions can be included if they're separated by commas.)

- *DataType* is a keyword corresponding to the type of data that will be included in the array.

For example, to declare a one-dimensional string array named *Employees* that has room for 10 employee names (numbered 0 through 9), you can type the following in an event procedure:

```
Dim Employees(9) As String
```

In a module, the same array declaration looks like this:

```
Public Employees(9) As String
```

You can also explicitly specify the lower bound of the array as zero by using the following code in an event procedure:

```
Dim Employees(0 To 9) As String
```

This "0 to 9" syntax is included to make your code more readable—newcomers to your program will understand immediately that the *Employees* array has 10 elements numbered 0 through 9. However, the lower bound of the array must always be zero. You cannot use this syntax to create a different lower bound for the array.

Setting Aside Memory

When you create an array, Visual Basic sets aside room for it in memory. The following screen shot shows conceptually how the 10-element *Employees* array is organized. The elements are numbered 0 through 9 rather than 1 through 10 because array indexes always start with 0.

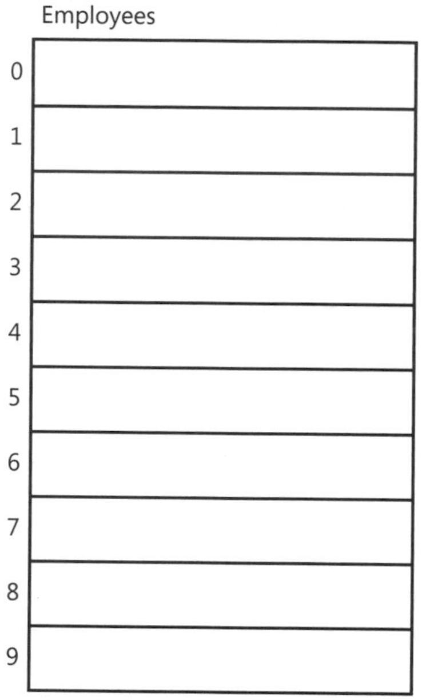

Employees

```
 0 ┌─────────────────────┐
   │                     │
 1 ├─────────────────────┤
   │                     │
 2 ├─────────────────────┤
   │                     │
 3 ├─────────────────────┤
   │                     │
 4 ├─────────────────────┤
   │                     │
 5 ├─────────────────────┤
   │                     │
 6 ├─────────────────────┤
   │                     │
 7 ├─────────────────────┤
   │                     │
 8 ├─────────────────────┤
   │                     │
 9 └─────────────────────┘
```

To declare a public two-dimensional array named *Scoreboard* that has room for two rows and nine columns of *Short* integer data, you can type this statement in an event procedure or at the top of the form:

```
Dim Scoreboard(1, 8) As Short
```

Using the syntax that emphasizes the lower (zero) bound, you can also declare the array as follows:

```
Dim Scoreboard(0 To 1, 0 To 8) As Short
```

After you declare such a two-dimensional array and Visual Basic sets aside room for it in memory, you can use the array in your program as if it were a table of values, as shown in the following screen shot. (In this case, the array elements are numbered 0 through 1 and 0 through 8.)

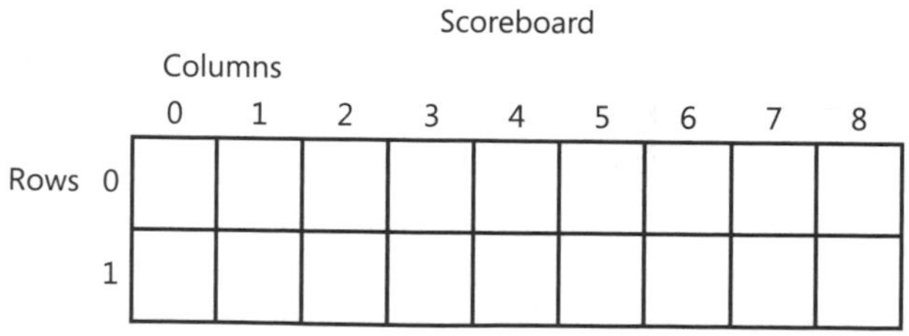

Scoreboard

```
        Columns
        0   1   2   3   4   5   6   7   8
      ┌───┬───┬───┬───┬───┬───┬───┬───┬───┐
Rows 0│   │   │   │   │   │   │   │   │   │
      ├───┼───┼───┼───┼───┼───┼───┼───┼───┤
    1 │   │   │   │   │   │   │   │   │   │
      └───┴───┴───┴───┴───┴───┴───┴───┴───┘
```

Working with Array Elements

To refer to an element of an array, you use the array name and an array index enclosed in parentheses. The index must be an integer or an expression that results in an integer. For example, the index could be a number such as 5, an integer variable such as *num*, or an expression such as *num-1*. (The counter variable of a *For … Next* loop is often used.) For example, the following statement assigns the value "Leslie" to the element with an index of 5 in the *Employees* array example in the previous section:

```
Employees(5) = "Leslie"
```

This statement produces the following result in our *Employees* array:

Employees

0	
1	
2	
3	
4	
5	Lesile
6	
7	
8	
9	

Similarly, the following statement assigns the number 4 to row 0, column 2 (the top of the third inning) in the *Scoreboard* array example in the previous section:

```
Scoreboard(0, 2) = 4
```

This statement produces the following result in our *Scoreboard* array:

Scoreboard

Columns

	0	1	2	3	4	5	6	7	8
Rows 0			4						
1									

You can use these indexing techniques to assign or retrieve any array element.

Declaring an Array and Assigning It Initial Values

It is also possible to declare an array and assign it initial values at the same time. This statement syntax is somewhat parallel to what you learned about assigning an initial value to a variable at the moment of declaration, and it is useful when you know in advance just how large an array needs to be and what its contents are.

To create an array in this manner, you use what is called an *array literal*. An array literal consists of a list of comma-separated values that are enclosed in braces ({}). When using this syntax, you can either supply the array type or let Visual Basic use *type inference* to determine what type the array should be. For example, to declare a one-dimensional array named *Waiters* of type *String* and fill it with seven names, you would use the following syntax:

```
Dim Waiters() As String = {"Ben", "Sue", "Lee", "Kim", "Pat", "Eve", "Sal"}
```

Note that the size of this array is determined automatically by Visual Basic when *Waiters* is declared. In addition, if you don't indicate an array type, Visual Basic will use type inference to determine the right array data type for you. Obviously if all the values are the same type, it should be clear to the compiler what data type should be used for the array. But if there is a mixture of types, such as an assortment of integer, single, and double-precision numbers, Microsoft Visual Studio will pick a data type for the array that is large enough to accommodate all the values. In many cases, this will be the data type *Object* because *Object* variables (and arrays) are specifically designed to hold any type of data.

The following statement declares an array named *Investments* and uses an array literal to add four values to the array when it is created. Since no type is specified, Visual Basic evaluates the array elements and determines that in this case, the *Object* type is most appropriate.

```
Dim Investments() = {5000, 20350.50, 499.99, 10000}
```

> **Note** If the compiler's Option Infer setting is set to On, the *Double* type will be specified when the above statement is executed. See Chapter 1 for help adjusting this setting.

A multi-dimensional array can also be declared in this way, although you need to take care to list the elements in the proper order (that is, row 0 first, then row 1, row 2, and so on). For example, the following statement declares a two-dimensional array named *Rectangle* and assigns four values to the array:

```
Dim Rectangle = {{10, 20}, {50, 60}}
```

This array has two rows and two columns. Array element (0, 0—that is, row 0, column 0) now contains a value of 10 and element (0, 1—that is, row 0, column 1) now contains a value of 20. Also, notice that there are three sets of braces used in the declaration; these braces clarify which elements are being assigned and keep them in the proper order.

The following screen shot shows the Visual Studio Code Editor with the three examples of array literal declarations that I have shown in this section. Notice that the Code Editor is in debugging mode (or break mode) and the Watch window is visible and shows the contents of the *Waiters* array. (Debugging mode and the Watch window were introduced in Chapter 8, "Debugging Visual Basic Programs.") A *For … Next* loop is also being used to display the contents of the *Waiters* array in a message box, although you cannot see the results of that loop on this screen. *For … Next* loops are excellent tools to process arrays, as you'll see in the next section.

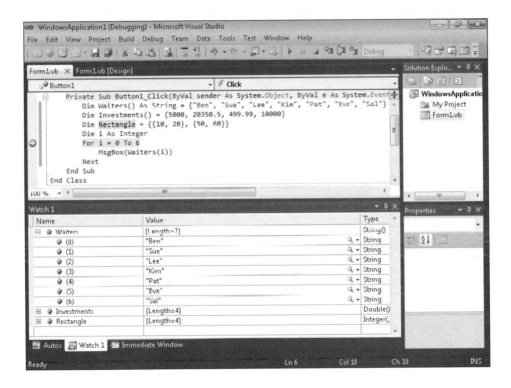

Creating a Fixed-Size Array to Hold Temperatures

The following exercise uses a one-dimensional array named *Temperatures* to record the daily high temperatures for a seven-day week. The program demonstrates how you can use an array to store and process a group of related values on a form. The *Temperatures* array variable is declared at the top of the form, and then temperatures are assigned to the array by using an *InputBox* function and a *For … Next* loop, which you learned about in Chapter 7,

"Using Loops and Timers." The loop counter is used to reference each element in the array. The array contents are then displayed on the form by using a *For … Next* loop and a text box object. The average high temperature is also calculated and displayed—how fun!

The *UBound* and *LBound* Functions

To simplify working with the array, the Fixed Array program uses the *UBound* function to check for the upper bound, or top index value, of the array. With *UBound,* you can process arrays without referring to the declaration statements that defined exactly how many values the array would hold. The closely related *LBound* function, which confirms the lower index value, or lower bound, of an array, is also available to you as a feature of early versions of Visual Basic. However, because all Visual Basic arrays now have a lower bound of zero (0), the function simply returns a value of 0. The *UBound* and *LBound* functions have the syntax

```
LBound(ArrayName)
UBound(ArrayName)
```

where *ArrayName* is the name of an array that's been declared in the project.

Use a fixed-size array

1. Start Visual Studio, and create a new Visual Basic Windows Forms Application project named **My Fixed Array**.

2. Draw a text box object on the form.

3. Set the *Multiline* property of the *TextBox1* object to True so that you can resize the object.

4. Resize the text box object so that it fills up most of the form.

5. Draw two wide button objects on the form below the text box object, oriented one beside the other.

6. Set the following properties for the form and its objects:

Object	Property	Setting
TextBox1	ScrollBars	Vertical
Button1	Text	"Enter Temps"
Button2	Text	"Display Temps"
Form1	Text	"Fixed Array Temps"

Your form looks like the one shown in the following screen shot:

7. In Solution Explorer, click the View Code button to display the Code Editor.

8. Scroll to the top of the form's program code, and directly below the *Public Class Form1* statement, type the following array declaration:

```
Dim Temperatures(0 To 6) As Single
```

This statement creates an array named *Temperatures* (of the type *Single*) that contains seven elements numbered 0 through 6. Because the array has been declared at the top of the form, it is available in all the event procedures in the form.

9. Display the form again, and then double-click the Enter Temps button (*Button1*).

The *Button1_Click* event procedure appears in the Code Editor.

10. Type the following program statements to prompt the user for temperatures and to load the input into the array:

```
Dim Prompt, Title As String
Dim i As Short
Prompt = "Enter the day's high temperature."
For i = 0 To UBound(Temperatures)
    Title = "Day " & (i + 1)
    Temperatures(i) = InputBox(Prompt, Title)
Next
```

The *For ... Next* loop uses the short integer counter variable *i* as an array index to load temperatures into array elements 0 through 6. Rather than using the simplified *For* loop syntax:

```
For i = 0 to 6
```

to process the array, I chose a slightly more complex syntax involving the *UBound* function for future flexibility. The *For* loop construction:

```
For i = 0 To UBound(Temperatures)
```

determines the upper bound of the array by using the *UBound* statement. This technique is more flexible because if the array is expanded or reduced later, the *For* loop automatically adjusts itself to the new array size.

To fill the array with temperatures, the event procedure uses an *InputBox* function, which displays the current day by using the *For* loop counter.

11. Display the form again, and then double-click the Display Temps button (*Button2*).

12. Type the following statements in the *Button2_Click* event procedure:

```
Dim Result As String
Dim i As Short
Dim Total As Single = 0
Result = "High temperatures for the week:" & vbCrLf & vbCrLf
For i = 0 To UBound(Temperatures)
    Result = Result & "Day " & (i + 1) & vbTab & _
      Temperatures(i) & vbCrLf
    Total = Total + Temperatures(i)
Next
Result = Result & vbCrLf & _
  "Average temperature: " & Format(Total / 7, "0.0")
TextBox1.Text = Result
```

This event procedure uses a *For ... Next* loop to cycle through the elements in the array, and it adds each element in the array to a string variable named *Result*, which is declared at the top of the event procedure. I've used several literal strings, constants, and string concatenation operators *(&)* to pad and format the string by using carriage returns *(vbCrLf)*, tab characters *(vbTab)*, and headings. The *vbCrLf* constant, used here for the first time, contains the carriage return and line feed characters and is an efficient way to create new lines. The *vbTab* constant is also used here for the first time to put some distance between the day and temperature values in the *Result* string. At the end of the event procedure, an average for the temperatures is determined, and the final string is assigned to the *Text* property of the text box object, as shown in this statement:

```
TextBox1.Text = Result
```

13. Click the Save All button on the Standard toolbar to save the project. Specify the C:\Vb10sbs\Chap11 folder as the location.

Now you'll run the program.

Tip The complete Fixed Array program is located in the C:\Vb10sbs\Chap11\Fixed Array folder.

14. Click the Start Debugging button on the Standard toolbar to run the program.

15. Click the Enter Temps button, and when prompted by the *InputBox* function, enter seven different temperatures. (How about using the temperatures from your last vacation?)

The *InputBox* function dialog box looks like this:

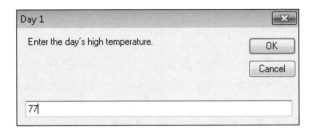

16. After you've entered the temperatures, click the Display Temps button.

Using the array, Visual Basic displays each of the temperatures in the text box and prints an average at the bottom. Your screen looks similar to this:

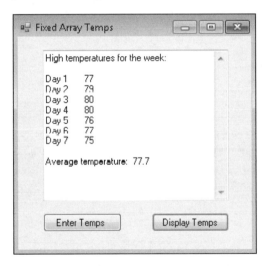

17. Click the Close button on the form to end the program.

Creating a Dynamic Array

As you can see, arrays are quite handy for working with lists of numbers, especially if you process them by using *For ... Next* loops. But what if you're not sure how much array space you'll need before you run your program? For example, what if you want to let the user choose how many temperatures are entered into the Fixed Array program?

Visual Basic handles this problem efficiently with a special elastic container called a *dynamic array*. Dynamic arrays are dimensioned at run time, either when the user specifies the size of the array or when logic you add to the program determines an array size based on specific conditions. Dimensioning a dynamic array takes several steps because although the size of the array isn't specified until the program is running, you need to make "reservations" for the array at design time. To create a dynamic array, you follow these basic steps:

1. Specify the name and type of the array in the program at design time, omitting the number of elements in the array. For example, to create a dynamic array named *Temperatures*, you type:

```
Dim Temperatures() As Single
```

2. Add code to determine the number of elements that should be in the array at run time. You can prompt the user by using an *InputBox* function or a text box object, or you can calculate the storage needs of the program by using properties or other logic. For example, the following statements get the array size from the user and assign it to the *Days* variable of type *Short*:

```
Dim Days As Short
Days = InputBox("How many days?", "Create Array")
```

3. Use the variable in a *ReDim* statement to dimension the array, subtracting 1 because arrays are zero-based. For example, the following statement sets the size of the *Temperatures* array at run time by using the *Days* variable:

```
ReDim Temperatures(Days - 1)
```

> **Important** With *ReDim*, you should not try to change the number of dimensions in an array that you've previously declared.

4. Use the *UBound* function to determine the upper bound in a *For ... Next* loop, and process the array elements as necessary, as shown here:

```
For i = 0 to UBound(Temperatures)
    Temperatures(i) = InputBox(Prompt, Title)
Next
```

In the following exercise, you'll use these steps to revise the Fixed Array program so that it can process any number of temperatures by using a dynamic array.

Use a dynamic array to hold temperatures

1. Open the Code Editor to display the program code for the Fixed Array project.

2. Scroll to the top of the form's code, in which you originally declared the *Temperatures* fixed array.

3. Remove *0 To 6* from the *Temperatures* array declaration so that the array is now a dynamic array.

   The statement looks like the following:

```
Dim Temperatures() As Single
```

4. Add the following variable declaration just below the *Temperatures* array declaration:

```
Dim Days As Integer
```

The integer variable *Days* will be used to receive input from the user and to dimension the dynamic array at run time.

5. Scroll down in the Code Editor to display the *Button1_Click* event procedure, and modify the code so that it looks like the following. (The changed or added elements are shaded.)

```
Dim Prompt, Title As String
Dim i As Short
Prompt = "Enter the day's high temperature."
Days = InputBox("How many days?", "Create Array")
If Days > 0 Then ReDim Temperatures(Days - 1)
For i = 0 To UBound(Temperatures)
    Title = "Day " & (i + 1)
    Temperatures(i) = InputBox(Prompt, Title)
Next
```

The fourth and fifth lines prompt the user for the number of temperatures he or she wants to save, and then the user's input is used to dimension a dynamic array. The *If ... Then* decision structure is used to verify that the number of days is greater than zero. (Dimensioning an array with a number less than zero or equal to zero generates an error.) Because index 0 of the array is used to store the temperature for the first day, the *Days* variable is decremented by 1 when dimensioning the array. The *Days* variable isn't needed to determine the upper bound of the *For ... Next* loop—as in the previous example, the *UBound* function is used instead.

6. Scroll down in the Code Editor to display the *Button2_Click* event procedure. Modify the code so that it looks like the following routine. (The changed elements are shaded.)

```
Dim Result As String
Dim i As Short
Dim Total As Single = 0
Result = "High temperatures:" & vbCrLf & vbCrLf
For i = 0 To UBound(Temperatures)
    Result = Result & "Day " & (i + 1) & vbTab & _
      Temperatures(i) & vbCrLf
    Total = Total + Temperatures(i)
Next
Result = Result & vbCrLf & _
  "Average temperature: " & Format(Total / Days, "0.0")
TextBox1.Text = Result
```

The *Days* variable replaces the number 7 in the average temperature calculation at the bottom of the event procedure. I also edited the "High temperatures" heading that will be displayed in the text box.

7. Display the form.

8. Change the *Text* property of *Form1* to "Dynamic Array."

9. Save your changes to disk.

 Tip On the companion CD, I gave this project a separate name to keep it distinct from the Fixed Array project. The complete Dynamic Array project is located in the C:\Vb10sbs\ Chap11\Dynamic Array folder.

10. Click the Start Debugging button to run the program.

11. Click the Enter Temps button.

12. Type **5** when you're prompted for the number of days you want to record, and then click OK.

13. Enter five temperatures when prompted.

14. When you've finished entering temperatures, click the Display Temps button.

    The program displays the five temperatures on the form, along with their average. Your screen looks similar to the following screen shot:

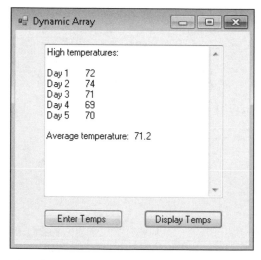

15. Click the Close button on the form to end the program.

You've practiced using the two most common array types in Visual Basic programming. When you write your own programs, you'll soon use much larger arrays, but the concepts are the same, and you'll be amazed at how fast Visual Basic can complete array-related computations.

Preserving Array Contents by Using *ReDim Preserve*

In the previous exercise, you used the *ReDim* statement to specify the size of a dynamic array at run time. However, one potential shortcoming associated with the *ReDim* statement is that if you redimension an array that already has data in it, all the existing data is irretrievably lost. After the *ReDim* statement is executed, the contents of a dynamic array are set to their default value, such as zero or *null*. Depending on your outlook, this can be considered a useful feature for emptying the contents of arrays, or it can be an irksome feature that requires a workaround.

Fortunately, Visual Basic provides the *Preserve* keyword, which you use to preserve the data in an array when you change its dimensions. The syntax for the *Preserve* keyword is as follows:

```
ReDim Preserve ArrayName(Dim1Elements, Dim2Elements, ...)
```

In such a *ReDim* statement, the array must continue to have the same number of dimensions and contain the same type of data. In addition, there's a caveat that you can resize only the last array dimension. For example, if your array has two or more dimensions, you can change the size of only the last dimension and still preserve the contents of the array. (Single-dimension arrays automatically pass this test, so you can freely expand the size of dynamic arrays by using the *Preserve* keyword.)

The following examples show how you can use *Preserve* to increase the size of the last dimension in a dynamic array without erasing any existing data contained in the array.

If you originally declared a dynamic string array named *Philosophers* by using the syntax:

```
Dim Philosophers() As String
```

you can redimension the array and add data to it by using code similar to the following:

```
ReDim Philosophers(200)
Philosophers(200) = "David Probst"
```

You can expand the size of the *Philosophers* array to 301 elements (0–300), and preserve the existing contents, by using the following syntax:

```
ReDim Preserve Philosophers(300)
```

Using *ReDim* for Three-Dimensional Arrays

A more complex example involving a three-dimensional array uses a similar syntax. Imagine that you want to use a three-dimensional, single-precision, floating-point array named *myCube* in your program. You can declare the *myCube* array by using the following syntax:

```
Dim myCube(,,) As Single
```

You can then redimension the array and add data to it by using the following code:

```
ReDim myCube(25, 25, 25)
myCube(10, 1, 1) = 150.46
```

after which you can expand the size of the third dimension in the array (while preserving the array's contents) by using this syntax:

```
ReDim Preserve myCube(25, 25, 50)
```

In this example, however, only the third dimension can be expanded—the first and second dimensions cannot be changed if you redimension the array by using the *Preserve* keyword. Attempting to change the size of the first or second dimension in this example produces a run-time error when the *ReDim Preserve* statement is executed.

Experiment a little with *ReDim Preserve*, and see how you can use it to make your own arrays flexible and robust.

One Step Further: Processing Large Arrays by Using Methods in the *Array* Class

In previous sections, you learned about using arrays to store information during program execution. In this section, you'll learn about using methods in the *Array* class of the .NET Framework, which you can use to quickly sort, search, and reverse the elements in an array, as well as perform other functions. The sample program I've created demonstrates how these features work especially well with very large arrays. You'll also learn how to use the *ProgressBar* control.

The *Array* Class

When you create arrays in Visual Basic, you are using a base class that is defined by Visual Basic for implementing arrays within user-created programs. This *Array* class also provides a collection of methods that you can use to manipulate arrays while they are active in programs. The most useful methods include *Array.Sort*, *Array.Find*, *Array.Reverse*, *Array* *.Copy*, and *Array.Clear*. You can locate other interesting methods by experimenting with the *Array* class in the Code Editor (by using Microsoft IntelliSense) and by checking the

Visual Studio Help documentation. The *Array* class methods function much like the .NET Framework methods you have already used in this book; that is, they are called by name and (in this case) require a valid array name as an argument. For example, to sort an array of temperatures (such as the *Temperatures* array that you created in the last exercise), you would use the following syntax:

```
Array.Sort(Temperatures)
```

You would make such a call after the *Temperatures* array had been declared and filled with data in the program. When Visual Basic executes the *Array.Sort* method, it creates a temporary storage location for the array in memory and uses a sorting routine to reorganize the array in alphanumeric order. After the sort is complete, the original array is shuffled in ascending order, with the smallest value in array location 0 and the largest value in the last array location. With the *Temperatures* example above, the sort would produce an array of daily temperatures organized from coolest to hottest.

In the following exercise, you'll see how the *Array.Sort* and *Array.Reverse* methods can be used to quickly reorder a large array containing six-digit numbers randomly selected between 0 and 1,000,000. You'll also experiment with the *ProgressBar* control, which provides useful visual feedback for the user during long sorts.

Use *Array* methods to sort an array of 3,000 elements

1. On the File menu, click Open Project, and then open the Array Class Sorts project, located in the C:\Vb10sbs\Chap11 folder.

2. Display the form if it is not already visible.

   Your screen looks like this:

   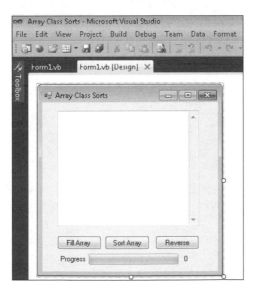

This form looks similar to the earlier projects in this chapter and features a test box for displaying array data. However, it also contains three buttons for manipulating large arrays and a progress bar object that gives the user feedback during longer array operations. (Visual feedback is useful when computations take longer than a few seconds to complete, and if you use this code to sort an array of 3,000 array elements, a slight delay is inevitable.)

3. Click the progress bar on the form.

The *ProgressBar1* object is selected on the form and is listed in the Properties window. I created the progress bar object by using the *ProgressBar* control on the Common Controls tab in the Toolbox. A progress bar is designed to display the progress of a computation by displaying an appropriate number of colored rectangles arranged in a horizontal progress bar. When the computation is complete, the bar is filled with rectangles. (In Windows 7 and Windows Vista, a smoothing effect is applied so that the progress bar is gradually filled with a solid band of color—an especially attractive effect.) You've probably seen the progress bar many times while you downloaded files or installed programs within Windows. Now you can create one in your own programs!

The important properties that make a progress bar work are the *Minimum*, *Maximum*, and *Value* properties, and these are typically manipulated using program code. (The other progress bar properties, which you can examine in the Properties window, control how the progress bar looks and functions.) You can examine how the *Minimum* and *Maximum* properties are set by looking at this program's *Form1_Load* event procedure.

4. Double-click the form to display the *Form1_Load* event procedure.

You see the following code:

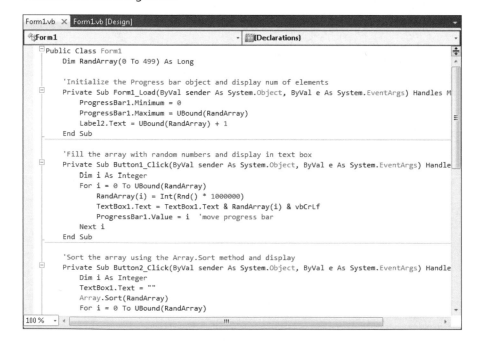

```vb
Public Class Form1
    Dim RandArray(0 To 499) As Long

    'Initialize the Progress bar object and display num of elements
    Private Sub Form1_Load(ByVal sender As System.Object, ByVal e As System.EventArgs) Handles M
        ProgressBar1.Minimum = 0
        ProgressBar1.Maximum = UBound(RandArray)
        Label2.Text = UBound(RandArray) + 1
    End Sub

    'Fill the array with random numbers and display in text box
    Private Sub Button1_Click(ByVal sender As System.Object, ByVal e As System.EventArgs) Handle
        Dim i As Integer
        For i = 0 To UBound(RandArray)
            RandArray(i) = Int(Rnd() * 1000000)
            TextBox1.Text = TextBox1.Text & RandArray(i) & vbCrLf
            ProgressBar1.Value = i   'move progress bar
        Next i
    End Sub

    'Sort the array using the Array.Sort method and display
    Private Sub Button2_Click(ByVal sender As System.Object, ByVal e As System.EventArgs) Handle
        Dim i As Integer
        TextBox1.Text = ""
        Array.Sort(RandArray)
        For i = 0 To UBound(RandArray)
```

For a progress bar to display an accurate indication of how long a computing task will take to complete, you need to set relative measurements for the beginning and the end of the bar. This is accomplished with the *Minimum* and *Maximum* properties, which are set to match the first and the last elements in the array that we are building. As I have noted, the first array element is always zero but the last array element depends on the size of the array, so I have used the *UBound* function to return that number and set the progress bar *Maximum* property accordingly. The array that we are manipulating in this exercise is *RandArray*, a *Long* integer array declared initially to hold 500 elements (0 to 499).

5. Click the Start Debugging button to run the program.

   The program runs, and the Array Class Sorts form opens on the screen. In its *Form1_Load* event procedure, the program declared an array named *RandArray* and dimensioned it with 500 elements. A progress bar object was calibrated to track a calculation of 500 units (the array size), and the number 500 appears to the right of the progress bar (the work of a label object and the *UBound* function).

6. Click the Fill Array button.

   The program loads *RandArray* with 500 random numbers (derived by the *Rnd* function), and displays the numbers in the text box. As the program processes the array and fills the text box object with data, the progress bar slowly fills with the color green. Your screen looks like this when the process is finished:

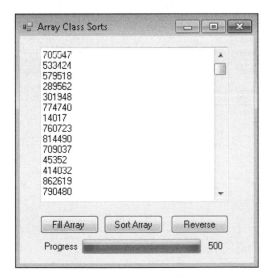

The code that produced this result is the *Button1_Click* event procedure, which contains the following program statements:

```
'Fill the array with random numbers and display in text box
Private Sub Button1_Click(ByVal sender As System.Object, _
    ByVal e As System.EventArgs) Handles Button1.Click
```

```
    Dim i As Integer
    For i = 0 To UBound(RandArray)
        RandArray(i) = Int(Rnd() * 1000000)
        TextBox1.Text = TextBox1.Text & RandArray(i) & vbCrLf
        ProgressBar1.Value = i 'move progress bar
    Next i
End Sub
```

To get random numbers that are integers, I used the *Int* and *Rnd* functions together, as I did in Chapter 2, "Writing Your First Program," and I multiplied the random number produced by *Rnd* by 1,000,000 to get whole numbers that are six digits or less. Assigning these numbers to the array is facilitated by using a *For … Next* loop with an array index that matches the loop counter (*i*). Filling the array is an extremely fast operation; the slowdown (and the need for the progress bar) is caused by the assignment of array elements to the text box object one at a time. This involves updating a user interface component on the form 500 times, and the process takes a few seconds to complete. It is instructional, however—the delay provides a way for me to show off the *ProgressBar* control. Since the progress bar object has been calibrated to use the number of array elements as its maximum, assigning the loop counter (*i*) to the progress bar's *Value* property allows the bar to display exactly how much of the calculation has been completed.

7. Click the Sort Array button.

   The program follows a similar process to sort *RandArray*, this time using the *Array.Sort* method to reorder the array in ascending order. (The 500 elements are listed from lowest to highest.) Your screen looks like this:

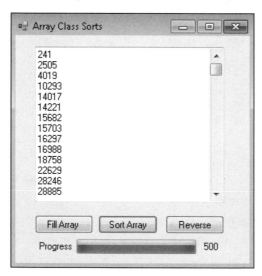

   The code that produced this result is the *Button2_Click* event procedure, which contains the following program statements:

```
'Sort the array using the Array.Sort method and display
Private Sub Button2_Click(ByVal sender As System.Object, _
```

```
ByVal e As System.EventArgs) Handles Button2.Click
    Dim i As Integer
    TextBox1.Text = ""
    Array.Sort(RandArray)
    For i = 0 To UBound(RandArray)
        TextBox1.Text = TextBox1.Text & RandArray(i) & vbCrLf
        ProgressBar1.Value = i 'move progress bar
    Next i
End Sub
```

This event procedure clears the text box object when the user clicks the Sort Array button, and then sorts the array by using the *Array.Sort* method described earlier. The sorting process is very quick. Again, the only slowdown is rebuilding the text box object one line at a time in the *For … Next* loop, a process that is reported by the *ProgressBar1* object and its *Value* property. See how simple it is to use the *Array.Sort* method?

8. Click the Reverse button.

The program uses the *Array.Reverse* method to manipulate *RandArray*, reordering the array in backward or reverse order; that is, the first element becomes last and the last element becomes first.

> **Note** This method does not always produce a sorted list; the array elements are in descending order only because *RandArray* had been sorted previously in ascending order by the *Array.Sort* method. (To examine the list more closely, use the scroll bars or the arrow keys.)

Your screen looks like this:

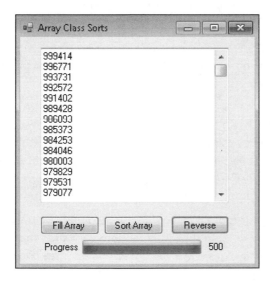

The code that produced this result is the *Button3_Click* event procedure, which contains the following program statements:

```
'Reverse the order of array elements using Array.Reverse
Private Sub Button3_Click(ByVal sender As System.Object, _
  ByVal e As System.EventArgs) Handles Button3.Click
    Dim i As Integer
    TextBox1.Text = ""
    Array.Reverse(RandArray)
    For i = 0 To UBound(RandArray)
        TextBox1.Text = TextBox1.Text & RandArray(i) & vbCrLf
        ProgressBar1.Value = i 'move progress bar
    Next i
End Sub
```

This event procedure is identical to the *Button2_Click* event procedure, with the following exception:

```
Array.Sort(RandArray)
```

has become:

```
Array.Reverse(RandArray)
```

9. Click the Stop Debugging button to end the program.

10. Scroll to the top of the Code Editor, and locate the program statement that declares the *RandArray* array:

```
Dim RandArray(0 To 499) As Long
```

11. Replace 499 in the array declaration statement with 2999.

    The statement now looks like this:

```
Dim RandArray(0 To 2999) As Long
```

12. Run the program again to see how declaring and filling an array with 3,000 elements affects program performance.

    Because processing 3,000 elements is much more work, Visual Basic takes a little while to update the text box object again and again as you fill, sort, and reverse *RandArray*. However, the progress bar keeps you posted, and you can see that with just a small change, you can adapt what you've learned in this chapter to different situations. (The secret was using the *UBound* function to report the size of the array to the program's event procedures, rather than "hard coding" the upper bound at 499.)

You can further experiment with this program by adding a *Randomize* statement to the *Form1_Load* event procedure (to make the results truly random each time that you run the program), or by trying additional array sizes and array types. (Try an array size of 100, 800, 2,000, or 5,000 elements, for example.) If you try larger numbers, you'll eventually exceed the amount of data that the text box object can display, but it takes a while before you exceed the maximum array size allowed by Visual Basic.

If you want to focus on array operations without displaying the results, place a comment character (') before each line of code that manipulates a text box object to "comment out" the text box (but not the progress bar) portions of the program. You'll be amazed at how fast array operations run when the results do not need to be displayed on the form. (An array of 100,000 elements loads in just a few seconds.)

Chapter 11 Quick Reference

To	Do This
Create an array	Dimension the array by using the *Dim* keyword. For example: ```Dim Employees(9) As String```
Create a public array	Dimension the array by using the *Public* keyword in a module. For example: ```Public Employees(9) As String```
Create a public array specifying upper and lower bounds	Dimension the array as described earlier, but also use the *To* keyword. For example: ```Public Employees(0 To 9) As String``` Note: The lower bound of the array must always be zero (0).
Assign a value to an array	Specify the array name, the index of the array element, and the value. For example: ```Employees(5) = "Leslie"```
Declare an array and assign values to it at the same time	Specify the array name, an array type (optional), and the values for the array enclosed in braces. For example: ```Dim Waiters() As String = {"Ben", "Sue", "Lee", "Kim", "Pat"}```
Format text strings with carriage return and tab characters	Use the *vbCrLf* and *vbTab* constants within your program code. (To add these values to strings, use the concatenation operator (&).)
Create a dynamic array	Specify the name and type of the array, but omit the number of elements. (If the array has multiple dimensions, insert commas but no numbers between the dimensions.) In your program code, specify the size of the array by using the *ReDim* statement. For example: ```ReDim Temperatures(10)```

Process the elements in an array	Write a *For … Next* loop that uses the loop counter variable to address each element in the array. For example:
	
	```Dim i As Short```
	```Dim Total As Single```
	```For i = 0 To UBound(Temperatures)```
	``` Total = Total + Temperatures(i)```
	```Next```

Redimension an array while preserving the data in it	Use the *Preserve* keyword in your *ReDim* statement. For example: ```ReDim Preserve myCube(25, 25, 50)```

To	Do This

Reorder the contents of an array	Use methods in the *Array* class of the .NET Framework. To sort an array named *RandArray* in ascending order, use the *Array.Sort* method as follows:
	
	`Array.Sort(RandArray)`
	
	To reverse the order of an array named *RandArray*, use the *Array.Reverse* method as follows:
	
	`Array.Reverse(RandArray)`

To give the user visual feedback during long calculations	Add a *ProgressBar* control to your form. (You can find the *ProgressBar* control on the Common Controls tab of the Toolbox.) Set the *Minimum*, *Maximum*, and *Value* properties for the control by using program code. The counter variable in a *For … Next* loop often offers a good way to set the *Value* property.

Chapter 12
Working with Collections

After completing this chapter, you will be able to:

- Manipulate the *Controls* collection on a form.

- Use a *For Each … Next* loop to cycle through objects in a collection.

- Create your own collections for managing Web site URLs and other information.

- Use VBA collections within Microsoft Office.

In this chapter, you'll learn how to use groups of objects called *collections* in a Microsoft Visual Basic program. You'll learn how to manage information with collections and process collection objects by using *For Each … Next* loops. When you combine collection-processing skills with what you learned about arrays in Chapter 11, "Using Arrays to Manage Numeric and String Data," you'll have much of what you need to know about managing data effectively in a program, and you'll have taken your first steps in manipulating the object collections exposed by Microsoft Visual Studio 2010 and popular Windows applications.

Working with Object Collections

In this section, you'll learn about collections, a powerful mechanism for controlling objects and other data in a Visual Basic program. The Microsoft .NET Framework maintains several standard object collections that you can use when you write your programs. You can use Visual Studio to browse your system for collections and other application objects.

You already know that objects on a form are stored together in the same file. But did you also know that Visual Basic considers the objects to be members of the same group? In Visual Studio terminology, the entire set of objects on a form is called the *Controls collection*. The *Controls* collection is created automatically when you open a new form, and when you add objects to the form, they become part of that collection.

Each collection in a program has its own name so that you can reference it as a distinct unit in the program code. For example, you use the *Controls* name to reference the collection of objects on a form. This grouping method is similar to the way arrays group a list of elements together under one name, and like Visual Basic arrays, the *Controls* collection is zero-based.

If you have more than one form in a project, you can create public variables associated with the form names and use those variables to differentiate one *Controls* collection from another. (You'll learn more about using public variables to store form data in Chapter 14, "Managing Windows Forms and Controls at Run Time.") You can even add controls programmatically to the *Controls* collection in a form.

Referencing Objects in a Collection

You can reference the objects in a collection, or the individual members of the collection, by specifying the *index position* of the object in the group. Visual Basic stores collection objects in the reverse order of that in which they were created, so you can use an object's "birth order" to reference the object individually, or you can use a loop to step through several objects. For example, to identify the last object created on a form, you can specify the 0 (zero) index, as shown in this example:

```
Controls(0).Text = "Business"
```

This statement sets the *Text* property of the last object on the form to "Business." (The second-to-last object created has an index of 1, the third-to-last object created has an index of 2, and so on.) Considering this logic, it's important that you don't always associate a particular object on the form with an index value because if a new object is added to the collection, the new object takes the 0 index spot and the remaining object indexes are incremented by 1.

The following *For ... Next* loop uses a message box to display the names of the last four controls added to a form:

```
Dim i As Integer
For i = 0 To 3
    MsgBox(Controls(i).Name)
Next i
```

Note that I've directed this loop to cycle from 0 to 3 because the last control object added to a form is in the 0 position. In the following section, you'll learn a more efficient method for writing such a loop.

Writing *For Each ... Next* Loops

Although you can reference the members of a collection individually, the most useful way to work with objects in a collection is to process them as a group. In fact, the reason that collections exist is so that you can process groups of objects efficiently. For example, you might want to display, move, sort, rename, or resize an entire collection of objects at once.

To handle this kind of task, you can use a special loop called *For Each ... Next* to cycle through objects in a collection one at a time. A *For Each ... Next* loop is similar to a *For ... Next* loop. When a *For Each ... Next* loop is used with the *Controls* collection, it looks like this:

```
Dim CtrlVar As Control
...
For Each CtrlVar In Controls
    process object
Next CtrlVar
```

The *CtrlVar* variable is declared as a *Control* type and represents the current object in the *For Each ... Next* loop. *Controls* (note the "s") is the collection class that I introduced earlier that represents all the control objects on the current form. The body of the loop is used to process the individual objects of the collection. For example, you might want to change the *Enabled*, *Left*, *Top*, *Text*, or *Visible* property of the objects in the collection, or you might want to list the name of each object in a list box.

Experimenting with Objects in the *Controls* Collection

In the following exercises, you'll use program code to manipulate the objects on a form by using the *Controls* collection. The project you'll create will have three button objects, and you'll create event procedures that change the *Text* properties of each object, move objects to the right, and give one object in the group special treatment. The program will use three *For Each … Next* loops to manipulate the objects each time the user clicks one of the buttons.

Use a *For Each … Next* loop to change *Text* properties

1. Create a new Visual Basic Windows Forms Application project named **My Controls Collection**.

2. Use the *Button* control to draw three button objects on the left side of the form, as shown here:

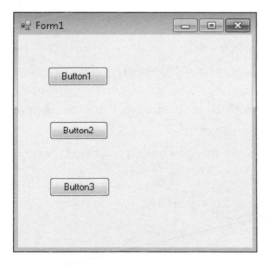

3. Use the Properties window to set the *Name* property of the third button object (*Button3*) to "btnMoveObjects."

4. Double-click the first button object (*Button1*) on the form.

   The *Button1_Click* event procedure appears in the Code Editor.

5. Type the following program statements:

```
For Each ctrl In Controls
    ctrl.Text = "Click Me!"
Next
```

This *For Each ... Next* loop steps through the *Controls* collection on the form one control at a time and sets each control's *Text* property to "Click Me!" The loop uses *ctrl* as an object variable in the loop, which you'll declare in the following step.

6. Scroll to the top of the form's program code, and directly above the statement *Public Class Form1*, type the following statement:

```
Option Infer Off
```

This statement tells the compiler that it should not try to infer the type of variables. Since you will be explicitly declaring the variable types, this infer option is not needed. If *Option Infer* is on and you try to run the code in this chapter, you may see a warning message indicating that the type for a variable you are using cannot be inferred. (For more information, see Chapter 1, "Exploring the Visual Studio Integrated Development Environment.")

7. Directly below the statement *Public Class Form1*, type the following comment and variable declaration:

```
'Declare a variable of type Control to represent form controls
Dim ctrl As Control
```

This global variable declaration creates a variable in the *Control* class type that represents the current form's controls in the program. You're declaring this variable in the general declarations area of the form so that it is valid throughout all the form's event procedures.

Now you're ready to run the program and change the *Text* property for each button on the form.

8. Click the Start Debugging button on the Standard toolbar to run the program.

9. Click the first button on the form (*Button1*).

The *Button1_Click* event procedure changes the *Text* property for each control in the *Controls* collection. Your form looks like this:

10. Click the Close button on the form.

The program ends.

 Note The *Text* property changes made by the program have not been replicated on the form within the Designer. Changes made at run time do not change the program's core property settings.

11. Click the Save All button on the Standard toolbar to save your changes. Specify the C:\Vb10sbs\Chap12 folder as the location.

Now you're ready to try a different experiment with the *Controls* collection: using the *Left* property to move each control in the *Controls* collection to the right.

Use a *For Each … Next* loop to move controls

1. Display the form again, and then double-click the second button object (*Button2*).

2. Type the following program code in the *Button2_Click* event procedure:

```
For Each ctrl In Controls
    ctrl.Left = ctrl.Left + 25
Next
```

Each time the user clicks the second button, this *For Each … Next* loop steps through the objects in the *Controls* collection one by one and moves them 25 pixels to the right. (To move objects 25 pixels to the left, you would subtract 25 instead.) A *pixel* is a device-independent measuring unit with which you can precisely place objects on a form.

As in the previous event procedure that you typed, the *ctrl* variable is a "stand-in" for the current object in the collection and contains the same property settings as the object it represents. In this loop, you adjust the *Left* property, which determines an object's position relative to the left side of the form.

3. Click the Start Debugging button.

The program runs, and three buttons appear on the left side of the form.

4. Click the first button, and then click the second button several times.

The buttons on the form change to "Click Me!", and then each time you click the second button, the objects on the form gradually move to the right. Your screen looks like this after five clicks:

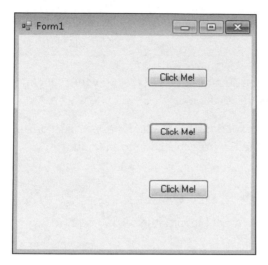

5. Click the Close button on the form to stop the program.

6. Click the Save All button to save your changes.

You won't always want to move all the objects on a form as a group. With Visual Basic, you can process collection members individually. In the next exercise, you'll learn how to keep the third button object in one place while the other two buttons move to the right.

Using the *Name* Property in a *For Each ... Next* Loop

If you want to process one or more members of a collection differently than you process the others, you can use the *Name* property, which uniquely identifies each object on the form. You've set the *Name* property periodically in this book to make your program code more readable, but *Name* also can be used programmatically to identify specific objects in your program.

To use the *Name* property programmatically, single out the objects to which you want to give special treatment, and then note their *Name* properties. Then as you loop through the objects on the form by using a *For Each ... Next* loop, you can use one or more *If* statements to test for the important *Name* properties and handle those objects differently. For example, let's say you want to construct a *For Each ... Next* loop that moves one object more slowly across the form than the other objects. You could use an *If ... Then* statement to spot the *Name* property of the slower object and then move that object a shorter distance, by not incrementing its *Left* property as much as those of the other objects.

> **Tip** If you plan to give several objects special treatment in a *For Each ... Next* loop, you can use *ElseIf* statements with the *If ... Then* statement, or you can use a *Select Case* decision structure.

In the following exercise, you'll test the *Name* property of the third button object (*btnMoveObjects*) to give that button special treatment in a *For Each ... Next* loop. The result will be an event procedure that moves the top two buttons to the right but keeps the bottom button stationary.

> **Tip** In addition to the *Name* property, most objects support the *Tag* property. Similar to the *Name* property, the *Tag* property is a location in which you can store string data about the object. The *Tag* property is empty by default, but you can assign information to it and test it to uniquely identify objects in your program that you want to process differently.

Use the *Name* property to give an object in the *Controls* collection special treatment

1. Display the form, and then double-click the third button object.

   The *btnMoveObjects_Click* event procedure appears in the Code Editor. Remember that you changed the *Name* property of this object from "Button3" to "btnMoveObjects" in an earlier exercise.

2. Type the following program code in the event procedure:

```
For Each ctrl In Controls
    If ctrl.Name <> "btnMoveObjects" Then
        ctrl.Left = ctrl.Left + 25
    End If
Next
```

   The new feature of this *For Each ... Next* loop is the *If ... Then* statement that checks each collection member to see whether it has a *Name* property called "btnMoveObjects." If the loop encounters this marker, it passes over the object without moving it. Note that, as in the previous examples, the *ctrl* variable was declared at the top of the form as a variable of the *Control* type with scope throughout the form.

3. Click the Save All button to save your edits.

> **Tip** The complete Controls Collection program is located in the C:\Vb10sbs\Chap12\ Controls Collection folder.

4. Click the Start Debugging button.

   The program runs, and the three button objects appear on the form.

5. Click the third button object six or seven times.

As you click the button, the top two button objects move across the screen. The third button stays in the same place, however, as shown here:

6. Click the Close button on the form to stop the program.

Giving one object in a collection special treatment can be very useful. In this case, using the *Name* property in the *For Each ... Next* loop improved the readability of the program code, suggesting numerous potential uses for a game or graphics program. As you use other types of collections in Visual Basic, be sure to keep the *Name* property in mind.

Creating Your Own Collections

With Visual Basic, you can also create your own collections to track data in a program and manipulate it systematically. Although collections are often created to hold objects, such as user interface controls, you can also use collections to store numeric or string values while a program is running. In this way, collections nicely complement the capabilities of arrays, which you learned about in Chapter 11.

Declaring New Collections

New collections are declared as variables in a program, and the location in which you declare them determines their scope, or the extent to which their assigned values persist. Because collections are so useful, I usually declare them at the top of a form or in a module.

New collection declarations require the syntax:

```
Dim CollectionName As New Collection()
```

where *CollectionName* is the name of your collection. If you place the collection declaration in a module, you use the *Public* keyword instead of the *Dim* keyword. After you create a collection, you can add members to it by using the *Add* method, and you can examine the individual members by using a *For Each … Next* loop.

The following exercise shows you how to create a collection that holds string data representing the Internet addresses (Uniform Resource Locators, or URLs) that you've recently used while surfing the Web. To connect to the Web, the program will use the Visual Basic *System.Diagnostics.Process.Start* method and your default Web browser, a technique that I first introduced in Chapter 3, "Working with Toolbox Controls."

Track Internet addresses by using a new collection

1. Click the Close Project command on the File menu.
2. Create a new Windows Forms Application project named **My URL Collection**.
3. Draw a wide text box object at the top of the form, centered within the form.
4. Draw two wide button objects below the text box object on the form, one button below the other.
5. Set the following properties for the form and its objects:

Object	Property	Setting
TextBox1	Text	"http://www.microsoft.com/learning/books/"
Button1	Text	"Visit Site"
Button2	Text	"List Recent Sites"
Form1	Text	"URL Collection"

Your form looks like this:

6. Click the View Code button in Solution Explorer to display the Code Editor.
7. Move the insertion point near the top of the form's program code, and directly below the statement *Public Class Form1*, type the following variable declaration, and then press ENTER:

```
Dim URLsVisited As New Collection()
```

This statement creates a new collection and assigns it the variable name *URLsVisited*. Because you're placing the declaration in the declaration area for the form, the collection has scope throughout all the form's event procedures.

8. Display the form again, double-click the Visit Site button, and then type the following code in the *Button1_Click* event procedure:

```
URLsVisited.Add(TextBox1.Text)
System.Diagnostics.Process.Start(TextBox1.Text)
```

This program code uses the *Add* method to fill up, or *populate*, the collection with members. When the user clicks the *Button1* object, the program assumes that a valid Internet address has been placed in the *TextBox1* object. Every time the *Button1* object is clicked, the current URL in *TextBox1* is copied to the *URLsVisited* collection as a string. Next, the *System.Diagnostics.Process.Start* method is called with the URL as a parameter. Because the parameter is a URL, the *Start* method attempts to open the URL by using the default Web browser on the system. (If the URL is invalid or an Internet connection cannot be established, the Web browser handles the error.)

> **Note** The only URLs that this program adds to the *URLsVisited* collection are those you've specified in the *TextBox1* object. If you browse to additional Web sites by using your Web browser, those sites won't be added to the collection.

9. Display the form again, and then double-click the List Recent Sites button.

10. Type the following program code using the Code Editor:

```
Dim URLName As String = "", AllURLs As String = ""
For Each URLName In URLsVisited
    AllURLs = AllURLs & URLName & vbCrLf
Next URLName
MsgBox(AllURLs, MsgBoxStyle.Information, "Web sites visited")
```

This event procedure prints the entire collection by using a *For Each … Next* loop and a *MsgBox* function. The routine declares a string variable named *URLName* to hold each member of the collection as it's processed and initializes the variable to empty (""). The value is added to a string named *AllURLs* by using the concatenation operator (&), and the *vbCrLf* string constant is used to place each URL on its own line.

Finally, the *AllURLs* string, which represents the entire contents of the *URLsVisited* collection, is displayed in a message box. I added the *MsgBoxStyle.Information* argument in the *MsgBox* function to emphasize that the text being displayed is general information and not a warning. (*MsgBoxStyle.Information* is also a built-in Visual Basic constant.)

11. Click the Save All button to save your changes. Specify the C:\Vb10sbs\Chap12 folder as the location.

>
>
> **Note** To run the URL Collection program, your computer must establish a connection to the Internet and be equipped with a Web browser, such as Windows Internet Explorer.

Run the URL Collection program

> **Tip** The complete URL Collection program is located in the C:\Vb10sbs\Chap12\URL Collection folder.

1. Click the Start Debugging button to run the program.

   The program displays a default Web site in the URL box, so it isn't necessary to type your own Internet address at first.

2. Click the Visit Site button.

   Visual Basic adds the Microsoft Press Web site (*http://www.microsoft.com/learning/books/*) to the *URLsVisited* collection, opens the default Web browser on your system, and loads the requested Web page, as shown here. (You can explore the Web site if you're interested.)

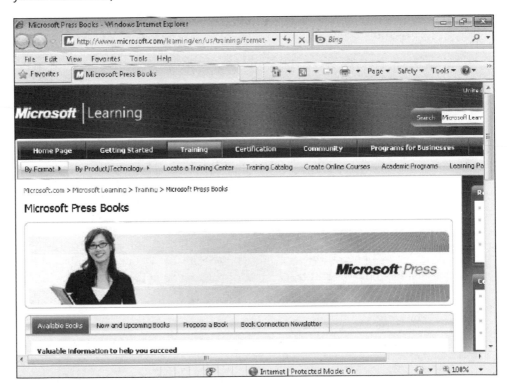

3. Click the form again. (You might need to click the form's icon on the Windows taskbar.)

4. Click the List Recent Sites button.

   Visual Basic executes the event procedure for the *Button2* object. You see a message box that looks like this:

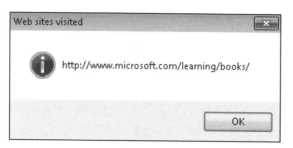

5. Click OK in the message box, type a different Web site in the form's text box, and then click the Visit Site button.

 Tip You might want to visit the Microsoft Visual Basic Developer Center site, located at *http://msdn.microsoft.com/vbasic/*, to learn more about Visual Basic.

6. Visit a few more Web sites by using the URL Collection form, and then click the List Recent Sites button.

   Each time you click List Recent Sites, the *MsgBox* function expands to show the growing URL history list, as shown here:

   If you visit more than a few dozen Web sites, you'll need to replace the *MsgBox* function with a multiline text box on the form. (Can you figure out how to write the code?)

7. When you're finished, click the Close button on the form, and then close your Web browser.

Congratulations! You've learned how to use the *Controls* collection and how to process collections by using a *For Each … Next* loop. These skills will be useful whenever you work with collections. As you become more familiar with classic computer science data structures and algorithms related to list management (stacks, queues, dictionaries, hash tables, and other structured lists), you'll find that Visual Studio and the .NET Framework provide equivalents to help you manage information in extremely innovative ways. (For a few book ideas related to data structures and algorithms, see the section entitled "General Books About Programming and Computer Science" in the Appendix, "Where to Go for More Information.")

One Step Further: VBA Collections

If you decide to write Visual Basic macros for Office applications in the future, you'll find that collections play a big role in the object models of Microsoft Word, Microsoft Excel, Microsoft Access, Microsoft PowerPoint, and several other applications that support the Visual Basic for Applications (VBA) programming language. In Word, for example, all the open documents are stored in the *Documents* collection, and each paragraph in the current document is stored in the *Paragraphs* collection. You can manipulate these collections with a *For Each ... Next* loop just as you did the collections in the preceding exercises. Office 2003, Office 2007, and Office 2010 offer a large installation base for solutions based on VBA.

> **Tip** As a software developer, you should be aware that companies and individual users often have a mixture of application versions that they use, including Office 2003, Office 2007, and Office 2010. In most cases, you'll need to offer solutions based on VBA for several Office versions, because a typical business or organization will have multiple versions of Office in use.

The following sample code comes from a Word VBA macro that uses a *For Each ... Next* loop to search each open document in the *Documents* collection for a file named MyLetter .doc. If the file is found in the collection, the macro saves the file by using the *Save* method. If the file isn't found in the collection, the macro attempts to open the file from the C:\Vb10sbs\Chap12 folder:

```
Dim aDoc As Document
Dim docFound As Boolean
Dim docLocation As String
docFound = False
docLocation = "c:\vb10sbs\chap12\myletter.doc"
For Each aDoc In Documents
    If InStr(1, aDoc.Name, "myletter.doc", 1) Then
        docFound = True
        aDoc.Save
        Exit For
    End If
Next aDoc
If docFound = False Then
    Documents.Open FileName:=docLocation
End If
```

The macro begins by declaring three variables. The *aDoc* object variable represents the current collection element in the *For Each ... Next* loop. The *docFound* Boolean variable assigns a Boolean value of True if the document is found in the *Documents* collection. The *docLocation* string variable contains the path of the MyLetter.doc file on disk. (This routine assumes that the MyLetter.doc file is with your book sample files in C:\Vb10sbs\Chap12.)

The *For Each … Next* loop cycles through each document in the *Documents* collection, searching for the MyLetter file. If the file is detected by the *InStr* function (which detects one string in another), the file is saved. If the file isn't found, the macro attempts to open it by using the *Open* method of the *Documents* object.

Also note the *Exit For* statement, which I use to exit the *For Each … Next* loop when the MyLetter file has been found and saved. *Exit For* is a special program statement that you can use to exit a *For … Next* loop or a *For Each … Next* loop when continuing will cause unwanted results. In this example, if the MyLetter.doc file is located in the collection, continuing the search is fruitless, and the *Exit For* statement affords a graceful way to stop the loop as soon as its task is completed.

Entering the Word Macro

I've included this sample Word macro to show you how you can use collections in Visual Basic for Applications, but the source code is designed for Word, not the Visual Studio Integrated Development Environment (IDE). If you aren't working in Word, the *Documents* collection won't have any meaning to the compiler.

The steps that you will follow to try the macro depend on the version of Word you are using. If you are using Word 2007 or Word 2010, you'll need to start Word, click the Developer tab, click the Macros command, specify a name for the macro (I used OpenMyDoc), click Create, and then enter the code by using the Visual Basic Editor. (If the Developer tab is not shown, you will need to enable it in the Word Options dialog box.) If you are using Word 2003, you'll need to start Word, go to the Macro submenu of the Tools menu, click the Macros command, specify a name for the macro, click Create, and then enter the code by using the Visual Basic Editor.

In the Visual Basic Editor, the completed macro looks like the following screen shot. You can run the macro by clicking the Run Sub/UserForm button on the toolbar, just as you would run a program in the Visual Studio IDE. After the macro runs, click the Word application again, and you'll see that the MyLetter document has been opened for you.

> **Tip** Word macros are generally compatible between versions, although I have sometimes run into problems when upgrading VBA macros or supporting multiple versions of Office. If you are using a different version of Word, you may need to slightly modify the sample code shown on the following page.

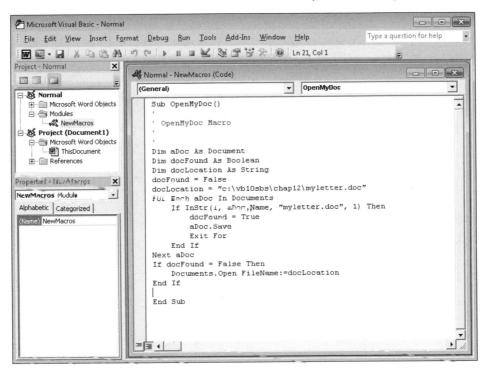

```
Sub OpenMyDoc()
'
' OpenMyDoc Macro
'
'
Dim aDoc As Document
Dim docFound As Boolean
Dim docLocation As String
docFound = False
docLocation = "c:\vb10sbs\chap12\myletter.doc"
For Each aDoc In Documents
    If InStr(1, aDoc.Name, "myletter.doc", 1) Then
        docFound = True
        aDoc.Save
        Exit For
    End If
Next aDoc
If docFound = False Then
    Documents.Open FileName:=docLocation
End If

End Sub
```

Chapter 12 Quick Reference

To	Do This

Process objects in a collection	Write a *For Each ... Next* loop that addresses each member of the collection individually. For example:
	
	```Dim ctrl As Control```
	```For Each ctrl In Controls```
	``` ctrl.Text = "Click Me!"```
	```Next```

Move objects in the *Controls* collection from left to right across the screen	Modify the *Control.Left* property of each collection object in a *For Each ... Next* loop. For example:
	
	```Dim ctrl As Control```
	```For Each ctrl In Controls```
	``` ctrl.Left = ctrl.Left + 25```
	```Next```

Give special treatment to an object in a collection	Test the *Name* property of the objects in the collection by using a *For Each ... Next* loop. For example:
	
	```Dim ctrl As Control```
	```For Each ctrl In Controls```
	``` If ctrl.Name <> "btnMoveObjects" Then```
	``` ctrl.Left = ctrl.Left + 25```
	``` End If```
	```Next```

To	Do This
Create a new collection and add members to it	Declare a variable by using the New Collection syntax. Use the *Add* method to add members. For example: ``` Dim URLsVisited As New Collection() URLsVisited.Add(TextBox1.Text) ```
Use Visual Basic for *Applications* collections in Word	If you are using Word 2007 or Word 2010, start the program, click the Developer tab, click the Macros command, give the macro a name, click Create, and then enter the macro code by using the Visual Basic Editor. If you are using Word 2003, start the program, go to the Macro submenu of the Tools menu, click the Macros command, give the macro a name, click Create, and then enter the macro code by using the Visual Basic Editor. Word exposes many useful collections, including *Documents* and *Paragraphs*.

Chapter 13

Exploring Text Files and String Processing

After completing this chapter, you will be able to:

- Use the *My* namespace, a time-saving "speed dial" feature within Visual Studio 2010.

- Display text from a file In a text box object by using the *ReadAllText* method and the *OpenFileDialog* control.

- Save notes in a text file by using the *WriteAllText* method and the *SaveFileDialog* control.

- Use string processing techniques in the *String* class to compare, combine, sort, and encrypt strings.

Managing electronic documents is an important function in any modern business, and Microsoft Visual Basic 2010 provides numerous mechanisms for working with different document types and manipulating the information in documents. The most basic document type is the *text file*, which is made up of non-formatted words and paragraphs, letters, numbers, and a variety of special-purpose characters and symbols.

In this chapter, you'll learn how to work with information stored in text files on your system. You'll learn how to open a text file and display its contents in a text box object, and you'll learn how to write to a text file on disk. You'll also learn more about managing strings in your programs, and you'll use methods in the Microsoft .NET Framework *String*, *StreamReader*, and *StreamWriter* classes to combine; sort; and display words, lines, and entire text files.

Reading Text Files

A *text file* consists of one or more lines of numbers, words, or characters. Text files are distinct from *document files* and *Web pages*, which contain formatting codes, and from *executable files*, which contain instructions for the operating system. Text files on your computer are typically identified by Windows Explorer as "Text Documents," or they have the file name extension .txt, .ini, .log, or .inf.

The simplest way to display a text file in a program is to use a text box object. As you have learned, you can create text box objects in any size. If the contents of the text file don't fit neatly in the text box, you can also add scroll bars to the text box so that the user can examine the entire file.

By using an *OpenFileDialog* control to prompt the user for the file's path, you can let the user choose which text file to open in a program. This control contains the *Filter* property, which controls the type of files displayed; the *ShowDialog* method, which displays the Open dialog box; and the *FileName* property, which returns the path specified by the user. The *OpenFileDialog* control doesn't open the file; it just gets the path.

There are several ways to read text files, but the two most common ways are to use the *My* namespace or the *StreamReader* class. The *StreamReader* class offers more features than the *My* namespace, in particular the ability to process files one line at a time (a capability that might be needed for sorting and parsing tasks). So it is best to master both methods for opening text files discussed in this chapter. The one that you use in actual programming practice will depend on the task at hand and the way you plan to use your code in the future.

The *My* Namespace

The *My* namespace is a rapid access feature designed to simplify accessing the .NET Framework to perform common tasks, such as manipulating forms, exploring the host computer and its file system, displaying information about the current application or its user, and accessing Web services. Most of these capabilities were previously available through the .NET Framework Base Class Library, but due to its complexity, many programmers found the features difficult to locate and use. The *My* namespace was added in Microsoft Visual Studio 2005 to make programming easier.

The *My* namespace is organized into several categories of functionality, as shown in Table 13-1. (*My.Log*, *My.Response*, and *My.Request* are not listed here because they are designed for ASP.NET applications only.)

TABLE 13-1 The *My* Namespace

Object	Description
My.Application	Information related to the current application, including the title, directory, and version number.
My.Computer	Information about the hardware, software, and files located on the current (local) computer. *My.Computer* includes *My.Computer.FileSystem*, which you can use to open text files and encoded files on the system.
My.Forms	Information about the forms in your current Visual Studio project. Chapter 14, "Managing Windows Controls and Forms at Run Time," shows how to use *My.Forms* to switch back and forth between forms at run time.
My.Resources	Information about your application's resources (read only). Allows you to dynamically retrieve resources for your application.
My.Settings	Information about your application's settings. Allows you to dynamically store and retrieve property settings and other information for your application.
My.User	Information about the current user active on *My.Computer*.
My.WebServices	Information about Web services active on *My.Computer*, and a mechanism to access new Web services.

The *My* namespace is truly a "speed dial" feature, fully explorable via the Microsoft IntelliSense feature of the Code Editor. For example, to use a message box to display the name of the current computer followed by the name of the current user in a program, you can simply type:

```
MsgBox(My.User.Name)
```

This produces output similar to the following:

The *My.Computer* object can display many categories of information about your computer and its files. For example, the following statement displays the current system time (the local date and time) maintained by the computer:

```
MsgBox(My.Computer.Clock.LocalTime)
```

This produces output like this (your date and time will probably be different):

You can use the *My.Computer.FileSystem* object along with the *ReadAllText* method to open a text file and display its contents within a text box object. Here's the syntax you can use if you have a text box object on your form named *txtNote* (as in the last sample program) and you plan to use an open file dialog object named *OpenFileDialog1* to get the name of the text file from the user:

```
Dim AllText As String = ""
OpenFileDialog1.Filter = "Text files (*.txt)|*.txt"
If OpenFileDialog1.ShowDialog() = DialogResult.OK Then 'display Open dialog box
    AllText = My.Computer.FileSystem.ReadAllText(OpenFileDialog1.FileName)
    txtNote.Text = AllText 'display file
End If
```

The *ReadAllText* method copies the entire contents of the specified text file to a string variable or object (in this case, a string variable named *AllText*), so in terms of performance and coding time, *ReadAllText* is faster than reading the file one line at a time.

Because of this speed factor, the *My* namespace provides an excellent shortcut to many common programming tasks. It is important to take note of this feature and its possible uses, but the *My* namespace is efficient here because we are reading the entire text file.

If you forget the syntax for the *ReadAllText* method, you can quickly insert an example by using the Insert Snippet command. As described in Chapter 7, "Using Loops and Timers," the Insert Snippet command allows you to insert common code snippets in the Code Editor. To insert the *ReadAllText* method, display the Code Editor, and on the Edit menu, click IntelliSense, and then click Insert Snippet. In the Insert Snippet list box, double-click Fundamentals – Collections, Data Types, File System, Math; double-click File System – Processing Drives, Folders, And Files; and then double-click Read Text From A File. This inserts the following code snippet:

```
Dim fileContents1 As String
fileContents1 = My.Computer.FileSystem.ReadAllText("C:\Test.txt")
```

The *StreamReader* Class

The *StreamReader* class in the .NET Framework library allows you to open and display text files in your programs. I'll use this technique several times in this book when I work with text files (for example, in Chapter 16, "Inheriting Forms and Creating Base Classes"). To make it easier to use the *StreamReader* class, you add the following *Imports* statement to the top of your code, as discussed in Chapter 5, "Visual Basic Variables and Formulas, and the .NET Framework":

```
Imports System.IO
```

Then, if your program contains a text box object, you can display a text file inside the text box by using the following program code. (The text file opened in this example is Badbills.txt, and the code assumes that an object named *TextBox1* has been created on your form.)

```
Dim StreamToDisplay As StreamReader
StreamToDisplay = New StreamReader("C:\vb10sbs\chap13\text browser\badbills.txt")
TextBox1.Text = StreamToDisplay.ReadToEnd
StreamToDisplay.Close()
```

In this *StreamReader* example, I declare a variable named *StreamToDisplay* of the type *StreamReader* to hold the contents of the text file, and then I specify a valid path for the file I want to open. Next, I read the contents of the text file into the *StreamToDisplay* variable by using the *ReadToEnd* method, which retrieves all the text in the file from the current location (the beginning of the text file) to the end of the text file and assigns it to the *Text* property of the text box object. The final statement closes the *StreamReader*. Closing the

StreamReader can be important because if you try to read or write to the file again, you might get an exception indicating that the process cannot access the file.

You can also use a combination of the *My* namespace and the *StreamReader* class. The following example reads text from a file line by line and displays it in a text box. The *OpenTextFileReader* method in the *My* namespace opens a *StreamReader*. The *EndOfStream* property indicates the end of the file. The *ReadLine* method reads one line from the file. When you are finished with a *StreamReader*, you should close it by calling the *Close* method:

```
Dim AllText As String = "", LineOfText As String = ""
Dim StreamToDisplay As StreamReader
StreamToDisplay = My.Computer.FileSystem.OpenTextFileReader( _
    "C:\vb10sbs\chap13\text browser\badbills.txt")
Do Until StreamToDisplay.EndOfStream 'read lines from file
    LineOfText = StreamToDisplay.ReadLine()
    'add each line to the AllText variable
    AllText = AllText & LineOfText & vbCrLf
Loop
TextBox1.Text = AllText 'display file
StreamToDisplay.Close()
```

> **Tip** Text files that are opened by using this syntax are called *sequential files* because you must work with their contents in sequential order. In contrast, you can access the information in a database file in any order. (You'll learn more about databases in Chapter 18, "Getting Started with ADO.NET.")

Using the *ReadAllText* Method

The following exercise demonstrates how you can use an *OpenFileDialog* control and the *ReadAllText* method to open a text file. The exercise also demonstrates how you can display the contents of a text file in a text box. (For more information about using controls on the Dialogs tab of the Toolbox to create standard dialog boxes, see Chapter 4, "Working with Menus, Toolbars, and Dialog Boxes.")

Run the Text Browser program

1. Start Visual Studio, and open the Text Browser project in the C:\Vb10sbs\Chap13\Text Browser folder.

    The project opens in the Integrated Development Environment (IDE).

2. If the project's form isn't visible, display it now.

The Text Browser form opens, as shown here:

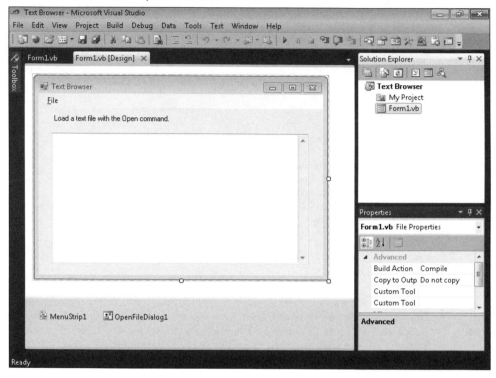

The form contains a large text box object that has scroll bars. It also contains a menu strip object that places Open, Close, and Exit commands on the File menu; an open file dialog object; and a label providing operating instructions. I also created the property settings shown in the following table. (Note especially the text box settings.)

Object	Property	Setting
txtNote	*Enabled*	False
	Multiline	True
	Name	txtNote
	ScrollBars	Both
CloseToolStripMenuItem	*Enabled*	False
lblNote	*Text*	"Load a text file with the Open command."
	Name	lblNote
Form1	*Text*	"Text Browser"

3. Click the Start Debugging button on the Standard toolbar.

The Text Browser program runs.

4. On the Text Browser File menu, click the Open command.

The Open dialog box opens.

5. Open the C:\Vb10sbs\Chap13\Text Browser folder.

The contents of the Text Browser folder are shown here:

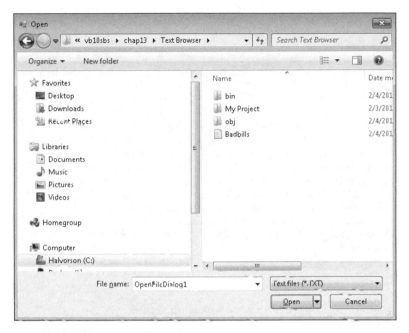

6. Double-click the Badbills file name.

Badbills, a text file containing an article written in 1951 in the United States about the dangers of counterfeit money, appears in the text box, as shown here:

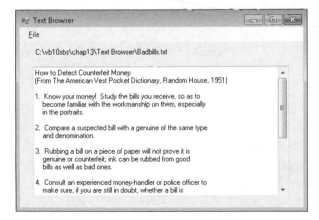

7. Use the scroll bars to view the entire document. Memorize number 5.

8. When you're finished, click the Close command on the File menu to close the file, and then click the Exit command to quit the program.

The program stops, and the IDE returns.

Now you'll look at two important event procedures in the program.

Examine the Text Browser program code

1. On the File menu of the Text Browser form, double-click the Open command.

The *OpenToolStripMenuItem_Click* event procedure appears in the Code Editor.

2. Resize the Code Editor to see more of the program code, if necessary.

The *OpenToolStripMenuItem_Click* event procedure contains the following program code:

```
Dim AllText As String = ""
OpenFileDialog1.Filter = "Text files (*.txt)|*.txt"
If OpenFileDialog1.ShowDialog() = DialogResult.OK Then 'display Open dialog box
    Try 'open file and trap any errors using handler
        AllText = My.Computer.FileSystem.ReadAllText(OpenFileDialog1.FileName)
        lblNote.Text = OpenFileDialog1.FileName  'update label
        txtNote.Text = AllText 'display file
        txtNote.Enabled = True 'allow text cursor
        CloseToolStripMenuItem.Enabled = True   'enable Close command
        OpenToolStripMenuItem.Enabled = False   'disable Open command
    Catch ex As Exception
        MsgBox("An error occurred." & vbCrLf & ex.Message)
    End Try
End If
```

This event procedure performs the following actions:

❑ Declares variables and assigns a value to the Filter property of the open file dialog object.

❑ Prompts the user for a path by using the *OpenFileDialog1* object.

❑ Traps errors by using a *Try … Catch* code block.

❑ Reads the entire contents of the specified file by using the *ReadAllText* method.

❑ Copies the contents of the file into a string named *AllText*. The *AllText* string has room for a very large file, but if an error occurs during the copying process, the *Catch* clause displays the error.

❑ Displays the *AllText* string in the text box, and enables the scroll bars and text cursor.

❑ Updates the File menu commands.

Take a moment to see how the statements in the *OpenToolStripMenuItem_Click* event procedure work—especially the *ReadAllText* method. The error handler in the procedure displays a message and aborts the loading process if an error occurs.

Tip For more information about the statements and methods, highlight the keyword you're interested in, and then press F1 to see a discussion of it in the Visual Studio Help documentation.

3. Display the *CloseToolStripMenuItem_Click* event procedure, which is executed when the Close menu command is clicked.

The event procedure looks like this:

```
txtNote.Text = ""                 'clear text box
lblNote.Text = "Load a text file with the Open command."
CloseToolStripMenuItem.Enabled = False  'disable Close command
OpenToolStripMenuItem.Enabled = True     'enable Open command
```

The procedure clears the text box, updates the *lblNote* label, disables the Close command, and enables the Open command.

Now you can use this simple program as a template for more advanced programs that process text files. In the next section, you'll learn how to type your own text into a text box and how to save the text in the text box to a file on disk.

Writing Text Files

To create and write to a new text file on disk by using Visual Basic, you can use many of the methods and keywords used in the last example. Creating new files on disk and saving data to them is useful if you plan to generate custom reports or logs, save important calculations or values, or create a special-purpose word processor or text editor. Here's an overview of the steps you'll need to follow in the program:

1. Get input from the user or perform mathematical calculations, or do both.

2. Assign the results of your processing to one or more variables. For example, you could assign the contents of a text box to a string variable.

3. Prompt the user for a path by using a *SaveFileDialog* control. You use the *ShowDialog* method to display the dialog box.

4. Use the path received in the dialog box to open the file for output.

5. Write one or more values to the open file.

6. If necessary, close the file when you're finished.

The *WriteAllText* Method

In the previous example, we used the *My.Computer.FileSystem* object with the *ReadAllText* method. Not surprisingly, this object also includes the *WriteAllText* method. The *WriteAllText* method writes text to a file. If a file does not exist, a new one is created. Here's the syntax you can use if you have a text box object on your form named *txtNote* (as in the last sample program) and you plan to use a save file dialog object named *SaveFileDialog1* to get the name of the text file from the user:

```
SaveFileDialog1.Filter = "Text files (*.txt)|*.txt"
If SaveFileDialog1.ShowDialog() = DialogResult.OK Then
    'copy text to disk
```

```
    My.Computer.FileSystem.WriteAllText( _
        SaveFileDialog1.FileName, txtNote.Text, False)
End If
```

WriteAllText takes three parameters. The first parameter specifies the file (in this case, the user specifies the file using *SaveFileDialog1*). The second parameter specifies the text to write to the file (in this case, the contents of the *txtNote* text box). The last parameter specifies whether to append the text or overwrite the existing text. A value of False for the last parameter directs Visual Basic to overwrite the existing text.

The *StreamWriter* Class

Similar to its companion, the *StreamReader* class, the *StreamWriter* class in the .NET Framework library allows you to write text to files in your programs. To make it easier to use the *StreamWriter* class, you add the following *Imports* statement to the top of your code:

```
Imports System.IO
```

Then, if your program contains a text box object, you can write the contents to a file by using the following program code. (The text file in this example is Output.txt, and the code assumes an object named *TextBox1* has been created on your form.)

```
Dim StreamToWrite As StreamWriter
StreamToWrite = New StreamWriter("C:\vb10sbs\chap13\output.txt")
StreamToWrite.Write(TextBox1.Text)
StreamToWrite.Close()
```

In this *StreamWriter* example, I declare a variable named *StreamToWrite* of the type *StreamWriter*, and then I specify a valid path for the file I want to write to. Next, I write the contents of the text box to the file by using the *Write* method. The final statement closes the *StreamWriter*. Closing the *StreamWriter* can be important because if you try to read or write to the file again, you might get an exception that indicates the process cannot access the file.

You can also use a combination of the *My* namespace and the *StreamWriter* class. The following example writes to a text file line by line. The *OpenTextFileWriter* method in the *My* namespace opens a *StreamWriter*. The *WriteLine* method writes one line to the file. When you are finished with a *StreamWriter*, you should close it by calling the *Close* method.

```
Dim LineOfText As String = ""
Dim StreamToWrite As StreamWriter
StreamToWrite = My.Computer.FileSystem.OpenTextFileWriter( _
    "C:\vb10sbs\chap13\output.txt", False)
'get line of text
LineOfText = InputBox("Enter line")
Do Until LineOfText = ""
    'write line to file
    StreamToWrite.WriteLine(LineOfText)
```

```
    LineOfText = InputBox("Enter line")
Loop
StreamToWrite.Close()
```

Using the *WriteAllText* Method

The following exercise demonstrates how you can use *TextBox* and *SaveFileDialog* controls to create a simple note-taking utility. The program uses the *WriteAllText* method to write string data in a file. You can use this program to take notes at home or at work and then to stamp them with the current date and time.

Run the Quick Note program

1. Click the Close Project command on the File menu.

2. Open the Quick Note project in the C:\Vb10sbs\Chap13\Quick Note folder.

   The project opens in the IDE.

3. If the project's form isn't visible, display it now.

   The Quick Note form opens, as shown in the following screen shot. It looks similar to the Text Browser form. However, I replaced the *OpenFileDialog* control with the *SaveFileDialog* control on the form. The File menu contains the Save As, Insert Date, and Exit commands.

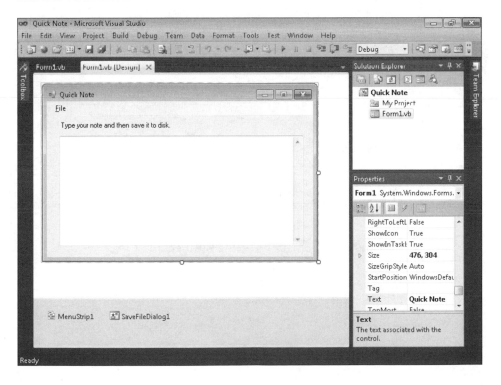

I set the following properties in the project:

Object	Property	Setting
txtNote	*Multiline*	True
	Name	txtNote
	ScrollBars	Vertical
lblNote	*Text*	"Type your note and then save it to disk."
Form1	*Text*	"Quick Note"

4. Click the Start Debugging button.

5. Type the following text, or some text of your own, in the text box:

How to Detect Counterfeit Coins

1. **Drop coins on a hard surface. Genuine coins have a bell-like ring; most counterfeit coins sound dull.**

2. **Feel all coins. Most counterfeit coins feel greasy.**

3. **Cut edges of questionable coins. Genuine coins are not easily cut.**

When you're finished, your screen looks similar to this:

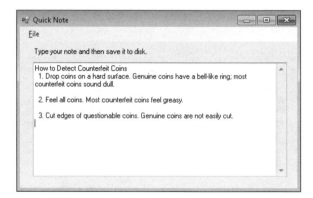

 Tip To paste text from the Clipboard into the text box, press CTRL+V or SHIFT+INSERT. To copy text from the text box to the Clipboard, select the text, and then press CTRL+C.

Now try using the commands on the File menu.

6. On the File menu, click the Insert Date command.

The current date and time appear as the first line in the text box, as shown here:

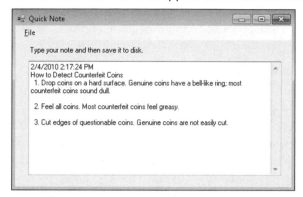

The Insert Date command provides a handy way to include the current time stamp in a file, which is useful if you're creating a diary or a logbook.

7. On the File menu, click the Save As command.

The program displays a Save As dialog box with all the expected features. The default file type is set to .txt. Your screen looks like the following:

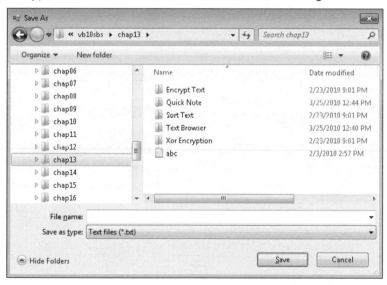

8. In the Save As dialog box, open the C:\Vb10sbs\Chap13\Quick Note folder if it isn't already open. Then type **Badcoins.txt** in the File Name text box, and click Save.

The text of your document is saved in the new Badcoins.txt text file.

9. On the File menu, click the Exit command.

The program stops, and the development environment returns.

Now you'll look at the event procedures in the program.

Examine the Quick Note program code

1. On the File menu of the Quick Note form, double-click the Insert Date command.

   The *InsertDateToolStripMenuItem_Click* event procedure appears in the Code Editor. You see the following program code:

   ```
   txtNote.Text = My.Computer.Clock.LocalTime & vbCrLf & txtNote.Text
   txtNote.Select(0, 0)   'remove selection
   ```

   This event procedure adds the current date and time to the text box by linking, or *concatenating*, the current date (generated by the *My.Computer.Clock* object and the *LocalTime* property), a carriage return (added by the *vbCrLf* constant), and the *Text* property. You could use a similar technique to add just the current date (by using *DateString*) or any other information to the text in the text box.

   When you insert the date using the Insert Date command, sometimes the text is selected. To remove this selection, the *Select* method is called. The selection is set to the beginning of the text box by specifying 0 in the first parameter, and the length of the selection is set to 0 in the second parameter. This removes any selections and positions the cursor at the beginning of the text box.

2. Take a moment to see how the concatenation statements work, and then examine the *SaveAsToolStripMenuItem_Click* event procedure in the Code Editor.

   You see the following program code:

   ```
   SaveFileDialog1.Filter = "Text files (*.txt)|*.txt"
   If SaveFileDialog1.ShowDialog() = DialogResult.OK Then
       'copy text to disk
       My.Computer.FileSystem.WriteAllText( _
           SaveFileDialog1.FileName, txtNote.Text, False)
   End If
   ```

   This block of statements uses a save file dialog object to display a Save As dialog box, verifies whether the user selected a file, and writes the value in the *txtNote.Text* property to disk by using the *WriteAllText* method. Note especially the statement:

   ```
   My.Computer.FileSystem.WriteAllText( _
       SaveFileDialog1.FileName, txtNote.Text, False)
   ```

   which assigns the entire contents of the text box to the file. The important point to note here is that the entire file is stored in the *txtNote.Text* property.

3. Close the program by using the Close Project command on the File menu.

You're finished with the Quick Note program.

Processing Strings with the *String* Class

As you learned in the preceding exercises, you can quickly open, edit, and save text files to disk with the *TextBox* control and a handful of well-chosen program statements. Visual Basic also provides a number of powerful statements and methods specifically designed for processing the textual elements in your programs. In this section, you'll learn about several ways to process strings.

The most common task you've accomplished so far with strings in this book is concatenating them by using the concatenation operator (&). For example, the following program statement concatenates three literal string expressions and assigns the result "Bring on the circus!" to the string variable *Slogan*:

```
Dim Slogan As String
Slogan = "Bring" & " on the " & "circus!"
```

You can also concatenate and manipulate strings by using methods in the *String* class of the .NET Framework library. For example, the *String.Concat* method allows equivalent string concatenation by using this syntax:

```
Dim Slogan As String
Slogan = String.Concat("Bring", " on the ", "circus!")
```

Visual Basic 2010 features two methods for string concatenation and many other string-processing tasks: You can use operators and functions from earlier versions of Visual Basic (*Mid*, *UCase*, *LCase*, and so on), or you can use newer methods from the .NET Framework (*Substring*, *ToUpper*, *ToLower*, and so on). There's no real penalty for using either string-processing technique, although the older methods exist primarily for compatibility purposes. (By supporting both methods, Microsoft hopes to welcome upgraders and their existing code base, allowing them to learn new features at their own pace.) In the rest of this chapter, I'll focus on the newer string-processing functions from the .NET Framework *String* class. However, you can use either string-processing method or a combination of both.

Table 13-2 lists several methods and one property in the *String* class that appear in subsequent exercises and their close equivalents in the Visual Basic programming language. The fourth column in the table provides sample code using the *String* class.

TABLE 13-2 Elements of the *String* Class and Visual Basic Equivalents

String Method or Property	Visual Basic Function	Description	*String* Example

ToUpper	UCase	Changes letters in a string to uppercase.	`Dim Name, NewName As String`
			`Name = "Kim"`
			`NewName = Name.ToUpper`
			`'NewName = "KIM"`

ToLower	LCase	Changes letters in a string to lowercase.	`Dim Name, NewName As String`
			`Name = "Kim"`
			`NewName = Name.ToLower`
			`'NewName = "kim"`

Length	Len	Determines the number of characters in a string.	`Dim River As String`
			`Dim Size As Short`
			`River = "Mississippi"`
			`Size = River.Length`
			`'Size = 11`

String Method or Property	Visual Basic Function	Description	*String* Example

Contains	*Instr*	Determines whether the specified string occurs in the current string.	```Dim region As String```
			 ```Dim result As Boolean```
			 ```region = "Germany"```
			 ```result = region.Contains("Ge")```
			 ```'result = True```

Substring	*Mid*	Returns a fixed number of characters in a string from a given starting point. (Note: The first element in a string has an index of 0.)	```Dim Cols, Middle As String```
			 ```Cols = "First Second Third"```
			 ```Middle = Cols.SubString(6, 6)```
			 ```'Middle = "Second"```

IndexOf	*InStr*	Finds the starting point of one string within a larger string.	```Dim Name As String```
			 ```Dim Start As Short```
			 ```Name = "Abraham"```
			 ```Start = Name.IndexOf("h")```
			 ```'Start = 4```

Trim	*Trim*	Removes leading and following spaces from a string.	```Dim Spacey, Trimmed As String```
			 ```Spacey = " Hello "```
			 ```Trimmed = Spacey.Trim```
			 ```'Trimmed = "Hello"```

Remove	*N/A*	Removes characters from the middle of a string.	```Dim RawStr, CleanStr As String```
			 ```RawStr = "Hello333 there"```
			 ```CleanStr = RawStr.Remove(5, 3)```
			 ```'CleanStr = "Hello there"```

Insert	*N/A*	Adds characters to the middle of a string.	```Dim Oldstr, Newstr As String```
			 ```Oldstr = "Hi Felix"```
			 ```Newstr = Oldstr.Insert(3, "there ")```
			 ```'Newstr = "Hi there Felix"```

Compare	*StrComp*	Compares strings and can disregard case differences.	```Dim str1 As String = "Soccer"```
			 ```Dim str2 As String = "SOCCER"```
			 ```Dim Match As Integer```
			 ```Match = String.Compare(str1, _```
			 ``` str2, True)```
			 ```'Match = 0 [strings match]```

CompareTo	*StrComp*	Compares a string to the current string and checks for case differences	```Dim str1 As String = "Soccer"```
			 ```Dim str2 As String = "SOCCER"```
			 ```Dim Match As Integer```
			 ```Match = str1.CompareTo(str2)```
			 ```'Match = -1 [strings do not match]```

Replace	*Replace*	Replaces all instances of a substring in a string with another string.	```Dim Oldstr, Newstr As String```
			 ```Oldstr= "*se*ll"```
			 ```Newstr = Oldstr.Replace(_```
			 ``` "*", "ba")```
			 ```'Newstr = "baseball"```

String Method or Property	Visual Basic Function	Description	*String* Example

StartsWith	N/A	Determines whether a string starts with a specified string.	```Dim str1 As String```
			```Dim result As Boolean```
			```str1 = "Hi Felix"```
			```result = str1.StartsWith("Hi")```
			```'result = True```

EndsWith	N/A	Determines whether a string ends with a specified string.	```Dim str1 As String```
			```Dim result As Boolean```
			```str1 = "Hi Felix"```
			```result = str1.EndsWith("Felix")```
			```'result = True```

Split	*Split*	Splits a string into substrings based on a specified separator and puts the substring in an array.	```Dim AllText As String = _```
			``` "a*b*c*1*2*3"```
			```Dim strArray() As String```
			```strArray = AllText.Split("*")```
			```'strArray =```
			```' {"a", "b", "c", "1", "2", "3"}```

Sorting Text

An extremely useful skill to develop when working with textual elements is the ability to sort a list of strings. The basic concepts in sorting are simple. You draw up a list of items to sort and then compare the items one by one until the list is sorted in ascending or descending alphabetical order.

In Visual Basic, you compare one item with another by using the same relational operators that you use to compare numeric values. The tricky part (which sometimes provokes long-winded discussions among computer scientists) is the specific sorting algorithm that you use to compare elements in a list. We won't get into the advantages and disadvantages of different sorting algorithms in this chapter. (The bone of contention is usually speed, which makes a difference only when several thousand items are sorted.) Instead, we'll explore how the basic string comparisons are made in a sort. Along the way, you'll learn the skills necessary to sort your own text boxes, list boxes, files, and databases.

Before Visual Basic can compare one character with another in a sort, it must convert each character into a number by using a translation table called the *ASCII character set* (also called the *ANSI character set*). (The acronym ASCII stands for American Standard Code for Information Interchange.) Each of the basic symbols that you can display on your computer has a different ASCII code. These codes include the basic set of "typewriter" characters (codes 32 through 127) and special "control" characters, such as tab, line feed, and carriage return (codes 0 through 31). For example, the lowercase letter *a* corresponds to the ASCII code 97, and the uppercase letter *A* corresponds to the ASCII code 65. As a result, Visual Basic treats these two characters quite differently when sorting or performing other comparisons.

In the 1980s, IBM extended ASCII with codes 128 through 255, which represent accented, Greek, and graphic characters, as well as miscellaneous symbols. ASCII and these additional characters and symbols are typically known as the *IBM extended character set.*

The ASCII character set is still the most important numeric code for beginning programmers to learn, but it isn't the only character set. As the market for computers and application software has become more global, a more comprehensive standard for character representation called *Unicode* has emerged. Unicode can hold up to 65,536 symbols—plenty of space to represent the traditional symbols in the ASCII character set plus most (written) international languages and symbols. A standards body maintains the Unicode character set and adds symbols to it periodically. Windows XP, Windows Vista, Windows 7, and Visual Studio have been specifically designed to manage ASCII and Unicode character sets. (For more information about the relationship between Unicode, ASCII, and Visual Basic data types, see the section entitled "Working with Specific Data Types" in Chapter 5.)

In the following sections, you'll learn more about using the ASCII character set to process strings in your programs. As your applications become more sophisticated and you start planning for the global distribution of your software, you'll need to learn more about Unicode and other international settings.

Working with ASCII Codes

To determine the ASCII code of a particular letter, you can use the Visual Basic *Asc* function. For example, the following program statement assigns the number 122 (the ASCII code for the lowercase letter *z*) to the *AscCode* short integer variable:

```
Dim AscCode As Short
AscCode = Asc("z")
```

Conversely, you can convert an ASCII code to a letter with the *Chr* function. For example, this program statement assigns the letter *z* to the letter character variable:

```
Dim letter As Char
letter = Chr(122)
```

The same result could also be achieved if you used the *AscCode* variable just declared, as shown here:

```
letter = Chr(AscCode)
```

How can you compare one text string or ASCII code with another? You simply use one of the six relational operators Visual Basic supplies for working with textual and numeric elements. These relational operators are shown in Table 13-3.

TABLE 13-3 **Visual Basic Relational Operators**

Operator	Meaning
< >	Not equal to
=	Equal to
<	Less than
>	Greater than
< =	Less than or equal to
> =	Greater than or equal to

A character is "greater than" another character if its ASCII code is higher. For example, the ASCII value of the letter *B* is greater than the ASCII value of the letter *A*, so the expression:

```
"A" < "B"
```

is true, and the expression:

```
"A" > "B"
```

is false.

When comparing two strings that each contain more than one character, Visual Basic begins by comparing the first character in the first string with the first character in the second string and then proceeds character by character through the strings until it finds a difference. For example, the strings *Mike* and *Michael* are the same up to the third characters (*k* and *c*). Because the ASCII value of *k* is greater than that of *c*, the expression:

```
"Mike" > "Michael"
```

is true.

If no differences are found between the strings, they are equal. If two strings are equal through several characters but one of the strings continues and the other one ends, the longer string is greater than the shorter string. For example, the expression:

```
"AAAAA" > "AAA"
```

is true.

Sorting Strings in a Text Box

The following exercise demonstrates how you can use relational operators, concatenation, and several string methods to sort lines of text in a text box. The program is a revision of the Quick Note utility and features an Open command that opens an existing file and a Close command that closes the file. There's also a Sort Text command on the File menu that you can use to sort the text currently displayed in the text box.

Because the entire contents of a text box are stored in one string, the program must first break that long string into smaller individual strings. These strings can then be sorted by using the *ShellSort* Sub procedure, a sorting routine based on an algorithm created by Donald Shell in 1959. To simplify these tasks, I created a module for the *ShellSort* Sub procedure so that I can call it from any event procedure in the project. (For more about using modules, see Chapter 10, "Creating Modules and Procedures.") Although you learned how to use the powerful *Array.Sort* method in Chapter 11, "Using Arrays to Manage Numeric and String Data," the *ShellSort* procedure is a more flexible and customizable tool. Building the routine from scratch also gives you a little more experience with processing textual values—an important learning goal of this chapter.

Another interesting aspect of this program is the routine that processes the lines in the text box object. I wanted the program to be able to sort a text box of any size. To accomplish this, I created the code that follows. The code uses the *Replace*, *EndsWith*, and *Substring* methods of the *String* class. The *Replace* method is used to replace the different newline characters (carriage return, line feed, or carriage return and line feed) with just the carriage return character. The *EndsWith* method checks for a carriage return at the very end of the text. The *Substring* method is used to remove the last carriage return if it exists:

```
sText = txtNote.Text
'replace different new line characters with one version
sText = sText.Replace(vbCrLf, vbCr)
sText = sText.Replace(vbLf, vbCr)
'remove last carriage return if it exists
If sText.EndsWith(vbCr) Then
    sText = sText.Substring(0, sText.Length - 1)
End If

'split each line in to an array
strArray = sText.Split(vbCr)
```

This code also uses the very handy *Split* method of the *String* class. The *Split* method breaks a string down into substrings and puts each substring into an array. The breaks are based on a separator string that you specify (in this case, a carriage return). The resulting array of strings then gets passed to the *ShellSort* Sub procedure for sorting, and *ShellSort* returns the string array in alphabetical order. After the string array is sorted, I can simply copy it back to the text box by using a *For* loop.

Run the Sort Text program

1. Open the Sort Text project located in the C:\Vb10sbs\Chap13\Sort Text folder.

2. Click the Start Debugging button to run the program.

3. Type the following text, or some text of your own, in the text box:

Zebra

Gorilla

Moon

Banana

Apple

Turtle

4. Click the Sort Text command on the File menu.

The text you typed is sorted and redisplayed in the text box as follows:

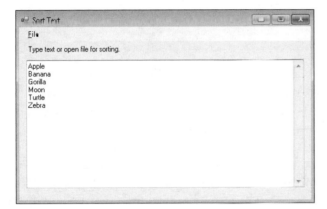

5. Click the Open command on the File menu, and then open the Abc.txt file in the C:\Vb10sbs\Chap13 folder, as shown here:

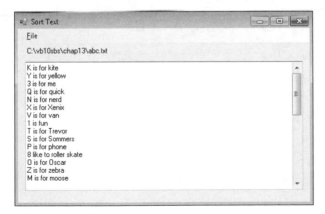

The Abc.txt file contains 36 lines of text. Each line begins with either a letter or a number from 1 through 10.

6. Click the Sort Text command on the File menu to sort the contents of the Abc.txt file.

The Sort Text program sorts the file in ascending order and displays the sorted list of lines in the text box, as shown here:

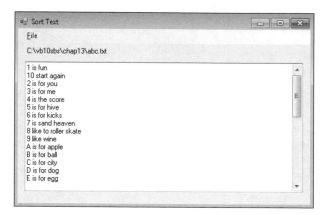

7. Scroll through the file to see the results of the alphabetical sort.

Notice that although the alphabetical portion of the sort ran perfectly, the sort produced a strange result for one of the numeric entries—the line beginning with the number 10 appears second in the list rather than tenth. What's happening here is that Visual Basic read the 1 and the 0 in the number 10 as two independent characters, not as a number. Because we're comparing the ASCII codes of these strings from left to right, the program produces a purely alphabetical sort. If you want to sort only numbers with this program, you need to prohibit textual input, modify the code so that the numeric input is stored in numeric variables, and then compare the numeric variables instead of strings.

Examining the Sort Text Program Code

OK—let's take a closer look at the code for this program now.

Examine the Sort Text program

1. On the File menu of the Sort Text program, click the Exit command to stop the program.

2. Open the Code Editor for Form1, and then display the code for the *SortTextToolStripMenuItem_Click* event procedure.

We've already discussed the first part of this event procedure, which splits each line into an array. The remainder of the event procedure calls a procedure to sort the array, and displays the reordered list in the text box.

The entire *SortTextToolStripMenuItem_Click* event procedure looks like this:

```
Dim strArray() As String
Dim sText As String
Dim i As Short

sText = txtNote.Text
'replace different new line characters with one version
sText = sText.Replace(vbCrLf, vbCr)
sText = sText.Replace(vbLf, vbCr)
'remove last carriage return if it exists
If sText.EndsWith(vbCr) Then
    sText = sText.Substring(0, sText.Length - 1)
End If

'split each line in to an array
strArray = sText.Split(vbCr)

'sort array
ShellSort(strArray, strArray.Length)

'then display sorted array in text box
sText = ""
For i = 0 To strArray.Length - 1
    sText = sText & strArray(i) & vbCrLf
Next i
txtNote.Text = sText
txtNote.Select(0, 0)    'remove text selection
```

The *Split* method creates an array that has the same number of elements as the text box has lines of text. After the array is full of text, I call the *ShellSort* procedure located in the Module1.vb module, which I discussed earlier in this chapter. After the array is sorted, I use a *For* loop (as discussed in Chapter 7) to reconstruct the lines and copy them into the text box.

3. Display the code for the Module1.vb module in the Code Editor.

This module defines the content of the *ShellSort* procedure. The *ShellSort* procedure uses an *If* statement and the <= relational operator (as discussed in Chapters 6, 8, and this chapter) to compare array elements and swap any that are out of order. The procedure looks like this:

```
Sub ShellSort(ByVal sort() As String, ByVal numOfElements As Short)
    Dim temp As String
    Dim i, j, span As Short
    'The ShellSort procedure sorts the elements of sort()
    'array in descending order and returns it to the calling
    'procedure.

    span = numOfElements \ 2
    Do While span > 0
```

```
        For i = span To numOfElements - 1
            For j = (i - span) To 0 Step -span
                If sort(j) <= sort(j + span) Then Exit For
                'swap array elements that are out of order
                temp = sort(j)
                sort(j) = sort(j + span)
                sort(j + span) = temp
            Next j
        Next i
        span = span \ 2
    Loop
End Sub
```

The method of the sort is to continually divide the main list of elements into sublists that are smaller by half. The sort then compares the tops and the bottoms of the sublists to see whether the elements are out of order. If the top and bottom are out of order, they're exchanged. The result is an array named *sort()* that's sorted alphabetically in descending order. To change the direction of the sort, simply reverse the relational operator (change <= to >=).

The remaining event procedures in Form1 (*OpenToolStripMenuItem_Click, CloseToolStripMenuItem_Click, SaveAsToolStripMenuItem_Click, InsertDateToolStripMenuItem_Click,* and *ExitToolStripMenuItem_Click*) are all similar to the procedures that you studied in the Text Browser and the Quick Note programs. (See my explanations earlier in this chapter for the details.)

Let's move on to another variation of this program that manipulates the strings in a text box or a file.

Protecting Text with Basic Encryption

Now that you've had some experience with ASCII codes, you can begin to write simple encryption routines that shift the ASCII codes in your documents and "scramble" the text to hide it from intruding eyes. This process, known as *encryption,* mathematically alters the characters in a file, making them unreadable to the casual observer. Of course, to use encryption successfully, you also need to be able to reverse the process—otherwise, you'll simply be trashing your files rather than protecting them. And you'll want to create an encryption scheme or *key* that can't be easily recognized, a complicated process that's only begun by the sample programs in this chapter.

The following exercises show you how to encrypt and decrypt text strings safely. You'll run the Encrypt Text program now to see a simple encryption scheme in action. As I note at the end of this chapter, these exercises are just the tip of the iceberg for using encryption, cryptography, and file security measures—and these issues have become major areas of interest for programmers in the last decade or so. Still, even basic encryption is fun and a useful demonstration of text-processing techniques.

Encrypt text by changing ASCII codes

1. Close the Sort Text project, and then open the Encrypt Text project located in the C:\Vb10sbs\Chap13\Encrypt Text folder.

2. Click the Start Debugging button to run the program.

3. Type the following text, or some text of your own, in the text box:

   Here at last, my friend, you have the little book long since expected and promised, a little book on vast matters, namely, "On my own ignorance and that of many others."

   Francesco Petrarca, c. 1368

   The resulting application window and text look something like this:

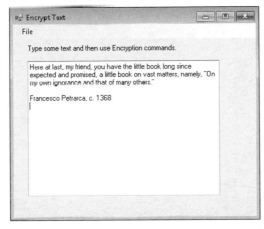

4. On the File menu, click the Save Encrypted File As command, and then save the file in the C:\Vb10sbs\Chap13 folder with the name **Padua.txt**.

   As you save the text file, the program scrambles the ASCII code and displays the results in the text box shown here:

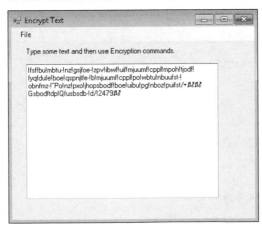

If you open this file in Microsoft Word or another text editor, you'll see the same result—the characters in the file have been encrypted to prevent unauthorized reading.

5. To restore the file to its original form, choose the Open Encrypted File command on the File menu, and then open the Padua.txt file in the C:\Vb10sbs\Chap13 folder.

The file appears again in its original form, as shown here:

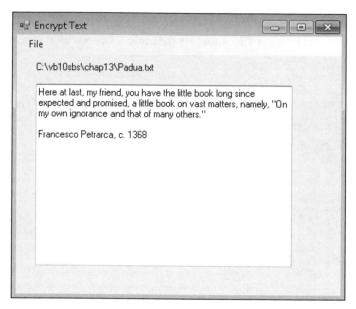

6. On the File menu, click the Exit command to end the program.

Examine the Encrypt program code

1. Open the *mnuSaveAsItem_Click* event procedure in the Code Editor to see the program code that produces the encryption that you observed when you ran the program.

Although the effect you saw might have looked mysterious, it was a very straightforward encryption scheme. Using the *Asc* and *Chr* functions and a *For* loop, I simply added one number to the ASCII code for each character in the text box and then saved the encrypted string to the specified text file.

The entire event procedure is listed here—in particular, note the items in bold:

```
Dim Encrypt As String = ""
Dim letter As Char
Dim i, charsInFile As Short

SaveFileDialog1.Filter = "Text files (*.txt)|*.txt"
If SaveFileDialog1.ShowDialog() = DialogResult.OK Then
    Try
        'save text with encryption scheme (ASCII code + 1)
        charsInFile = txtNote.Text.Length
```

```
        For i = 0 To charsInFile - 1
            letter = txtNote.Text.Substring(i, 1)
            'determine ASCII code and add one to it
            Encrypt = Encrypt & Chr(Asc(letter) + 1)
        Next
        'write encrypted text to file
        My.Computer.FileSystem.WriteAllText(SaveFileDialog1.FileName, Encrypt, False)
        txtNote.Text = Encrypt
        txtNote.Select(0, 0)    'remove text selection
        mnuCloseItem.Enabled = True
    Catch ex As Exception
        MsgBox("An error occurred." & vbCrLf & ex.Message)
    End Try
End If
```

Note especially the statement:

```
Encrypt = Encrypt & Chr(Asc(letter) + 1)
```

which determines the ASCII code of the current letter, adds 1 to it, converts the ASCII code back to a letter, and then adds it to the *Encrypt* string.

2. Now display the *mnuOpenItem_Click* event procedure in the Code Editor to see how the program reverses the encryption.

This program code is nearly identical to that of the Save Encrypted File As command, but rather than adding 1 to the ASCII code for each letter, it subtracts 1. Here's the complete *mnuOpenItem_Click* event procedure, with noteworthy statements in bold:

```
Dim AllText As String
Dim i, charsInFile As Short
Dim letter As Char
Dim Decrypt As String = ""

OpenFileDialog1.Filter = "Text files (*.txt)|*.txt"
If OpenFileDialog1.ShowDialog() = DialogResult.OK Then 'display Open dialog box
    If My.Computer.FileSystem.FileExists(OpenFileDialog1.FileName) Then
        Try 'open file and trap any errors using handler
            AllText = My.Computer.FileSystem.ReadAllText(OpenFileDialog1.FileName)
            'now, decrypt string by subtracting one from ASCII code
            charsInFile = AllText.Length 'get length of string
            For i = 0 To charsInFile - 1 'loop once for each char
                letter = AllText.Substring(i, 1) 'get character
                Decrypt = Decrypt & Chr(Asc(letter) - 1) 'subtract 1
            Next i 'and build new string
            txtNote.Text = Decrypt 'then display converted string
            lblNote.Text = OpenFileDialog1.FileName
            txtNote.Select(0, 0)    'remove text selection
            txtNote.Enabled = True 'allow text cursor
            mnuCloseItem.Enabled = True  'enable Close command
            mnuOpenItem.Enabled = False  'disable Open command
        Catch ex As Exception
            MsgBox("An error occurred." & vbCrLf & ex.Message)
        End Try
    End If
End If
```

This type of simple encryption might be all you need to conceal the information in your text files. However, files encrypted in this way can easily be decoded. By searching for possible equivalents of common characters such as the space character, determining the ASCII shift required to restore the common character, and running the conversion for the entire text file, a person experienced in encryption could readily decipher the file's content. Also, this sort of encryption doesn't prevent a malicious user from physically tampering with the file—for example, simply by deleting it if it's unprotected on your system or by modifying it in significant ways. But if you just want to hide information quickly, this simple encryption scheme should do the trick.

One Step Further: Using the *Xor* Operator

The preceding encryption scheme is quite safe for text files because it shifts the ASCII character code value up by just 1. However, you'll want to be careful about shifting ASCII codes more than a few characters if you store the result as text in a text file. Keep in mind that dramatic shifts in ASCII codes (such as adding 500 to each character code) won't produce actual ASCII characters that can be decrypted later. For example, adding 500 to the ASCII code for the letter *A* (65) would give a result of 565. This value couldn't be translated into a character by the *Chr* function and would generate an error.

One way around this problem is to convert the letters in your file to numbers when you encrypt the file so that you can reverse the encryption no matter how large (or small) the numbers are. If you followed this line of thought, you could then apply mathematical functions—multiplication, logarithms, and so on—to the numbers so long as you knew how to reverse the results.

One tool for encrypting numeric values is already built into Visual Basic. This tool is the *Xor operator*, which performs the "exclusive or" operation, a function carried out on the bits that make up the number itself. The *Xor* operator can be observed by using a simple *MsgBox* function. For example, the program statement:

```
MsgBox(Asc("A") Xor 50)
```

would display a numeric result of 115 in a message box when the Visual Basic compiler executes it. Likewise, the program statement:

```
MsgBox(115 Xor 50)
```

would display a result of 65 in a message box, the ASCII code for the letter *A* (our original value). In other words, the *Xor* operator produces a result that can be reversed—if the original *Xor* code is used again on the result of the first operation. This interesting behavior of the *Xor* function is used in many popular encryption algorithms. It can make your secret files more difficult to decode.

Run the Xor Encryption program now to see how the *Xor* operator works in the note-taking utility you've been building.

Encrypt text with the *Xor* operator

1. Close the Encrypt Text project, and then open the Xor Encryption project in the C:\Vb10sbs\Chap13\Xor Encryption folder.

2. Click the Start Debugging button to run the program.

3. Type the following text (or some of your own) in the encrypted text file:

   Rothair's Edict (Lombard Italy, c. 643) 296.

   On Stealing Grapes. He who takes more than three grapes from another man's vine shall pay six soldi as compensation. He who takes less than three shall bear no guilt.

4. On the File menu, click the Save Encrypted File As command, and then save the file in the C:\Vb10sbs\Chap13 folder with the name **Oldlaws.txt**.

   The program prompts you for a secret encryption code (a number) that will be used to encrypt the file and decrypt it later. (Take note—you'll need to remember this code to decode the file.)

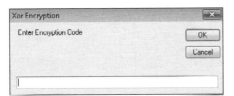

5. Type **500**, or another numeric code, and then press ENTER.

   Visual Basic encrypts the text by using the *Xor* operator and then stores it on disk as a series of numbers. You won't see any change on your screen, but rest assured that the program created an encrypted file on disk. (You can verify this with a word processor or a text editor.)

6. Click the Close command on the program's File menu to clear the text in the text box.

   Now you'll restore the encrypted file.

7. On the File menu, click the Open Encrypted File command.

8. Open the C:\Vb10sbs\Chap13 folder, and then double-click the Oldlaws.txt file.

9. Type **500** (or the encryption code that you specified, if different) in the Xor Encryption dialog box when it appears, and then click OK.

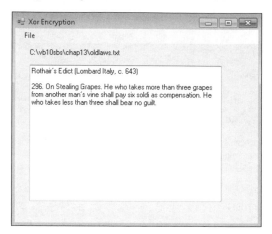

The program opens the file and restores the text by using the *Xor* operator and the encryption code you specified.

10. On the File menu, click the Exit command to end the program.

Examining the Encryption Program Code

The *Xor* operator is used in both the *mnuSaveAsItem_Click* and the *mnuOpenItem_Click* event procedures. By now, these generic menu processing routines will be fairly familiar to you. The *mnuSaveAsItem_Click* event procedure consists of these program statements (noteworthy lines in bold):

```
Dim letter As Char
Dim strCode As String
Dim i, charsInFile, Code As Short
Dim StreamToWrite As StreamWriter = Nothing

SaveFileDialog1.Filter = "Text files (*.txt)|*.txt"
If SaveFileDialog1.ShowDialog() = DialogResult.OK Then
    Try
        strCode = InputBox("Enter Encryption Code")
        If strCode = "" Then Exit Sub 'if cancel clicked
        'save text with encryption scheme
        Code = CShort(strCode)
        charsInFile = txtNote.Text.Length
        StreamToWrite = My.Computer.FileSystem.OpenTextFileWriter( _
            SaveFileDialog1.FileName, False)
        For i = 0 To charsInFile - 1
            letter = txtNote.Text.Substring(i, 1)
            'convert to number w/ Asc, then use Xor to encrypt
            StreamToWrite.Write(Asc(letter) Xor Code) 'and save in file
            'separate numbers with a space
            StreamToWrite.Write(" ")
        Next
        mnuCloseItem.Enabled = True
    Catch ex As Exception
```

```
                MsgBox("An error occurred." & vbCrLf & ex.Message)
        Finally
            If StreamToWrite IsNot Nothing Then
                StreamToWrite.Close()
            End If
        End Try
End If
```

In the *Write* method the *Xor* operator is used to convert each letter in the text box
to a numeric code, which is then saved to disk one number at time. The numbers are
separated with spaces.

The final result of this encryption is no longer textual, but numeric—guaranteed to bewilder
even the nosiest snooper. For example, the following screen shot shows the encrypted file
produced by the preceding encryption routine, displayed in Notepad. (I've enabled Word
Wrap so that you can see all the code.)

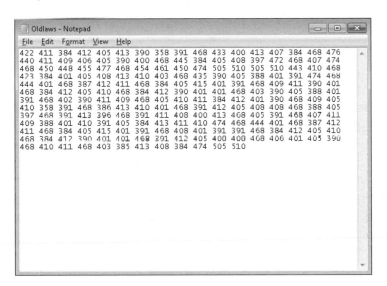

The *mnuOpenItem_Click* event procedure contains the following program statements.
(Again, pay particular attention to the lines in bold.)

```
Dim AllText As String
Dim i As Short
Dim ch As Char
Dim strCode As String
Dim Code, Number As Short
Dim Numbers() As String
Dim Decrypt As String = ""

OpenFileDialog1.Filter = "Text files (*.txt)|*.txt"
If OpenFileDialog1.ShowDialog() = DialogResult.OK Then 'display Open dialog box
    Try 'open file and trap any errors using handler
        strCode = InputBox("Enter Encryption Code")
        If strCode = "" Then Exit Sub 'if cancel clicked
```

```
        Code = CShort(strCode)
        'read encrypted numbers
        AllText = My.Computer.FileSystem.ReadAllText(OpenFileDialog1.FileName)
        AllText = AllText.Trim
        'split numbers in to an array based on space
        Numbers = AllText.Split(" ")
        'loop through array
        For i = 0 To Numbers.Length - 1
            Number = CShort(Numbers(i)) 'convert string to number
            ch = Chr(Number Xor Code) 'convert with Xor
            Decrypt = Decrypt & ch 'and build string
        Next
        txtNote.Text = Decrypt 'then display converted string
        lblNote.Text = OpenFileDialog1.FileName
        txtNote.Select(0, 0)    'remove text selection
        txtNote.Enabled = True 'allow text cursor
        mnuCloseItem.Enabled = True  'enable Close command
        mnuOpenItem.Enabled = False  'disable Open command
    Catch ex As Exception
        MsgBox("An error occurred." & vbCrLf & ex.Message)
    End Try
End If
```

When the user clicks the Open Encrypted File command, this event procedure opens the encrypted file, prompts the user for an encryption code, and displays the translated file in the text box object. The *ReadAllText* method reads the encrypted file. The *Split* method splits the numbers as strings into an array and uses the space as a separator. The *For* loop reads each string in the array, converts the string to a number, and stores it in the *Number* short integer variable. The *Number* variable is then combined with the *Code* variable by using the *Xor* operator, and the result is converted to a character by using the *Chr* function. These characters (stored in the *ch* variable of type *Char*) are then concatenated with the *Decrypt* string variable, which eventually contains the entire decrypted text file, as shown here:

```
ch = Chr(Number Xor Code) 'convert with Xor
Decrypt = Decrypt & ch 'and build string
```

Encryption techniques like this are useful, and they can also be very instructional. Because encryption relies so much on string-processing techniques, it's a good way to practice a fundamental and important Visual Basic programming skill. As you become more experienced, you can also use the encryption services provided by the .NET Framework to add much more sophisticated security and cryptography services to your programs. For an introduction to these topics, search for "Cryptographic Tasks" in the Visual Studio Help documentation. Because these services rely somewhat on your understanding of classes, containers, and Internet transactions, I recommend that you finish the chapters in Parts III and IV of this book before you experiment with them.

Well, now—congratulations! If you've worked from Chapters 5 to here, you've completed the programming fundamentals portion of this book, and you are now ready to focus specifically on creating professional-quality user interfaces in your programs. You have come a long way in your study of Visual Basic programming skills and in your use of the Visual Studio IDE. Take a short break, and I'll see you again in Part III, "Designing the User Interface"!

Chapter 13 Quick Reference

To	Do This
Display an Open dialog box	Add an *OpenFileDialog* control to your form, and then use the *ShowDialog* method of the open file dialog object. For example:
| | ```
If OpenFileDialog1.ShowDialog() = DialogResult.OK Then
``` |
| Read a text file by using the *My* namespace | Use the *My.Computer.FileSystem* object and the *ReadAllText* method. For example (assuming that you are also using an open file dialog object named *ofd* and a text box object named *txtNote*): |
| | ```
Dim AllText As String = ""
ofd.Filter = "Text files (*.txt)|*.txt"
If ofd.ShowDialog() = DialogResult.OK Then
    AllText = _
        My.Computer.FileSystem.ReadAllText(ofd.FileName)
    txtNote.Text = AllText 'display file
End If
``` |
| Read a text file by using the *StreamReader* class | Add the statement *Imports System.IO* to your form's declaration section, and then use *StreamReader*. Use the *ReadToEnd* method to read the entire file. When finished, call the *Close* method. For example, to display the file in a text box object named *TextBox1*: |
| | ```
Dim StreamToDisplay As StreamReader
StreamToDisplay = New StreamReader( _
    "c:\vb10sbs\chap13\text browser\badbills.txt")
TextBox1.Text = StreamToDisplay.ReadToEnd
StreamToDisplay.Close()
``` |
| Read a text file line by line | Use *StreamReader* and the *ReadLine* method. Use the *OpenTextFileReader* method in the *My* namespace to open a *StreamReader*. To check for the end of the file, use the *EndOfStream* property: |
| | ```
Dim AllText As String = "", LineOfText As String = ""
Dim StreamToDisplay As StreamReader
StreamToDisplay = My.Computer.FileSystem.OpenTextFileReader( _
    "C:\vb10sbs\chap13\text browser\badbills.txt")
Do Until StreamToDisplay.EndOfStream 'read lines from file
    LineOfText = StreamToDisplay.ReadLine()
    AllText = AllText & LineOfText & vbCrLf
Loop
TextBox1.Text = AllText 'display file
StreamToDisplay.Close()
``` |
| Display a Save As dialog box | Add a *SaveFileDialog* control to your form, and then use the *ShowDialog* method of the save file dialog object. For example: |
| | ```
If SaveFileDialog1.ShowDialog() = DialogResult.OK Then
``` |
```

To	Do This
Write a text file by using the *My* namespace	Use the *My.Computer.FileSystem* object and the *WriteAllText* method. For example (assuming that you are also using a save file dialog object named *sfd* and a text box object named *txtNote*): ```\nsfd.Filter = "Text files (*.txt)|*.txt"\nIf sfd.ShowDialog() = DialogResult.OK Then\n My.Computer.FileSystem.WriteAllText(_\n sfd.FileName, txtNote.Text, False)\nEnd If\n```
Write a text file by using the *StreamWriter* class	Add the statement *Imports System.IO* to your form's declaration section, and then use *StreamWriter*. Use the *Write* method to write the text. When finished, call the *Close* method. For example, to write the contents of a text box object named *TextBox1* to a file: ```\nDim StreamToWrite As StreamWriter\nStreamToWrite = New StreamWriter(_\n "c:\vb10sbs\chap13\output.txt")\nStreamToWrite.Write(TextBox1.Text)\nStreamToWrite.Close()\n```
Write a text file line by line	Use *StreamWriter* and the *WriteLine* method. Use the *OpenTextFileWriter* method in the *My* namespace to open a *StreamWriter*: ```\nDim LineOfText As String = ""\nDim StreamToWrite As StreamWriter\nStreamToWrite = My.Computer.FileSystem.OpenTextFileWriter(_\n "C:\vb10sbs\chap13\output.txt", False)\nLineOfText = InputBox("Enter line")\nDo Until LineOfText = ""\n StreamToWrite.WriteLine(LineOfText)\n LineOfText = InputBox("Enter line")\nLoop\nStreamToWrite.Close()\n```
Process strings	Use the *String* class. Some of the members of *String* include: ■ *Compare* ■ *Remove* ■ *CompareTo* ■ *Replace* ■ *Contains* ■ *StartsWith* ■ *EndsWith* ■ *Substring* ■ *IndexOf* ■ *ToLower* ■ *Insert* ■ *ToUpper* ■ *Length* ■ *Trim*
Convert a string with separators to an array	Use the *Split* method on the *String* class. For example: ```\nDim AllText As String = "a*b*c*1*2*3"\nDim strArray() As String\nstrArray = AllText.Split("*")\n'strArray = {"a", "b", "c", "1", "2", "3"}\n```

To	Do This
Convert text characters to ASCII codes	Use the *Asc* function. For example: ``` Dim Code As Short Code = Asc("A") 'Code equals 65 ```
Convert ASCII codes to text characters	Use the *Chr* function. For example: ``` Dim Letter As Char Letter = Chr(65) 'Letter equals "A" ```

Encrypt text	Use the *Xor* operator and a user-defined encryption code. For example, this code block uses *Xor* and a user code to encrypt the text in the *txtNote* text box and to save it in the encrypt.txt file as a series of numbers:
	
	``
	strCode = InputBox("Enter Encryption Code")
	Code = CShort(strCode)
	charsInFile = txtNote.Text.Length
	StreamToWrite = My.Computer.FileSystem.OpenTextFileWriter(_
	  SaveFileDialog1.FileName, False)
	For i = 0 To charsInFile - 1
	    letter = txtNote.Text.Substring(i, 1)
	    StreamToWrite.Write(Asc(letter) Xor Code)
	    StreamToWrite.Write(" ")
	Next
	StreamToWrite.Close()
	``

Decrypt text	Request the code that the user chose to encrypt the text, and use *Xor* to decrypt the text. For example, this code block uses *Xor* and a user code to reverse the encryption created in the preceding example:
	
	``
	strCode = InputBox("Enter Encryption Code")
	Code = CShort(strCode)
	AllText = My.Computer.FileSystem.ReadAllText(_
	  OpenFileDialog1.FileName)
	Numbers = AllText.Split(" ")
	For i = 0 To Numbers.Length - 1
	    Number = CShort(Numbers(i))
	    ch = Chr(Number Xor Code)
	    Decrypt = Decrypt & ch
	Next
	txtNote.Text = Decrypt
	``

Part III
Designing the User Interface

In this part:

In Part II, you learned many of the core development skills necessary for writing Microsoft Visual Basic applications. You learned how to use variables, operators, decision structures, and the Microsoft .NET Framework; how to manage code flow with loops, timers, procedures, and structured error handlers; how to debug your programs; and how to organize information with arrays, collections, text files, and string processing techniques.

Each exercise you have worked with so far concentrated on one or more of these core skills in a simple, stand-alone program. Real-world programs are rarely so simple. They usually require you to combine the techniques in various ways and with various enhancements. Your programs will quite often require multiple forms, used as dialog boxes, input and output forms, reports, and other elements. Because Visual Basic treats each form as a separate object, you can think of them as simple building blocks that you can combine to create powerful programs.

In Part III, you'll focus again on the user interface, and you'll learn how to add multiform projects, animation effects, visual inheritance, and printing support to your Visual Basic applications.

Chapter 14
Managing Windows Forms and Controls at Run Time

After completing this chapter, you will be able to:

- Add new forms to a program and switch between multiple forms.

- Change the position of a form on the Windows desktop.

- Add controls to a form at run time.

- Change the alignment of objects within a form at run time.

- Use the Project Designer to specify the startup form.

In this chapter, you'll learn how to add additional forms to an application to handle input, output, and special messages. You'll also learn how to use the *Me* and *My.Forms* objects to switch between forms, how to use the *DesktopBounds* property to resize a form, how to add Toolbox controls to a form at run time, how to change the alignment of objects within a form, and how to specify which form runs when a program is started.

Adding New Forms to a Program

Each program you've written so far has used one form and a series of general-purpose dialog boxes for input and output. In many cases, dialog boxes and a form are sufficient for communicating with the user. But if you need to exchange more information with the user in a more customized manner, you can add additional forms to your program. Each new form is considered an object that inherits its capabilities from the *System.Windows.Forms.Form* class. By default, the first form in a program is named Form1.vb. Subsequent forms are named Form2.vb, Form3.vb, and so on. (You can change the specific name for a form by using the Add New Item dialog box or by using Solution Explorer.) Each new form has a unique name and its own set of objects, properties, methods, and event procedures.

Table 14-1 lists several practical uses for additional forms in your programs.

TABLE 14-1 Practical Uses for Extra Forms

Form or Forms	Description
Introductory form	A form that displays a welcome message, artwork, or copyright information when the program starts
Program instructions	A form that displays information and tips about how the program works
Dialog boxes	Custom dialog boxes that accept input and display output in the program
Document contents	A form that displays the contents of one or more files and artwork used in the program

How Forms Are Used

Microsoft Visual Basic gives you significant flexibility when using forms. You can make all the forms in a program visible at the same time, or you can load and unload forms as the program needs them. If you display more than one form at once, you can allow the user to switch between the forms, or you can control the order in which the forms are used. A form that must be addressed when it's displayed on the screen is called a *dialog box*. Dialog boxes (sometimes called *modal forms*) retain the focus until the user clicks OK, clicks Cancel, or otherwise dispatches them. To display an existing form as a dialog box in Visual Basic, you open it by using the *ShowDialog* method.

If you want to display a form that the user can switch away from, you use the *Show* method instead of the *ShowDialog* method. (Forms that can lose the application focus are sometimes also called *non-modal forms* or *modeless forms*.) Most Windows applications use regular, non-modal forms when displaying information because they give the user more flexibility, so this style is the default when you create a new form in Microsoft Visual Studio. Because forms are simply members of the *System.Windows.Forms.Form* class, you can also create and display forms by using program code.

Working with Multiple Forms

The following exercises demonstrate how you can use a second form to display Help information for the Lucky Seven program that you worked with in Chapter 2, "Writing Your First Program," and Chapter 10, "Creating Modules and Procedures." You'll add a second form by using the Add Windows Form command on the Project menu, and you'll display the form in your program code by using the *My* namespace and the *ShowDialog* method. The second form will display a short Readme.txt file that I created to display help and copyright information for the program (the type of information you typically see in an About or a Help dialog box).

Add a second form

1. Start Visual Studio, and then open the Lucky Seven Help project in the C:\Vb10sbs\ Chap14\Lucky Seven Help folder.

    The Lucky Seven Help project is the same slot machine game that you built in Chapter 10. The program uses a module and a function to calculate the win rate as you try to spin one or more 7s.

2. Display the primary form (LuckySeven.vb) in the Designer, if it isn't already visible.

3. Click the Add Windows Form command on the Project menu to add a second form to the project.

You'll see a dialog box similar to the following:

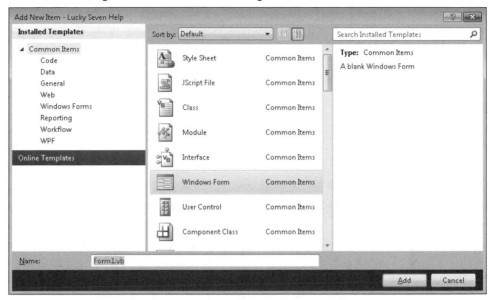

You use the Add New Item dialog box to add forms, classes, modules, and other components to your Visual Basic project. Although you selected the Add Windows Form command, forms aren't the only components listed here. (The Windows Form template is selected by default, however.) To view the available templates by category, click the items in the left pane of the Add New Item dialog box.

Tip I especially recommend that you experiment with the Explorer Form template in the Windows Forms category, which allows you to add a Windows Explorer–style browser to your application, complete with menus, toolbar, and a folder hierarchy pane.

4. Type **HelpInfo.vb** in the Name text box, and then click Add.

A second form named HelpInfo.vb is added to the Lucky Seven Help project, and the form opens in Solution Explorer, as shown here:

> **Tip** You can rename or delete form files by using Solution Explorer. To rename a file, right-click the file, and then click the Rename command. To remove a file from your project, right-click the file, and then click the Exclude From Project command. (However, this command is not available in Visual Basic 2010 Express.) To remove a file from your project and permanently delete it from your computer, select the file, and then press DELETE.

Now you'll add some controls to the HelpInfo.vb form.

5. Use the *Label* control to create a label at the top of the HelpInfo.vb form. Place the label near the left edge of the form, but leave a small indent so that there is room for a descriptive label.

6. Use the *TextBox* control to create a text box object.

7. Set the *Multiline* property for the text box object to True so that you can resize the object easily.

8. Resize the text box object so that it covers most of the form.

9. Use the *Button* control to create a button at the bottom of the form.

10. Set the following properties for the objects on the HelpInfo.vb form:

Object	Property	Setting
Label1	*Text*	"Operating Instructions for Lucky Seven Slot Machine"
TextBox1	*ScrollBars*	Vertical
Button1	*Text*	"OK"
HelpInfo	*Text*	"Help"

The HelpInfo.vb form looks similar to this:

Now you'll enter a line of program code for the HelpInfo.vb form's *Button1_Click* event procedure.

11. Double-click OK to display the *Button1_Click* event procedure in the Code Editor.

12. Type the following program statement:

```
Me.DialogResult = DialogResult.OK
```

The HelpInfo.vb form acts as a dialog box in this project because the Lucky Seven form opens it using the *ShowDialog* method. After the user has read the Help information displayed by the dialog box, he or she will click OK, which sets the *DialogResult* property of the current form to DialogResult.OK. (The *Me* keyword is used here to refer to the HelpInfo.vb form, and you'll see this shorthand syntax from time to time when a reference is being made to the current *instance* of a class or structure in which the code is executing.)

DialogResult.OK is a Visual Basic constant that indicates the dialog box has been closed and should return a value of "OK" to the calling procedure. A more sophisticated dialog box might allow for other values to be returned by parallel button event procedures, such as *DialogResult.Cancel*, *DialogResult.No*, and *DialogResult.Yes*. When the *DialogResult* property is set, however, the form is automatically closed.

13. At the top of the Code Editor, type the following *Imports* statement above the *Public Class* declaration:

```
Imports System.IO
```

This statement makes it easier to reference the *StreamReader* class in your code. The *StreamReader* class isn't specifically related to defining or using additional forms—I'm just using it as a quick way to add textual information to the new form I'm creating.

14. Display the HelpInfo.vb form again, and then double-click the form background.

The *HelpInfo_Load* event procedure appears in the Code Editor. This is the event procedure that runs when the form is first loaded into memory and displayed on the screen.

15. Type the following program statements:

```
Dim StreamToDisplay As StreamReader
StreamToDisplay = _
    New StreamReader("c:\vb10sbs\chap14\lucky seven help\readme.txt")
TextBox1.Text = StreamToDisplay.ReadToEnd
StreamToDisplay.Close()
TextBox1.Select(0, 0)
```

Rather than type the contents of the Help file into the *Text* property of the text box object (which would take a long time), I've used the *StreamReader* class to open, read, and display an appropriate Readme.txt file in the text box object. This file contains operating instructions and general contact information.

The *StreamReader* class was introduced in Chapter 13, "Exploring Text Files and String Processing," but you might not have experimented with it yet. As you learned, *StreamReader* is a .NET Framework alternative to opening a text file with the *My.Computer.FileSystem* object. To make it easier to use *StreamReader* in code, you include the *System.IO* namespace at the top of the code for your form. Next, you declare a *StreamToDisplay* variable of the type *StreamReader* to hold the contents of the text file, and open the text file by using a specific path. Finally, you read the contents of the text file into the *StreamToDisplay* variable by using the *ReadToEnd* method, which reads all the text in the file from the current location (the beginning of the text file) to the end of the text file and assigns it to the *Text* property of the text box object. The *StreamReader.Close* statement closes the text file, and the *Select* method removes the selection from the text in the text box object.

You're finished with the HelpInfo.vb form. Now you'll add a button object and some code to the LuckySeven.vb form.

Display the second form by using an event procedure

1. Click LuckySeven.vb in Solution Explorer, and then click the View Designer button.

    The LuckySeven.vb form opens in the Integrated Development Environment (IDE). Now you'll add a Help button to the user interface.

2. Use the *Button* control to draw a small button object in the lower-right corner of the form.

3. Use the Properties window to set the button object's *Text* property to "Help."

    Your form looks something like this:

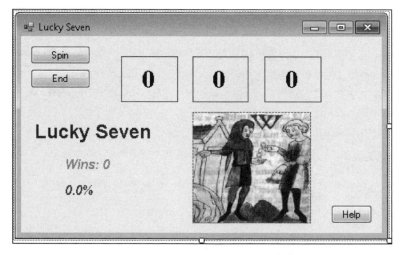

4. Double-click the Help button to display the *Button3_Click* event procedure in the Code Editor.

5. Type the following program statement:

    ```
    My.Forms.HelpInfo.ShowDialog()
    ```

    This statement uses the *My* namespace (introduced in Chapter 13) to access the forms active within the current project. As you type the statement, the Microsoft IntelliSense feature lists the forms available in the *Forms* collection, as shown in the following screen shot:

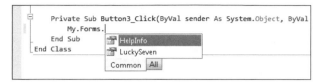

Note that you can also open and manipulate forms directly by using the following syntax:

```
HelpInfo.ShowDialog()
```

This statement opens the HelpInfo.vb form as a dialog box by using the *ShowDialog* method.

Alternatively, you can use the *Show* method to open the form, but in that case, Visual Basic won't consider HelpInfo.vb to be a dialog box; the form is a non-modal form that the user can switch away from and return to as needed. In addition, the *DialogResult* property in the HelpInfo.vb form's *Button1_Click* event procedure won't close the HelpInfo.vb form. Instead, the program statement *Me.Close* is required.

 Tip Keep the differences between modal and non-modal forms in mind as you build your own projects. There are differences between each type of form, and you'll find that each style provides a benefit to the user.

Now you'll run the program to see how a multiple-form application works.

Run the program

1. Click the Start Debugging button on the Standard toolbar.

   The first form, LuckySeven.vb, in the Lucky Seven project appears.

2. Click the Spin button seven or eight times to play the game.

   Your screen looks similar to this:

3. Click the Help button.

   Visual Basic opens the second form in the project, HelpInfo.vb, and displays the Readme.txt file in the text box object. The form looks like this:

4. Use the vertical scroll bar to view the entire Readme file.

5. Try to click the Spin button on the LuckySeven.vb form.

   Notice that you cannot activate the LuckySeven.vb form while the HelpInfo.vb form is active. Because the HelpInfo.vb form is a dialog box (a modal form), you must address it before you can continue with the program.

6. Click OK to close the HelpInfo.vb form.

   The form closes, and the LuckySeven.vb form becomes active again.

7. Click the Spin button a few more times, and then click the Help button again.

   The HelpInfo.vb form opens again and is fully functional.

8. Click OK, and then click End on the LuckySeven.vb form.

   The program stops, and the development environment returns.

Using the *DialogResult* Property in the Calling Form

Although I didn't demonstrate it in the sample program, you can use the *DialogResult* property that you assigned to the dialog box to great effect in a Visual Basic program. As I mentioned earlier, a more sophisticated dialog box might provide additional buttons to the user—Cancel, Yes, No, Abort, and so on. Each dialog box button can be associated with a different type of action in the main program. And in each of the dialog box's button event procedures, you can assign the *DialogResult* property for the form that corresponds to the button name, such as the following program statement:

```
Me.DialogResult = DialogResult.Cancel    'user clicked Cancel button
```

In the calling event procedure—in other words, in the *Button3_Click* event procedure of LuckySeven.vb—you can write additional program code to detect which button the user clicked in the dialog box. This information is stored in the form's *DialogResult* property, which can be evaluated using a basic decision structure such as *If … Then* or *Select … Case*. For example, the following code can be used in the *Button3_Click* event procedure to verify whether the user clicked OK, Cancel, or another button in the dialog box. (The first line isn't new, but reminds you of the HelpInfo form name that you are using in this example.)

```
My.Forms.HelpInfo.ShowDialog()

If HelpInfo.DialogResult = DialogResult.OK Then
    MsgBox("The user clicked OK")
ElseIf HelpInfo.DialogResult = DialogResult.Cancel Then
    MsgBox("The user clicked Cancel")
Else
    MsgBox("Another button was clicked")
End If
```

By using creative event procedures that declare, open, and process dialog box choices, you can add any number of forms to your programs, and you can create a user interface that looks professional and feels flexible and user friendly.

Positioning Forms on the Windows Desktop

You've learned how to add forms to your Visual Basic project and how to open and close forms by using program code. But which tool or setting determines the placement of forms on the Windows desktop when your program runs? As you might have noticed, the placement of forms on the screen at run time is different from the placement of forms within the Visual Studio development environment at design time. In this section, you'll learn how to position your forms just where you want them at run time so that users see just what you want them to see.

The tool you use isn't a graphical layout window but a property named *DesktopBounds* that is maintained for each form in your project. *DesktopBounds* can be read or set only at run time, and it takes the dimensions of a rectangle as an argument—that is, two point pairs that specify the coordinates of the upper-left corner of the window and the lower-right corner of the window. The coordinate points are expressed in pixels, and the distances to the upper-left and lower-right corners are measured from the upper-left corner of the screen. (You'll learn more about the Visual Basic coordinate system in the next chapter.) Because the *DesktopBounds* property takes a rectangle structure as an argument, you can set both the size and the location of the form on the Windows desktop.

In addition to the *DesktopBounds* property, you can use a simpler mechanism with fewer capabilities to set the location of a form at design time. This mechanism, the *StartPosition* property, positions a form on the Windows desktop by using one of the following property settings: Manual, CenterScreen, WindowsDefaultLocation, WindowsDefaultBounds, or CenterParent. The default setting for the *StartPosition* property, WindowsDefaultLocation, lets Windows position the form on the desktop where it chooses—usually the upper-left corner of the screen.

If you set *StartPosition* to Manual, you can manually set the location of the form by using the *Location* property, in which the first number (*x*) is the distance from the left edge of the screen and the second number (*y*) is the distance from the top edge of the screen. (You'll learn more about the *Location* property in the next chapter.) If you set *StartPosition* to CenterScreen, the form opens in the middle of the Windows desktop. (This is my preferred *StartPosition* setting.) If you set *StartPosition* to WindowsDefaultBounds, the form is resized to fit the standard window size for a Windows application, and then the form is opened in the default location for a new Windows form. If you set *StartPosition* to CenterParent, the form is centered within the parent form. This final setting is especially useful in so-called multiple document interface (MDI) applications in which parent and child windows have a special relationship.

The following exercises demonstrate how you can set the *StartPosition* and *DesktopBounds* properties to position a Visual Basic form. You can use either technique to position your forms on the Windows desktop at run time.

Use the *StartPosition* property to position the form

1. Click the Close Project command on the File menu, and then create a new Windows Forms Application project named **My Desktop Bounds**.

2. If the project's form isn't visible, display it now.

3. Click the form to display its properties in the Properties window.

4. Set the *StartPosition* property to CenterScreen.

Changing the *StartPosition* property to CenterScreen directs Visual Basic to display the form in the center of the Windows desktop when you run the program.

5. Click the Start Debugging button to run the application.

Visual Basic loads the form and displays it in the middle of the screen, as shown here:

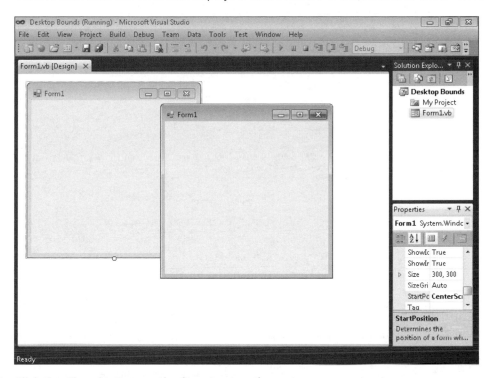

6. Click the Close button on the form to stop the program.

The IDE returns.

7. Set the *StartPosition* property to Manual.

The *Manual* property setting directs Visual Basic to position the form based on the values in the *Location* property.

8. Set the *Location* property to 100, 50.

The *Location* property specifies the position, in pixels, of the upper-left corner of the form.

9. Click the Start Debugging button to run the application.

Visual Basic loads the form and then displays it on the Windows desktop 100 pixels from the left and 50 pixels from the top, as shown in the screen shot on the following page.

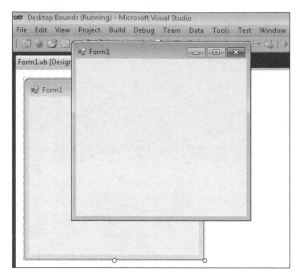

10. Click the Close button on the form to close the program.

You've experimented with a few basic *StartPosition* settings for positioning a form at run time. Now you'll use the *DesktopBounds* property to size and position a second form window while the program is running. You'll also learn how to create a new form at run time without using the Add Windows Form command on the Project menu.

Set the *DesktopBounds* property

1. Use the *Button* control to add a button object to the form, and then change the *Text* property of the button object to "Create Form."

2. Double-click the Create Form button to display the *Button1_Click* event procedure in the Code Editor.

3. Type the following program code:

```
'Create a second form named form2
Dim form2 As New Form

'Define the Text property and border style of the form
form2.Text = "My New Form"
form2.FormBorderStyle = FormBorderStyle.FixedDialog

'Specify that the position of the form will be set manually
form2.StartPosition = FormStartPosition.Manual

'Declare a Rectangle structure to hold the form dimensions
'Upper left corner of form (200, 100)
'Width and height of form (300, 250)
Dim Form2Rect As New Rectangle(200, 100, 300, 250)

'Set the bounds of the form using the Rectangle object
form2.DesktopBounds = Form2Rect
```

```
'Display the form as a modal dialog box
form2.ShowDialog()
```

When the user clicks the Create Form button, this event procedure creates a new form with the title "My New Form" and a fixed border style. To use program code to create a new form, you use the *Dim* statement and specify a variable name for the form and the *Form* class, which is automatically included in projects as part of the *System.Windows.Forms* namespace. You can then set properties such as *Text*, *FormBorderStyle*, *StartPosition*, and *DesktopBounds*.

The *StartPosition* property is set to *FormStartPosition.Manual* to indicate that the position will be set manually. The *DesktopBounds* property sizes and positions the form and requires an argument of type *Rectangle*. The *Rectangle* type is a structure that defines a rectangular region and is automatically included in Visual Basic projects. Using the *Dim* statement, the *Form2Rect* variable is declared of type *Rectangle* and initialized with the form position and size values. At the bottom of the event procedure, the new form is opened as a dialog box using the *ShowDialog* method.

Although I usually recommend placing your *Dim* statements together at the top of the form, here I have placed one a little lower in the code to make it easier to understand the context and use of the variable.

> **Tip** The complete Desktop Bounds program is located in the C:\Vb10sbs\Chap14\Desktop Bounds folder.

4. Click the Start Debugging button to run the program.

   Visual Basic displays the first form on the desktop.

5. Click the Create Form button.

   Visual Basic displays the My New Form dialog box with the size and position you specified in the program code, as shown here:

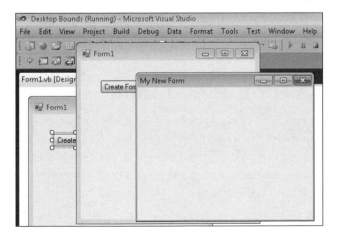

Notice that you can't resize the second form because *FormBorderStyle* was set to FixedDialog.

6. Close the second form, and then close the first form.

Your program stops running, and the IDE returns.

7. Click the Save All button, and then specify the C:\Vb10sbs\Chap14 folder as the location.

Minimizing, Maximizing, and Restoring Windows

In addition to establishing the size and location of a Visual Basic form, you can minimize a form to the Windows taskbar, maximize a form so that it takes up the entire screen, or restore a form to its normal shape. These settings can be changed at design time or at run time based on current program conditions.

To allow a form to be both minimized and maximized, you must first verify that the form's minimize and maximize boxes are available. Using the Properties window or program code, you specify the following settings:

```
form2.MaximizeBox = True
form2.MinimizeBox = True
```

Then, in program code or by using the Properties window, you set the *WindowState* property for the form to Minimized, Maximized, or Normal. (In code, you need to add the *FormWindowState* constant, as shown below.) For example, the following program statement minimizes form2 to the Windows taskbar:

```
form2.WindowState = FormWindowState.Minimized
```

If you want to control the maximum or minimum size of a form, set the *MaximumSize* or *MinimumSize* properties at design time by using the Properties window. To set the *MaximumSize* or *MinimumSize* in code, you'll need to use a *Size* structure (which is similar to the *Rectangle* structure used in the previous exercise), as shown here:

```
Dim FormSize As New Size(400, 300)
form2.MaximumSize = FormSize
```

Adding Controls to a Form at Run Time

Throughout this book, you've added objects to forms by using the Toolbox and the Designer. However, as the previous exercise demonstrated, you can also create Visual Basic objects on forms at run time, either to save development time (if you're copying routines you have used before) or to respond to a current need in the program. For example, you might want to generate a simple dialog box containing objects that process input only under certain conditions.

Creating objects is very simple because the fundamental classes that define controls in the Toolbox are available to all programs. Objects are declared and *instantiated* (or brought into being) by using the *Dim* and *New* keywords. The following program statement shows how this process works when a new button object named *button1* is created on a form:

```
Dim button1 As New Button
```

After you create an object at run time, you can also use code to customize it with property settings. In particular, it's useful to specify a name and location for the object because you didn't specify them manually by using the Designer. For example, the following program statements configure the *Text* and *Location* properties for the new *button1* object:

```
button1.Text = "Click Me"
button1.Location = New Point(20, 25)
```

Finally, your code must add the following new object to the *Controls* collection of the form where it will be created. This will make the object visible and active in the program:

```
form2.Controls.Add(button1)
```

If you are adding the new button to the current form (that is, if you are adding a button to Form1 and your code is located inside a *Form1* event procedure), you can use the *Me* object instead. For example,

```
Me.Controls.Add(button1)
```

adds the *button1* object to the *Controls* collection of the current form. When you do this, be sure that a *button1* object doesn't already exist on the form you are adding it to. (Each object must have its own unique name.)

You can use this process to add any control in the Toolbox to a Visual Basic form. The class name you use to declare and instantiate the control is a variation of the name that appears in the *Name* property for each control.

The following exercise demonstrates how you can add a *Label* control and a *Button* control to a new form at run time. The new form will act as a dialog box that displays the current date.

Create new *Label* and *Button* controls

1. Click the Close Project command on the File menu, and then create a new Windows Forms Application project named **My Add Controls**.

2. Display the form (Form1.vb).

3. Use the *Button* control to add a button object to the form, and then change the *Text* property of the button object to "Display Date."

4. Double-click the Display Date button to display the *Button1_Click* event procedure in the Code Editor.

5. Type the following program code:

```
'Declare new form and control objects
Dim form2 As New Form
Dim lblDate As New Label
Dim btnCancel As New Button

'Set label properties
lblDate.Text = "Current date is: " & DateString
lblDate.Size = New Size(150, 50)
lblDate.Location = New Point(80, 50)

'Set button properties
btnCancel.Text = "Cancel"
btnCancel.Location = New Point(110, 100)

'Set form properties
form2.Text = "Current Date"
form2.CancelButton = btnCancel
form2.StartPosition = FormStartPosition.CenterScreen

'Add new objects to Controls collection
form2.Controls.Add(lblDate)
form2.Controls.Add(btnCancel)

'Display form as a dialog box
form2.ShowDialog()
```

This event procedure displays a new form containing a label object and a button object on the screen. The label object contains the current date as recorded by your computer's system clock (returned through *DateString*). The *Text* property of the button object is set to "Cancel."

As I mentioned earlier, you add controls to a form by declaring a variable to hold the control, setting object properties, and adding the objects to the *Controls* collection. In this exercise, I also demonstrate the *Size* and *CancelButton* properties for the first time. The *Size* property requires a *Size* structure. The *New* keyword is used to immediately create the *Size* structure. The *CancelButton* property allows the user to close the dialog box by pressing ESC or clicking the Cancel button. (The two actions are equivalent.)

6. Click the Save All button, and then specify the C:\Vb10sbs\Chap14 folder as the location.

> **Tip** The complete Add Controls program is located in the C:\Vb10sbs\Chap14\Add Controls folder.

7. Click the Start Debugging button to run the program.

Visual Basic displays the first form on the desktop.

8. Click the Display Date button.

Visual Basic displays the second form. This form contains the label and button objects that you defined by using program code. The label object contains the current date, as shown here:

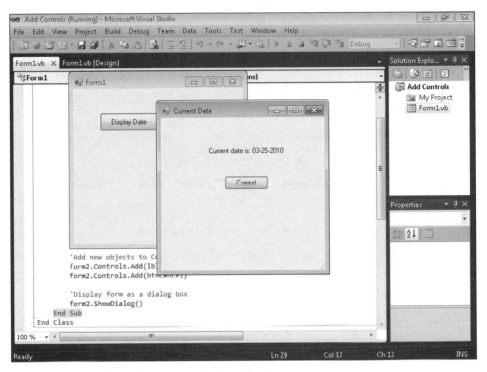

9. Click the Cancel button to close the new form.

10. Click the Display Date button again.

    The new form opens as it did the first time.

11. Press ESC to close the form.

    Because you set the *CancelButton* property to the *btnCancel* object, clicking Cancel and pressing ESC produce the same result.

12. Click the Close button on the form to end the program.

    The program stops, and the development environment returns.

Organizing Controls on a Form

When you add controls to a form programmatically, it takes a bit of trial and error to position the new objects so that they're aligned properly and look nice. After all, you don't have the Visual Studio Designer to help you—just the (*x, y*) coordinates of the *Location* and *Size* properties, which are clumsy values to work with unless you have a knack for two-dimensional thinking or have the time to run the program repeatedly to verify the placement of your objects.

Fortunately, Visual Basic contains several property settings that you can use to organize objects on the form at run time. These include the *Anchor* property, which forces an object on the form to remain at a constant distance from the specified edges of the form, and the *Dock* property, which forces an object to remain attached to one edge of the form. You can use the *Anchor* and *Dock* properties at design time, but I find that they're also very helpful for programmatically aligning objects at run time. The following exercise shows how these properties work.

Anchor and dock objects at run time

1. Click the Close Project command on the File menu, and then create a new Windows Forms Application project named **My Anchor and Dock**.

2. Display the form.

3. Click the *PictureBox* control, and then add a picture box object in the top middle of the form.

4. Click the *Image* property in the Properties window, and then click the ellipsis button in the second column.

   The Select Resource dialog box appears.

5. Click the Local Resource radio button, and then click the Import button.

6. In the Open dialog box, navigate to the C:\Vb10sbs\Chap15 folder.

7. In the Files Of Type list box, select All Files.

8. Select Sun.ico, and then click Open.

9. Click OK in the Select Resource dialog box.

   The Sun icon appears in the *PictureBox*.

10. Set the *SizeMode* property on the *PictureBox* to StretchImage.

11. Use the *TextBox* control to create a text box object.

12. Set the *Multiline* property for the text box object to True so that you can resize the object appropriately.

13. Resize the text box object so that it covers most of the bottom half of the form.

14. Click the *Button* control, and then add a button object to the lower-right corner of the form.

15. Set the following properties for the button and text box objects.

Object	Property	Setting
Button1	*Text*	"Align Now"
TextBox1	*Text*	"Anchor and Dock Samples"

Your form looks similar to this:

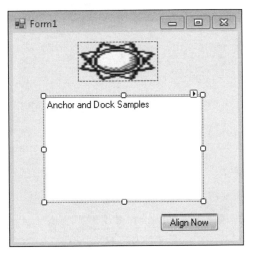

16. Double-click the Align Now button to open the *Button1_Click* event procedure in the Code Editor.

17. Type the following program code:

```
PictureBox1.Dock = DockStyle.Top
TextBox1.Anchor = AnchorStyles.Bottom Or _
    AnchorStyles.Left Or AnchorStyles.Right Or _
    AnchorStyles.Top
Button1.Anchor = AnchorStyles.Bottom Or _
    AnchorStyles.Right
```

When this event procedure is executed, the *Dock* property of the *PictureBox1* object is used to dock the picture box to the top of the form. This forces the top edge of the picture box object to touch and adhere to the top edge of the form—much as the Visual Studio docking feature works in the IDE. The only surprising behavior here is that the picture box object is also resized so that its sides adhere to the left and right edges of the form.

Next, the *Anchor* property for the *TextBox1* and *Button1* objects is used. The *Anchor* property maintains the current distance from the specified edges of the form, even if the form is resized. Note that the *Anchor* property maintains the object's current distance from the specified edges—it doesn't attach the object to the specified edges unless it's already there. In this example, I specify that the *TextBox1* object should be anchored to all four edges of the form (bottom, left, right, and top). I use the *Or* operator to combine my edge selections. I anchor the *Button1* object to the bottom and right edges of the form.

18. Save the project, and then specify the C:\Vb10sbs\Chap14 folder as the location.

> **Tip** The complete Anchor and Dock program is located in the C:\Vb10sbs\Chap14\Anchor and Dock folder.

19. Click the Start Debugging button to run the program.

The form opens, just as you designed it.

20. Move the pointer to the lower-right corner of the form until it changes into a Resize pointer, and then enlarge the form.

Notice that the size and position of the objects on the form do not change.

21. Return the form to its original size.

22. Click the Align Now button on the form.

The picture box object is now docked at the top edge of the form. The picture box is also resized so that its sides adhere to the left and right edges of the form, as shown here:

Notice that the Sun icon in the picture box is now distorted, which is a result of the docking process.

23. Enlarge the form again.

As you resize the form, the picture box and text box objects are also resized. Because the text box is anchored on all four sides, the distance between the edges of the form and the text box remains constant. During the resizing activity, it also becomes apparent that the button object is being repositioned. Although the distance between the button object and the top and left edges of the form changes, the distance to the bottom and right edges remains constant, as shown here:

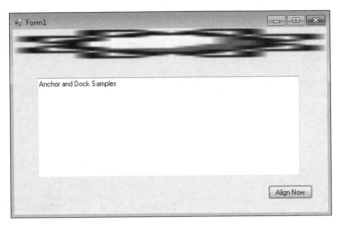

24. Experiment with the *Anchor* and *Dock* properties for a while, and try a different bitmap image if you like. When you're finished, click the Close button on the form to end the program.

You now have the skills necessary to add new forms to a project, position them on the Windows desktop, populate them with new controls, and align the controls by using program code. You've gained a number of useful skills for working with Windows forms in a program.

One Step Further: Specifying the Startup Object

If your project contains more than one form, which form is loaded and displayed first when you run the application? Although Visual Basic normally loads the first form that you created in a project (Form1.vb), you can change the form that Visual Basic loads first by adjusting a setting in the Visual Studio Project Designer, a handy tool that I'll introduce here.

The following exercise shows you how to change the first form, or *startup form*, by using the Project Designer.

Switch the startup form from Form1 to Form2

1. Click the Close Project command on the File menu, and then create a new Windows Forms Application project named **My Startup Form**.

2. Display Form1.vb, if it isn't already visible.

3. Click the Add Windows Form command on the Project menu.

   You'll add a new form to the project to demonstrate how switching the startup form works.

4. Click Add to add the second form (Form2.vb) to Solution Explorer.

5. Click My Startup Form Properties on the Project menu.

The Project Designer opens, as shown here:

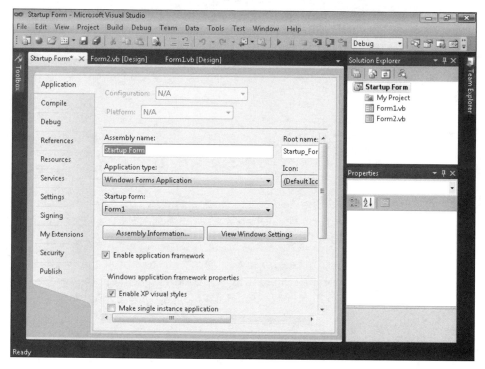

The Project Designer lets you adjust settings that apply to the entire project in one place. Here you'll use the Application tab and the Startup Form list box to specify a new startup form.

6. On the Application tab, click the Startup Form arrow, and then click Form2.

Visual Basic changes the startup form in your project from Form1 to Form2. When the program runs, Form2 will be displayed, and Form1 will appear only if it's opened using the *Show* or *ShowDialog* method.

7. Click the Close button to close the Project Designer.

8. Click the Start Debugging button.

The program runs in the development environment, and Form2 opens.

9. Click the Close button on the form to end the program.

10. Close the project, and discard your changes—it is not necessary to save this simple demonstration project, and you're finished managing forms for now.

Although this demonstration exercise was fairly simple, you can see that Visual Basic offers you some flexibility in how you start your programs. You can specify the startup form, and you can place code within that form's *Load* event procedure to configure the program or adjust its settings before the first form is actually loaded.

Console Applications

If you want to write a Visual Basic application that displays no graphical user interface at all, consider writing a *console* application. This Visual Studio project type processes input and output by using a command-line console (a character-based window also known as the *command prompt*).

You can specify the console application type when you create your project by using the New Project command on the File menu (select the Console Application template), and you can convert an existing project into a console application by displaying the Project Designer, clicking the Application tab, and then selecting Console Application in the Application Type list box. Console applications begin execution within the *Sub Main* procedure inside a code module, because there are no forms to display. You can find out more about this topic by reviewing "Building Console Applications" in the Visual Studio Help documentation.

Chapter 14 Quick Reference

To	Do This
Add a new form to a program	On the Project menu, click Add Windows Form, and then click Add.

Switch between forms in your project, or open hidden forms by using program code	Use the *Show* or *ShowDialog* method. For example:
	`form2.ShowDialog()`
	You can also use the *My.Forms* object to display a form. For example:
	`My.Forms.HelpInfo.ShowDialog()`
	Hide the current form by using the *Me* object. For example:
	`Me.Visible = False`
	Display a form that is hidden by using the *Me* object. For example:
	`Me.ShowDialog()`
	Note that to use the *Me* object, your program code must be located within the form you are manipulating.

To	Do This
| Create a new form with program code and set its properties | Create the form by using the *Dim* and *New* keywords and the *Form* class, and then set any necessary properties. For example:<br><br>```
Dim form2 As New Form
form2.Text = "My New Form"
``` |
| Position a startup form on the Windows desktop | Set the *StartPosition* property to one of the available options, such as CenterScreen or CenterParent. |
| Size and position a startup form on the Windows desktop by using code | Set the *StartPosition* to Manual, declare a *Rectangle* structure that defines the form's size and position, and then use the *DesktopBounds* property to size and position the form on the desktop. For example:<br><br>```
form2.StartPosition = FormStartPosition.Manual
Dim Form2Rect As New Rectangle(200, 100, 300, 250)
form2.DesktopBounds = Form2Rect
``` |
| Minimize, maximize, or restore a form at run time | Set the *MaximizeBox* and *MinimizeBox* properties for the form to True in design mode to allow for maximize and minimize operations. In the program code, set the form's *WindowState* property to FormWindowState.Minimized, FormWindowState.Maximized, or FormWindowState.Normal when you want to change the window state of the form. |
| Add controls to a form at run time | Create a control of the desired type, set its properties, and then add it to the form's *Controls* collection. For example:<br><br>```
Dim button1 as New Button
button1.Text = "Click Me"
button1.Location = New Point(20, 25)
form2.Controls.Add(button1)
``` |
| Anchor an object a specific distance from specific edges of the form | Set the *Anchor* property of the object, and specify the edges you want to remain a constant distance from. Use the *Or* operator when specifying multiple edges. For example:<br><br>```
Button1.Anchor = AnchorStyles.Bottom Or AnchorStyles.Right
``` |
| Dock an object to one of the form's edges | Set the *Dock* property of the object, and then specify the edge you want the object to be attached to. For example:<br><br>```
PictureBox1.Dock = DockStyle.Top
``` |
| Specify the startup form in a project | Click the Properties command on the Project menu to open the Project Designer. For a Windows Forms Application project, you can specify any form in your project as the startup form by clicking the form name in the Startup Form list box. |
| Create a Visual Basic program with no user interface (or only a command-line interface) | Create a console application project by clicking the New Project command on the File menu, clicking the Console Application template, and then clicking OK. You then add the program code to one or more modules, not forms, and execution begins with a procedure named *Sub Main*. |
```

Chapter 15
Adding Graphics and Animation Effects

After completing this chapter, you will be able to:

- Use the *System.Drawing* namespace to add graphics to your forms.

- Create animation effects on your forms.

- Expand or shrink objects on a form at run time.

- Change the transparency of a form.

For many developers, adding artwork and special effects to an application is the most exciting—and addictive—part of programming. Fortunately, creating impressive and useful graphical effects with Microsoft Visual Basic 2010 is both satisfying and easy.

In this chapter, you'll learn how to add a number of visually interesting features to your programs. You'll learn how to create artwork on a form using the *System.Drawing* namespace, how to create simple animation effects by using *PictureBox* and *Timer* controls, and how to expand or shrink objects at run time by using the *Height* and *Width* properties. You'll also learn how to change the transparency of the form and change a form's background image and color. When you've finished, you'll have many of the skills you need to create a visually exciting user interface.

What will you be able to do on your own? This is the point when your imagination takes over. One of my favorite results is from a reader of a previous version of this book who used what he had learned about Visual Basic and graphics to build his own electrocardiograph machine, complete with analog circuitry and a Windows form displaying digital data from the homemade electrocardiogram. If this isn't your idea of fun, you might decide on a more modest goal: to enhance your application's start page so that it contains custom artwork and visual effects—perhaps in combination with one or more digital photographs loaded into picture box objects on a form.

Even game programmers can have some serious fun using graphics in Visual Basic and Microsoft Visual Studio. However, if you're planning on creating the next version of Microsoft Zoo Tycoon or Microsoft Halo, you had better plan for much more than visual output. Modern video games contain huge libraries of objects and complex formulas for rendering graphical images that go well beyond the scope of this book. But that still leaves a lot of room for experimentation and fun!

Adding Artwork by Using the *System.Drawing* Namespace

Adding ready-made artwork to your programs is easy in Visual Basic. Throughout this book, you've experimented with adding bitmaps and icons to a form by using picture box objects. Now you'll learn how to create original artwork on your forms by using the GDI+ functions in the *System.Drawing* namespace, an application programming interface (API) provided by the Microsoft .NET Framework for creating two-dimensional vector graphics, imaging, and typography within the Windows operating system. The effects that you create can add color, shape, and texture to your forms.

Using a Form's Coordinate System

The first thing to learn about creating graphics is the layout of the form's predefined coordinate system. In Visual Basic, each form has its own coordinate system. The coordinate system's starting point, or *origin*, is the upper-left corner of a form. The default coordinate system is made up of rows and columns of device-independent picture elements, or *pixels*, which represent the smallest points that you can locate, or *address*, on a Visual Basic form.

In the Visual Basic coordinate system, rows of pixels are aligned to the *x*-axis (horizontal axis), and columns of pixels are aligned to the *y*-axis (vertical axis). You define locations in the coordinate system by identifying the intersection of a row and a column with the notation (*x*, *y*). For example, if you decide to place a picture box object on a form in your project, the (*x*, *y*) coordinates for the object will indicate where the upper-left corner of the picture box is located on the form. Also keep in mind that the (*x*, *y*) coordinates of the upper-left corner of a form are always (0, 0)—that is the origin that everything is measured from.

Visual Basic works in collaboration with your computer's video display driver software to determine how pixels are displayed on the form and how shapes such as lines, rectangles, curves, and circles are displayed. Occasionally, more than one neighboring pixel is turned on to display a particular shape, such as a diagonal line that appears on a form. The logic that handles this type of rendering isn't your responsibility—it's handled by your display adapter and the drawing routines in the GDI+ graphics library. Occasionally, this will produce a distorted or jagged result, but it is rarely anything more than a slight visual glitch.

The *System.Drawing.Graphics* Class

The *System.Drawing* namespace includes numerous classes for creating artwork and special effects in your programs. In this section, you'll learn a little about the *System.Drawing. Graphics* class, which provides methods and properties for drawing shapes on your forms. You can learn about the other classes by referring to the Visual Studio Help documentation.

Whether you're creating simple screen shots or building complex drawings, it's important to be able to render many of the standard geometric shapes in your programs. Table 15-1 lists several of the fundamental drawing shapes and the methods you use in the *System.Drawing.Graphics* class to create them.

TABLE 15-1 Useful Shapes and Methods in the *System.Drawing.Graphics* Class

Shape	Method	Description
Line	*DrawLine*	Simple line connecting two points.
Rectangle	*DrawRectangle*	Rectangle or square connecting four points.
Arc	*DrawArc*	Curved line connecting two points (a portion of an ellipse).
Circle/Ellipse	*DrawEllipse*	Elliptical shape that is "bounded" by a rectangle.
Polygon	*DrawPolygon*	Complex shape with a variable number of points and sides (stored in an array).
Curve	*DrawCurve*	A curved line that passes through a variable number of points (stored in an array); complex curves called *cardinal splines* can also be drawn with this method.
Bézier splines	*DrawBezier*	A curve drawn by using four points. (Points two and three are "control" points.)

In addition to the preceding methods, which create empty or "non-filled" shapes, there are several methods for drawing shapes that are filled with color. These methods usually have a "Fill" prefix, such as *FillRectangle*, *FillEllipse*, and *FillPolygon*.

When you use a graphics method in the *System.Drawing.Graphics* class, you need to create a *Graphics* object in your code to represent the class and either a *Pen* or *Brush* object to indicate the attributes of the shape you want to draw, such as line width and fill color. The *Pen* object is passed as one of the arguments to the methods that aren't filled with color. The *Brush* object is passed as an argument when a fill color is desired. For example, the following call to the *DrawLine* method uses a *Pen* object and four integer values to draw a red line that starts at pixel (20, 30) and ends at pixel (100, 80). The *Graphics* object is declared by using the name *GraphicsFun*, and the *Pen* object is declared by using the name *PenColor*.

```
Dim GraphicsFun As Graphics
Dim PenColor As New Pen(Color.Red)
GraphicsFun = Me.CreateGraphics
GraphicsFun.DrawLine(PenColor, 20, 30, 100, 80)
```

The syntax for the *DrawLine* method is important, but also note the three lines above it, which are required to use a method in the *System.Drawing.Graphics* class. You must create variables to represent both the *Graphics* and *Pen* objects, and the *Graphics* variable needs to be instantiated by using the *CreateGraphics* method for the Windows form. Note that the *System.Drawing.Graphics* namespace is included in your project automatically—you don't need to include an *Imports* statement in your code to reference the class.

Using the Form's Paint Event

If you test the previous *DrawLine* method in a program, you'll notice that the line you created lasts, or *persists*, on the form only so long as nothing else covers it up. If a dialog box opens on the form momentarily and covers the line, the line is no longer visible when the entire form is visible again. The line also disappears if you minimize the form window and then maximize it again. To address this shortcoming, you need to place your graphics code in the form's *Paint* event procedure so that each time the form is refreshed, the graphics are repainted, too.

In the following exercise, you'll create three shapes on a form by using the form's *Paint* event procedure. The shapes you draw will continue to persist even if the form is covered or minimized.

Create line, rectangle, and ellipse shapes

1. Start Visual Studio, and create a new Windows Forms Application project named **My Draw Shapes**.

2. Resize the form so that it's longer and wider than the default form size.

   You'll need a little extra space to create the graphics shapes. You won't be using any Toolbox controls, however. You'll create the shapes by placing program code in the form's *Form1_Paint* event procedure.

3. Set the *Text* property of Form1 to "Draw Shapes."

4. Click the View Code button in Solution Explorer to display the Code Editor.

5. At the top of the Code Editor, just below the Form1.vb tab, click the Class Name arrow, and then click Form1 Events.

   Form1 Events is the list of events in your project associated with the *Form1* object.

6. Click the Method Name arrow, and then click the *Paint* event.

7. The *Form1_Paint* event procedure appears in the Code Editor.

   This event procedure is where you place code that should be executed when Visual Basic refreshes the form.

8. Within the *Form1_Paint* event procedure, type the following program code:

```
'Prepare GraphicsFun variable for graphics calls
Dim GraphicsFun As Graphics
GraphicsFun = Me.CreateGraphics

'Use a red pen color to draw a line and an ellipse
Dim PenColor As New Pen(Color.Red)
GraphicsFun.DrawLine(PenColor, 20, 30, 100, 80)
GraphicsFun.DrawEllipse(PenColor, 10, 120, 200, 160)
```

```
'Use a green brush color to create a filled rectangle
Dim BrushColor As New SolidBrush(Color.Green)
GraphicsFun.FillRectangle(BrushColor, 150, 10, 250, 100)

'Create a blue cardinal spline curve with four points
Dim Points() As Point = {New Point(358, 280), _
  New Point(300, 320), New Point(275, 155), New Point(350, 180)}
For tension As Single = 0 To 2.5 Step 0.5
    GraphicsFun.DrawCurve(Pens.DodgerBlue, Points, tension)
Next
```

This sample event procedure draws four graphic shapes on your form: a red line, a red ellipse, a green-filled rectangle, and a blue cardinal spline (a complex curve made up of five lines). To enable graphics programming, the routine declares a variable named *GraphicsFun* in the code and uses the *CreateGraphics* method to activate or instantiate the variable. The *PenColor* variable of type *Pen* is used to set the drawing color in the line and ellipse, and the *BrushColor* variable of type *SolidBrush* is used to set the fill color in the rectangle. These examples are obviously just the tip of the graphics library iceberg—there are many more shapes, colors, and variations that you can create by using the methods in the *System.Drawing.Graphics* class.

 Tip The complete Draw Shapes program is located in the C:\Vb10sbs\Chap15\Draw Shapes folder.

9. Click the Start Debugging button on the Standard toolbar to run the program.

Visual Basic loads the form and executes the form's *Paint* event. Your form looks like this:

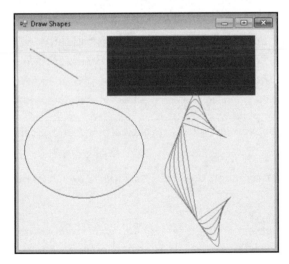

10. Minimize the form, and then restore it again.

The form's *Paint* event is executed again, and the graphics shapes are refreshed on the form.

11. Click the Close button to end the program.

12. Click the Save All button on the Standard toolbar to save the project, and then specify the C:\Vb10sbs\Chap15 folder as the location.

Now you're ready to move on to some simple animation effects.

Adding Animation to Your Programs

Displaying bitmaps and drawing shapes adds visual interest to a program, but for programmers, the king of graphical effects has always been animation. *Animation* is the simulation of movement produced by rapidly displaying a series of related images on the screen. Real animation involves moving objects programmatically, and it often involves changing the size or shape of the images along the way.

In this section, you'll learn how to add simple animation to your programs. You'll learn how to update the *Top* and *Left* properties of a picture box, control the rate of animation by using a timer object, and sense the edge of your form's window.

Moving Objects on the Form

In Visual Studio 2010, a group of special properties named *Left*, *Top*, and *Location*, and the *SetBounds* method allow you to move objects in the coordinate system. Table 15-2 offers a description of these keywords and how they support basic animation effects.

TABLE 15-2 Useful Properties and Methods for Moving Objects on a Form

Keyword	Description
Left	This property can be used to move an object horizontally (left or right).
Top	This property can be used to move an object vertically (up or down).
Location	This property can be used to move an object to the specified location.
SetBounds	This method sets the boundaries of an object to the specified location and size.

In the following sections, you'll experiment with using the *Left*, *Top*, and *Location* properties to move objects.

To move an object in a horizontal direction, use the *Left* property, which uses the syntax:

```
object.Left = horizontal
```

where *object* is the name of the object on the form that you want to move, and *horizontal* is the new horizontal, or *x*-axis, coordinate of the left edge of the object, measured in pixels. For example, the following program statement moves a picture box object to a location 300 pixels to the right of the left window edge:

```
PictureBox1.Left = 300
```

To move a relative distance to the right or left, you would add or subtract pixels from the current *Left* property setting. For example, to move an object 50 pixels to the right, you add 50 to the *Left* property, as follows:

```
PictureBox1.Left = PictureBox1.Left + 50
```

In a similar way, you can change the vertical location of an object on a form by setting the *Top* property, which takes the syntax:

```
object.Top = vertical
```

where *object* is the name of the object on the form that you want to move, and *vertical* is the new vertical, or *y*-axis, coordinate of the top edge of the object, measured in pixels. For example, the following program statement moves a picture box object to a location 150 pixels below the window's title bar:

```
PictureBox1.Top = 150
```

Relative movements down or up are easily made by adding or subtracting pixels from the current *Top* property setting. For example, to move 30 pixels in a downward direction, you add 30 to the current *Top* property, as follows:

```
PictureBox1.Top = PictureBox1.Top + 30
```

The *Location* Property

To move an object in both vertical and horizontal directions, you can use a combination of the *Left* and *Top* property settings. For example, to relocate the upper-left corner of a picture box object to the (*x*, *y*) coordinates (300, 200), you enter the following program code:

```
PictureBox1.Left = 300
PictureBox1.Top = 200
```

However, the designers of Visual Studio don't recommend using two program statements to relocate an object if you plan to make numerous object movements in a program (for example, if you plan to move an object hundreds or thousands of times during an elaborate animation effect). Instead, you should use the *Location* property with the syntax:

```
object.Location = New Point(horizontal, vertical)
```

where *object* is the name of the object, *horizontal* is the horizontal *x*-axis coordinate, *vertical* is the vertical *y*-axis coordinate, and *Point* is a structure identifying the pixel location for the upper-left corner of the object. For example, the following program statement moves a picture box object to an (*x*, *y*) coordinate of (300, 200):

```
PictureBox1.Location = New Point(300, 200)
```

To perform a relative movement using the *Location* property, the *Location.X* and *Location.Y* properties are needed. For example, the program statement:

```
PictureBox1.Location = New Point(PictureBox1.Location.X - 50, _
  PictureBox1.Location.Y - 40)
```

moves the picture box object 50 pixels left and 40 pixels up on the form. Although this construction seems a bit unwieldy, it's the recommended way to relocate objects in relative movements on your form at run time.

Creating Animation by Using a *Timer* Object

The trick to creating animation in a program is placing one or more *Location* property updates in a timer event procedure so that at set intervals the timer causes one or more objects to drift across the screen. In Chapter 7, "Using Loops and Timers," you learned how to use a timer object to update a simple clock utility every second so that it displayed the correct time. When you create animation, you set the *Interval* property of the timer to a much faster rate—1/5 second (200 milliseconds), 1/10 second (100 milliseconds), or less. The exact rate that you choose depends on how fast you want the animation to run.

Another trick is to use the *Top* and *Left* properties and the size of the form to "sense" the edges of the form. By using these values in an event procedure, you can stop the animation (disable the timer) when an object reaches the edge of the form. And by using the *Top* property, the *Left* property, form size properties, and an *If … Then* or *Select … Case* decision structure, you can make an object appear to bounce off one or more edges of the form.

The following exercise demonstrates how you can animate a picture box containing a Sun icon (Sun.ico) by using the *Location* property and a timer object. In this exercise, you'll use the *Top* property to detect the top edge of the form, and you'll use the *Size.Height* property to detect the bottom edge. The Sun icon will move back and forth between these extremes each time you click a button.

Animate a Sun icon on your form

1. Click the Close Project command on the File menu, and then create a new Windows Forms Application project named **My Moving Icon**.

2. Using the *Button* control, draw two button objects in the lower-left corner of the form.

3. Using the *PictureBox* control, draw a small rectangular picture box object in the lower-right corner of the form.

   This is the object that you'll animate in the program.

4. Click the *Image* property in the Properties window, and then click the ellipsis button in the second column.

   The Select Resource dialog box appears.

5. Click the Local Resource radio button, and then click the Import button.

6. In the Open dialog box, navigate to the C:\Vb10sbs\Chap15 folder.

7. In the Files Of Type list box, select All Files.

8. Select Sun.ico, and then click Open.

9. Click OK in the Select Resource dialog box.

   The Sun icon appears in the *PictureBox*.

10. Set the *SizeMode* property on the *PictureBox* to StretchImage.

11. Double-click the *Timer* control on the Components tab of the Toolbox to add it to the component tray below the form.

    The timer object is the mechanism that controls the pace of the animation. Recall that the timer object itself isn't visible on the form, so it's shown below the form in the component tray reserved for objects that are not visible.

12. Set the following properties for the button, timer, and form objects.

Object	Property	Setting
Button1	*Text*	"Move Up"
Button2	*Text*	"Move Down"
Timer1	*Interval*	75
Form1	*Text*	"Basic Animation"

After you set these properties, your form looks similar to this:

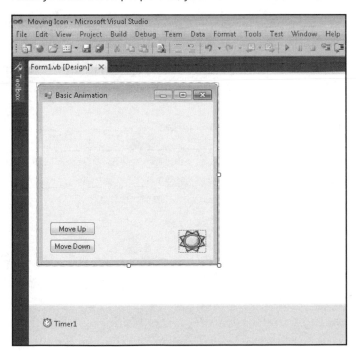

13. Double-click the Move Up button to edit its event procedure.

    The *Button1_Click* event procedure appears in the Code Editor.

14. Type the following program code:

```
GoingUp = True
Timer1.Enabled = True
```

This simple event procedure sets the *GoingUp* variable to True and enables the timer object. The actual program code to move the picture box object and sense the correct direction is stored in the *Timer1_Tick* event procedure. The *GoingUp* variable has a jagged underline now because you have not declared it yet.

15. Near the top of the form's program code (below the statement *Public Class Form1*), type the following variable declaration:

```
Dim GoingUp As Boolean   'GoingUp stores current direction
```

This variable declaration makes *GoingUp* available to all the event procedures in the form, so the jagged underline in the *Button1_Click* event procedure is removed. I've used a *Boolean* variable because there are only two possible directions for movement in this program—up and down.

16. Display the form again, double-click the Move Down button, and then enter the following program code in the *Button2_Click* event procedure:

```
GoingUp = False
Timer1.Enabled = True
```

This routine is very similar to the *Button1_Click* event procedure, except that it changes the direction from up to down.

17. Display the form again, double-click the *Timer1* object, and then enter the following program code in the *Timer1_Tick* event procedure:

```
If GoingUp = True Then
    'move picture box toward the top
    If PictureBox1.Top > 10 Then
        PictureBox1.Location = New Point _
          (PictureBox1.Location.X - 10, _
          PictureBox1.Location.Y - 10)
    End If
Else
    'move picture box toward the bottom
    If PictureBox1.Top < (Me.Size.Height - 75) Then
        PictureBox1.Location = New Point _
          (PictureBox1.Location.X + 10, _
          PictureBox1.Location.Y + 10)
    End If
End If
```

So long as the timer is enabled, this *If… Then* decision structure is executed every 75 milliseconds. The first line in the procedure checks whether the *GoingUp* Boolean variable is set to True, indicating that the icon is moving toward the top of the form. If it's set to True, the procedure moves the picture box object to a relative position 10 pixels closer to both the top and left edges of the form.

If the *GoingUp* variable is currently set to False, the decision structure moves the icon down instead. In this case, the picture box object moves until the edge of the form is detected. The height of the form can be determined by using the *Me.Size.Height* property. (I subtract 75 from the form height so that the icon is still displayed on the form.) The *Me* object in this example represents the form (*Form1*).

As you'll see when you run the program, this movement gives the icon animation a steady drifting quality. To make the icon move faster, you decrease the *Interval* setting for the timer object. To make the icon move slower, you increase the *Interval* setting.

Run the Moving Icon program

 Tip The complete Moving Icon program is located in the C:\Vb10sbs\Chap15\Moving Icon folder.

1. Click the Start Debugging button to run the program.

    The Moving Icon program runs in the IDE.

2. Click the Move Up button.

    The picture box object moves up the form on a diagonal path, as indicated here:

After a few moments, the button comes to rest at the upper edge of the form.

Note If you placed the picture box object in the lower-right corner of the form, as instructed in step 3 of the previous exercise, you see something similar to this screen shot. However, if you placed the picture box object in another location, or created a smaller form, the image might drift off the screen when you click Move Up or Move Down. Can you tell why?

3. Click the Move Down button.

   The picture box moves back down again to the lower-right corner of the screen.

4. Click both buttons again several times, and ponder the animation effects.

   Note that you don't need to wait for one animation effect to end before you click the next button. The *Timer1_Tick* event procedure uses the *GoingUp* variable immediately to manage your direction requests, so it doesn't matter whether the picture box has finished going in one direction. Consider this effect for a moment, and imagine how you could use a similar type of logic to build your own Visual Basic video games. You could increase or decrease the animation rates according to specific conditions or "collisions" on screen, and you could force the animated objects to move in different directions. You could also change the picture displayed by the picture box object based on where the icon is on the screen or what conditions it encounters.

5. When you're finished running the program, click the Close button on the form to stop the demonstration.

6. Click the Save All button to save the project, and then specify the C:\Vb10sbs\Chap15 folder as the location.

Expanding and Shrinking Objects While a Program Is Running

In addition to maintaining a *Top* property and a *Left* property, Visual Basic maintains a *Height* property and a *Width* property for most objects on a form. You can use these properties in clever ways to expand and shrink objects while a program is running. The following exercise shows you how to do it.

Expand a picture box at run time

1. On the File menu, click the Close Project command.

2. Create a new Windows Forms Application project named **My Zoom In**.

3. Display the form, click the *PictureBox* control in the Toolbox, and then draw a small picture box object near the upper-left corner of the form.

4. Set the following properties for the picture box and the form.

When you set the properties for the picture box, note the current values in the *Height* and *Width* properties within the *Size* property. (You can set these at design time, too.) Since this is an image from space, we're using a black background for the form, and a JPEG image of stars in the background. These two form properties, *BackColor* and *BackgroundImage*, are being introduced for the first time in this chapter.

Object	Property	Setting
PictureBox1	Image	"C:\Vb10sbs\Chap15\Earth.jpg"
	SizeMode	StretchImage
Form1	Text	"Approaching Earth"
	BackColor	Black
	BackgroundImage	"C:\Vb10sbs\Chap15\Space.jpg"

Your form looks like this:

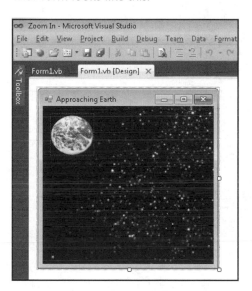

5. Double-click the *PictureBox1* object on the form.

The *PictureBox1_Click* event procedure appears in the Code Editor.

6. Type the following program code in the *PictureBox1_Click* event procedure:

```
PictureBox1.Height = PictureBox1.Height + 15
PictureBox1.Width = PictureBox1.Width + 15
```

7. These two lines increase the height and width of the Earth icon by 15 pixels each time the user clicks the picture box. If you stretch your imagination a little, watching the effect makes you feel like you're approaching Earth in a spaceship.

8. Click the Save All button, and then save the project in the C:\Vb10sbs\Chap15 folder.

Tip The complete Zoom In program is located in the C:\Vb10sbs\Chap15\Zoom In folder.

9. Click the Start Debugging button to run the program.

The Earth image appears alone on the form.

Stars appear in the background because you have loaded the Space.jpg file onto the form with the *BackImage* property. Any area not covered by the *BackImage* property on the form will be black because you've used the *BackColor* property to simulate the quiet melancholy of outer space.

10. Click the Earth image several times to expand it on the screen.

After 10 or 11 clicks, your screen looks similar to this:

Because the image has a relatively low resolution, it will eventually become somewhat blurry if you magnify it much more. You can address this limitation by saving smaller images at a higher resolution. The wispy clouds on Earth mitigate the blurring problem in this example, however. (In print, this will not look that great, so be sure to try it out on your computer and see the image in color!)

11. When you get close enough to establish a standard orbit, click the Close button to quit the program.

The program stops, and the development environment returns.

One Step Further: Changing Form Transparency

Interested in one last special effect? With GDI+, you can do things that are difficult or even impossible in earlier versions of Visual Basic. For example, you can make a form partially transparent so that you can see through it. Let's say you're designing a photo-display program that includes a separate form with various options to manipulate the photos. You can make the option form partially transparent so that the user can see any photos beneath it while still having access to the options.

In the following exercise, you'll change the transparency of a form by changing the value of the *Opacity* property.

Set the *Opacity* property

1. On the File menu, click the Close Project command.

2. Create a new Windows Forms Application project named **My Transparent Form**.

3. Display the form, click the *Button* control in the Toolbox, and then draw two buttons on the form.

4. Set the following properties for the two buttons and the form:

Object	Property	Setting
Button1	*Text*	"Set Opacity"
Button2	*Text*	"Restore"
Form1	*Text*	"Transparent Form"

5. Double-click the Set Opacity button on the form.

6. Type the following program code in the *Button1_Click* event procedure:

```
Me.Opacity = 0.75
```

Opacity is specified as a percentage, so it has a range of 0 to 1. This line sets the *Opacity* of Form1 (*Me*) to 75 percent.

7. Display the form again, double-click the Restore button, and then enter the following program code in the *Button2_Click* event procedure:

```
Me.Opacity = 1
```

This line restores the opacity to 100 percent.

8. Click the Save All button, and then save the project in the C:\Vb10sbs\Chap15 folder.

> **Tip** The complete Transparent Form program is located in the C:\Vb10sbs\Chap15\ Transparent Form folder.

9. Click the Start Debugging button to run the program.

10. Click the Set Opacity button.

Notice how you can see through the form, as shown here:

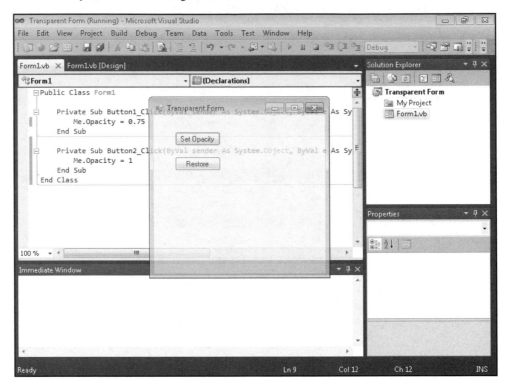

11. Click the Restore button.

The transparency effect is removed.

12. When you're done testing the transparency effect, click the Close button to quit the program.

The program stops, and the development environment returns.

Chapter 15 Quick Reference

To	Do This
Create lines or shapes on a form	Use methods in the *System.Drawing.Graphics* namespace. For example, the following program statements draw a red ellipse on the form:

	<pre>Dim GraphicsFun As Graphics
	GraphicsFun = Me.CreateGraphics
	Dim PenColor As New Pen(System.Drawing.Color.Red)
	GraphicsFun.DrawEllipse(PenColor, 10, 120, 200, 160)</pre>

Create lines or shapes that persist on the form during window redraws	Place the graphics methods in the *Paint* event procedure for the form.

To	Do This
Move an object on a form	Relocate the object by using the *Location* property, the *New* keyword, and the *Point* structure. For example: `PictureBox1.Location = New Point(300, 200)`
Animate an object	Use a timer event procedure to modify the *Left*, *Top*, or *Location* property for an object on the form. The timer's *Interval* property controls animation speed.
Expand or shrink an object at run time	Change the object's *Height* property or *Width* property.
Set the background color on a form	Change the form's *BackColor* property.
Set the background image on a form	Change the form's *BackgroundImage* property.
Change the transparency of a form	Change the form's *Opacity* property.

Chapter 16
Inheriting Forms and Creating Base Classes

After completing this chapter, you will be able to:

- Use the Inheritance Picker to incorporate existing forms in your projects.

- Create your own base classes with custom properties and methods.

- Derive new classes from base classes by using the *Inherits* statement.

An important skill for virtually all professional software developers today is the ability to understand and utilize *object-oriented programming* (OOP) techniques. The changes associated with OOP have been gaining momentum in recent versions of Microsoft Visual Basic, including features that support *inheritance*, a mechanism that allows one class to acquire the interface and behavior characteristics of another class.

Inheritance in Visual Basic 2010 is facilitated by both the Visual Basic language and tools within the Integrated Development Environment (IDE). What this means is that you can build one form in the development environment and pass on its characteristics and functionality to other forms. In addition, you can build your own classes and inherit properties, methods, and events from them.

In this chapter, you'll experiment with both types of inheritance. You'll learn how to integrate existing forms into your projects by using the Inheritance Picker dialog box that is part of Microsoft Visual Studio 2010, and you'll learn how to create your own classes and derive new ones from them by using the *Inherits* statement. With these skills, you'll be able to utilize many of the forms and coding routines you've already developed, making Visual Basic programming a faster and more flexible endeavor. These improvements will help you design compelling user interfaces rapidly and will extend the work that you have done in other programming projects.

Inheriting a Form by Using the Inheritance Picker

In OOP syntax, *inheritance* means having one class receive the objects, properties, methods, and other attributes of another class. As I mentioned in the section "Adding New Forms to a Program" in Chapter 14, "Managing Windows Forms and Controls at Run Time," Visual Basic goes through this process routinely when it creates a new form in the development environment. The first form in a project (*Form1*) relies on the

System.Windows.Forms.Form class for its definition and default values. In fact, this class is identified in the Properties window when you select a form in the Designer, as shown in the following screen shot:

Although you haven't realized it, you've been using inheritance all along to define the Windows forms that you've been using to build Visual Basic applications. Although existing forms can be inherited by using program code as well, the designers of Visual Studio considered the task to be so important that they designed a special dialog box in the development environment to facilitate the process. This dialog box is called the *Inheritance Picker,* and it's accessed through the Add New Item command on the Project menu. In the following exercise, you'll use the Inheritance Picker to create a second copy of a dialog box in a project.

Inherit a simple dialog box

1. Start Visual Studio, and create a new Visual Basic Windows Forms Application project named **My Form Inheritance**.

2. Display the form in the project, and then use the *Button* control to add two button objects at the bottom of the form, positioned side by side.

3. Change the *Text* properties of the *Button1* and *Button2* buttons to "OK" and "Cancel," respectively.

4. Double-click OK to display the *Button1_Click* event procedure in the Code Editor.

5. Type the following program statement:

   ```
   MsgBox("You clicked OK")
   ```

6. Display the form again, double-click the Cancel button, and then type the following program statement in the *Button2_Click* event procedure:

   ```
   MsgBox("You clicked Cancel")
   ```

7. Display the form again, and set the *Text* property of the form to "Dialog Box."

   You now have a simple form that can be used as the basis of a dialog box in a program. With some customization, you can use this basic form to process several tasks—you just need to add the controls that are specific to your individual application.

8. Click the Save All button to save your project, and then specify the C:\Vb10sbs\Chap16 folder as the location.

Now you'll practice inheriting the form. The first step in this process is building, or *compiling*, the project because you can inherit only from forms that are compiled into .exe or .dll files. Each time the base form is recompiled, changes made to the base form are passed to the derived (inherited) form.

9. Click the Build My Form Inheritance command on the Build menu.

   Visual Basic compiles your project and creates an .exe file.

10. Click the Add New Item command on the Project menu, and then click the Windows Forms category on the left side of the dialog box and the Inherited Form template in the middle of the dialog box.

   The Add New Item dialog box looks as shown in the following screen shot:

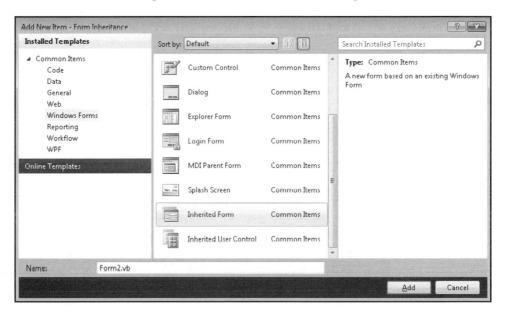

Note Visual Basic 2010 Express does not include the Inherited Form template. If you are looking for justification to upgrade to Visual Studio Professional, this may provide some. (In general, Professional and the other full versions of Visual Studio provide a number of additional templates that are useful.) At this point, you may want to simply review the sample project that I have included on the Practice Files CD and examine the code. However there is a work-around that you can attempt to create an inherited form manually. To try it, add a Windows Form named Form2.vb to your project instead of Inherited Form. At the top of Solution Explorer, click the Show All Files toggle button. Expand Form2.vb and then open Form2.Designer.vb. Change "Inherits System.Windows.Forms.Form" to "Inherits My_Form_Inheritance.Form1." Click Save All, close Form2.Designer.vb, and then click Show All Files again to hide the advanced files. Since you performed the steps manually, you can now skip to the next section, "Customize the Inherited Form."

As usual, Visual Studio lists all the possible templates you could include in your projects, not just those related to inheritance. The Inherited Form template gives you access to the Inheritance Picker dialog box.

You can also use the Name text box at the bottom of the dialog box to assign a name to your inherited form, although it is not necessary for this example. This name will appear in Solution Explorer and in the file name of the form on disk.

11. Click Add to accept the default settings for the new, inherited form.

Visual Studio displays the Inheritance Picker dialog box, as shown here:

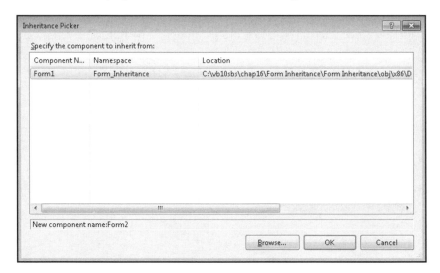

This dialog box lists all the inheritable forms in the current project. If you want to browse for another compiled form, click the Browse button and locate the .dll file on your system.

Note If you want to inherit a form that isn't a component of the current project, the form must be compiled as a .dll file.

12. Click Form1 in the Inheritance Picker dialog box, and then click OK.

Visual Studio creates the Form2.vb entry in Solution Explorer and displays the inherited form in the Designer. Notice in the screen shot at the top of the following page that the form looks identical to the Form1 window you created earlier except that the two buttons contain tiny icons, which indicate that the objects come from an inherited source.

It can be difficult to tell an inherited form from a base form (the tiny inheritance icons aren't that obvious), but you can also use Solution Explorer and the IDE tabs to distinguish between the forms.

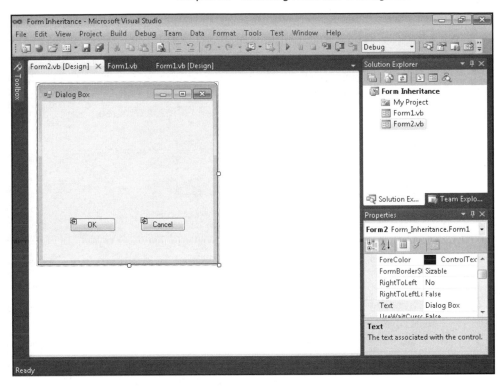

Now you'll add a few new elements to the inherited form.

Customize the inherited form

1. Use the *Button* control to add a third button object near the middle of Form2 (the inherited form).

2. Set the *Text* property for the button object to "Click Me!"

3. Double-click the Click Me! button.

4. In the *Button3_Click* event procedure, type the following program statement:

```
MsgBox("This is the inherited form!")
```

5. Display Form2 again, and then try double-clicking the OK and Cancel buttons on the form.

   Notice that you can't display or edit the event procedures or properties for these inherited objects without taking additional steps that are beyond the scope of this chapter. (Tiny "lock" icons indicate that the inherited objects are *read-only*.) However, you can add new objects to the form or customize it in other ways.

6. Enlarge the form.

   This works just fine. And in addition to modifying the size, you can change the location and other display or operational characteristics of the form. Notice that if you use the Properties window to customize a form, the Object list box in the Properties window displays the form from which the current form is derived. Here's what the Properties window looks like in your project when Form2 is selected:

   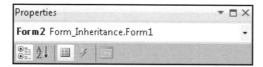

   Now set the startup object in your project to Form2.

7. Click the My Form Inheritance Properties command on the Project menu.

   The Project Designer, introduced in Chapter 14, appears.

8. On the Application tab, click the Startup Form list box, click Form2, and then close the Project Designer by clicking the Close button on the tab.

   There is no Save button in the Project Designer because Visual Studio saves your changes as you make them in the dialog box. Now run the new project.

 Tip The complete Form Inheritance program is located in the C:\Vb10sbs\Chap16\Form Inheritance folder.

9. Click the Start Debugging button.

   The inherited form opens, as shown here. (My version is shown slightly enlarged after following step 6 earlier in this exercise.)

   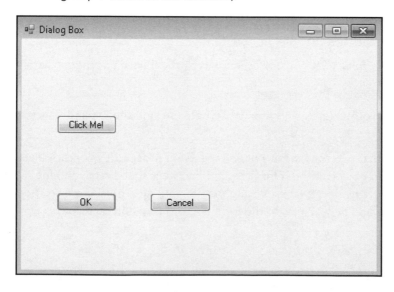

10. Click OK.

The inherited form runs the event procedure that it inherited from Form1, and the event procedure displays the following message:

11. Click OK, and then click the Click Me! button.

Form2 displays the inherited form message.

What this demonstrates is that Form2 (the inherited form) has its own characteristics (a new Click Me! button and an enlarged size). Form2 also uses two buttons (OK and Cancel) that were inherited from Form1 and contain the code from Form1, as well as the exact visual representation of the buttons. This means that you can redeploy the user interface and code features that you have previously created without cumbersome cutting and pasting. In other words, you've encountered one of the main benefits of OOP—reusing and extending the functionality of existing forms, program code, and projects. You've also learned to use the Visual Studio Inheritance Picker dialog box, which offers a handy way to select objects you want to reuse.

12. Click OK to close the message box, and then click Close on the form to end the program.

The program stops, and the IDE returns.

Creating Your Own Base Classes

The Inheritance Picker managed the inheritance process in the previous exercise by creating a new class in your project named *Form2*. To build the *Form2* class, the Inheritance Picker established a link between the *Form1* class in the My Form Inheritance project and the new form. Here's what the new *Form2* class looks like in the Code Editor:

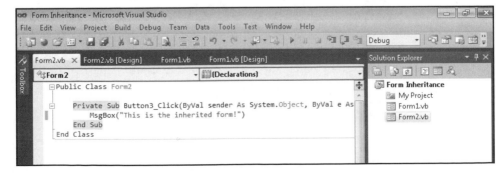

The *Button3_Click* event procedure that you added is also a member of the new class. But recall for a moment that the *Form1* class itself relied on the *System.Windows.Forms.Form* class for its fundamental behavior and characteristics. So the last exercise demonstrates that one derived class (*Form2*) can inherit its functionality from another derived class (*Form1*), which in turn inherited its core functionality from an original base class (*Form*), which is a member of the *System.Windows.Forms* namespace in the Microsoft .NET Framework.

In addition to the Inheritance Picker, Visual Studio offers the *Inherits* statement, which causes the current class to inherit the properties, procedures, and variables of another class. To use the *Inherits* statement to inherit a form, you must place the *Inherits* statement at the top of the form as the first statement in the class. Although you might choose to use the Inheritance Picker for this sort of work with forms, it is useful to know about *Inherits* because it can be used for classes and interfaces other than forms, and you will probably run into it now and then in your colleagues' program code. You'll see an example of the *Inherits* statement near the end of this chapter.

Recognizing that classes are such a fundamental building block in Visual Basic programs, you might very well ask how new classes are created and how these new classes might be inherited down the road by subsequently derived classes. To ponder these possibilities, I'll devote the remainder of this chapter to discussing the syntax for creating classes in Visual Basic 2010 and introducing how these user-defined classes might be inherited later by still more classes. Along the way, you'll learn how very useful creating your own classes can be.

Nerd Alert

There's a potential danger for terminology overload when discussing class creation and inheritance. A number of very smart computer scientists have been thinking about these OOP concepts for several years, and there are numerous terms and definitions in use for the concepts that I plan to cover. However, if you stick with me, you'll find that creating classes and inheriting them is quite simple in Visual Basic 2010 and that you can accomplish a lot of useful work by adding just a few lines of program code to your projects. Understanding OOP terminology will also help you make sense of some of the advanced features of Visual Basic 2010, such as covariance and contravariance, Language Integrated Query (LINQ), anonymous types, extension methods, and lambda expressions, which facilitate the use of classes, objects, and methods, and are sometimes emphasized in marketing announcements and new feature lists.

Adding a New Class to Your Project

Simply stated, a *class* in Visual Basic is a representation or *blueprint* that defines the structure of one or more objects. Creating a class allows you to define your own objects in a program—objects that have properties, methods, fields, and events, just like the objects that the Toolbox controls create on Windows forms. To add a new class to your project, you click the Add Class command on the Project menu, and then you define the class by using program code and a few Visual Basic keywords.

In the following exercise, you'll create a program that prompts a new employee for his or her first name, last name, and date of birth. You'll store this information in the properties of a new class named *Person*, and you'll create a method in the class to compute the current age of the new employee. This project will teach you how to create your own classes and also how to use the classes in the event procedures of your program.

Build the Person Class project

1. Click the Close Project command on the File menu, and then create a new Windows Forms Application project named **My Person Class**.

2. Use the *Label* control to add a label object to the top of Form1.

3. Use the *TextBox* control to draw two wide text box objects below the label object.

4. Use the *DateTimePicker* control to draw a date time picker object below the text box objects.

   You last used the *DateTimePicker* control to enter dates in Chapter 3, "Working with Toolbox Controls." Go to that chapter if you want to review this control's basic methods and properties.

5. Use the *Button* control to draw a button object below the date/time picker object.

6. Set the following properties for the objects on the form:

Object	Property	Setting
Label1	Text	"Enter employee first name, last name, and date of birth."
TextBox1	Text	"First name"
TextBox2	Text	"Last name"
Button1	Text	"Display record"
Form1	Text	"Person Class"

Your form looks something like this:

This is the basic user interface for a form that defines a new employee record for a business application. The form isn't connected to a database, however, so only one record can be stored at a time. You'll learn to make database connections in Chapter 18, "Getting Started with ADO.NET."

Now you'll add a class to the project to store the information in the record.

7. Click the Add Class command on the Project menu.

Visual Studio displays the Add New Item dialog box, with the Class template selected, as shown here:

The Add New Item dialog box gives you the opportunity to name your class. Because you can store more than one class in a new class module, you might want to specify a name that is somewhat general.

8. Type **Person.vb** in the Name box, and then click Add.

Visual Studio opens a blank class module in the Code Editor and lists a file named Person.vb in Solution Explorer for your project, as shown here:

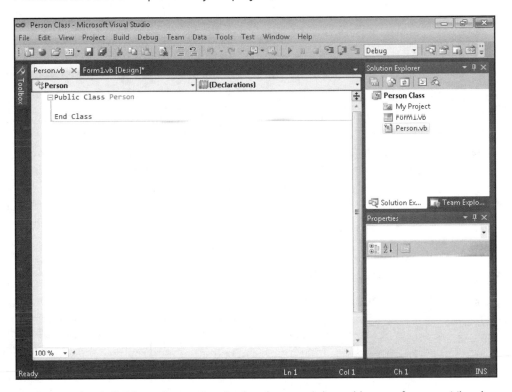

Now you'll type the definition of your class in the class module and learn a few new Visual Basic keywords. You'll follow four steps: declare class variables, create properties, create a method, and finally, create an object based on the new class.

Step 1: Declare class variables

- Below the *Public Class Person* program statement, type the following variable declarations:

```
Private Name1 As String
Private Name2 As String
```

Here, you declare two variables that will be used exclusively within the class module to store the values for two string property settings. I've declared the variables by using the *Private* keyword because, by convention, Visual Basic programmers keep their internal class variables private—in other words, not available for inspection outside the class module itself. These variables are sometimes call *fields* or *backing fields* because they provide storage for properties.

Step 2: Create properties

1. Below the variable declarations, type the following program statement, and then press ENTER:

```
Public Property FirstName() As String
```

This statement creates a property named *FirstName*, which is of type *String*, in your class. This is all you need to do to implement a simple property. (A backing field is not required.)

In Visual Studio 2008, what happens next is that Visual Basic creates a code template for the remaining elements in the property declaration. These elements include a *Get* block, which determines what other programmers see when they check the *FirstName* property; a *Set* block, which determines what happens when the *FirstName* property is set or changed; and an *End Property* statement, which marks the end of the property procedure. However, in Visual Studio 2010, these elements are created automatically when you use the *Property* statement. The process happens internally (you don't see it in the Code Editor), and in the documentation, it is referred to as the new *auto-implemented properties* feature. This enables you to quickly specify a property of a class without having to write *Get* and *Set* code blocks on your own.

Auto-implemented properties are very handy for those of us who create or manipulate classes and properties often. However, there are situations in which you cannot use auto-implemented properties but must instead use standard, or *expanded*, property syntax (that is, the syntax that we used routinely in Visual Basic 2008). These situations include the following scenarios:

❑ You need to add code to the *Get* or *Set* procedure of a property (for example, when you are validating values in a *Set* code block).

❑ You want to make a *Set* procedure *Private* or a *Get* procedure *Public*.

❑ You want to create properties that are *WriteOnly* or *ReadOnly*.

❑ You want to add special *parameterized* properties.

❑ You want to place an attribute or Extensible Markup Language (XML) comment in a hidden, private field.

Although these uses may seem advanced or esoteric at this point, they are important enough that I want to teach you what the standard syntax for *Get* and *Set* code blocks is. You may not need to use it at first, but as you create more advanced classes and properties of your own, you may need to use it. (In addition, the Visual Studio Help documentation often shows these *Get* and *Set* code blocks when discussing classes, so you should learn the standard syntax now.)

2. Type in the following *FirstName* property procedure structure that uses the *Get* and *Set* keywords. You'll notice that much of the structure is added automatically after you type the first *Get* statement:

```
Get
     Return Name1
End Get
Set(ByVal value As String)
     Name1 = value
End Set
End Property
```

In this structure, the *Return* keyword specifies that the *Name1* string variable will be returned when the *FirstName* property is referenced. The *Set* block assigns a string value to the *Name1* variable when the property is set. Notice here especially the *value* variable, which is used in property procedures to stand for the value that's assigned to the class when a property is set. Although this syntax might look strange, trust me for now—this is the formal way to create property settings in controls, and more sophisticated properties would even add additional program logic here to test values or make computations.

3. Below the *End Property* statement, type a second property procedure for the *LastName* property in your class. Again, after you type the *Get* keyword, much of the structure for the property procedure will be added automatically:

```
Public Property LastName() As String
    Get
         Return Name2
    End Get
    Set(ByVal value As String)
         Name2 = value
    End Set
End Property
```

This property procedure is similar to the first one except that it uses the second string variable (*Name2*) that you declared at the top of the class.

You're finished defining the two properties in your class. Now let's move on to a method named *Age* that will determine the new employee's current age based on his or her birth date.

Step 3: Create a method

■ Below the *LastName* property procedure, type the following function definition:

```
Public Function Age(ByVal Birthday As Date) As Integer
    Return Int(Now.Subtract(Birthday).Days / 365.25)
End Function
```

To create a method in the class that performs a specific action, you add a function or a Sub procedure to your class. Although many methods don't require arguments to accomplish their work, the *Age* method I'm defining requires a *Birthday* argument of type *Date* to complete its calculation. The method uses the *Subtract* method to subtract the new employee's birth date from the current system time, and it returns the value expressed in days divided by 365.25—the approximate length in days of a single year. The *Int* function returns the integer portion of a number, and this value is returned to the calling procedure via the *Return* statement—just like a typical function. (For more information about function definitions, see Chapter 10, "Creating Modules and Procedures.")

Your class definition is finished, and in the Code Editor, the *Person* class now looks like the following:

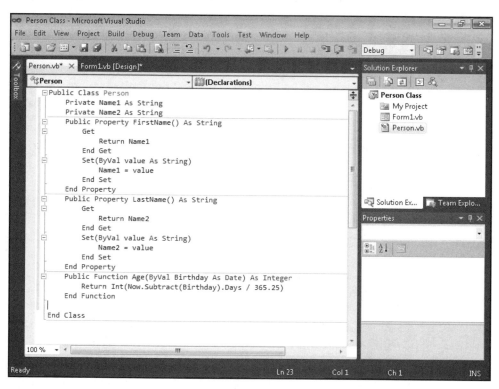

Now you'll return to Form1 and use the new class in an event procedure.

Tip Although you didn't do it for this example, it's usually wise to add some type-checking logic to class modules in actual projects so that properties or methods that are improperly used don't trigger run-time errors that halt the program.

Step 4: Create an object based on the new class

1. Click the Form1.vb icon in Solution Explorer, and then click View Designer.

   The Form1 user interface appears.

2. Double-click the Display Record button to open the *Button1_Click* event procedure in the Code Editor.

3. Type the following program statements:

   ```
   Dim Employee As New Person
   Dim DOB As Date

   Employee.FirstName = TextBox1.Text
   Employee.LastName = TextBox2.Text
   DOB = DateTimePicker1.Value.Date

   MsgBox(Employee.FirstName & " " & Employee.LastName _
     & " is " & Employee.Age(DOB) & " years old.")
   ```

   This routine stores the values entered by the user in an object named *Employee* that's declared as type *Person*. The *New* keyword indicates that you want to immediately create a new instance of the *Employee* object. You've declared variables often in this book—now you get to declare one based on a class you created yourself! The routine then declares a *Date* variable named *DOB* to store the date entered by the user, and the *FirstName* and *LastName* properties of the *Employee* object are set to the first and last names returned by the two text box objects on the form. The value returned by the date/time picker object is stored in the *DOB* variable, and the final program statement displays a message box containing the *FirstName* and *LastName* properties plus the age of the new employee as determined by the *Age* method, which returns an integer value when the *DOB* variable is passed to it. After you define a class in a class module, it's a simple matter to use it in an event procedure, as this routine demonstrates.

4. Click the Save All button to save your changes, and then specify the C:\Vb10sbs\Chap16 folder as the location.

5. Click the Start Debugging button to run the program.

   The user interface appears in the IDE, ready for your input.

6. Type a first name in the First Name text box and a last name in the Last Name text box.

7. Click the date/time picker object's arrow, and then scroll in the list box to a sample birth date (the date I'm selecting is July 12, 1970).

> **Tip** You can scroll faster into the past by clicking the Year field when the date/time picker dialog box is open. Scroll arrows appear, and you can move one year at a time backward or forward. You can also move quickly to the month you want by clicking the Month field and then clicking the month name.

Your form looks similar to this:

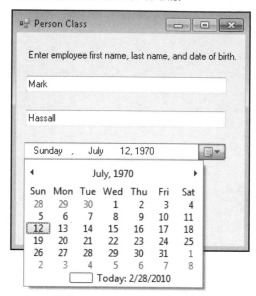

8. Click the Display Record button.

   Your program stores the first name and last name values in property settings and uses the *Age* method to calculate the new employee's current age. A message box displays the result, as shown here:

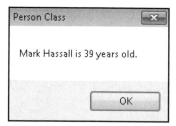

9. Click OK to close the message box, and then experiment with a few different date values, clicking Display Record each time you change the Birth Date field.

10. When you're finished experimenting with your new class, click the Close button on the form.

    The development environment returns.

One Step Further: Inheriting a Base Class

As promised at the beginning of this chapter, I have one more trick to show you regarding user-defined classes and inheritance. Just as forms can inherit form classes, they can also inherit classes that you've defined by using the Add Class command and a class module. The mechanism for inheriting a base (parent) class is to use the *Inherits* statement to include the previously defined class in a new class. You can then add additional properties or methods to the derived (child) class to distinguish it from the base class. I realize that this may be sounding a bit abstract, so let's try an example.

In the following exercise, you'll modify the My Person Class project so that it stores information about new teachers and the grades they teach. First, you'll add a second user-defined class, named *Teacher*, to the *Person* class module. This new class will inherit the *FirstName* property, the *LastName* property, and the *Age* method from the *Person* class and will add an additional property named *Grade* to store the grade in which the new teacher teaches.

Use the *Inherits* keyword

1. Click the Person.vb class in Solution Explorer, and then click the View Code button.

2. Scroll to the bottom of the Code Editor so that the insertion point is below the *End Class* statement.

   As I mentioned earlier, you can include more than one class in a class module, so long as each class is delimited by *Public Class* and *End Class* statements. You'll create a class named *Teacher* in this class module, and you'll use the *Inherits* keyword to incorporate the method and properties you defined in the *Person* class.

3. Type the following class definition in the Code Editor. As before, after you type the *Get* keyword and press ENTER, some of the *Property* structure will be provided for you:

```
Public Class Teacher
    Inherits Person
    Private Level As Short

    Public Property Grade() As Short
        Get
            Return Level
        End Get
        Set(ByVal value As Short)
            Level = value
        End Set
    End Property
End Class
```

   The *Inherits* statement links the *Person* class to this new class, incorporating all of its variables, properties, and methods. If the *Person* class were located in a separate module or project, you could identify its location by using a namespace designation, just as you identify classes when you use the *Imports* statement at the top of a program that uses classes in the .NET Framework class libraries. Basically, I've defined the *Teacher* class as a special type of *Person* class—in addition to the *FirstName* and *LastName* properties, the *Teacher* class has a *Grade* property that records the level at which the teacher teaches.

   Now you'll use the new class in the *Button1_Click* event procedure.

4. Display the *Button1_Click* event procedure in Form1.

   Rather than create a new variable to hold the *Teacher* class, I'll just use the *Employee* variable as is—the only difference will be that I can now set a *Grade* property for the new employee.

5. Modify the *Button1_Click* event procedure as follows. (The shaded lines are the ones that you need to change.)

```
Dim Employee As New Teacher
Dim DOB As Date

Employee.FirstName = TextBox1.Text
Employee.LastName = TextBox2.Text
DOB = DateTimePicker1.Value.Date
Employee.Grade = InputBox("What grade do you teach?")

MsgBox(Employee.FirstName & " " & Employee.LastName _
  & " teaches grade " & Employee.Grade)
```

In this example, I've removed the current age calculation—the *Age* method isn't used—but I did this only to keep information to a minimum in the message box. When you define properties and methods in a class, you aren't required to use them in the program code.

Now you'll run the program.

> **Tip** The revised Person Class program is located in the C:\Vb10sbs\Chap16\Person Class folder.

6. Click the Start Debugging button to run the program.

The new employee form opens on the screen:

7. Type your first name in the First Name text box and your last name in the Last Name text box.

8. Click the date/time picker object, and then scroll to your birth date.

9. Click Display Record.

Your program stores the first name and last name values in property settings and then displays the following input box, which prompts the new teacher for the grade he or she teaches:

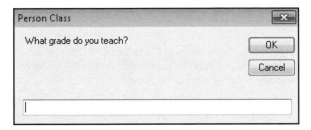

10. Type **3**, and then click OK to close the input box.

The application stores the number 3 in the new *Grade* property and uses the *FirstName*, *LastName*, and *Grade* properties to display the new employee information in a confirming message box. You see this message:

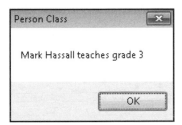

11. Experiment with a few more values if you like, and then click the Close button on the form.

The program stops, and the development environment returns. You're finished working with classes and inheritance in this chapter. Nice job!

Further Experiments with OOP

If you've enjoyed this foray into object-oriented coding techniques, more fun awaits you in Visual Basic 2010, a truly OOP language. In particular, you might want to add events to your class definitions, create default property values, declare and use named and anonymous types, and experiment with a polymorphic feature called *method overloading*. These and other OOP features can be explored by using the Visual Studio Help documentation or by perusing an advanced book on Visual Basic programming. (See the Appendix, "Where to Go for More Information," for a reading list.) You'll also find that a thorough knowledge of classes and how they are created will serve you well as you move more deeply into the .NET Framework and advanced topics like database programming. For the relationship between OOP and databases in Visual Basic, see Part IV, "Database and Web Programming."

Chapter 16 Quick Reference

To	Do This
Inherit an existing form's interface and functionality	Click the Add New Item command on the Project menu, click the Inherited Form template, specify a name for the inherited form, and then click Add. Use the Inheritance Picker to select the form you want to inherit, and then click OK.
	Note that to be eligible for inheritance, base forms must be compiled as .exe or .dll files. If you want to inherit a form that isn't a component in the current project, the form must be compiled as a .dll file.
Customize an inherited form	Add Toolbox controls to the form, and set property settings. Note that you won't be able to set the properties of inherited objects on the form. These objects are identified by small icons and are inactive.
Create your own base classes	Click the Add Class command on the Project menu, specify the class name, and then click Add. Define the class in a class module by using program code.
Hide declared variables in a class	Use the *Private* keyword to hide class variables from other programmers who examine your class. For example:
	`Private Name1 As String`
Create a new property in the class	Define a public property procedure in the class. For example:
| | ```
Public Property FirstName() As String
    Get
        Return Name1
    End Get
    Set(ByVal value As String)
        Name1 = value
    End Set
End Property
``` |
| | Note that the first line shown in this example (containing the *Property* statement) is all that you may need to enter if you are creating a new property with few custom settings. In other words, Visual Studio 2010 automatically recognizes the *Property* keyword when you enter it and uses the new auto-implemented properties feature to create a basic property definition for you. However, in this chapter, I have shown the complete *Get* and *Set* syntax because it is useful in many real-world coding scenarios. |
| Create a new method in the class | Define a Sub or Function procedure in the class. For example: |
| | ```
Public Function Age(ByVal Birthday As Date) As Integer
    Return Int(Now.Subtract(Birthday).Days / 365.25)
End Function
``` |
| Declare an object variable to use the class | Use the *Dim* and *New* keywords, a variable name, and the user-defined class in a program statement. For example: |
| | `Dim Employee As New Person` |

To	Do This
Set properties for an object variable	Use the regular syntax for setting object properties. For example: `Employee.FirstName = TextBox1.Text`
Inherit a base class in a new class	Create a new class, and use the *Inherits* keyword to incorporate the base class's class definitions. For example: ``` Public Class Teacher Inherits Person Private Level As Short Public Property Grade() As Short Get Return Level End Get Set(ByVal value As Short) Level = value End Set End Property End Class ```

Chapter 17
Working with Printers

After completing this chapter, you will be able to:

- Print graphics from a Visual Basic program.

- Print text from a Visual Basic program.

- Print multipage documents.

- Create Print, Page Setup, and Print Preview dialog boxes in your programs.

In the following sections, you'll complete your survey of user interface design and components by learning how to add printer support to your Windows applications. Microsoft Visual Basic 2010 supports printing with the *PrintDocument* class. The *PrintDocument* class and its many methods, properties, and supporting classes handle sending text and graphics to printers.

In this chapter, you'll learn how to print graphics and text from Visual Basic programs, manage multipage printing tasks, and add printing dialog boxes to your user interface. In my opinion, this chapter is one of the most useful in the book, with lots of practical code that you can immediately incorporate into real-world programming projects. Printing support doesn't come automatically in Visual Basic 2010, but the routines in this chapter will help you print longer text documents and display helpful dialog boxes such as Page Setup, Print, and Print Preview from within your programs. I'll start the chapter with two very simple printing routines to show you the basics, and then I'll get considerably more sophisticated

Using the *PrintDocument* Class

Most Windows applications allow users to print documents after they create them, and by now you might be wondering just how printing works in Visual Basic programs. This is one area where Visual Basic 2010 has lots of power and flexibility, but this impressive technical sophistication comes at a little cost. Producing printed output from Visual Basic programs isn't a trivial process, and the technique you use depends on the type and amount of printed output you want to generate. In all cases, however, the fundamental mechanism that regulates printing in Visual Basic 2010 is the *PrintDocument* class, which you can create in a project in two ways:

- By adding the *PrintDocument* control to a form

- By defining it programmatically with a few lines of Visual Basic code

The *PrintDocument* class is located in the *System.Drawing.Printing* namespace. The *System.Drawing.Printing* namespace provides several useful classes for printing text and graphics, including the *PrinterSettings* class, which contains the default print settings for a printer; the *PageSettings* class, which contains print settings for a particular page; and the *PrintPageEventArgs* class, which contains event information about the page that's about to be printed. The *System.Drawing.Printing* namespace is automatically incorporated into your project. To make it easier to reference the printing classes and other important values in this namespace, add the following *Imports* statement to the top of your form:

```
Imports System.Drawing.Printing
```

To learn how to use the *PrintDocument* class in a program, complete the following exercise, which teaches you how to add a *PrintDocument* control to your project and use it to print a graphics file on your system.

Use the *PrintDocument* control

1. Start Microsoft Visual Studio, and then create a new Visual Basic Windows Forms Application project named **My Print Graphics**.

   A blank form opens in the Visual Studio Integrated Development Environment (IDE).

2. Use the *Label* control to draw a label object near the top of the form.

3. Use the *TextBox* control to draw a text box object below the label object.

   The text box object will be used to type the name of the artwork file that you want to open. A single-line text box will be sufficient.

4. Use the *Button* control to draw a button object below the text box.

   This button object will print the graphics file. Now you'll add a *PrintDocument* control.

5. Scroll down until you see the Printing tab of the Toolbox, and then double-click the *PrintDocument* control.

   Like the *Timer* control, the *PrintDocument* control is invisible at run time, so it's placed in the component tray beneath the form when you create it. Your project now has access to the *PrintDocument* class and its useful printing functionality.

6. Set the following properties for the objects on your form:

Object	Property	Setting
Label1	Text	"Type the name of a graphic file to print."
TextBox1	Text	"C:\Vb10sbs\Chap15\Sun.ico"
Button1	Text	"Print Graphics"
Form1	Text	"Print Graphics"

Your form looks similar to this:

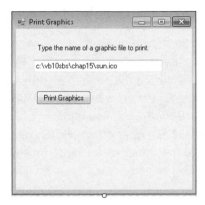

Now add the program code necessary to print a graphic file (bitmap, icon, metafile, JPEG file, and so on).

7. Double-click the Print Graphics button.

The *Button1_Click* event procedure appears in the Code Editor.

8. Move the insertion point to the top of the form's code, and then type the following program statement:

```
Imports System.Drawing.Printing
```

This *Imports* statement declares the *System.Drawing.Printing* namespace, which makes it easier to reference the printing classes.

9. Now move the insertion point down to the *Button1_Click* event procedure, and enter the following program code:

```
' Print using an error handler to catch problems
Try
    AddHandler PrintDocument1.PrintPage, AddressOf Me.PrintGraphic
    PrintDocument1.Print() 'print graphic
Catch ex As Exception 'catch printing exception
    MessageBox.Show("Sorry--there is a problem printing", ex.ToString())
End Try
```

> **Note** After you enter this code, you'll see a jagged line under *Me.PrintGraphic* indicating an error. Don't worry, you'll be adding the *PrintGraphic* procedure in the next step.

This code uses the *AddHandler* statement, which specifies that the *PrintGraphic* event procedure (also called an event handler) should be called when the *PrintPage* event of the *PrintDocument1* object fires. An *event procedure* is a mechanism that handles events that represent crucial actions in the life cycle of an object. You have been working with event procedures several times already. For example, you just created the *Click* event procedure for the *Button1* object. The *AddHandler* statement is a way to manually "wire up" an event procedure.

In this case, the event procedure being specified is related to printing services, and the request comes with specific information about the page to be printed, the current printer settings, and other attributes of the *PrintDocument* class. Technically, the *AddressOf* operator is used to identify the *PrintGraphic* event procedure by determining its internal address and storing it. The *AddressOf* operator implicitly creates an object known as a *delegate* that forwards calls to the appropriate event procedure when an event occurs.

The third line of the code you just entered uses the *Print* method of the *PrintDocument1* object to send a print request to the *PrintGraphic* event procedure. This print request is located inside a *Try* code block to catch any printing problems that might occur during the printing activity. I introduced the *Try … Catch* error handler in Chapter 9, "Trapping Errors by Using Structured Error Handling." Here the *ex* variable is being declared of type *Exception* to get a detailed message about any errors that occur.

10. Scroll above the *Button1_Click* event procedure in the Code Editor to the general declaration space below the *Public Class Form1* statement. Then type the following *PrintGraphic* event procedure:

```
'Sub for printing graphic
Private Sub PrintGraphic(ByVal sender As Object, _
  ByVal ev As PrintPageEventArgs)
    ' Create the graphic using DrawImage
    ev.Graphics.DrawImage(Image.FromFile(TextBox1.Text), _
      ev.Graphics.VisibleClipBounds)
    ' Specify that this is the last page to print
    ev.HasMorePages = False
End Sub
```

This routine handles the printing event generated by the *PrintDocument1.Print* method. I've declared the Sub procedure within the form's code, but you can also declare the Sub as a general-purpose procedure in a module. Note the *ev* variable in the argument list for the *PrintGraphic* procedure. This variable is the crucial carrier of information about the current print page, and it's declared of type *PrintPageEventArgs*, a class in the *System.Drawing.Printing* namespace.

To actually print the graphic, the procedure uses the *Graphics.DrawImage* method associated with the current print page to load a graphics file by using the file name stored in the *Text* property of the *TextBox1* object. (By default, I set this property to C:\Vb10sbs\Chap15\Sun.ico—the same Sun icon used in Chapter 15, "Adding Graphics and Animation Effects"—but you can change this value at run time and print any artwork files that you like.) Finally, I set the *ev.HasMorePages* property to False so that Visual Basic understands that the print job doesn't have multiple pages.

11. Click the Save All button on the Standard toolbar to save your changes, and then specify the C:\Vb10sbs\Chap17 folder as the location.

Now you're ready to run the program. Before you do so, you might want to locate a few graphics files on your system that you can print. (Just jot down the paths for now and type them in when you test the project.)

Run the Print Graphics program

 Tip The complete Print Graphics program is located in the C:\Vb10sbs\Chap17\Print Graphics folder.

1. Click the Start Debugging button on the Standard toolbar.

    Your program runs in the IDE. You see this form:

    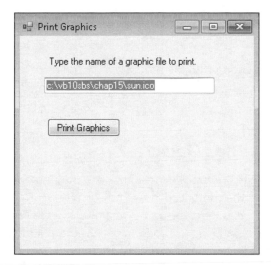

2. Turn on your printer, and then verify that it is online and has paper.

3. If you installed your sample files in the default C:\Vb10sbs folder, click the Print Graphics button now to print the Sun.ico icon graphic.

    If you didn't use the default sample file location, or if you want to print a different artwork file, modify the text box path accordingly, and then click the Print Graphics button.

    The *DrawImage* method expands the graphic to the maximum size your printer can produce on one page and then sends the graphic to the printer. (This "expansion feature" fills up the page and gives you a closer look at the image.) Admittedly, this might not be that interesting for you, but we'll get more sophisticated in a moment. (If you want to modify the location or size of your output, search the Visual Studio Help documentation for the "Graphics.DrawImage Method" topic, study the different argument variations available, and then modify your program code.)

If you look closely, you see the following dialog box appear when Visual Basic sends your print job to the printer:

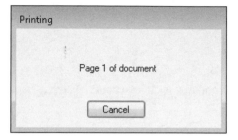

This status box is also a product of the *PrintDocument* class, and it provides users with a professional-looking print interface, including the page number for each printed page.

4. Type additional paths if you like, and then click the Print Graphics button for more printouts.

5. When you're finished experimenting with the program, click the Close button on the form.

The program stops. Not bad for your first attempt at printing from a Visual Basic program!

Printing Text from a Text Box Object

You've had a quick introduction to the *PrintDocument* control and printing graphics. Now try using a similar technique to print the contents of a text box on a Visual Basic form. In the following exercise, you'll build a simple project that prints text by using the *PrintDocument* class, but this time you'll define the class by using program code without adding the *PrintDocument* control to your form. In addition, you'll use the *Graphics.DrawString* method to send the entire contents of a text box object to the default printer.

> **Note** The following program is designed to print one page or less of text. To print multiple pages, you need to add additional program code, which will be explored later in the chapter. My goal is to introduce one new printing feature at a time.

Use the *Graphics.DrawString* method to print text

1. Click the Close Project command on the File menu, and then create a new Windows Forms Application project named **My Print Text**.

   A blank form opens.

2. Use the *Label* control to draw a label object near the top of the form.

   This label will display a line of instructions for the user.

3. Use the *TextBox* control to draw a text box object below the label object.

The text box object will contain the text you want to print.

4. Set the *Multiline* property of the text box object to True, and then expand the text box so that it's large enough to enter several lines of text.

5. Use the *Button* control to draw a button object below the text box.

This button object will print the text file.

6. Set the following properties for the objects on your form:

Object	Property	Setting
Label1	Text	"Type some text in this text box object, then click Print Text."
TextBox1	ScrollBars	Vertical
Button1	Text	"Print Text"
Form1	Text	"Print Text"

Your form looks similar to this:

Now add the program code necessary to print the contents of the text box.

7. Double-click the Print Text button.

The *Button1_Click* event procedure appears in the Code Editor.

8. Scroll to the very top of the form's code, and then type the following *Imports* declaration:

```
Imports System.Drawing.Printing
```

This makes it easier to reference the classes in the *System.Drawing.Printing* namespace, which includes the *PrintDocument* class.

9. Now scroll back down to the *Button1_Click* event procedure, and then enter the following program code:

```
' Print using an error handler to catch problems
Try
    ' Declare PrintDoc variable of type PrintDocument
    Dim PrintDoc As New PrintDocument
    AddHandler PrintDoc.PrintPage, AddressOf Me.PrintText
    PrintDoc.Print() 'print text
Catch ex As Exception 'catch printing exception
    MessageBox.Show("Sorry--there is a problem printing", ex.ToString())
End Try
```

The lines that are new or changed from the Print Graphics program are shaded. Rather than add a *PrintDocument* control to your form, this time you simply created the *PrintDocument* programmatically by using the *Dim* keyword and the *PrintDocument* type, which is defined in the *System.Drawing.Printing* namespace. From this point on, the *PrintDoc* variable represents the *PrintDocument* object, and it is used to declare the error handler and to print the text document. Note that for clarity, I renamed the Sub procedure that will handle the print event *PrintText* (rather than *PrintGraphic*).

10. Scroll above the *Button1_Click* event procedure in the Code Editor to the general declaration area. Type the following *PrintText* event procedure:

```
'Sub for printing text
Private Sub PrintText(ByVal sender As Object, _
  ByVal ev As PrintPageEventArgs)
    'Use DrawString to create text in a Graphics object
    ev.Graphics.DrawString(TextBox1.Text, New Font("Arial", _
      11, FontStyle.Regular), Brushes.Black, 120, 120)
    ' Specify that this is the last page to print
    ev.HasMorePages = False
End Sub
```

This routine handles the printing event generated by the *PrintDoc.Print* method. The changes from the *PrintGraphic* procedure in the previous exercises are also shaded. As you can see, when you print text, you need to use a new method.

Rather than use *Graphics.DrawImage*, which renders a graphics image, you must use *Graphics.DrawString*, which prints a text string. I've specified the text in the *Text* property of the text box object to print some basic font formatting (Arial, 11 point, regular style, black color), and (*x*, *y*) coordinates (120, 120) on the page to start drawing. These specifications will give the printed output a default look that's similar to the text box on the screen. Like last time, I've also set the *ev.HasMorePages* property to False to indicate that the print job doesn't have multiple pages.

11. Click the Save All button on the toolbar to save your changes, and then specify C:\Vb10sbs\Chap17 as the folder location.

Now you'll run the program to see how a text box object prints.

Run the Print Text program

> **Tip** The complete Print Text program is located in the C:\Vb10sbs\Chap17\Print Text folder.

1. Click the Start Debugging button on the toolbar.

   Your program runs in the IDE.

2. Verify that your printer is on.

3. Type some sample text in the text box. If you type multiple lines, be sure to include a carriage return at the end of each line.

   Wrapping isn't supported in this demonstration program—very long lines will potentially extend past the right margin. (Again, we'll solve this problem soon.) Your form looks something like this:

4. Click the Print Text button.

   The program displays a printing dialog box and prints the contents of your text box.

5. Modify the text box, and try additional printouts, if you like.

6. When you're finished, click the Close button on the form to stop the program.

Now you know how to print both text and graphics from a program.

Printing Multipage Text Files

The printing techniques that you've just learned are useful for simple text documents, but they have a few important limitations. First, the method I used doesn't allow for long lines—in other words, text that extends beyond the right margin. Unlike the text box object, the *PrintDocument* object doesn't automatically wrap lines when they reach the edge of the paper. If you have files that don't contain carriage returns at the end of lines, you'll need to write the code that handles these long lines.

The second limitation is that the Print Text program can't print more than one page of text. Indeed, it doesn't even understand what a page of text *is*—the printing procedure simply sends the text to the default printer. If the text block is too long to fit on a single page, the additional text won't be printed. To handle multipage printouts, you need to create a virtual page of text called the *PrintPage* and then add text to it until the page is full. When the page is full, it is sent to the printer, and this process continues until there is no more text to print. At that point, the print job ends.

If fixing these two limitations sounds complicated, don't despair yet—there are a few handy mechanisms that help you create virtual text pages in Visual Basic and help you print text files with long lines and several pages of text. The first mechanism is the *PrintPage* event, which occurs when a page is printed. *PrintPage* receives an argument of the type *PrintPageEventArgs*, which provides you with the dimensions and characteristics of the current printer page. Another mechanism is the *Graphics.MeasureString* method. The *MeasureString* method can be used to determine how many characters and lines can fit in a rectangular area of the page. By using these mechanisms and others, it's relatively straightforward to construct procedures that process multipage print jobs.

Complete the following steps to build a program named Print File that opens text files of any length and prints them. The Print File program also demonstrates how to use the *RichTextBox*, *PrintDialog*, and *OpenFileDialog* controls. The *RichTextBox* control is a more robust version of the *TextBox* control you just used to display text. The *PrintDialog* control displays a standard Print dialog box so that you can specify various print settings. The *OpenFileDialog* control lets you select a text file for printing. (You used *OpenFileDialog* in Chapter 4, "Working with Menus, Toolbars, and Dialog Boxes.")

Manage print requests with *RichTextBox*, *OpenFileDialog*, and *PrintDialog* controls

1. Click the Close Project command on the File menu, and then create a new Windows Forms Application project named **My Print File**.

   A blank form opens.

2. Use the *Button* control in the Toolbox to draw two buttons in the upper-left corner of the form.

   This program has a simple user interface, but the printing techniques you'll learn are easily adaptable to much more complex solutions.

3. Click the *RichTextBox* control in the Toolbox, and then draw a rich text box object that covers the bottom half of the form.

4. Double-click the *OpenFileDialog* control on the Dialogs tab to add an open file dialog object to the component tray below your form.

   You'll use the open file dialog object to browse for text files on your system.

5. Double-click the *PrintDocument* control on the Printing tab to add a print document object to the component tray.

   You'll use the print document object to support printing in your application.

6. Double-click the *PrintDialog* control on the Printing tab to add a print dialog object to the component tray.

   You'll use the print dialog object to open a Print dialog box in your program.

7. Now set the following properties for the objects on your form:

Object	Property	Setting
Button1	*Name*	btnOpen
	Text	"Open"
Button2	*Name*	btnPrint
	Enabled	False
	Text	"Print"
Form1	*Text*	"Print File"

Your form looks something like this:

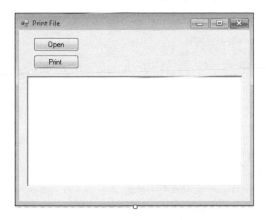

Now add the program code necessary to open the text file and print it.

8. Double-click the Open button.

   The *btnOpen_Click* event procedure appears in the Code Editor.

9. Scroll to the top of the form, and then enter the following code:

```
Imports System.IO 'for FileStream class
Imports System.Drawing.Printing
```

These statements make it easier to reference the *FileStream* class and the classes for printing.

10. Move the cursor below the *Public Class Form1* statement, and then enter the following variable declarations:

```
Private PrintPageSettings As New PageSettings
Private StringToPrint As String
Private PrintFont As New Font("Arial", 10)
```

These statements define important information about the pages that will be printed.

11. Scroll to the *btnOpen_Click* event procedure, and then type the following program code:

```
Dim FilePath As String
'Display Open dialog box and select text file
OpenFileDialog1.Filter = "Text files (*.txt)|*.txt"
OpenFileDialog1.ShowDialog()
'If Cancel button not selected, load FilePath variable
If OpenFileDialog1.FileName <> "" Then
    FilePath = OpenFileDialog1.FileName
    Try
        'Read text file and load into RichTextBox1
        Dim MyFileStream As New FileStream(FilePath, FileMode.Open)
        RichTextBox1.LoadFile(MyFileStream, _
          RichTextBoxStreamType.PlainText)
        MyFileStream.Close()
        'Initialize string to print
        StringToPrint = RichTextBox1.Text
        'Enable Print button
        btnPrint.Enabled = True
    Catch ex As Exception
        'display error messages if they appear
        MessageBox.Show(ex.Message)
    End Try
End If
```

When the user clicks the Open button, this event procedure displays an Open dialog box using a filter that displays only text files. When the user selects a file, the file name is assigned to a public string variable named *FilePath*, which is declared at the top of the event procedure. The procedure then uses a *Try ... Catch* error handler to load the text file into the *RichTextBox1* object. To facilitate the loading process, I've used the *FileStream* class and the *Open* file mode, which places the complete contents of the text file into the *MyFileStream* variable. Finally, the event procedure enables the Print button (*btnPrint*) so that the user can print the file. In short, this routine opens the file and enables the print button on the form but doesn't do any printing itself.

Now you'll add the necessary program code to display the Print dialog box and print the file by using logic that monitors the dimensions of the current text page.

Add code for the *btnPrint* and *PrintDocument1* objects

1. Display the form again, and then double-click the Print button (*btnPrint*) to display its event procedure in the Code Editor.

2. Type the following program code:

```
Try
    'Specify current page settings
    PrintDocument1.DefaultPageSettings = PrintPageSettings
    'Specify document for print dialog box and show
    StringToPrint = RichTextBox1.Text
    PrintDialog1.Document = PrintDocument1
    Dim result As DialogResult = PrintDialog1.ShowDialog()
    'If click OK, print document to printer
    If result = DialogResult.OK Then
        PrintDocument1.Print()
    End If
Catch ex As Exception
    'Display error message
    MessageBox.Show(ex.Message)
End Try
```

This event procedure sets the default print settings for the document and assigns the contents of the *RichTextBox1* object to the *StringToPrint* string variable (defined at the top of the form) in case the user changes the text in the rich text box. It then opens the Print dialog box and allows the user to adjust any print settings (printer, number of copies, the print-to-file option, and so on). If the user clicks OK, the event procedure sends this print job to the printer by issuing the following statement:

```
PrintDocument1.Print()
```

3. Display the form again, and then double-click the PrintDocument1 object in the component tray.

   Visual Studio adds the *PrintPage* event procedure for the *PrintDocument1* object.

4. Type the following program code in the *PrintDocument1_PrintPage* event procedure:

```
Dim numChars As Integer
Dim numLines As Integer
Dim stringForPage As String
Dim strFormat As New StringFormat
'Based on page setup, define drawable rectangle on page
Dim rectDraw As New RectangleF( _
    e.MarginBounds.Left, e.MarginBounds.Top, _
    e.MarginBounds.Width, e.MarginBounds.Height)
'Define area to determine how much text can fit on a page
'Make height one line shorter to ensure text doesn't clip
Dim sizeMeasure As New SizeF(e.MarginBounds.Width, _
    e.MarginBounds.Height - PrintFont.GetHeight(e.Graphics))

'When drawing long strings, break between words
strFormat.Trimming = StringTrimming.Word
```

```
'Compute how many chars and lines can fit based on sizeMeasure
e.Graphics.MeasureString(StringToPrint, PrintFont, _
  sizeMeasure, strFormat, numChars, numLines)
'Compute string that will fit on a page
stringForPage = StringToPrint.Substring(0, numChars)
'Print string on current page
e.Graphics.DrawString(stringForPage, PrintFont, _
  Brushes.Black, rectDraw, strFormat)
'If there is more text, indicate there are more pages
If numChars < StringToPrint.Length Then
    'Subtract text from string that has been printed
    StringToPrint = StringToPrint.Substring(numChars)
    e.HasMorePages = True
Else
    e.HasMorePages = False
    'All text has been printed, so restore string
    StringToPrint = RichTextBox1.Text
End If
```

This event procedure handles the actual printing of the text document, and it does so by carefully defining a printing area (or printing rectangle) based on the settings in the Page Setup dialog box. Any text that fits within this area can be printed normally; text that's outside this area needs to be wrapped to the following lines, or pages, as you'd expect to happen in a standard Windows application.

The printing area is defined by the *rectDraw* variable, which is based on the *RectangleF* class. The *strFormat* variable and the *Trimming* method are used to trim strings that extend beyond the edge of the right margin. The actual text strings are printed by the *DrawString* method, which you've already used in this chapter. The *HasMorePages* property is used to specify whether there are additional pages to be printed. If no additional pages remain, the *HasMorePage* property is set to False, and the contents of the *StringToPrint* variable are restored to the contents of the *RichTextBox1* object.

5. Click the Save All button on the toolbar to save your changes, and then specify the C:\Vb10sbs\Chap17 folder as the location.

That's a lot of typing! But now you're ready to run the program and see how printing text files on multiple pages works.

Run the Print File program

 Tip The complete Print File program is located in the C:\Vb10sbs\Chap17\Print File folder.

1. Click the Start Debugging button on the toolbar.

Your program runs in the IDE. Notice that the Print button is currently disabled because you haven't selected a file yet.

2. Click the Open button.

The program displays an Open dialog box.

3. Browse to the C:\Vb10sbs\Chap17 folder, and then click the Longfile.txt file.

In Windows 7, your Open dialog box looks like this:

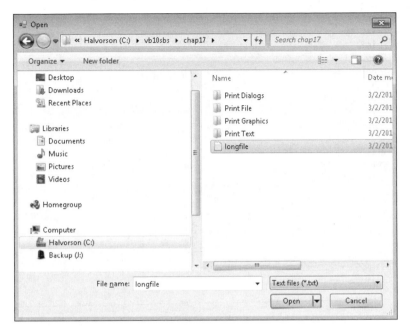

4. Click Open to select the file.

Your program loads the text file into the rich text box object on the form and then enables the Print button. This file is long and has a few lines that wrap so that you can test the wide margin and multipage printing options. Your form looks like this:

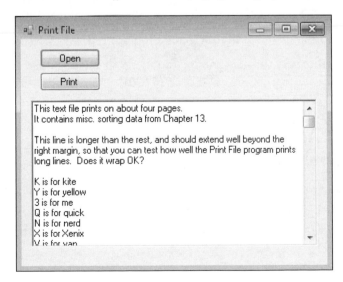

5. Verify that your printer is on, and then click the Print button.

Visual Basic displays the Print dialog box, customized with the name and settings for your printer, as shown in the following screen shot:

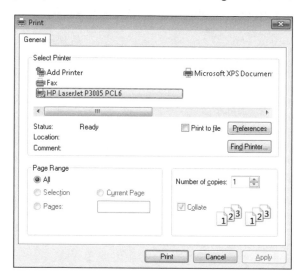

Many of the options in the Print dialog box are active, and you can experiment with them as you would a regular Windows application.

6. Click Print to print the document.

Your program submits the four-page print job to the Windows print queue. After a moment (and if your printer is ready), the printer begins printing the document. As in previous exercises, a dialog box automatically opens to show you the printing status and gives you an indication of how many pages your printed document will be.

7. Click the Close button on the form to stop the program.

You've just created a set of very versatile printing routines that can be added to any Visual Basic application that needs to print multiple pages of text!

One Step Further: Adding Print Preview and Page Setup Dialog Boxes

The Print File application is ready to handle several printing tasks, but its interface isn't as visually compelling as that of a commercial Windows application. You can make your program more flexible and interesting by adding a few extra dialog box options to supplement the Print dialog box that you experimented with in the previous exercise.

Two additional printing controls are available on the Printing tab of the Toolbox, and they work much like the familiar *PrintDialog* and *OpenFileDialog* controls that you've used in this book:

- The *PrintPreviewDialog* control displays a custom Print Preview dialog box.
- The *PageSetupDialog* control displays a custom Page Setup dialog box.

As with other dialog boxes, you can add these printing controls to your form by using the Toolbox, or you can create them programmatically.

In the following exercise, you'll add Print Preview and Page Setup dialog boxes to the Print File program you've been working with. In the completed practice files, I've named this project Print Dialogs so that you can distinguish the code of the two projects, but you can add the dialog box features directly to the Print File project if you want.

Add *PrintPreviewDialog* and *PageSetupDialog* controls

1. If you didn't complete the previous exercise, open the Print File project from the C:\Vb10sbs\Chap17\Print File folder.

   The Print File project is the starting point for this project.

2. Display the form, and then use the *Button* control to add two additional buttons to the top of the form.

3. Double-click the *PrintPreviewDialog* control on the Printing tab of the Toolbox.

   A print preview dialog object is added to the component tray.

4. Double-click the *PageSetupDialog* control on the Printing tab of the Toolbox.

   A page setup dialog object is added to the component tray. If the objects in the component tray obscure one another, you can drag them to a better (more visible) location, or you can right-click the component tray and select Line Up Icons.

5. Set the following properties for the button objects on the form:

Object	Property	Setting
Button1	*Name*	btnSetup
	Enabled	False
	Text	"Page Setup"
Button2	*Name*	btnPreview
	Enabled	False
	Text	"Print Preview"

Your form looks like this:

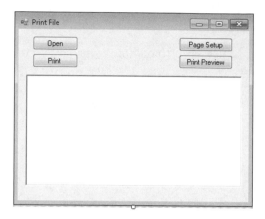

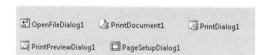

6. Double-click the Page Setup button (*btnSetup*) to display the *btnSetup_Click* event procedure in the Code Editor.

7. Type the following program code:

```
Try
    'Load page settings and display page setup dialog box
    PageSetupDialog1.PageSettings = PrintPageSettings
    PageSetupDialog1.ShowDialog()
Catch ex As Exception
    'Display error message
    MessageBox.Show(ex.Message)
End Try
```

The code for creating a Page Setup dialog box in this program is quite simple because the *PrintPageSettings* variable has already been defined at the top of the form. This variable holds the current page definition information, and when it's assigned to the *PageSettings* property of the *PageSetupDialog1* object, the *ShowDialog* method automatically loads a dialog box that allows the user to modify what the program has selected as the default page orientation, margins, and so on. The *Try … Catch* error handler simply handles any errors that might occur when the *ShowDialog* method is used.

8. Display the form again, and then double-click the Print Preview button (*btnPreview*) to display the *btnPreview_Click* event procedure.

9. Type the following program code:

```
Try
    'Specify current page settings
    PrintDocument1.DefaultPageSettings = PrintPageSettings
    'Specify document for print preview dialog box and show
    StringToPrint = RichTextBox1.Text
    PrintPreviewDialog1.Document = PrintDocument1
    PrintPreviewDialog1.ShowDialog()
Catch ex As Exception
    'Display error message
    MessageBox.Show(ex.Message)
End Try
```

In a similar way, the *btnPreview_Click* event procedure assigns the *PrintPageSettings* variable to the *DefaultPageSettings* property of the *PrintDocument1* object, and then it copies the text in the rich text box object to the *StringToPrint* variable and opens the Print Preview dialog box. Print Preview automatically uses the page settings data to display a visual representation of the document as it will be printed—you don't need to display this information manually.

Now you'll make a slight modification to the program code in the *btnOpen_Click* event procedure.

10. Scroll up to the *btnOpen_Click* event procedure in the Code Editor.

This is the procedure that displays the Open dialog box, opens a text file, and enables the printing buttons. Because you just added the Page Setup and Print Preview buttons, you have to add program code to enable those two printing buttons as well.

11. Scroll to the bottom of the event procedure, just before the final *Catch* code block, and then locate the following program statement:

```
btnPrint.Enabled = True
```

12. Below that statement, add the following lines of code:

```
btnSetup.Enabled = True
btnPreview.Enabled = True
```

Now your program will enable the print buttons when there's a document available to print.

13. Click the Save All button on the toolbar to save your changes.

Test the Page Setup and Print Preview features

 Tip The complete Print Dialogs program is located in the C:\Vb10sbs\Chap17\Print Dialogs folder.

1. Click the Start Debugging button on the toolbar.

   The program opens, with only the first button object enabled.

2. Click the Open button, and then open the Longfile.txt file in the C:\Vb10sbs\Chap17 folder.

   The remaining three button objects are now enabled, as shown here:

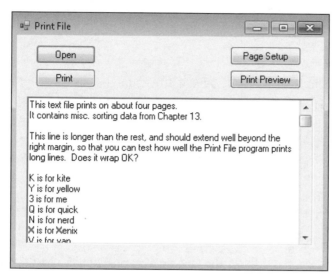

3. Click the Page Setup button.

   Your program displays the Page Setup dialog box, as shown here:

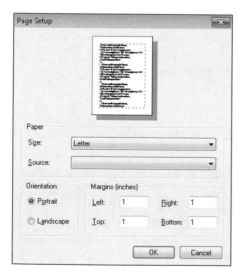

Page Setup provides numerous useful options, including the ability to change the paper size and source, the orientation of the printing (Portrait or Landscape), and the page margins (Left, Right, Top, and Bottom).

4. Change the Left margin to 2, and then click OK.

The left margin will now be 2 inches.

5. Click the Print Preview button.

Your program displays the Print Preview dialog box, as shown in the following screen shot:

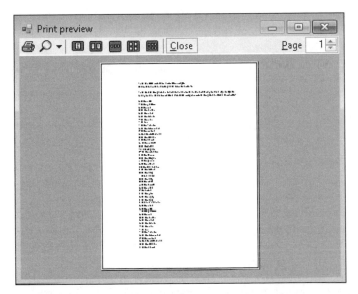

If you've used the Print Preview command in Microsoft Word or Microsoft Excel, you will recognize several of the buttons and preview features in this Print Preview dialog box. For example, the helpful toolbar contains (from left to right) the Print and Zoom buttons; the One Page, Two Pages, Three Pages, Four Pages, and Six Pages buttons (to adjust how many pages are visible at one time); the Close button; and the Page Select control. No program code is required to make these helpful features operate.

6. Click the Four Pages button to display your document four pages at a time.

7. Click the Maximize button on the Print Preview title bar to make the window full size.

8. Click the Zoom arrow, and then click 150%.

Your screen looks like this:

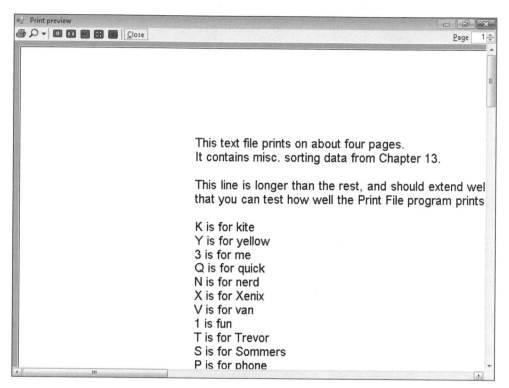

9. Click the Zoom arrow and return the view to Auto.

10. Click the Three Pages button, and then click the Up arrow in the Page Select box to view pages 2 through 4.

As you can see, this Print Preview window is quite impressive—and you incorporated it into your program with just a few lines of code!

11. If you want to test printing the entire document again, click the Print button.

12. When you're finished experimenting, click the Close button to close the Print Preview dialog box, and then click the Close button to close the program.

You're done working with printers for now.

Chapter 17 Quick Reference

To	Do This
Make it easier to reference the printing classes in your projects	Add the following *Imports* statement to the top of your form: ```Imports System.Drawing.Printing```

Create a printing event procedure	Double-click the *PrintDocument1* object in the component tray
	or
	Use the *AddHandler* statement and the *AddressOf* operator. For example:
	
	```AddHandler PrintDocument1.PrintPage, _```
	``` AddressOf Me.PrintGraphic```

Create a *PrintDocument* object in your project	Double-click the *PrintDocument* control on the Printing tab of the Toolbox. *or* Include the following variable declaration in your program code. ```Dim PrintDoc As New PrintDocument```

Print graphics from a printing event procedure	Use the *Graphics.DrawImage* method. For example:
	
	```ev.Graphics.DrawImage(Image.FromFile _```
	``` (TextBox1.Text), ev.Graphics.VisibleClipBounds)```

Print text from a printing event procedure	Use the *Graphics.DrawString* method in an event procedure. For example:
	
	```ev.Graphics.DrawString(TextBox1.Text, _```
	``` New Font("Arial", 11, FontStyle.Regular), _```
	``` Brushes.Black, 120, 120)```

Call a printing event procedure	Use the *Print* method of an object of type *PrintDocument*. For example: ```PrintDoc.Print()```
Print multipage text documents	Write a handler for the *PrintPage* event, which receives an argument of the type *PrintPageEventArgs*. Compute the rectangular area on the page for the text, use the *MeasureString* method to determine how much text will fit on the current page, and use the *DrawString* method to print the text on the page. If additional pages are needed, set the *HasMorePages* property to True. When all text has been printed, set *HasMorePages* to False.

Open a text file by using the *FileStream* class, and then load it into a *RichTextBox* object	Create a variable of type *FileStream*, specifying the path and file mode, load the stream into a *RichTextBox*, and then close the stream. For example:
	
	```Imports System.IO 'at the top of the form```
	```...```
	```Dim MyFileStream As New FileStream(_```
	``` FilePath, FileMode.Open)```
	```RichTextBox1.LoadFile(MyFileStream, _```
	``` RichTextBoxStreamType.PlainText)```
	```MyFileStream.Close()```

Display printing dialog boxes in your programs	Use the *PrintDialog*, *PrintPreviewDialog*, and *PageSetupDialog* controls on the Printing tab of the Toolbox.

Part IV

Database and Web Programming

In Part IV, you'll learn how to work with information stored in databases and Web sites. First, you'll learn about Microsoft ADO.NET, an important paradigm for working with database information, and you'll learn how to display, modify, and search for database content by using a combination of program code and Windows Forms controls. Microsoft Visual Studio 2010 was specifically designed to create applications that provide access to a rich variety of data sources. These custom interfaces have traditionally been called *database front ends*, meaning that through your Microsoft Visual Basic application, the user is given a more useful window into database information than simply manipulating raw database records. However, a more appropriate description in Visual Studio 2010 is that you can build *datacentric* applications, meaning that through your application, the user is invited to explore the full potential of any number of rich data source connections, whether to local or remote locations, and that the application places this data at the center of the user's computing experience.

Chapter 18
Getting Started with ADO.NET

After completing this chapter, you will be able to:

- Use the Data Source Configuration Wizard to establish a connection to a database and build a dataset.

- Use the Dataset Designer and the Data Sources window to examine dataset members and create bound objects on forms.

- Create datacentric applications by using dataset and data navigator objects.

- Use bound *TextBox* and *MaskedTextBox* controls to display database information on a Windows form.

- Write SQL statements to filter and sort dataset information by using the Visual Studio Query Builder tool.

In this chapter, you'll take your first steps with ADO.NET and with datacentric applications. You'll use the Data Source Configuration Wizard to establish a connection to a Microsoft Access database on your system, you'll create a dataset that represents a subset of useful fields and records from a database table, and you'll use the Dataset Designer and Data Sources window to examine dataset members and create bound objects on your forms. You'll also learn how to use *TextBox* and *MaskedTextBox* controls to present database information to your user, and you'll learn to write Structured Query Language (SQL) SELECT statements that filter datasets (and therefore what your user sees and uses) in interesting ways.

Database Programming with ADO.NET

A *database* is an organized collection of information stored in a file. You can create powerful databases by using any of a variety of database products, including Access, Microsoft SQL Server, and Oracle. You can also store and transmit database information by using Extensible Markup Language (XML), a file format designed for exchanging structured data over the Internet and in other settings.

Creating and maintaining databases has become an essential task for all major corporations, government institutions, nonprofit agencies, and most small businesses. Rich data resources—for example, customer addresses, manufacturing inventories, account balances, employee records, donor lists, and order histories—have become the lifeblood of the business world.

You can use Microsoft Visual Studio 2010 to create new databases, but Visual Studio 2010 is primarily designed for displaying, analyzing, and manipulating the information in existing databases. ADO.NET, first introduced in Microsoft Visual Studio .NET 2002, is still the standard data model for database programming in Visual Studio 2010. ADO.NET has been improved over the years to work with a large number of data access scenarios, and it has been carefully optimized for Internet use. For example, it uses the same basic method for accessing local, client-server, and Internet-based data sources, and the internal data format of ADO.NET is XML.

Fortunately, most of the database applications that programmers created using Microsoft Visual Basic 2008 and ADO.NET still function very well, and the basic techniques for accessing a database are mostly the same in Visual Basic 2010. However, there are two new database technologies in Visual Studio 2010 that will be of considerable use to experienced database programmers. These technologies are Language-Integrated Query (LINQ) and the ADO.NET Entity Framework.

LINQ is included with Visual Studio 2010 and offers the capability to write object-oriented database queries directly within Visual Basic code. The ADO.NET Entity Framework introduces a new object model, powerful new features, and tools that will make database applications even freer from hard-coded dependencies on a particular data engine or logical model. As database technology and the Internet continue to advance, ADO.NET will continue to evolve, and Visual Basic programmers should be well-positioned to benefit.

Database Terminology

An underlying theme in the preceding section is that database programmers are often faced with new technologies to decode and master, a reorientation often initiated by the terms *new paradigm* or *new database model*. Although continually learning new techniques can be a source of frustration, the rapid pace of change can be explained partially by the relative newness of distributed and multiple-tier database application programming in Windows, as well as technical innovations, security needs, and Web programming challenges that are beyond the control of the Visual Studio development team. In this chapter, however, we'll be starting at the *beginning*, and with database programming more than almost any other subject, you really need to be exposed to topics *step by step*. Let's start by understanding some basic database terminology.

A *field* (also called a *column*) is a category of information stored in a database. Typical fields in a faculty member database might contain ID numbers, the names of faculty members, e-mail names, business phone numbers, and department names. All the information about a particular faculty member is called a *record* (less commonly called a *row*). When a database is created, information is entered in a *table* of fields and records.

Records correspond to rows in the table, and fields correspond to columns, as shown in the following faculty database (Faculty2010) in Access 2007:

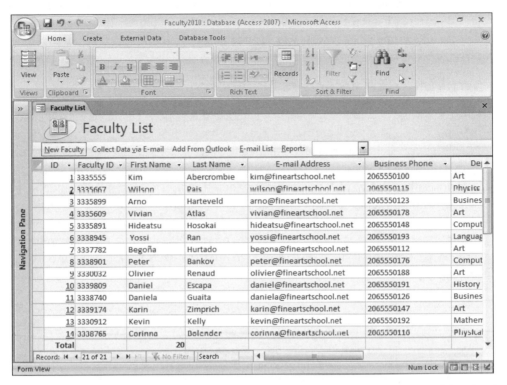

A *relational database* can consist of multiple linked tables. In general, most of the databases that you connect to from Visual Studio will probably be relational databases that contain multiple tables of data organized around a particular theme.

In ADO.NET, various objects are used to retrieve and modify information in a database. First, a *connection* is made, which specifies connection information about the database and creates something for other controls and components to bind to. Next, the Data Sources Configuration Wizard creates a *dataset*, which is a representation of one or more database tables you plan to work with in your program. (You don't manipulate the actual data, but rather a copy of it.) The Data Sources Configuration Wizard also adds an *XML schema file* to your project and associates a *table adapter* and *data navigator* with the dataset to handle retrieving data from the database, posting changes, and moving from one record to the next in the dataset. You can then bind information in the dataset to controls on a form by using the Data Sources window or *DataBindings* property settings.

Although in this chapter we will be experimenting with this process in a Windows Forms application, in Visual Basic 2010, you can also bind dataset information to Windows Presentation Foundation (WPF) client applications and Web applications (ASP.NET or Silverlight). You'll learn about databases and ASP.NET in Chapter 20, "Creating Web Sites and Web Pages by Using Visual Web Developer and ASP.NET."

Working with an Access Database

In the following sections, you'll learn how to use the ADO.NET data access technology in Visual Basic 2010. You'll get started by using the Data Source Configuration Wizard to establish a connection to a database named Faculty2010.accdb that I created in Access 2007 format. (It will also work in Access 2010, the newest version of Access.) Faculty2010.accdb contains various tables of academic information that would be useful for an administrator or teacher who is organizing faculty schedules or workloads, or important contact information for the employees at a college or school. You'll learn how to create a dataset based on a table of information in the Faculty2010 database, and you'll display this information on a Windows form. When you've finished, you'll be able to put these skills to work in your own database projects.

> **Tip** Although the sample in this chapter uses an Access database, you don't have to have Access installed. However, a few Microsoft connectivity components may be required on your computer to work with Access files, depending on how your system has been configured. If you try to complete the exercises below and receive an error message indicating that Microsoft.Jet.OLEDB is not registered on your computer or the Access database format is not recognized, you should complete Step 1 below to install the necessary connectivity components before you work with ADO.NET. Also, note that Faculty2010.accdb is in Access 2007 format. If you want to open the file in Access and work with it, you'll need to have Access 2007 or Access 2010 installed on your system.

Establish a connection by using the Data Source Configuration Wizard

1. Make sure that you have Access 2007 or later installed. If you don't have Access 2007 installed, download and install the 2007 System Driver: Data Connectivity Components from Microsoft.com.

2. Start Visual Studio, and then create a new Visual Basic Windows Forms Application project named **My ADO Faculty Form**.

   A new project opens in the Integrated Development Environment (IDE).

3. On the Data menu, click the Add New Data Source command.

The Data Source Configuration Wizard starts in the development environment, as shown in the following screen shot:

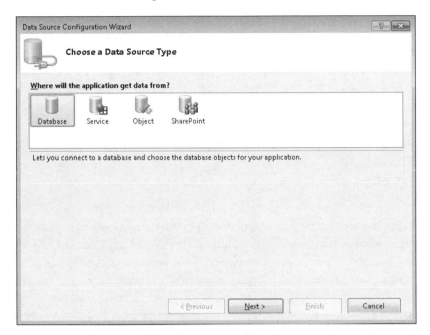

The Data Source Connection Wizard is a feature within the Visual Studio 2010 IDE that automatically prepares your Visual Basic program to receive database information. The wizard prompts you for the type of database that you will be connecting to (a local or remote database, Web service, custom data object that you have created, or Microsoft SharePoint site), establishes a connection to the data, and then creates a dataset or data entity within the program to hold specific database tables and fields. The result is that the wizard opens the Data Sources window and fills it with a visual representation of each database object that you can use in your program.

4. Click the Database icon (if it is not already selected) in the Data Source Configuration Wizard, and then click Next.

The wizard displays a screen prompting you to choose a database model for your application and the connection that your program will make to the database information. This is a new screen in Visual Studio 2010; your options are now to choose a dataset to make the connection or an entity data model. We will be using the dataset option here, but the entity data model can also be useful because it allows developers to work with data in the form of domain-specific objects and properties without concerning themselves with the format of underlying database tables and columns. The entity data model option is made possible by the ADO.NET Entity Framework, which is a subset of the ADO.NET database technology.

5. Click Dataset, and then click Next to select the dataset model.

   The wizard now displays a screen that helps you establish a connection to your database by building a statement called a *connection string*. A connection string contains the information that Visual Studio needs to open and extract information from a database file. This includes a path name and file name, but also potentially sensitive data such as a user name and password. For this reason, the connection string is treated carefully within the Data Source Connection Wizard, and you should take care to protect it from unauthorized access as you copy your source files from place to place.

6. Click the New Connection button.

   The first time that you click the New Connection button, the Choose Data Source dialog box opens, prompting you to select the database format that you plan to use. If you see the Add Connection dialog box instead of the Choose Data Source dialog box, it simply means that your copy of Visual Studio has already been configured to favor a particular database format. No problem; simply click the Change button in the Add Connection dialog box, and you'll see the same thing that first-time wizard users see, except that the title bar reads Change Data Source. In this example, however, I'll assume that you haven't selected a data source format; in that case, your screen looks like the following screen shot:

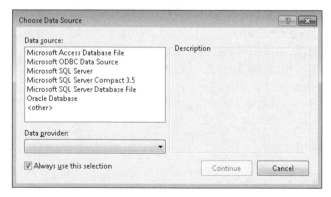

The Change/Choose Data Source dialog box is the place where you select your preferred database format, which Visual Studio uses as the default format. In this chapter, you'll select the Access format, but note that you can change the database format to one of the other choices at any time. You can also establish more than one database connection—each to a different type of database—within a single project.

7. Click Microsoft Access Database File, and then click Continue (or OK).

The Add Connection dialog box opens, as shown in the following screen shot:

Now you'll specify the location and connection settings for your database, so that Visual Studio can build a valid connection string.

8. Click Browse.

The Select Microsoft Access Database File dialog box opens, which functions like an Open dialog box.

9. Browse to the C:\Vb10sbs\Chap18 folder, click the Faculty2010.accdb database, and then click Open.

You have selected the Access database in 2007 format that I built to demonstrate how database fields and records are displayed within a Visual Basic program. The Add Connection dialog box opens again with the path name recorded. I don't restrict access to this file in any way, so a user name and password are not necessary with Faculty2010 .accdb. However, if your database requires a user name, a password, or both for use, you can specify it now in the User Name and Password boxes. These values are then included in the connection string.

10. Click the Test Connection button.

Visual Studio attempts to open the specified database file with the connection string that the wizard has built for you. If the database is in a recognized format and the user name and password entries (if any) are correct, you see the message shown in the illustration on the next page.

Note If you get a message that says "Unrecognized database format", you might not have Access 2007 or later installed. If you don't have Access 2007 or later installed, you will need to download and install the 2007 Office System Driver: Data Connectivity Components from Microsoft.com. (See Step 1 above.)

11. Click OK to close the message box, and then click OK to close the Add Connection dialog box.

Visual Studio displays the Data Source Configuration Wizard again.

12. Click the plus sign (+) next to the Connection String item in the dialog box to display your completed connection string.

Your wizard page looks similar to the following:

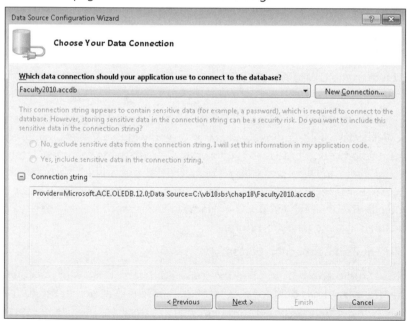

The connection string identifies a *provider* (also called a *managed provider*) named Microsoft.ACE.OLEDB.12.0, which is an underlying database component that understands how to connect to a database and extract data from it. The two most popular providers offered by Visual Studio are Microsoft OLE DB and SQL Server, but third-party providers are available for many of the other popular database formats.

13. Click the Next button.

The wizard displays an alert message indicating that a new local database (or local data file) has been selected that is not in the current project, and you are asked if the database should be copied to your project folders. (This message appears only the first time that you make a connection to a local database file. If you are repeating this exercise, you probably won't see the message.) In a commercial application that uses a database, you might want to control how this works a little more carefully. (To learn more about your options, you would click the Help button or press F1.)

14. Click No to avoid making an extra copy of the database at this time.

You are not commercially distributing this project; it is only a sample program, and an extra copy is not needed.

The Data Source Configuration Wizard now asks you the following question: "Do you want to save the connection string to the application configuration file?" Saving the connection string is the default selection, and in this example, the recommended string name is Faculty2010ConnectionString. You usually want to save this string within your application's default configuration file, because then if the location of your database changes, you can edit the string in your configuration file (which is listed in Solution Explorer), as opposed to tracking down the connection string within your program code and recompiling the application.

15. Click Next to save the default connection string.

You are now prompted to select the subset of database objects that you want to use for this particular project, as shown in the following dialog box:

> **Note** Visual Studio allows you to use just part of a database or to combine different databases—a useful feature when you're working to build datacentric applications.

The items you select in this dialog box are referred to within the project as *database objects*. Database objects can include tables of fields and records, database views, stored procedures, functions, and other items unique to your database. The collective term for all the database objects that you select is a *dataset*. In this project, the dataset is assigned the default name *Faculty2010DataSet*, which you can adjust in the DataSet Name box.

> **Tip** Note that the dataset you create now only *represents* the data in your database—if you add, delete, or modify database records in the dataset, you don't actually modify the underlying database tables until you issue a command that writes your changes back to the original database. Database programmers call this kind of arrangement a *disconnected data source*, meaning that there is a layer of abstraction between the actual database and your dataset.

16. Click the arrow next to the Tables node to expand the list of the tables included in the Faculty2010.accdb database.

    In this case, there is only one table listed, named *Faculty*, which we'll use in our sample program.

17. Click the arrow next to the Faculty node, and then select the check boxes for the *Last Name* and *Business Phone* fields.

    You'll add these two fields to the *Faculty2010DataSet* dataset. The wizard page looks like the following screen shot:

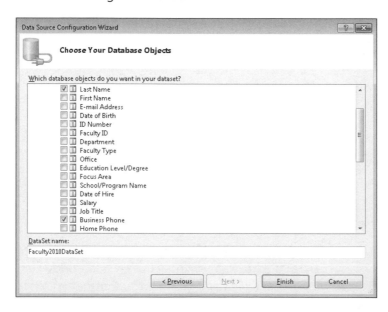

18. Click the Finish button to complete and close the Data Source Configuration Wizard.

Visual Studio finishes the tasks of adding a database connection to your project and configuring the dataset with the selected database objects. (Depending on how the Visual Studio IDE has been used and configured, you might see a Data Sources tab or window now.)

19. Click the Save All button on the Standard toolbar to save your changes. Specify the C:\Vb10sbs\Chap18 folder as the location.

20. If Solution Explorer is not currently visible, open it now to display the major files and components contained in the ADO Faculty Form project.

Your screen looks like this:

In addition to the standard Solution Explorer entries for a project, you see a new file named Faculty2010DataSet.xsd. This file is an XML schema that describes the tables, fields, data types, and other elements in the dataset that you have just created. The presence of the schema file means that you have added a *typed dataset* to your project. (Typed datasets have a schema file associated with them, but untyped datasets don't.) Typed datasets are advantageous because they enable the Microsoft IntelliSense feature of the Visual Studio Code Editor, and they give you specific information about the fields and tables you're using.

21. Click the Faculty2010DataSet.xsd schema file in Solution Explorer, and then click the View Designer button.

You see a visual representation of the tables, fields, and data adapter commands related to your new dataset in a visual tool called the *Dataset Designer*. The Dataset Designer contains tools for creating components that communicate between your database and your application—what database programmers call *data access layer components*. You can create and modify table adapters, table adapter queries, data tables, data columns, and data relationships with the Dataset Designer. You can also use the Dataset Designer to review and set important properties related to objects in a dataset, such as the length of database fields and the data types associated with fields.

22. Click the *Last Name* field, and then press F4 to highlight the Properties window.

23. Click the *MaxLength* property. Your screen looks similar to the following screen shot:

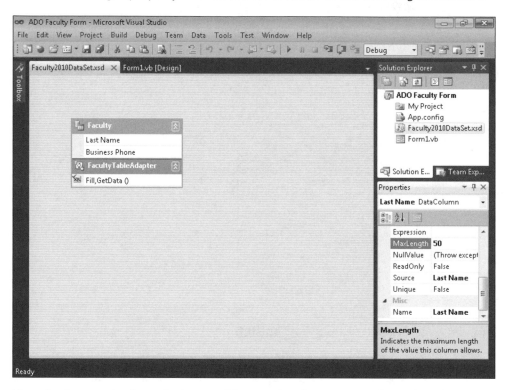

Here the Dataset Designer is shown with an active dataset named *Faculty2010DataSet*, and the Properties window shows that the *MaxLength* property is set to allow for a maximum of 50 characters in the *Last Name* field. Although this length seems sufficient, you can adjust this property (and others, too) if you find that the underlying database settings are inadequate for your application.

Setting the Dataset Designer aside for a moment, let's continue building the sample database application in the Data Sources window.

The Data Sources Window

The Data Sources window is a useful and timesaving feature of the Visual Studio 2010 IDE. Its purpose is to display a visual representation of the datasets that have been configured for use within your project, and to help you bind these datasets to controls on the form. Remember that a dataset is just a temporary representation of database information in your program, and that each dataset contains only a subset of the tables and fields within your entire database file; that is, only the items that you selected while using the Data Source Configuration Wizard. The dataset is displayed in a hierarchical (tree) view in the Data Sources window, with a root node for each of the objects that you selected in the wizard. Each time you run the wizard to create a new dataset, a new dataset tree is added to the Data Sources window, giving you potential access to a wide range of data sources and views within a single program.

If you have been following the instructions for selecting fields in the *Faculty* table of the Faculty2010 database, you have something interesting to display in the Data Sources window now. To prepare for the following exercises and display the Data Sources window, display the form again (click the Form1.vb [Design] tab), and then click the Show Data Sources command on the Data menu. (You can also click the Data Sources tab if it is visible.) When the Data Sources window is open, expand the *Faculty* table so that you can see the two fields that we selected. Your Data Sources window looks like this:

Across the top of the window are four helpful tools that allow you to work with datasets. From left to right, these toolbar buttons allow you to add a new dataset to your project, edit the selected dataset in the Dataset Designer, add or remove dataset fields, and refresh the dataset.

The easiest way to display the information in a dataset on a form (and therefore for your users) is to drag objects from the Data Sources window to the Windows Forms Designer. (This is the Designer you used in earlier chapters, but I am calling it the *Windows Forms Designer* here to distinguish it from the Dataset Designer.)

Chapter 19, "Data Presentation Using the *DataGridView* Control," describes how you can display entire tables of data on a form. In the remainder of this chapter, however, you'll experiment with dragging individual fields of data to the Windows Forms Designer to bind controls to select fields in the Faculty2010 database. Give it a try now.

Use the Data Sources window to create database objects on a form

1. In the Data Sources window, click the arrow next to the *Faculty* node to display the available fields in *Faculty2010DataSet* (if you have not already done so).

   Your Data Sources window looks like the previous screen shot. In Visual Studio 2010, you can display individual fields or an entire table of data by simply dragging the desired database objects onto your form.

2. Click the *Last Name* field, which contains the name of each instructor in the Faculty2010 database. An arrow appears to the right of the *Last Name* field in the Data Sources window. If the arrow does not appear, make sure that the Form1.vb [Design] tab is active in the Designer window, and then click Last Name again.

3. Click the *Last Name* arrow.

   Clicking this arrow displays a list of options related to how a database field is displayed on the form when you drag it, as shown in the following screen shot:

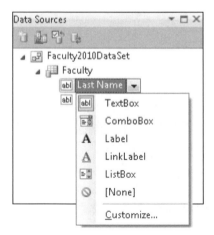

   Although I haven't discussed it yet, most of the controls on the Common Controls tab of the Toolbox have the built-in ability to display database information. In Visual Studio terminology, these controls are called *bound controls* when they are connected to data-ready fields in a dataset. The list of controls you see now is a group of popular options for displaying string information from a database, but you can add additional controls to the list (or remove items) by clicking the Customize command. In this case, however, you'll simply use the *TextBox* control, the default bound control for string data.

4. Click *TextBox* in the list, and then drag the *Last Name* field to the middle of the form in the Windows Forms Designer.

   As you drag the field over the form, a plus sign (+) below the pointer indicates that adding this database object to a form is a valid operation. When you release the mouse button, Visual Studio creates a data-ready text box object and places a professional-looking navigation bar at the top of the form. The form looks something like this (your Data Sources window might be in a different location):

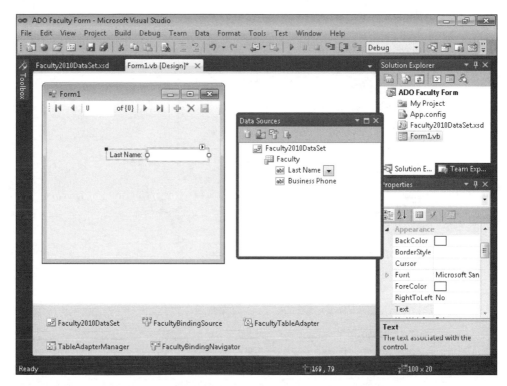

Visual Studio has actually created two objects for this *Last Name* field: a descriptive label object containing the name of the field, and a bound text box object that will display the contents of the field when you run the program. Below the form in the component tray, Visual Studio has also created several objects to manage internal aspects of the data access process. These objects include:

❑ *Faculty2010DataSet*, the dataset that you created with the Data Source Configuration Wizard to represent fields in the Faculty2010 database

❑ *FacultyBindingSource*, an intermediary component that acts as a conduit between the *Faculty* table and bound objects on the form

❑ *FacultyTableAdapter* and *TableAdapterManager*, intermediary components that move data between *Faculty2010DataSet* and tables in the underlying Faculty2010 database

❑ *FacultyBindingNavigator*, which provides navigation services and properties related to the navigation toolbar and the *Faculty* table

Now you'll run the program to see how all these objects work.

5. Click the Start Debugging button on the Standard toolbar.

The ADO Faculty Form program runs in the IDE. The text box object is loaded with the first *Last Name* record in the database (Abercrombie), and a navigation toolbar with several buttons and controls appears at the top of the form, as shown in the following screen shot:

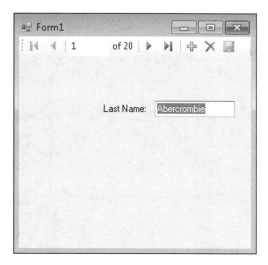

The navigation toolbar is a helpful feature in the Visual Studio 2010 database programming tools. From left to right, it contains Move First and Move Previous buttons; a current position indicator; and Move Next, Move Last, Add New, Delete, and Save Data buttons. You can change or delete these toolbar buttons by setting the Items property for the binding navigator object in the Properties window, which displays a visual tool called the *Items Collection Editor*. You can also enable or disable individual toolbar buttons.

6. Click the Move Next button to scroll to the second faculty name in the dataset.

The Pais record appears.

7. Continue scrolling through the dataset one record at a time. As you scroll through the list of names, notice that the position indicator keeps track of where you are in the list of records.

8. Click the Move First and Move Last buttons to move to the first and last records of the dataset, respectively.

9. Delete the last record from the dataset (Skinner) by clicking the Delete button when the record is visible.

The record is deleted from the dataset, and the position indicator shows that there are now 19 records remaining. (Lan has become the last and current record.) Your form looks like this:

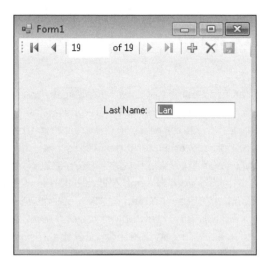

As I mentioned earlier, the dataset represents only the subset of tables from the Faculty2010 database that have been used in this project—the dataset is a disconnected image of the database, not the database itself. Accordingly, the record that you deleted has been deleted only from the dataset that is loaded in memory while the program is running. However, to verify that the program is actually working with disconnected data and is not modifying the original database, you'll stop and restart the program now.

10. Click the Close button on the form to end the program.

    The program terminates, and the IDE returns.

11. Click Start Debugging to run the program again.

    When the program restarts and the form loads, the navigation toolbar shows that the dataset contains 20 records, as it did originally. In other words, it works as expected.

12. Click the Move Last button to view the last record in the dataset.

    The record for Skinner appears again. This final faculty name was deleted only from memory and has reappeared because the underlying database still contains the name.

13. Click the Close button again to close the program.

Congratulations! Without writing any program code, you have built a functioning database application that displays specific information from a database. Setting up a dataset has taken many steps, but the dataset is now ready to be used in many useful ways in the program. Although I selected only one table and two fields from the Faculty2010 database to reduce screen clutter and focus our attention, you will probably want to select a much wider range of objects from your databases when you build datasets using the Data Source Configuration Wizard. As you can see, it is not necessary to create bound objects for each dataset item on a form—you can decide which database records you want to use and display.

Using Bound Controls to Display Database Information

As I mentioned earlier, Visual Studio can use a variety of the controls in the Visual Studio Toolbox to display database information. You can bind controls to datasets by dragging fields from the Data Sources window (the easiest method), and you can create controls separately on your forms and bind them to dataset objects at a later time. This second option is an important feature, because occasionally you will be adding data sources to a project after the basic user interface has been created. The procedure I'll demonstrate in this section handles that situation, while giving you additional practice with binding data objects to controls within a Visual Basic application. You'll create a masked text box object on your form, configure the object to format database information in a useful way, and then bind the *Business Phone* field in *Faculty2010DataSet* to the object.

Bind a masked text box control to a dataset object

1. Display the form in the Windows Forms Designer, and then open the Toolbox, if it is not already visible.

2. Click the *MaskedTextBox* control on the Common Controls tab, and then create a masked text box object on the form below the *Last Name* label and text box.

   As you might recall from Chapter 6, "Using Decision Structures," the *MaskedTextBox* control is similar to the *TextBox* control, but it gives you more ability to regulate or limit the information entered by the user into a program. The input format for the *MaskedTextBox* control is adjusted by setting the *Mask* property. In this exercise, you'll use *Mask* to prepare the masked text box object to display formatted phone numbers from the *Business Phone* field. (By default, phone numbers in the Faculty2010 database are stored without the spacing, parentheses, or dashes of North American phone numbers, but you want to see this formatting in your program.)

3. Click the smart tag in the upper-right corner of the masked text box object, and then click the Set Mask command.

   Visual Studio displays the Input Mask dialog box, which lists a number of pre-defined formatting masks. Visual Studio uses these masks to format output in the masked text box object, as well as input received from users.

4. Click the Phone Number input mask, and then click OK.

   The masked text box object now appears with input formatting guidelines for the country and language settings stored within Windows. (These settings might vary from country to country, but for me it looks like a North American telephone number with area code.)

5. Add a label object in front of the new masked text box object, and set its *Text* property to "Phone:" (including the colon).

   The first descriptive label was added automatically by the Data Sources window, but we need to add this one manually.

6. Adjust the spacing between the two labels and text boxes so that they are aligned consistently. When you're finished, your form looks similar to the following:

   Now you'll bind the *Business Phone* field in *Faculty2010DataSet* to the new masked text box object. The process is easy—you simply drag the *Business Phone* field from the Data Sources window onto the object that you want to bind to the data—in this case, the *MaskedTextBox1* object.

7. Display the Data Sources window if it is not visible, and then drag the *Business Phone* field onto the *MaskedTextBox1* object.

   When you drag a dataset object onto an object that already exists on the form (what we might call the *target object*), a new bound object is not created. Instead, the *DataBindings* properties for the target object are set to match the dragged dataset object in the Data Sources window.

   After this drag-and-drop operation, the masked text box object is bound to the *Business Phone* field, and the masked text box object's *Text* property contains a small database icon in the Properties window (a sign that the object is bound to a dataset).

8. Verify that the *MaskedTextBox1* object is selected on the form, and then press F4 to highlight the Properties window.

9. Scroll to the *DataBindings* category within the Properties window, and then click the arrow to expand it.

Visual Studio displays the properties typically associated with data access for a masked text box object. Your Properties window looks similar to the following:

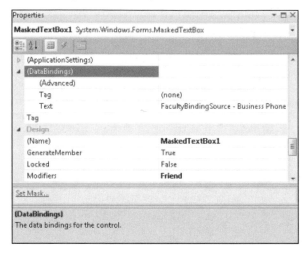

The noteworthy bound property here is the *Text* property, which has been set to FacultyBindingSource – Business Phone as a result of the drag-and-drop operation. (Note that the tiny database icon does not appear here; it appears only in the *Text* property at the bottom of the alphabetical list of properties.) In addition, if you click the arrow in the *Text* property now, you'll see a representation of the masked text box object. (This useful visual display allows you to quickly change the data source that the control is bound to, but don't adjust that setting now.)

10. Click the form to close any open Properties window panels.

11. Click the Start Debugging button to run the program.

Visual Studio runs the program in the IDE. After a moment, the two database fields are loaded into the text box and masked text box objects, as shown in the following screen shot:

Importantly, the masked text box object correctly formats the phone number information so that it is in the expected format for North American phone numbers.

12. Click the Move Next button a few times.

Another important feature is also demonstrated here: The two dataset fields scroll together, and the displayed faculty names match the corresponding business phone numbers recorded in the Faculty2010 database. This synchronization is handled by the *FacultyBindingNavigator* object, which keeps track of the current record for each bound object on the form.

13. Click the Close button to stop the program, and then click the Save All button to save your changes.

You've learned to display multiple database fields on a form, use the navigation toolbar to browse through a dataset, and format database information with a mask. Before you leave this chapter and move on to the useful *DataGridView* control discussed in Chapter 19, take a moment to see how you can further customize your dataset by using a few SQL statements.

One Step Further: SQL Statements, LINQ, and Filtering Data

You have used the Data Source Configuration Wizard to extract just the table and fields you wanted from the Faculty2010 database by creating a custom dataset named *Faculty2010DataSet*. In addition to this filtering, however, you can further organize and fine-tune the data displayed by bound controls by using SQL statements and the Visual Studio Query Builder. This section introduces these tools.

For Visual Basic users who are familiar with Access or SQL Server, filtering data with SQL statements is nothing new. But the rest of us need to learn that *SQL statements* are commands that extract, or *filter*, information from one or more structured tables in a database. The reason for this filtering is simple: Just as Web users are routinely confronted with a bewildering amount of data on the Internet (and use clever search keywords in their browsers to locate just the information they need), database programmers are routinely confronted with tables containing tens of thousands of records that need refinement and organization to accomplish a particular task. The SQL SELECT statement is one traditional mechanism for organizing database information. By chaining together a group of these statements, programmers can create complex search directives, or *queries*, that extract just the data that is needed from a database.

Realizing the industry-wide acceptance of SQL statements, previous versions of the Visual Studio and Visual Basic IDEs have included mechanisms for using SQL statements. In addition, Visual Studio 2008 and 2010 offer a powerful technology called *Language-Integrated Query (LINQ)*, which allows experienced programmers to write SQL-styled database queries directly within Visual Basic code. Although LINQ is a leading database technology in Visual Studio, it is not a feature that you can easily master until you have had a little more experience with SQL statements. In the following exercise, I'll provide some of this background using a powerful Visual Studio feature called *Query Builder*. Query Builder is a visual tool that helps programmers construct database queries, and it is especially useful for programmers who have had relatively little exposure to SQL code. In the following example, you'll use Query Builder to further organize your *Faculty2010DataSet* dataset by sorting it alphabetically.

Create SQL statements with Query Builder

1. On the form, click the *Last_NameTextBox* object (the first bound object that you created to display the last names of faculty members in the Faculty2010 database).

2. Click the Add Query command on the Data menu.

   The Add Query command is available when a bound object, such as *Last_NameTextBox*, is selected in the Designer. The Search Criteria Builder dialog box opens, as shown in the following screen shot:

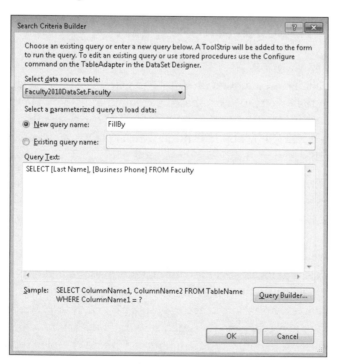

This dialog box helps you organize and view your queries, which are created by the Query Builder and consist of SQL statements. The table that your query will filter and organize by default (*Faculty2010DataSet.Faculty*) is selected in the Select Data Source

Table box, near the top of the dialog box. You'll recognize the object hierarchy format used by the table name, which is read as "the *Faculty* table within the *Faculty2010DataSet* dataset." If you had other tables to choose among, they would be in the list box displayed when you click the Select Data Source Table arrow.

3. Type **SortLastNames** in the New Query Name box.

   This text box assigns a name to your query, and forms the basis of toolbar buttons added to the form. (For easy access, the default arrangement is that new queries are assigned to toolbar buttons within the application you are building.)

4. Click the Query Builder button in the dialog box to open the Query Builder tool.

   The Query Builder allows you to create SQL statements by typing them directly into a large SQL statement text box or by clicking list boxes and other visual tools.

5. In the *Last Name* row representing the *Last Name* field in your dataset, click the cell under Sort Type, and then click the arrow to display the Sort Type list box.

   Your screen looks like this:

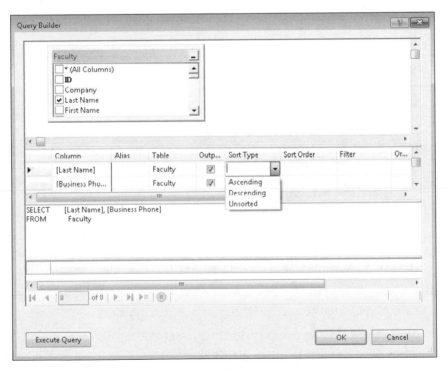

6. In the Sort Type list box, click Ascending.

   You'll sort records in the *Last Name* field in ascending order.

7. Click the SQL statement text box below the grid pane to update the Query Builder window.

A new clause (ORDER BY [Last Name]) is added to the SQL statement box, and your screen looks like this:

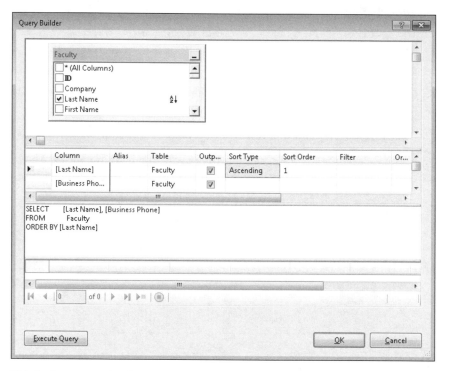

This is the strength of the Query Builder tool—it automatically builds the SQL statements for you in the SQL statement box.

8. Click OK to complete your query.

Visual Studio closes the Query Builder and displays your new query in the Search Criteria Builder dialog box. The name of the query (*SortLastNames*) is listed, as well as the SQL statements that make up the sort.

9. Click OK to close the Search Criteria Builder dialog box, and then configure the *Last_NameTextBox* object to list names in ascending alphabetical order.

The process has also created a *SortLastNamesToolStrip* object in the component tray below the form. The Designer and component tray now look like the screen shot shown on the following page.

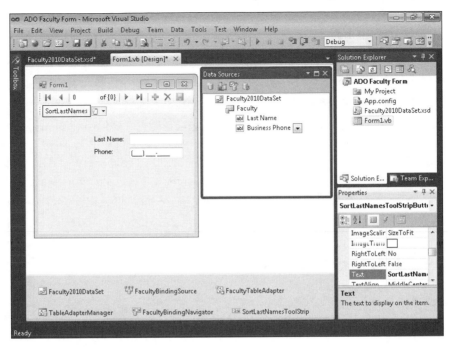

10. Click the Start Debugging button to run the program.

Visual Studio loads the form and displays the first record for two dataset objects.

11. Click the SortLastNames button on the new toolbar.

Your new SQL statement sorts the *Last Name* records in the dataset and displays the records in their new order. The first record is still Abercrombie, but now the second and third names are Atlas and Bankov, respectively.

12. Click the Move Last button on the toolbar.

Now Zimprich appears, as shown in the following screen shot:

Since the names are listed alphabetically from A to Z, Zimprich is now last in the list of faculty members.

13. Scroll through the remainder of the records, and then verify that it is now in ascending alphabetical order.

14. Click the Close button to end the program.

You're on your way with building custom queries by using SQL statements and Query Builder. Database programming is a complex topic, but you have already learned much that will help you build datacentric applications—highly personalized collections of data that benefit *the user* and his or her computing needs—in Visual Basic. You will continue exploring the theme of rich data access in Chapter 19. And in Chapter 20, your final project will be displaying database records on a Web site.

Chapter 18 Quick Reference

To	Do This
Establish a connection to a database	Click the Add New Data Source command on the Data menu, and then use the Data Source Configuration Wizard to browse to the database you want to provide access for by building a connection string.
Create a dataset	Using the Data Source Configuration Wizard, specify a name for the dataset in the DataSet Name box, expand the Tables node in the tree view of your database presented by the wizard, and then specify the tables and fields that you want to include in your dataset. (A dataset need not include all database tables and fields.)
Create bound objects capable of displaying data from a dataset on a Windows form	After running the Data Source Configuration Wizard, open the Data Sources window, and drag tables, fields, or both to the Windows form. To control the type of bound control created by Visual Studio for a table or field, click its arrow and select a control from the list box before dragging it. If you placed a control on the form before adding data sources to the project, bind a database object to the control by dragging the database objects from the Data Sources window onto the control on the form. Alternatively, set an object's *DataBinding* properties to a valid field (column) in the dataset. (One of the most useful *DataBinding* properties is *Text*.)
Add navigation controls to a Windows form	When a valid database object is dragged from the Data Sources window to a Windows form in the Designer, a navigation toolbar is added automatically to the form. To customize the buttons on this toolbar, right-click the *BindingNavigator* object in the component tray, and then click Edit Items.
Format database information on a form	Use a *MaskedTextBox* control to format the content of string data in the dataset. The *MaskedTextBox* control offers many useful input masks and the ability to create custom string formats.
Filter or sort database information stored in a dataset	Use SQL statements to create custom queries in the Visual Studio Query Builder, and then add these queries to a toolbar on a Windows form. After you master Query Builder, you'll be ready to experiment with LINQ.

Chapter 19

Data Presentation Using the *DataGridView* Control

After completing this chapter, you will be able to:

- Create a data grid view object on a Windows form, and use it to display a database table.

- Sort database tables by column.

- Change the format and color of cells in a data grid view object.

- Add and remove columns and column headings.

- Display multiple data grid view objects on a form.

- Permit changes in data grid view cells, and write updates to the underlying database.

In Chapter 18, "Getting Started with ADO.NET," you learned how to use Microsoft ADO.NET database programming techniques to establish a connection to a Microsoft Access database and display columns from the database in a Windows form. You also learned how to add a navigation bar to a form and how to organize database information using Structured Query Language (SQL) statements and the Query Builder tool.

In this chapter, you'll continue working with the database programming features of Microsoft Visual Studio 2010 and the useful classes, objects, and design tools in ADO.NET. In particular, you'll learn how to use the *DataGridView* control, which allows you to present an entire table of database information to the user.

Using *DataGridView* to Display Database Records

The *DataGridView* control presents information by establishing a grid of rows and columns on a form to display data as you might see it in a program such as Microsoft Excel or Access. A *DataGridView* control can be used to display any type of tabular data: text, numbers, dates, or the contents of an array. In programming terms, *DataGridView* is also quite convenient because the underlying data adapter and dataset objects associated with *DataGridView* handle all the data access functionality automatically.

In this chapter, you'll focus on the ability of the *DataGridView* control to display the columns (fields) and rows (records) of the Faculty2010.accdb database, the file of structured employee information that you started working with in Chapter 18. You'll start by filling a simple data grid view object with text records from the Access 2007 database, and then you'll set a few formatting options. Next you'll move on to sorting records in data grid view objects and learning how to add multiple data grid view objects to a form. Finally, you'll learn how to adjust *DataGridView* properties, including the *ReadOnly* property, which allows or prevents a user from saving changes back to the original database.

The *DataGridView* control is connected, or bound, to underlying data access components through its *BindingSource* property. This property contains useful information only after your program has established a connection to a valid data source by using the Data Source Configuration Wizard and the Data Sources window. (The steps involved in establishing this connection will be reviewed quickly here but are described in greater detail in Chapter 18; if you want more information, read the section "Working with an Access Database" in that chapter.) After a data grid view object is bound to a valid data source, Visual Studio fills, or *populates*, the data grid view object automatically by using the *Fill* method when the form is loaded into memory.

Establish a connection to a database table

1. Start Visual Studio, and then create a new Microsoft Visual Basic Windows Forms Application project named **My DataGridView Sample**.

   A new project appears in the Integrated Development Environment (IDE).

2. Click the Add New Data Source command on the Data menu.

   The Data Source Configuration Wizard opens in the development environment. You used this tool in Chapter 18 to link the Faculty2010.accdb database to your project and fill the Data Sources window with tables and columns from the database. This time, you'll select a broader range of information from the sample Access database.

3. Click the Database icon, and then click Next.

4. Click the Dataset icon, and then click Next.

   The wizard prompts you to build a connection string, but if you completed the exercises in Chapter 18, the Faculty2010.accdb database is offered to you automatically, as shown in the screen shot on the following page:

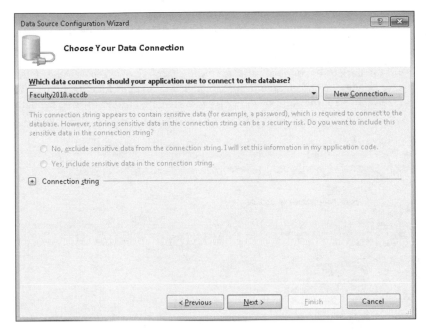

If you don't see the Faculty2010 database connection, click the New Connection button, and then browse to the Faculty2010.accdb file, located in the C:\Vb10sbs\ Chap18 folder. (Detailed steps for establishing this connection are given in Chapter 18, if you'd like additional information.)

5. With the Faculty2010.accdb connection selected, click Next.

   The wizard asks whether you want to save your connection string.

6. Click Next to save the string in the default location (your project's configuration file).

   You are now prompted to select the database objects that you want to use for this particular project. Remember that the Data Source Configuration Wizard allows you to pick and choose database tables and columns at this point—you can select all the objects in the database or just a subset.

7. Expand the Tables node and the *Faculty* table to see the lengthy list of fields in the database that contain faculty employee information.

8. Select the *ID*, *Last Name*, *First Name*, *E-mail Address*, *Faculty ID*, *Department*, *Faculty Type*, and *Business Phone* fields.

   Although this Access database has been designed to contain all sorts of information about school employees, you only want to extract these specific fields for the exercise you're completing.

> **Tip** It is important that you include the *ID* field because it is the *primary key* of the Access database that you are using. The primary key does not need to be displayed on your form, but it needs to be included in the dataset so that information from the table can be written back to the original database if you choose to give the user this option. (I discuss save operations at the end of this chapter.) If you don't include the primary key, you may receive an error message when you try to write data back to the original database.

Your wizard page looks as shown in the following screen shot:

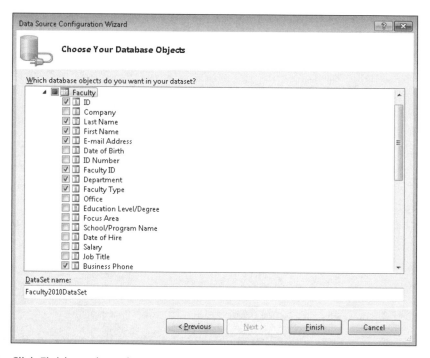

9. Click Finish to close the Data Source Configuration Wizard.

   Visual Studio creates a dataset named *Faculty2010DataSet* to represent the eight database objects that you selected. Visual Studio also adds an Extensible Markup Language (XML) schema file named Faculty2010DataSet.xsd to your project and the Solution Explorer window. You have now established a connection to the Faculty2010 .accdb database that you can use for the remainder of this chapter.

10. Click the Save All button on the Standard toolbar to save the project. Specify the C:\Vb10sbs\Chap19 folder as the location.

11. Click the Data Source tab to open the Data Sources window, and then expand the Faculty node. (If the Data Sources tab is not visible, click the Show Data Sources command on the Data menu.)

The Data Sources window displays the objects in *Faculty2010DataSet*, as shown in the following screen shot:

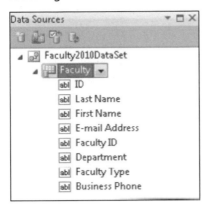

In Chapter 18, you dragged individual fields from the Data Sources window to a Windows form to bind data objects to controls in the user interface. In the next exercise, you'll follow a similar procedure, but this time you'll drag an entire table to the form, and you'll bind the table to a *DataGridView* control so that the fields that you have selected can be displayed at once.

Create a data grid view object

1. Resize the form so that it covers most of the screen.

   Before this chapter is complete, you'll place two data grid view objects side by side on the form, each with several columns and about 20 rows of data. Remember that the form can be larger than the room allotted for it within the IDE, and you can close programming tools or use the scroll bars to see portions of the form that are hidden. (However, you'll want to keep the Data Sources window open for the next step.)

2. In the Data Sources window, click the *Faculty* table, and then click the arrow to its right to display the list of controls that can be bound to the *Faculty* table on the form.

   The Data Sources window looks like this:

Because you have selected an entire table, you do not see individual bound controls in this list box. Instead you see the following options:

❑ DataGridView, the default selection, which displays a grid of columns and rows representing the fields and records in the *Faculty* table.

❑ Details, which configures Visual Basic to create individual controls (with associated labels) automatically for each field in a table that you drag to the form. Although I won't demonstrate Details now, it is a useful option if you want to present tabular data in a slightly more approachable format.

❑ None, which removes any association between the table and a user interface element or control. (If you select None for a table, you will not be able to drag the table from the Data Sources window to the form, and a Null icon will appear next to the table name.)

❑ Customize, which lets you select a different control that might be suitable for displaying multiple database fields (such as the *ListBox* control).

3. Click the *DataGridView* option, and then drag the *Faculty* table to the left side of your form.

Visual Studio creates a navigation bar at the top of the form, adds dataset, binding source, table adapter, table adapter manager, and binding navigator components to the component tray, and creates a data grid view object named *FacultyDataGridView* on the form. Your screen looks similar to the following screen shot:

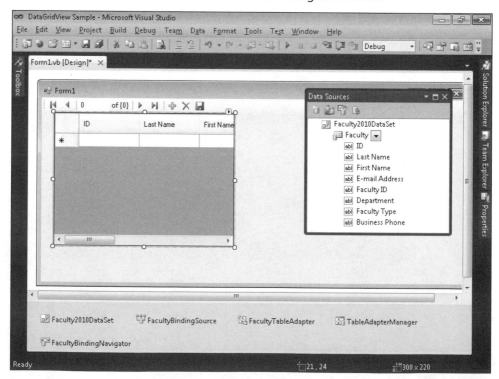

As you can see, the data grid view object does not contain any information at this point, and it is probably not the right size either. (My data grid view object is not wide enough to display all eight columns, for example.) However, you can clearly see that Visual Studio has organized the *Faculty* table in the data grid view so that its fields appear as columns and its rows represent individual records. A blank row is reserved for the first record in the table, and additional rows will be added as soon as the program is run and the data grid view is filled with data.

4. Move and resize the data grid view object so that you can see as many columns as possible and there is ample room for at least 10 rows of data.

   Depending on how your screen resolution is set, you may need to hide some of the programming tools in the IDE to accomplish this, or use the Visual Studio IDE scroll bars that appear when you work with large application windows.

5. Use the Properties window to set the form's *Text* property to "The Faculty Table."

   Your form looks similar to the following:

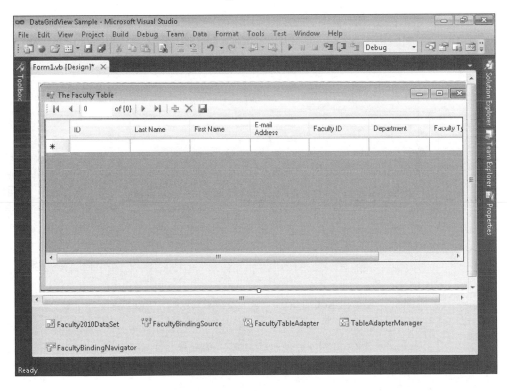

You have completed the basic steps necessary to create a data grid view object on a form and size it appropriately. Next, you'll preview the data and customize your table. The ability to preview data and adjust basic settings is made easy by the smart tag feature.

Preview the data bound to a data grid view object

1. Select the data grid view object on the form, and then click the smart tag in the upper-right corner of the object.

   Visual Studio displays DataGridView Tasks, a list of common property settings and commands related to the data grid view object. The DataGridView Tasks list looks like this:

   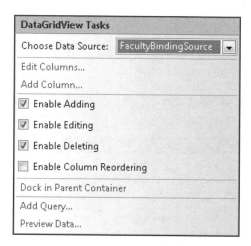

   You can use the settings and commands in this list to change the table that is bound to the data grid view object and to enable or disable editing within the data grid view. (The default setting is to give the user limited abilities to edit information in the table, although you can still control whether the changes he or she makes are written to the underlying database.) You can also adjust the columns shown, dock (attach) the data grid view to the parent container (in this case, the form), filter records with a query (SQL statement), and preview the data in the table.

2. Click Preview Data to open the Preview Data dialog box.

   You display this dialog box when you want to examine the data in a table before you actually run the program—a handy feature.

3. Click the Preview button.

Visual Studio loads the *Faculty* table from *Faculty2010DataSet*, as shown in the following screen shot:

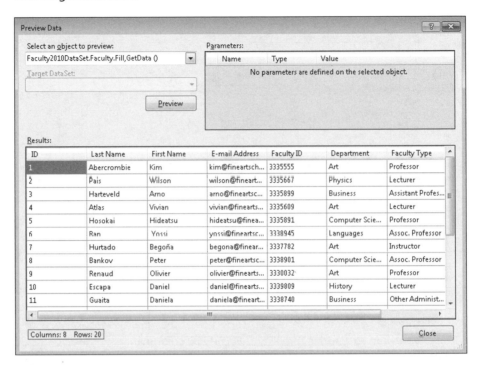

You should be familiar with some of this data already from Chapter 18, but you now may be able to see eight columns that you have selected, all in one place. Seeing all the columns at once is interesting, but it also could amount to information overload—it is up to you to decide how much database information your users should see, and how it should be formatted. In fact, you might not even be able to see all eight columns right now, as is the case in the screen shot. In Visual Studio, it is easy to tailor the data grid view's output so that the proper information is visible.

4. Click the Close button to close the Preview Data dialog box.

Now you'll remove the *ID* and *Faculty ID* columns from the data grid view to show only the information that a typical "directory lookup" feature would display on the screen. Recall that you only included the *ID* field so that your dataset would have a primary key, which is useful when data is written back to the original database.

Remove columns from a data grid view object

1. Open the DataGridView Tasks list again, and then click the Edit Columns command.

You see the following Edit Columns dialog box:

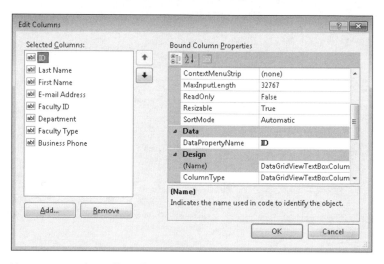

You can use the Edit Columns dialog box to add or remove columns from those displayed by the data grid view object. (As you'll learn later in the chapter, you also use this dialog box to change the properties of the *FacultyDataGridView* object.) Right now, you want to remove the *ID* and *Faculty ID* columns.

> **Note** Although you are removing the *ID* and *Faculty ID* columns from the data grid view object, they still exist in the underlying Faculty2010.accdb database.

2. Click the *ID* column in the Selected Columns list box, and then click the Remove button.

3. Click the *Faculty ID* column, and then click the Remove button.

Visual Studio removes both columns from the list.

4. Click OK to confirm your change, and then press the ESC key to close the DataGridView Tasks list.

The *FacultyDataGridView* object appears again, but without the *ID* and *FacultyID* columns. You now have more room on the form to display database information.

5. Resize the *FacultyDataGridView* object so that it takes up less space.

Your form looks similar to the following screen shot:

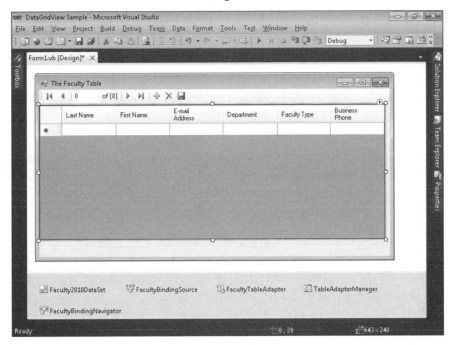

6. Click the Save All button to save your changes.

You've previewed and customized your table using database tools. Now you'll run the program to see what the data grid view looks like at run time. You'll also learn how to sort records in a data grid view object.

Manage a data grid view object at run time

1. Click the Start Debugging button.

Visual Studio runs your project in the IDE. The *Faculty* database table appears within the data grid view object, just as you configured it. Your form looks something like this:

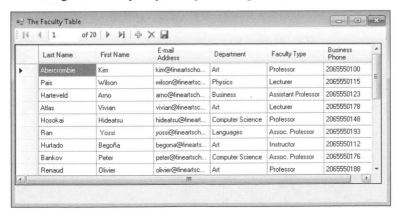

The program statement in the *Form1_Load* event procedure that populated the data grid view with information from the *Faculty* table looks like this:

```
Me.FacultyTableAdapter.Fill(Me.Faculty2010DataSet.Faculty)
```

This line was added to your program by Visual Studio when you dragged the *Faculty* table to the form from the Data Sources window.

Each row in the data grid view represents a record of data from the *Faculty* table in the database. Scroll bars are provided so that you can view any records or columns that aren't immediately visible. This is a handy ease-of-use feature that comes automatically with the *DataGridView* control.

2. Scroll down the list of records to view all 20 rows, which represent faculty employee data for a university.

3. Reduce the size of the First Name column by placing the pointer between the First Name and E-mail Address column headings and dragging the column border to the left.

   When you place the pointer between the column headings, it changes to a resizing handle. You can resize columns at run time because the data grid view object's *AllowUserToResizeColumns* property is by default set to True. If you want to prevent resizing, you can set this property to False.

4. Widen the E-mail Address column to see more of the e-mail name for each faculty member.

   When a data grid view object is filled with data, you can also take advantage of the *DataGridView* control's sorting feature.

5. Click the Last Name column heading.

   The data grid view is sorted alphabetically by the last names of the faculty members. Your form looks something like the following screen shot:

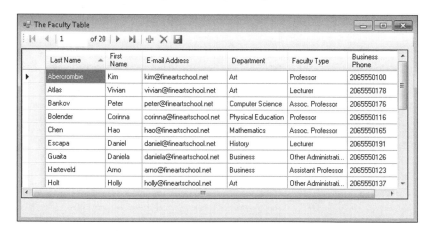

When database records are sorted, a sorting column, or *key*, is required—you establish this key by clicking the heading of the column on which you want to base the sort. The *DataGridView* control provides visual identification for the current sort key—a tiny arrow to the right of the column header. If the sort order is currently an ascending alphabetical (A–Z) list, the arrow points up. Clicking the column heading will reverse the sort order to create a descending alphabetical (Z–A) list. The arrow acts like a toggle, so you can switch back and forth between sorting directions.

6. Click the Last Name column several times to see how the sort order can be switched back and forth.

7. Click other column headings, such as Department and Faculty Type, to sort the database based on those keys.

8. When you're finished experimenting with the scrolling, resizing, and sorting features of the *DataGridView* control, click the Close button on the form to stop the program.

   The program closes, and the development environment returns.

Formatting *DataGridView* Cells

To customize the appearance of your dataset on a form, you can control the look and orientation of several *DataGridView* characteristics by setting properties at design time. For example, you can change the default width of cells in the data grid view, add or remove column headers, change the data grid view or header background colors, and change the color of the gridlines. The following exercise guides you through some of these useful property settings.

Set data grid view properties at design time

1. Display the form, and then click the data grid view object (if it is not already selected).

2. In the Properties window, click the *Columns* property, and then click the ellipsis (…) button in the second column to open the Edit Columns dialog box.

   You used this dialog box earlier to remove the *ID* and *Faculty ID* columns from the *Faculty* table. (This dialog box is also used to set property settings for individual columns.) Now, you'll change the default width of the *First Name* and *E-mail Address* columns.

3. Select the *First Name* column, and then set the *Width* property to 60.

   A width of 60 (measured in pixels) will provide plenty of room for the names that you have in the *First Name* column.

4. Select the *E-mail Address* column, and then set the *Width* property to 140.

   This will provide a little more room for the longer e-mail addresses.

5. Click OK to close the Edit Columns dialog box.

Now, you'll set properties that control the appearance of all the columns in the table.

> **Note** You use the Edit Columns dialog box to configure individual columns. To modify properties that apply to all the columns in a table, you adjust property settings for the data grid view object in the Properties window.

6. In the Properties window, set the *ColumnHeadersVisible* property to False.

Although the column names are somewhat useful in this particular database, sometimes column names don't clearly identify their contents or they contain abbreviations or words that you want to hide from your users. Setting this property removes the column names from the table.

7. Click the *AlternatingRowsDefaultCellStyle* property, and then click the ellipsis button.

The *AlternatingRowsDefaultCellStyle* property controls the color that appears in the background of data grid view cells in alternating rows. Changing this setting produces an alternating effect (white and the color you select) from row to row in the data grid view. In my opinion, this effect makes it easy to read records in longer tables.

Visual Studio displays the CellStyle Builder dialog box, a tool used to set the properties of column cells in data grid view tables.

8. Click the *BackColor* property, click its arrow in the second column, click the Custom tab, and then click the light yellow color.

Your dialog box looks like this. The yellow shading is not visible in this book, but you'll see it in parts of the dialog box.

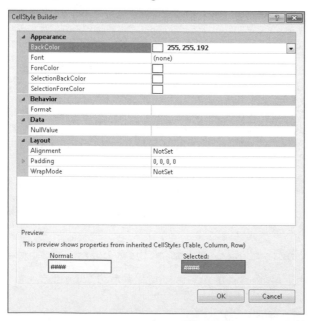

   9. Click OK to close the dialog box.

   When you run the program, the rows in the data grid view will be displayed in
   alternating colors of white and yellow.

> **Note** The color that appears around the edges of the cell is controlled by the
> *BackgroundColor* property. To change the color of all the cells in a data grid view, you can
> adjust the *DefaultCellStyle* property. To change the background color used for the header
> cells (if you display them), you can modify the *ColumnHeadersDefaultCellStyle* property.

   10. Click the *GridColor* property, click the arrow in the second column, click the Custom
   tab, and then click Navy (a dark blue color).

   This property setting controls the color of the gridlines. If you change the background
   color of the cells, you might also want to modify the gridline color.

   Now, you'll run the program to see the effect of your formatting changes.

   11. Click the Start Debugging button.

   After a few moments, the data grid view appears with information from the *Faculty*
   table. Your screen looks similar to the following screen shot:

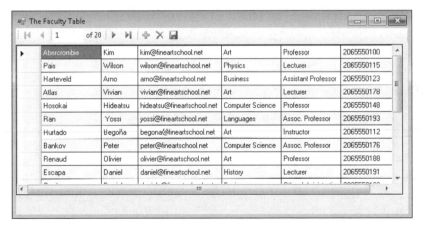

   Notice that the column headers have been removed, the second column is a
   little narrower, and the third column is a little wider. Notice also the alternating
   white-and-yellow row pattern and the blue gridlines (they are not too discernible in
   the printed book, alas, but you can see them on the screen).

   12. Click the Close button on the form to stop the program.

You might want to scan the Properties window for additional property settings and customizations. There are several possibilities if you look closely at the list of formatting options. Remember, these property settings affect all the columns in a table, not just individual columns.

Adding a Second Data Grid View Object

To provide your users with a data-rich user interface containing multiple views of your database, you should consider adding a second data grid view object to your form. After you have established a dataset in the Data Sources window, it is relatively straightforward to add an additional *DataGridView* control bound to a second table within the dataset. If you connect to a second database table (rather than a second copy of the first table), you can also add a second navigation bar to the form and use it to control the second data grid view separately. In the following exercise, you'll add a second version of the *Faculty* table to your form that contains a different set of fields with faculty information.

Bind a second *DataGridView* control to the *Faculty* table

1. Expand the size of the form or reduce the height of the *FacultyDataGridView* object to make room on the form for a second data grid view object below the first.

   Because my screen resolution is probably smaller than yours, I'm reducing the height of the *FacultyDataGridView* object and making the form a little bigger to accommodate the second data grid view.

2. Open the Data Sources window, if it is not currently visible.

3. Drag the *Faculty* table from the Data Sources window to below the *FacultyDataGridView* object.

   Visual Studio creates a second data grid view object named *FacultyDataGridView1* on the form. In this case, you're adding a second copy of the *Faculty* table to your program. However, if your database has multiple tables, an interesting thing to do is add a second table to the form, which will give you completely different database records to look at.

4. Right-click the new *FacultyDataGridView1* object, and then click the Edit Columns command.

   The Edit Columns dialog box opens.

5. Select and remove the *ID*, *E-mail Address*, *Department*, *Faculty Type*, and *Business Phone* columns.

This time, you'll show some different information from the *Faculty* table. When you're finished, just the *Last Name*, *First Name*, and *Faculty ID* columns are left, as shown in the following screen shot:

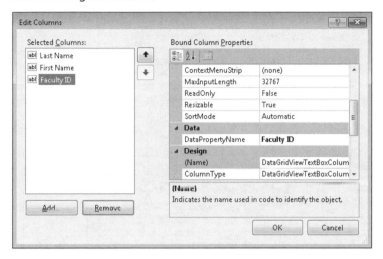

6. Click OK to close the Edit Columns dialog box.

7. Move and resize the second data grid view object on the form so that all three rows are displayed and the data grid views are next to each other.

   Your form looks something like the following screen shot. (Because I am running Visual Studio at a screen resolution of 800 x 600, I needed to hide many of the Visual Studio tool windows to show the form.)

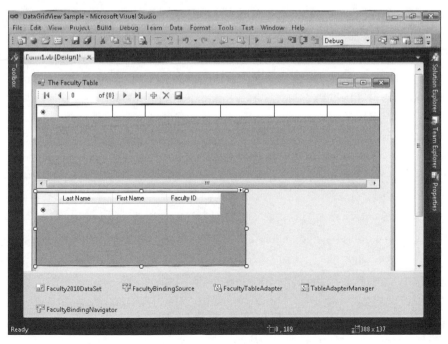

If you want to run your program now and have the two data grid view controls linked, you don't need to add any additional controls to your project. With one navigation bar, the two tables will be linked and both will scroll automatically, even though they display slightly different fields. Let's see how this works.

8. Click the Save All button to save your changes.

9. Click the Start Debugging button on the toolbar.

Visual Studio runs the DataGridView Sample program in the IDE. You see two data grid view objects on the form, as shown in the following screen shot:

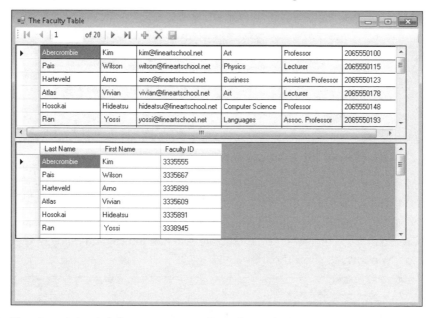

10. Use the navigation bar to start scrolling through the *Faculty* table records.

You can see that the two data grid view objects are linked, because they share the same table and underlying data adapter and binding navigator. This is a feature of the way dataset navigation works in this particular implementation; however, if you choose to display two separate database tables, you can add a second navigation bar and move through the records separately.

11. Use the top scroll bar to move through the contents of the top data grid view object on its own.

The scroll bars allow you to view the two data grid view objects independently, so you always don't have to be looking at the records for the same employee.

12. When you're finished experimenting with the two data grid view objects, click the Close button to close the DataGridView Sample application.

You can perhaps appreciate how useful two data grid view objects might be for the user who wants to compare two very large tables of information. If the data is further filtered by SQL SELECT statements, the application quickly becomes quite powerful.

Adding a *BindingNavigator* Control to Create a Second Navigation Bar on the Form

If you choose to add a second database table to your form, keep in mind that you can also add a second navigation bar to the form so that your user can use two different navigation bars at once. To make this work, you need to be using a database that contains more than one table. (In the Faculty2010.accdb database, there was only one table, but it is common for databases to have several tables to choose among.) Follow these steps to add a second table and navigation bar to your program:

1. Use the Data Sources window to create a second data grid view object on your form, representing a second table in the database.

2. Customize the table's fields by setting properties and using the Edit Columns command.

3. Double-click the *BindingNavigator* control on the Data tab of the Toolbox. Visual Studio adds a binding navigator object named *BindingNavigator1* to the component tray and adds a second navigation bar to the top of your form. You may need to move the data grid view objects down slightly if the new navigation bar is covering them.

4. Change the *BindingSource* property of the second binding navigator object to the binding source of the second table. This is made easy by the *BindingSource* arrow in the Properties window, which shows the names of the two valid binding sources in the program, so you can simply pick it from the list. Once a link has been established between the second navigation bar and the binding source object representing the second table, your program is ready to run.

One Step Further: Updating the Original Database

As I mentioned earlier, the dataset object in your program is only a representation of the data in your original database. This is also true of the information stored in the data grid view objects on your form—if the user makes a change to this data, the change isn't written back to the original database unless you have set the data grid view object's *ReadOnly* property to False and the user clicks the Save Data button on the navigation bar. The designers of ADO.NET and Visual Studio created this relationship to protect the original database and to allow your users to manipulate data freely in your programs—whether you plan to save the changes or not.

In the following exercise, you'll examine the first data grid view object's *ReadOnly* property, which enables or disables changes in the *FacultyDataGridView* object. You'll also learn how to use the Save Data button, which writes changes back to the original database tables on disk.

Enable updates to the database

1. Click the first data grid view object on the form (*FacultyDataGridView*).

2. In the Properties window, scroll to the *ReadOnly* property, and then examine its property setting.

   If the *ReadOnly* property is set to False, the user is free to make changes to the information in the data grid view cells. If you want to allow your users to modify the information and write it back to the database your program is connected to, you should keep this default setting. If you want to disable editing, you should set the *ReadOnly* property to True.

   You'll keep the default setting of False in this case—you want to test updating the underlying Faculty2010.accdb database.

> **Tip** The complete DataGridView Sample program is located in the C:\Vb10sbs\Chap19\ Datagridview sample folder.

3. Click the Start Debugging button to test the first grid's *ReadOnly* property.

   The two data grid view objects appear with data from the *Faculty* table.

4. In the first data grid view object, in the record for Physics faculty member Wilson Pais, click the cell containing Lecturer (the *Faculty Type* field), type **Assistant Professor**, and then press Enter.

   As you make the change, a tiny pencil icon appears in the row header to the left, indicating that a change is being made. Your screen looks similar to this:

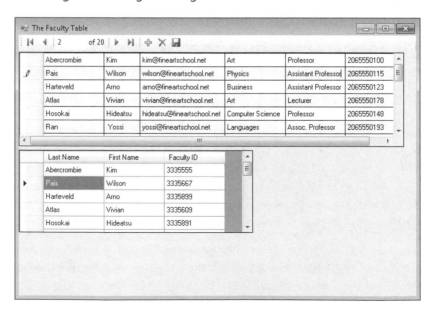

When you press Enter or click a different cell in the data grid view object, the change is stored in the *Faculty2010DataSet* dataset.

5. Click the Save Data button on the navigation bar.

Visual Studio uses the *UpdateAll* method in the data grid view's table adapter object to write the changed dataset to the underlying database. The program statement used to accomplish this save operation in the *FacultyBindingNavigatorSaveItem_Click* event procedure looks like this:

```
Me.TableAdapterManager.UpdateAll(Me.Faculty2010DataSet)
```

TableAdapterManager is the component in Visual Studio 2010 that allows you to control one or more database tables in a program. The *UpdateAll* method saves changes in all open tables in a program, which means that it saves changes not only in the *Faculty* table, but any other table that you have open. You do not have to accept the default saving behavior here. If you would like to save only the changes in the *Faculty* table when your user clicks the Save Data button, replace the statement above with the following line of code:

```
Me.FacultyTableAdapter.Update(Me.Faculty2010DataSet.Faculty)
```

If you use the *Update* method for a named table adapter object, then just that table adapter's associated data will be saved. (And remember, you can also control user edits within tables by using the *ReadOnly* property.)

6. Click the Close button to end the program.

The program closes and the Visual Studio IDE returns. Now, you'll run the program again to see whether the *Faculty* table in the Faculty2010.accdb database has indeed been modified. (When you restart the program, it will load data from the database file.)

7. Click the Start Debugging button.

After a moment, the data grid view objects are loaded with data. You will see that the row in the *Faculty* table containing the name Wilson Pais has been updated with the change to Assistant Professor. The program works!

8. Click the Close button to end the program.

If you want to continue experimenting with the *ReadOnly* property for one or both of the data grid view objects, set *ReadOnly* to True now, and see what happens when you try to modify the database. (You won't be able to make edits or save any changes.) You might also experiment with adding new rows of data to the database by using the built-in editing features and toolbar buttons associated with the *DataGridView* and *BindingNavigator* controls. (Before you add new rows, set the *ReadOnly* property back to False.)

Now take stock of your accomplishments. You've learned to display multiple tables and records by using the *DataGridView* and *BindingNavigator* controls, and you've learned how to customize the data grid view objects with property settings and how to write table updates from the data grid view back to the original database. As you can begin to see, database programming with ADO.NET and Visual Studio is straightforward but also somewhat involved. There are many tools, components, and programming techniques related to viewing, manipulating, and updating database records, and we haven't even begun to talk seriously about important issues such as security and what happens when you work with large databases that are being used by many users at the same time.

Although you've been able to accomplish a lot with little or no program code, there is still much to learn if you plan to make extensive use of databases within Visual Basic applications. For a list of books I recommend for you to continue your studies, see the Appendix, "Where to Go for More Information."

Data Access in a Web Forms Environment

The data access techniques discussed in Chapter 18 and this chapter were designed for use in the Windows Forms Designer—the Visual Studio environment that you've used to build most of the programs in this book. However, you can also use ADO.NET programming techniques in a Web Forms environment, which allows you to share data resources over the Internet and datacentric applications that are accessible through a Web browser such as Internet Explorer. I'll show you how to do this near the end of the next chapter, and you'll learn how to use a few new tools there too, including the *GridView* control, a version of the *DataGridView* control designed for displaying database tables on Web sites.

Chapter 19 Quick Reference

To	Do This
Establish a connection to database tables in a project	Use the Data Source Configuration Wizard to link the project to a database, create a dataset, and fill the Data Sources window with a representation of the selected tables.
Create a data grid view object on a form to display an entire database table	Drag a table icon from the Data Sources window to the form. Then resize the data grid view object so that each column is visible.
Preview data bound to a data grid view object	Click the data grid view object's smart tag to display the DataGridView Tasks list. Click the Preview Data command, and then click the Preview button in the Preview Data dialog box.
Remove a column from a data grid view object	Click the data grid view object's smart tag to display the DataGridView Tasks list. Click the Edit Columns command, click the column that you want to remove in the Selected Columns box, and then click the Remove button.

To	Do This
Sort the records in a data grid view object at run time	Click the column header that you want to sort by. Visual Studio sorts the data grid view object alphabetically based on that column.
Reverse the direction of a data grid view sort at run time	Click the column header a second time to reverse the direction of the sort (from A–Z to Z–A).
Change the default column width for a column in a data grid view object	In the Properties window, click the *Columns* property, and then the ellipsis button. In the Edit Columns dialog box, adjust the *Width* property.
Hide column headers in a data grid view object	Set the *ColumnHeadersVisible* property to False.
Create an alternating color scheme for rows within a data grid view object	Pick a color scheme for alternating rows by using the *AlternatingRowsDefaultCellStyle* property. In the CellStyle Builder dialog box, adjust the *BackColor* property. The color that you select will alternate with white.
Change the color of gridlines in a data grid view object	Adjust the *GridColor* property.
Add a second data grid view object to a form	Drag a second table from the Data Sources window to the form. (It can be the same table that you used in the first data grid view object, or a second table within the database.) Resize and customize the table, taking care to make the form large enough to display all the database columns and records that your user will want to see. If you want to add a second navigation bar to the form to provide access to the table, create a second *BindingNavigator* control on the form, and set its *BindingSource* property to the binding source representing the new table you created.
Prevent the user from editing or changing the data in a data grid view object	Set the data grid view object's *ReadOnly* property to True.
Write changes made in the data grid view object back to the underlying database	Verify that the data grid view object's *ReadOnly* property has been set to False. Then at run time, use the Save Data button on the navigation bar to save your changes and update the database. Alternatively, you can use the table adapter's *Update* method or the *Me.TableAdapterManager.UpdateAll* method within program code.

Chapter 20

Creating Web Sites and Web Pages by Using Visual Web Developer and ASP.NET

After completing this chapter, you will be able to:

- Start Visual Web Developer and create a new Web site.
- Use Visual Web Developer tools and windows, including the Web Page Designer.
- Use the Visual Web Developer Toolbox to add server controls to Web pages.
- Add text, formatting effects, and Visual Basic code to a Web page that calculates loan payments for a car loan.
- Create a Web page that displays Help information.
- Use the *HyperLink* control to link one Web page to another on a Web site.
- Use the *GridView* control to display a table of database information on a Web page.
- Set the *Title* for a Web page and edit the master page.

In this chapter, you'll learn how to build Web sites and Web pages by using the Visual Web Developer tool included with Microsoft Visual Studio 2010. Visual Web Developer has the look and feel of the Visual Studio Integrated Development Environment (IDE), but it is customized for Web programming and Microsoft ASP.NET 4, the Microsoft .NET Framework component designed to provide state-of-the-art Internet functionality. Although a complete description of Web programming and ASP.NET isn't possible here, there's enough in common between Web programming and Windows programming to allow you to do some useful experimentation—even if you have little or no experience with Hypertext Markup Language (HTML). Invest a few hours in this chapter, and you'll see how quickly you can build a Web site that calculates loan payments for car loans, create a Web page with Help information, and display loan prospects from a Microsoft Access database by using the *GridView* control.

Inside ASP.NET

ASP.NET 4, Microsoft's Web development platform, has been enhanced in this release. Some of the improvements include how Web pages are created in the Web Page Designer; various feature enhancements to ASP.NET Web pages and ASP.NET MVC; support for recently introduced browsers and handheld devices; a new ASP.NET *Chart* server control; enhancements to the *FormView*, *ListView*, and *QueryExtender* controls; new dynamic data controls and enhancements; and improvements to the AJAX (Asynchronous JavaScript and XML) programming model. Although ASP.NET has some similarities with an earlier Web programming technology named Active Server Pages (ASP), ASP.NET has been significantly enhanced since its first release in Visual Studio .NET 2002, and continues to evolve as new features are added to the .NET Framework and Visual Studio software. Visual Web Developer is the tool that you use to create and manage ASP.NET user interfaces, commonly called *Web pages* or (in a more comprehensive sense) *Web sites*.

> **Tip** In programming books about ASP.NET, you'll sometimes see Web pages referred to as *Web Forms* and Web sites referred to as *Web applications* or *ASP.NET applications*.

By using Visual Web Developer, you can create a Web site that displays a user interface, processes data, and provides many of the commands and features that a standard application for Windows might offer. However, the Web site you create is viewed in a Web browser, such as Internet Explorer, Mozilla Firefox, Apple Safari, or even one of the new mobile device types, including Google Chrome, the Research in Motion BlackBerry smart phone, and the Apple iPhone. These Web sites are typically stored on one or more *Web servers*, which use Microsoft Internet Information Services (IIS) to display the correct Web pages and handle most of the computing tasks required by your Web site. (In Visual Studio 2010, Web sites can also be located and run on a local computer that does not require IIS, giving you more options for development and deployment.) This distributed strategy allows your Web sites to potentially run on a wide range of Internet-based or stand-alone computers—wherever your users and their rich data sources are located.

To create a Web site in Visual Studio 2010, you click the New Web Site command on the File menu, and then use the Visual Web Developer to build one or more Web pages that will collectively represent your Web site. Each Web page consists of two pieces:

- A Web Forms page, which contains HTML, ASP.NET markup, and controls to create the user interface.

- A code-behind file, which is a code module that contains program code that "stands behind" the Web Forms page.

This division is conceptually much like the Windows Forms you've been creating in Microsoft Visual Basic—there's a UI component and a code module component. The code for both of these components can be stored in a single .aspx file, but typically the Web Forms page code is stored in an .aspx file, and the code-behind file is stored in an .aspx.vb file.

In addition to Web pages, Web sites can contain code modules (.vb files), HTML pages (.htm files), configuration information (Web.config files), global Web application information (Global.asax files), cascading style sheet (CSS) information, scripting files (JavaScript), master pages, and other components. You can use the Web Page Designer and Solution Explorer to switch back and forth between these components quickly and efficiently.

Web Pages vs. Windows Forms

What are the important differences between Web pages and Windows Forms? To begin with, Web pages offer a slightly different programming paradigm than Windows Forms. Whereas Windows Forms use a Windows application window as the primary user interface for a program, a Web site presents information to the user through one or more Web pages with supporting program code. These pages are viewed through a Web browser, and you can create them by using the Web Page Designer.

Like a Windows Form, a Web page can include text, graphic images, buttons, list boxes, and other objects that are used to provide information, process input, or display output. However, the basic set of controls you use to create a Web page is not the set on the Common Controls tab of the Toolbox. Instead, ASP.NET Web sites must use controls on one of the tabs in the Visual Web Developer Toolbox, including Standard, Data, HTML, and many others. Each of the Visual Web Developer controls has its own unique methods, properties, and events, and although there are many similarities between these controls and Windows Forms controls, there are also several important differences. For example, the Visual Studio *DataGridView* control is called *GridView* in Visual Web Developer and has different properties and methods.

Many Web page controls are *server controls*, meaning that they run on the Web server. Server controls have an "asp" prefix in their tag. HTML controls (located on the HTML tab of the Visual Web Developer Toolbox) are *client controls* by default, meaning that they run only within the user's browser. For now, however, you simply need to know that you can use server controls, HTML controls, or a combination of both in your Web site projects. As you gain experience in Web programming, you may want to investigate AJAX programming in Visual Studio, which can enhance the efficiency of your Web applications and add advanced user-interface elements for users.

Server Controls

Server controls are more capable than HTML controls and function in many ways like the Windows Forms controls. Indeed, many of the server controls have the same names as the Windows Forms controls and offer many of the same properties, methods, and events. In addition to simple controls such as *Button*, *TextBox*, and *Label*, more sophisticated controls such as *Chart*, *FileUpload*, *LoginView*, and *RequiredFieldValidator* are provided on a number of tabs in the Toolbox; Visual Studio 2010 has added a number of controls to the list. The screen shot on the following page shows a sample of the server controls in the Visual Web Developer Toolbox. (Dynamic Data and Reporting controls are not shown.)

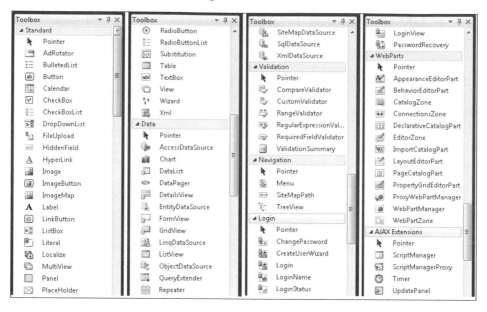

HTML Controls

The HTML controls are a set of older user interface (UI) controls that are supported by all Web browsers and conform closely to the early HTML standards developed for managing UI elements on a typical Web page. They include *Button*, *Text*, and *Checkbox*—useful basic controls for managing information on a Web page that can be represented entirely with HTML code. Indeed, you might recognize these controls if you've coded in HTML before. However, although they're easy to use and have the advantage of being a "common denominator" for Web browsers, they're limited by the fact that they have no ability to maintain their own state. (In other words, the data that they contain will be lost between views of a Web page.) The following screen shot shows the HTML controls offered on the HTML tab of the Toolbox in Visual Web Developer:

Building a Web Site by Using Visual Web Developer

The best way to learn about Visual Web Developer and ASP.NET is to get some hands-on practice. In the exercises in this chapter, you'll create a simple car loan calculator that determines monthly payments and contains an About tab that explains how the program works. Later in the chapter, you'll use the *GridView* control to display a table of data on a Web page in the same Web site. You'll begin by verifying that Visual Studio is properly configured for ASP.NET programming, and then you'll create a new Web site project. Next, you'll use the Web Page Designer to create a Web page with text and links on it, and you'll use controls in the Visual Web Developer Toolbox to add controls to the Web page.

Considering Software Requirements for ASP.NET Programming

Before you can create your first ASP.NET Web site, you need to make sure your computer is set up properly. To perform ASP.NET programming, you need to have Visual Web Developer installed. Visual Web Developer is a component of Visual Studio 2010 Professional, Premium, and more advanced editions. You can also download Visual Web Developer 2010 Express at *http://www.microsoft.com/express/Web/*, and it contains almost all the features described in this chapter (I'll point out any differences as we go). If you are using Visual Web Developer 2010 Express, be sure to set the settings to Expert by clicking the Tools menu, clicking Settings, and then clicking Expert Settings. This will ensure that the steps in this chapter more closely match your software.

Visual Studio 2010 and Visual Web Developer include their own local Web server, so setting up and configuring a Web server with Microsoft Internet Information Services (IIS) and the .NET Framework is not required. Having a local Web server makes it easy to create and test your ASP.NET Web sites, and you'll see it described below as the ASP.NET Development Server.

In Visual Studio 2010, you can create and run your Web site in one of three locations:

- Your own computer (via the ASP.NET Development Server)
- An HTTP server that contains IIS and related components
- An FTP site (a remote file server)

The first location is the option we'll use in this book because it requires no additional hardware or software. In addition, when you develop your Web site on the local file system, all the Web site files are stored in one location. When you're finished testing the application, you can deploy the files to a Web server of your choosing.

Create a new Web site

1. Start Visual Studio, and then click the New Web Site command on the File menu.

> **Note** If you don't see the New Web Site command on the File menu, then you don't have Visual Web Developer installed. To download Visual Web Developer Express, visit *http://www.microsoft.com/express/Web/* and follow the installation instructions.

Although you might have seen the New Web Site command before, we haven't used it yet in this book. This command starts Visual Web Developer and prepares Visual Studio to build a Web site. You see a New Web Site dialog box similar to the following:

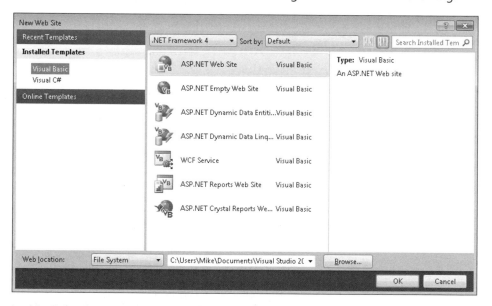

In this dialog box, you can select the Web site or application template, the location for the Web site (local file system, HTTP server, or FTP site), and the programming language that you want to use (Visual Basic or Microsoft Visual C#). You can also identify the version of the .NET Framework that you want to target with your Web application. (Version 4 offers the most features, but there are times that you may need to design specifically for platforms with an earlier version of the .NET Framework. However, Visual Web Developer 2010 Express does not provide the option of targeting a specific version of the .NET Framework.)

2. In the New Web Site dialog box, verify that Visual Basic is the selected language and that ASP.NET Web Site is the selected template.

3. In the Web Location list, make sure that File System is selected.

4. Type **C:\Vb10sbs\MyChap20** in the File Name text box.

Although you have been specifying the folder location for projects *after* you have built the projects in this book, in Visual Web Developer, projects are saved up front.

The "my" prefix in the path will avoid a conflict with the solution Web site in the practice files (C:\Vb10sbs\Chap20) that I've built for you.

5. Click OK to accept your selections.

    Visual Studio loads Visual Web Developer and creates a Web page (Default.aspx) to contain the user interface and a code-behind file (Default.aspx.vb) that will store the code for your Web page.

6. If you don't see Default.aspx open in the Web Page Designer, double-click Default.aspx in Solution Explorer now to open it.

7. At the bottom of the Web Page Designer, click the Design tab.

    Your screen looks something like the one shown in the following screen shot:

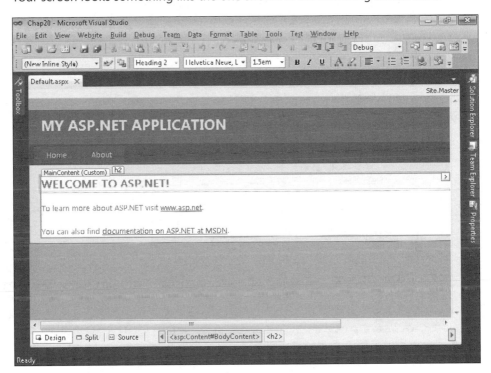

Unlike the Windows Forms Designer, the Web Page Designer displays the Web page in three possible views in the IDE, and three tabs at the bottom of the Designer (Design, Split, and Source) allow you to change your view of the Web page.

The Design tab shows you approximately how your Web page will look when a Web browser displays it. When the Design tab is selected, a basic template page ("My ASP.NET Application") appears in the Designer with the result of source-code formatting, and you can add controls to your Web page and adjust how objects on the page are arranged.

On the Source tab, you can view and edit the HTML and ASP.NET markup that's used to display the Web page in a Web browser. If you've used Microsoft Expression Web, you'll be familiar with these two ways of displaying a Web page and perhaps also with some of the HTML tags that control how Web pages are actually displayed. The Split tab offers a composite view of the Design and Source tabs.

A few additional differences between the Windows Forms Designer and the Web Page Designer are worth noting at this point. The Toolbox now contains several collections of controls used exclusively for Web programming. Solution Explorer also contains a different list of project files for the Web site you're building, as shown in the following screen shot. In particular, notice the Default.aspx file in Solution Explorer; this file contains the UI code for the active Web page. Nested under the Default.aspx file, you'll find a file named Default.aspx.vb. A configuration file named Web.config and a master page file named Site.master are also listed.

Note When you close your new Web site and exit Visual Web Developer, note that you open the Web site again by clicking the Visual Studio File menu and then clicking the Open Web Site command. Web sites are not opened by using the Open Project command on the File menu.

Now you're ready to add some text to the Web page by using the Web Page Designer.

Using the Web Page Designer

Unlike a Windows Form, a Web page can have text added directly to it when it is in the Web Page Designer. In Source view, the text appears within HTML and ASP.NET tags somewhat as it does in the Visual Studio Code Editor. In Design view, the text appears in top-to-bottom fashion within a grid as it does in a word processor such as Microsoft Word, and you'll see no HTML. In the next exercises, you'll type text in Design view, edit it, and then make formatting changes by using buttons on the Formatting toolbar. Manipulating text in this way is usually much faster than adding a *Label* control to the Web page to contain the text. You'll practice entering the text for your car loan calculator in the following exercise.

Add text in Design view

1. Click the Design tab, if it is not currently selected, to view the Web Page Designer in Design view.

   A faint rectangle appears at the top of the Web page, near the template text "WELCOME TO ASP.NET." The template text is there to show you how text appears on a Web Form, and where you can go to get additional information about ASP.NET. You'll also notice that your Web page has Home and About tabs, which are provided for you as part of your default page.

2. Position your insertion point at the end of the text "WELCOME TO ASP.NET."

   A blinking I-beam appears at the end of the line.

3. Press the BACKSPACE key to remove "WELCOME TO ASP.NET," and then type **Car Loan Calculator**.

   Visual Studio displays the title of your Web page exactly as it will appear when you open the Web site in your browser.

4. Delete the line beginning with "To learn more about ASP.NET…," and in its place, type the following sentence:

   Enter the required information and click Calculate!

5. Delete the sentence in the template beginning with "You can also find documentation…"

   Now you'll use the Formatting toolbar to format the title with italic formatting and a different color.

6. Right-click the Standard toolbar in Visual Web Developer to display the list of toolbars available in the IDE.

7. If you do not see a check mark next to Formatting in this list, click Formatting to add the Formatting toolbar.

   The Formatting toolbar now appears in the IDE if it was not already visible. Notice that it contains a few features not usually found on a text formatting toolbar.

8. Select the text "Car Loan Calculator."

   Before you can format text in Visual Web Developer, you must select it.

9. Click the Italic button on the Formatting toolbar.

10. On the Format menu, click the Font command, click Red in the Color list box, and then click OK.

Your screen looks like this:

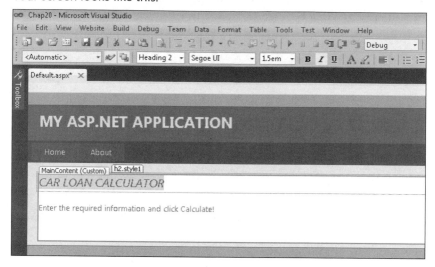

Now, you'll examine the HTML and ASP.NET markup for the text and formatting you entered.

View the HTML and ASP.NET markup for a Web page

1. Click the Source tab at the bottom of the Designer.

   The Source tab displays the actual HTML and ASP.NET markup for your Web page. To see more of the markup, you might want to resize a few programming tools temporarily and use the document scroll bars. The markup looks like the following screen shot. Your markup might have some differences.

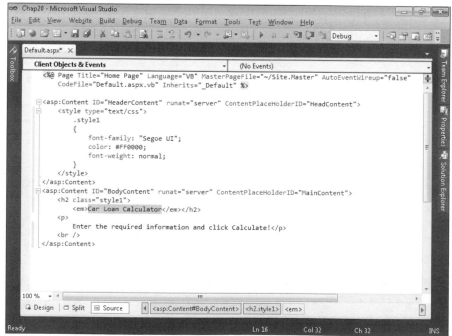

A Web page is made up of page information, scripting code, cascading style sheet (CSS) information, HTML tags, ASP.NET tags, image references, objects, and text. The @ *Page* directive contains information about the language you selected when creating the Web application, the name of any code-behind file, and any inherited forms.

HTML and ASP.NET tags typically appear in pairs so that you can see clearly where a section begins and ends. For example, the *<style>* tag identifies the beginning of text formatting, and the *</style>* tag identifies the end. Notice that the "Car Loan Calculator" text appears within *<em></em>* tags to make the text italic. Below the "Car Loan Calculator" text, the second line of text you entered is displayed.

> **Tip** Remember that the Source tab is an actual editor, so you can change the text that you entered by using standard text editing techniques. If you know something about HTML and ASP.NET, you can add other tags and content as well.

2. Click the Design tab to display your Web page in Design view, and open the Toolbox if it is not visible.

Adding Server Controls to a Web Site

Now you'll add *TextBox*, *Label*, and *Button* controls to the car loan calculator. Although these controls are located in the Visual Web Developer Toolbox, they're very similar to the Windows Forms controls of the same name that you've used throughout this book. (I'll cover a few of the important differences as they come up.) The most important thing to remember is that in the Web Page Designer, controls are inserted at the insertion point if you double-click the control name in the Toolbox. After you add the controls to the Web page, you'll set property settings for the controls.

Use *TextBox*, *Label*, and *Button* controls

1. Display the Standard tab of the Toolbox, if it isn't already visible.

2. Position the insertion point below the last line of text on the Web page, and then press ENTER to create a little blank space below the text for the controls.

   Because controls are placed at the insertion point, you need to use the text editing keys to position the insertion point appropriately before double-clicking a control in the Toolbox.

> **Note** By default, the Web Page Designer positions controls relative to other controls. This is an important difference between the Web Page Designer and the Windows Forms Designer. The Windows Forms Designer allows you to position controls wherever you like on a form. You can change the Web Page Designer so that you can position controls wherever you like on a Web page (called *absolute positioning*); however, you might get different behavior in different Web browsers.

3. Double-click the *TextBox* control on the Standard tab of the Toolbox to create a text box object at the insertion point on the Web page.

Notice the *asp:textbox#TextBox1* text that appears above the text box object. The "asp" prefix indicates that this object is an ASP.NET server control. (This text disappears when you run the program.)

4. Click the right side of the text box object to place the insertion point at the outside edge, and then press ENTER.

5. Double-click the *TextBox* control again to add a second text box object to the Web page.

6. Repeat Steps 4 and 5 to create a third text box object below the second text box.

Now you'll use the *Label* control to insert labels that identify the purpose of the text boxes.

7. Click to the right of the first text box object to place the insertion point at the right edge of the text box.

8. Press the SPACEBAR key twice to add two blank spaces, and then double-click the *Label* control in the Toolbox to add a label object to the Web page.

9. Repeat Steps 7 and 8 to add label objects to the right of the second and third text boxes.

10. Click to the right of the third label object to place the insertion point to the right of the label, and then press ENTER.

11. Double-click the *Button* control to create a button object at the bottom of the Web page.

The *Button* control, like the *TextBox* and *Label* controls, is very similar to its Windows Forms counterpart. Your screen looks like this:

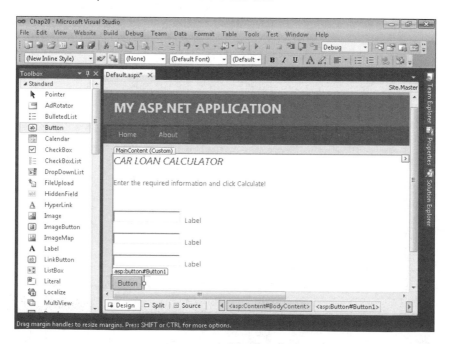

Now you'll set a few properties for the seven new controls you have created on the Web page. If it is not already visible, open the Properties window by pressing F4. As you set the properties, you'll notice one important difference between Web pages and Windows Forms—the familiar *Name* property has been changed to *ID* in Visual Web Developer. Despite their different names, the two properties perform the same function.

12. Set the following properties for the objects on the form:

Object	Property	Setting
TextBox1	*ID*	txtAmount
TextBox2	*ID*	txtInterest
TextBox3	*ID*	txtPayment
Label1	*ID*	lblAmount
	Text	"Loan Amount"
Label2	*ID*	lblInterest
	Text	"Interest Rate (for example, 0.09)"
Label3	*ID*	lblPayment
	Text	"Monthly Payment"
Button1	*ID*	btnCalculate
	Text	"Calculate"

Your Web page looks like this:

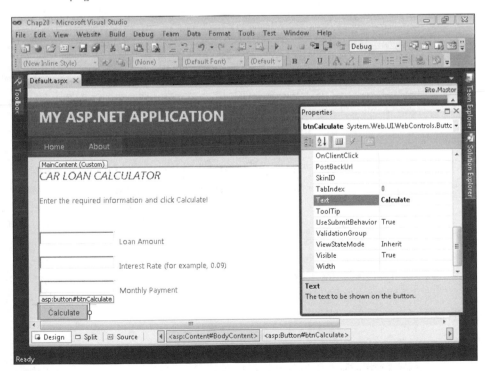

Writing Event Procedures for Web Page Controls

You write default event procedures (or event handlers) for controls on a Web page by double-clicking the objects on the Web page and typing the necessary program code in the Code Editor. Although the user will see the controls on the Web page in his or her own Web browser, the actual code that's executed will be located on the local test computer or a Web server, depending on how you configured your project for development and how it is eventually deployed. For example, when the user clicks a button on a Web page that is hosted by a Web server, the browser sends the button click event back to the server, which processes the event and sends a new Web page back to the browser. Although the process seems similar to that of Windows Forms, there's actually a lot going on behind the scenes when a control is used on an ASP.NET Web page!

In the following exercise, you'll practice creating the default event procedure for the *btnCalculate* object on the Web page.

Create the *btnCalculate_Click* event procedure

1. Double-click the Calculate button on the Web page.

   The code-behind file (Default.aspx.vb) opens in the Code Editor, and the *btnCalculate_Click* event procedure appears.

2. Type the following program code:

   ```
   Dim LoanPayment As Double
   'Use Pmt function to determine payment for 36 month loan
   LoanPayment = Pmt(CDbl(txtInterest.Text) / 12, 36, CDbl(txtAmount.Text))
   txtPayment.Text = Format(Abs(LoanPayment), "$0.00")
   ```

   This event procedure uses the *Pmt* function, a financial function that's part of the Visual Basic language, to determine what the monthly payment for a car loan would be by using the specified interest rate (*txtInterest.Text*), a three-year (36-month) loan period, and the specified principal amount (*txtAmount.Text*). The result is stored in the *LoanPayment* double-precision variable, and then it is formatted with appropriate monetary formatting and displayed by using the *txtPayment* text box object on the Web page.

   The two *Text* properties are converted from string format to double-precision format by using the *CDbl* function. The *Abs* (absolute value) function is used to make the loan payment a positive number. (*Abs* currently has a jagged underline in the Code Editor because it relies on the *System.Math* class, which you'll specify next.) Why make the loan payment appear as a positive number? The *Pmt* function returns a negative number by default (reflecting money that's owed), but I think negative formatting looks strange when it isn't part of a balance sheet, so I'm converting it to positive.

Notice that the program statements in the code-behind file are just regular Visual Basic code—the same stuff you've been using throughout this book. Basically, the process feels similar to creating a Windows application.

3. Scroll to the top of the Code Editor, and then enter the following program statement as the first line of the file:

```
Imports System.Math
```

As you learned in Chapter 5, "Visual Basic Variables and Formulas, and the .NET Framework," the *Abs* function isn't included in Visual Basic by default, but it is part of the *System.Math* class in the .NET Framework and can be more easily referenced in your project by the *Imports* statement. Web applications can make use of the .NET Framework class libraries just as Windows applications can.

The Code Editor looks like this:

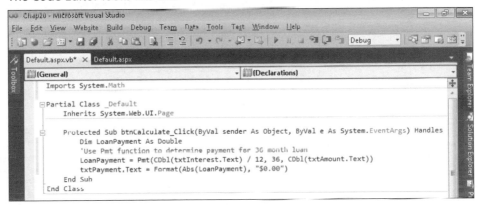

4. Click the Save All button on the Standard toolbar.

That's it! You've entered the program code necessary to run the car loan calculator and make your Web page interactive. Now you'll build and run the project and see how it works. You'll also learn a little bit about security settings within Internet Explorer, a topic closely related to Web development.

Build and view the Web site

1. Click the Start Debugging button on the Standard toolbar.

Visual Studio starts the ASP.NET Development Server, which runs ASP.NET applications locally (on your own computer) so that you can test this application. A status balloon appears at the bottom of your screen and lets you know the local Uniform Resource

Locator (URL) on your computer that has been established, as shown in the following screen shot. You'll also see a message about debugging:

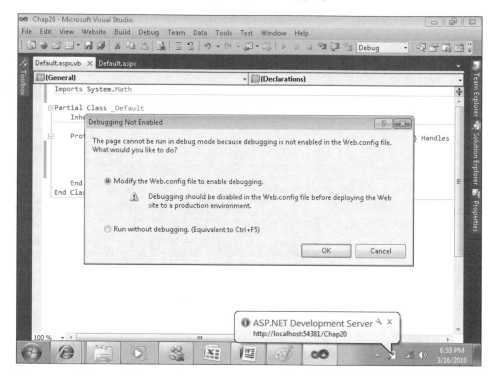

The potentially confusing Debugging Not Enabled dialog box is not a major concern. Visual Web Developer is just indicating that the Web.config file in your project does not currently allow debugging (a standard security feature). Although you can bypass this dialog box each time that you test the application within Visual Web Developer by clicking the Run Without Debugging button, I recommend that you modify the Web. config file now.

 Security Tip Before you widely distribute or deploy a real Web site, be sure to disable debugging in Web.config to keep your application safe from unauthorized tampering.

2. Click OK to modify the Web.config file.

Visual Studio modifies the file, builds your Web site, and displays the opening Web page in Internet Explorer.

The car loan calculator looks like the screen shot on the following page. If Internet Explorer does not appear, you might need to select it on the Windows taskbar.

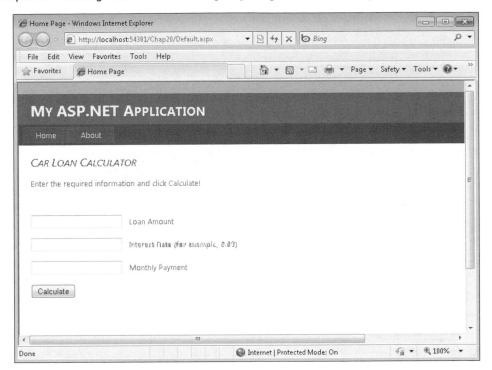

Security Tip You might see the Information Bar at the top of Internet Explorer indicating that intranet settings are turned off by default. An intranet warning is again related to Internet Explorer's design to protect you from rogue programs or unauthorized access. An intranet is a local network (typically a home network or small workgroup network), and because Visual Studio uses intranet-style addressing when you test Web sites built on your own computer, you're likely to see this warning message. To suppress the warning temporarily, click the Information Bar and then click Don't Show Me This Again. To remove intranet warnings more permanently, click the Internet Options command on the Tools menu of Internet Explorer, click the Security tab, and then click Local Intranet. Click the Sites button, and clear the check mark from Automatically Detect Intranet Network in the Local Intranet dialog box. However, exercise caution whenever you disable security warnings, as they are meant to protect you.

Now, let's get back to testing our Web page.

3. Type **18000** in the Loan Amount text box, and then type **0.09** in the Interest Rate text box.

You'll compute the monthly loan payment for an $18,000 loan at 9 percent interest for 36 months.

4. Click the Calculate button.

Visual Basic calculates the payment amount and displays $572.40 in the Monthly Payment text box. Your screen looks like this:

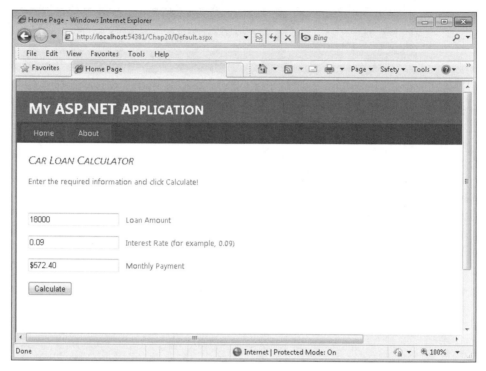

5. Close Internet Explorer.

You're finished testing your Web site for now. When Internet Explorer closes, your program is effectively ended. As you can see, building and viewing a Web site is basically the same as building and running a Windows application, except that the Web site is executed in the browser. You can even set break points and debug your application just as you can in a Windows application.

Curious about installing a Web site like this on an actual Web server? The basic procedure for deploying Web sites is to copy the .aspx files and any necessary support files for the project to a properly configured virtual directory on a Web server running IIS and .NET Framework 4. There are a couple of ways to perform deployment in Visual Web Developer. To get started, click Copy Web Site on the Website menu, or click Publish Web Site on the Build menu. (Visual Web Developer 2010 Express does not include the Publish Web Site command.) For more information about your options, see "ASP.NET Deployment Content Map" in the Visual Studio Help documentation. To find a hosting company that can host ASP.NET Web applications, you can check out *http://www.asp.net*.

> ### Validating Input Fields on a Web Page
>
> Although this Web page is useful, it runs into problems if the user forgets to enter a principal amount or an interest rate or specifies data in the wrong format. To make Web sites like this more robust, I usually add one or more *validator controls* that force users to enter input in the proper format. The validator controls are located on the Validation tab of the Visual Web Developer Toolbox and include controls that require data entry in a field (*RequiredFieldValidator*), require entry in the proper range (*RangeValidator*), and so on. For information on the validator controls, search the Visual Studio Help documentation. They are straightforward to use.

Customizing the Web Site Template

Now the fun begins! Only very simple Web sites consist of just one Web page. Using Visual Web Developer, you can expand your Web site quickly to include additional information and resources, including HTML pages, XML pages, text files, database records, Web services, login sessions, site maps, and more. If you want to add a Web page, you have three options:

- You can create a new Web page by using the HTML Page template or the Web Form template. You select these templates by using the Add New Item command on the Website menu. After you create the page, you add text and objects to the page by using the Web Page Designer.

- You can add a Web page that you have already created by using the Add Existing Item command on the Web site menu, and then customize the page in the Web Page Designer. You use this method if you want to include one or more Web pages that you have already created in a tool such as Expression Web. (If possible, add pages that don't rely on external style sheets and resources, or you'll need to add those items to the project as well.)

- You can use an existing Web page that is part of the Web site template that you are using. For example, in the Web site template that you have open now, there is an About Web page and various Login Web pages that you can customize and use quickly.

In the following exercise, you'll display the About Web page supplied by the template that you are using, and you will customize it with some information about how the car loan calculator application works.

Customize the About.aspx Web page

1. Display Solution Explorer, click the About.aspx file, and click the View Designer button.

   Visual Web Designer displays About.aspx in the Designer, and it displays a line of placeholder text ("Put content here.").

2. Delete the placeholder text, and then type the following information:

Car Loan Calculator

The Car Loan Calculator Web site was developed for the *book Microsoft Visual Basic 2010 Step by Step*, by Michael Halvorson (Microsoft Press, 2010). The Web site is best viewed using Microsoft Internet Explorer version 6.0 or later. To learn more about how this ADO.NET application was created, read Chapter 20 in the book.

Operating Instructions:

Type a loan amount, without dollar sign or commas, into the Loan Amount box.

Type an interest rate in decimal format into the Interest Rate text box. Do not include the "%" sign. For example, to specify a 9% interest rate, type "0.09."

Note that this loan calculator assumes a three-year, 36-month payment period.

Click the Calculate button to compute the basic monthly loan payment that does not include taxes or other fees.

3. Using buttons on the Formatting toolbar, add bold formatting for the headings and italic for the book title, as shown here:

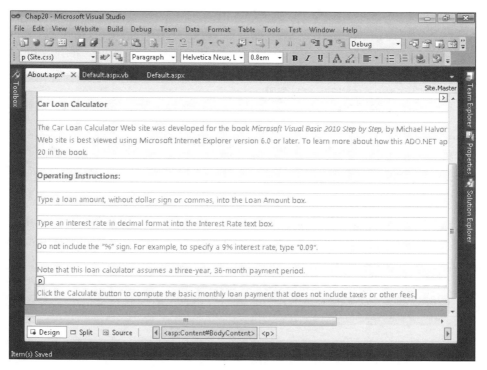

4. Click the Save All button on the Standard toolbar to save your changes.

5. Click the Start Debugging button.

Visual Studio builds the Web site and displays it in Internet Explorer.

6. Click the Home tab on the Web page.

Visual Studio displays the Home page for your Web site, the car loan calculator.

7. Compute another loan payment to experiment further with the loan calculator.

If you want to test another set of numbers, try entering **20000** for the loan amount and **0.075** for the interest rate. The result should be $622.12.

8. Now click the About tab to view the About Web page with instructions for your program.

Internet Explorer displays the About page on the screen. Your browser looks something like this:

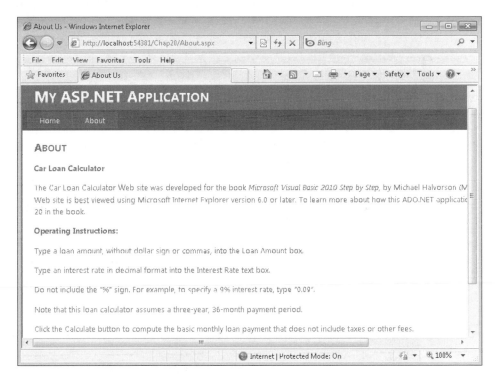

9. Read the text, and then click the Back button in Internet Explorer.

Just like any Web site, this one lets you click the Back and Forward buttons to jump from one Web page to the next.

10. Close Internet Explorer to close the Web site.

You've added a simple About page to your Web site, and you have experimented with moving from one page to the next. Pretty cool so far. Now, try something more sophisticated that shows how far you can take your Web site if you choose to include information from a database.

Displaying Database Records on a Web Page

For many users, one of the most exciting aspects of the World Wide Web is the ability to access large amounts of information rapidly through a Web browser. Often, of course, the quantity of information that needs to be displayed on a commercial Web site far exceeds what a developer can realistically prepare using simple text documents. In these cases, Web programmers add database objects to their Web sites to display tables, fields, and records of database information on Web pages, and they connect the objects to a secure database residing on the Web server or another location.

Visual Studio 2010 makes it easy to display simple database tables on a Web site, so as your computing needs grow, you can use Visual Studio to process orders, handle security, manage complex customer information profiles, and create new database records—all from the Web. Importantly, Visual Web Developer delivers this power very effectively. For example, by using the *GridView* control, you can display a database table containing dozens or thousands of records on a Web page without any program code. You'll see how this works by completing the following exercise, which adds a Web page containing loan contact data to the Car Loan Calculator project. If you completed the database programming exercises in Chapter 18, "Getting Started with ADO.NET," and Chapter 19, "Data Presentation Using the *DataGridView* Control," be sure to notice the similarities (and a few differences) between database programming in a Windows environment and database programming on the Web.

Add a new Web page for database information

1. Click the Add New Item command on the Website menu.

    Visual Web Developer displays a list of components that you can add to your Web site.

2. Click the Web Form template, type **FacultyLoanLeads.aspx** in the Name text box, and then click Add.

    Visual Web Developer adds a new Web page to your Web site. You'll customize it with some text and server controls.

3. Click the Design tab to switch to Design view.

4. Enter the following text at the top of the Web page:

    The following grid shows instructors who want loans and their contact phone numbers:

5. Press ENTER twice to add two blank lines below the text.

    Remember that Web page controls are added to Web pages at the insertion point, so it is always important to create a few blank lines when you are preparing to add a control.

Next, you'll display two fields from the *Faculty* table of the Faculty2010.accdb database by adding a *GridView* control to the Web page. *GridView* is similar to the *DataGridView* control you used in Chapter 19, but *GridView* has been optimized for use on the Web. (There are also a few other differences, which you can explore by using the Properties window and Visual Studio Help documentation.) Note that I'm using the same Access database table I used in Chapters 18 and 19, so you can see how similar database programming is in Visual Web Developer. Many programmers also use SQL databases on their Web sites, and Visual Web Developer also handles that format very well.

Add a *GridView* control

1. With the new Web page open and the insertion point in the desired location, double-click the *GridView* control on the Data tab of the Visual Web Developer Toolbox.

   Visual Web Developer adds a grid view object named *GridView1* to the Web page. The grid view object currently contains placeholder information.

2. If the GridView Tasks list is not already displayed, click the *GridView1* object's smart tag to display the list.

3. Click the Choose Data Source arrow, and then click the <New Data Source> option.

4. Visual Web Developer displays the Data Source Configuration Wizard, a tool that you used in Chapters 18 and 19 to establish a connection to a database and select the tables and fields that will make up a dataset.

   Your screen looks like this:

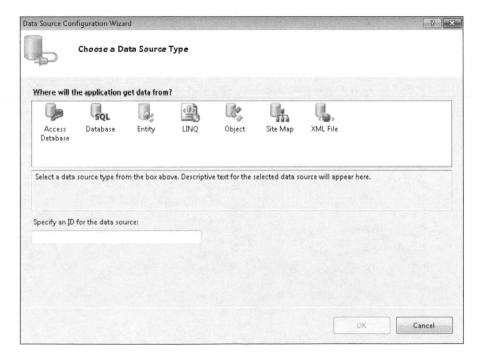

5. Click the Access Database icon, type **Faculty2010** in the Specify An ID For The Data Source box, and then click OK.

   You are now prompted to specify the location of the Access database on your system. (This dialog box is slightly different than the one you used in Chapter 18.)

6. Type **C:\Vb10sbs\Chap18\Faculty2010.accdb,** and then click Next.

> **Note** If you get a message that says "The Microsoft.ACE.OLEDB.12.0 provider is not registered on the local machine," you might not have Access 2007 or later installed. If you don't have Access 2007 or later installed, you will need to download and install the 2007 Office System Driver: Data Connectivity Components from Microsoft.com.

You are now asked to configure your data source; that is, to select the table and fields that you want to display on your Web page. Here, you'll use two fields from the *Faculty* table. (Remember that in Visual Studio, database fields are often referred to as *columns*, so you'll see the word *columns* used in the IDE and the following instructions.)

7. Click the Name list box arrow, and then click Faculty. (There is probably only one or two database tables here, but if there are several, click the Name arrow to view them.)

8. Select the Last Name and Business Phone check boxes in the Columns list box.

   Your screen looks like this:

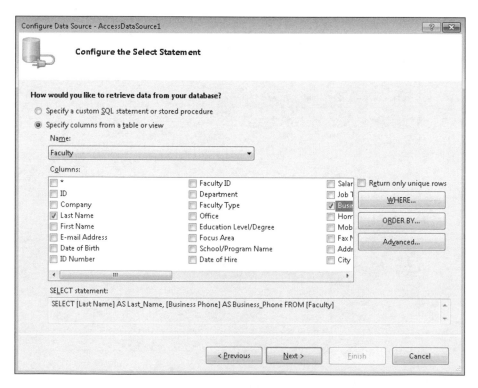

Through your actions here, you are creating an SQL SELECT statement that configures a dataset representing a portion of the Faculty2010.accdb database. You can see the SELECT statement at the bottom of this dialog box.

9. Click Next to see the Test Query screen.

10. Click the Test Query button to see a preview of your data.

    You'll see a preview of actual *Last Name* and *Business Phone* fields from the database. This data looks as expected, although if we were preparing this Web site for wider distribution, we would take the extra step of formatting the Business Phone column so that it contains standard spacing and phone number formatting.

11. Click Finish.

    Visual Web Developer closes the wizard and adjusts the number of columns and column headers in the grid view object to match the selections that you have made. However, it continues to display placeholder information ("abc") in the grid view cells.

12. With the GridView Tasks list still open, click the Auto Format command.

13. Click the Professional scheme.

    The AutoFormat dialog box looks like this:

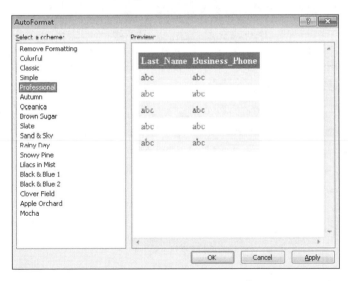

The ability to format, adjust, and preview formatting options quickly is a great feature of the *GridView* control.

14. Click OK, and then close the GridView Tasks list.

    The FacultyLoanLeads.aspx Web page is complete now, and looks like the screen shot on the following page. (My *GridView* control is within a *<div>* tag, but yours might be within a *<p>* tag.)

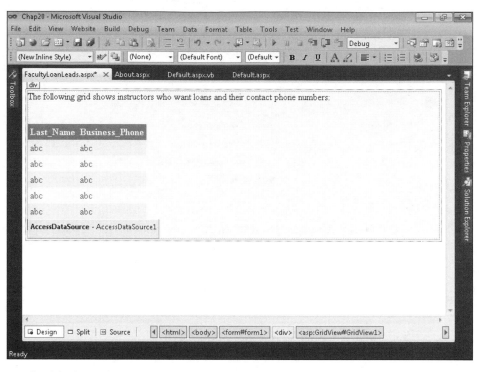

Now, you'll add a hyperlink on the first Web page (or home page) that will display this Web page when the user wants to see the database table. You'll create the hyperlink with the *HyperLink* control, which has been designed to allow users to jump from the current Web page to a new one with a simple mouse click.

How does the *HyperLink* control work? The *HyperLink* control is located in the Standard Toolbox. When you add a *HyperLink* control to your Web page, you set the text that will be displayed on the page by using the *Text* property, and then you specify the desired Web page or resource to jump to (either a URL or a local path) by using the *NavigateUrl* property. That's all there is to it.

Add a hyperlink to the home page

1. Click the Default.aspx tab at the top of the Designer.

   The home page for your Web site opens in the Designer.

2. Click to the right of the Calculate button object to place the insertion point after that object.

3. Press ENTER to create space for the hyperlink object.

4. Double-click the *HyperLink* control on the Standard tab of the Toolbox to create a hyperlink object at the insertion point.

5. Select the hyperlink object, and then set the *Text* property of the object to "Display Loan Prospects."

   We'll pretend that your users are bank loan officers (or well-informed car salespeople) looking to sell auto loans to university professors. Display Loan Prospects will be the link that they click to view the selected database records.

6. Set the *ID* property of the hyperlink object to "lnkProspects."

7. Click the *NavigateUrl* property, and then click the ellipsis button in the second column.

   The Select URL dialog box opens.

8. Click the FacultyLoanLeads.aspx file in the Contents Of Folder list box, and then click OK.

9. Click Save All to save your changes.

Your link is finished, and you're ready to test the Web site and *GridView* control in your browser.

Test the final Car Loan Calculator Web site

 Tip The complete Car Loan Calculator Web site is located in the C:\Vb10sbs\Chap20\ Chap20 folder. Use the Open Web Site command on the File menu to open an existing Web site.

1. Click the Start Debugging button.

   Visual Studio builds the Web site and displays it in Internet Explorer.

2. Enter **8000** for the loan amount and **0.08** for the interest rate, and then click Calculate.

   The result is $250.69. Whenever you add to a project, it is always good to go back and test the original features to verify that they have not been modified inadvertently. Your screen looks like the screen shot on the following page.

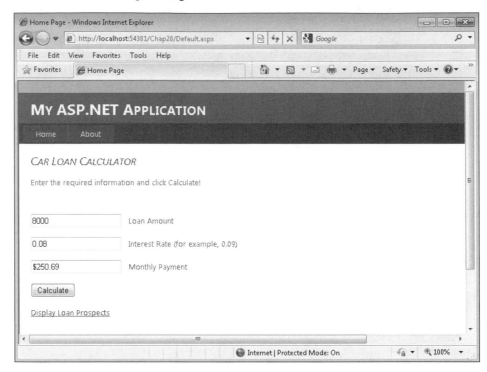

The new hyperlink (Display Loan Prospects) is visible at the bottom of the Web page.

3. Click Display Loan Prospects to load the database table.

Internet Explorer loads the *Last Name* and *Business Phone* fields from the Faculty2010. accdb database into the grid view object. Your Web page looks something like this:

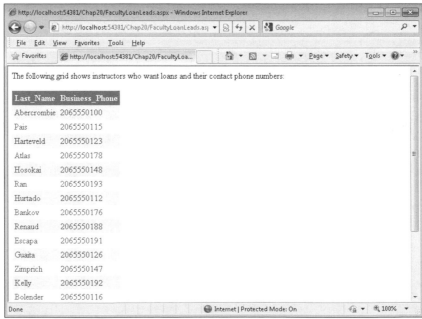

The information is nicely formatted and appears useful. By default, you'll find that the data in this table cannot be sorted, but you can change this option by selecting the Enable Sorting check box in GridView Tasks. If your database contains many rows (records) of information, you can select the Enable Paging check box in GridView Tasks to display a list of page numbers at the bottom of the Web page (like a list that you might see in a search engine that displays many pages of "hits" for your search).

4. Click the Back and Forward buttons in Internet Explorer.

    As you learned earlier, you can jump back and forth between Web pages in your Web site, just as you would in any professional Web site.

5. When you're finished experimenting, close Internet Explorer to close the Web site.

You've added a table of custom database information without adding any program code!

One Step Further: Setting Web Site Titles in Internet Explorer

Haven't had enough yet? Here are two last Web programming tips to enhance your Web site and send you off on your own explorations.

You might have noticed while testing the Car Loan Calculator Web site that Internet Explorer displayed "Home Page" in the title bar and window tab when displaying your Web site. Your program also displays the very large template title "MY ASP.NET APPLICATION" at the top of the window. In other words, your screen looked like this:

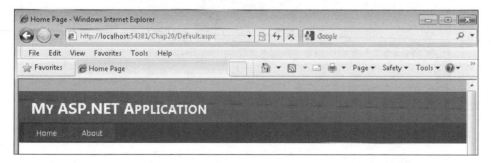

You can customize what Internet Explorer and other browsers display in the title bar by setting the *Title* property of the *DOCUMENT* object for your Web page; and you can modify the "MY ASP.NET APPLICATION" string by editing the site master page. Give editing both values a try now.

Set the *Title* property

1. With the Default.aspx Web page open in Design view, click the *DOCUMENT* object in the Object list box at the top of the Properties window.

Each Web page in a Web site contains a *DOCUMENT* object that holds important general settings for the Web page. However, the *DOCUMENT* object is not selected by default in the Designer, so you might not have noticed it. One of the important properties for the *DOCUMENT* object is *Title*, which sets the title of the current Web page in the browser.

2. Set the *Title* property to "Car Loan Calculator."

The change does not appear on the screen, but Visual Web Developer records it internally. Now, change the title of your application in the site master page.

Edit the master page title

1. Click the Site.Master file in Solution Explorer, and then click the View Designer button.

Visual Studio displays the master page in the Designer. The master page is a template that provides default settings for your Web site and lets you adjust characteristics such as appearance, banner titles, menus, and links. For example, you can click smart tags associated with the Web site's menu items and adjust them much as you customized menus in Chapter 4, "Working with Menus, Toolbars, and Dialog Boxes."

Your screen looks like this:

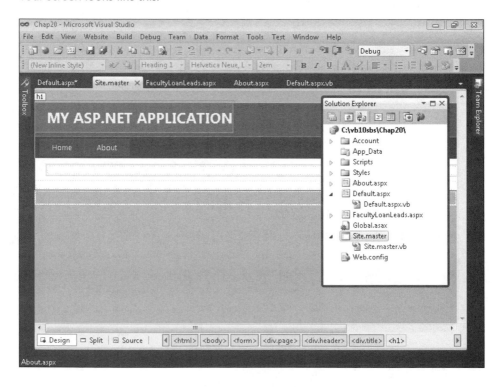

2. Delete the title "MY ASP.NET APPLICATION" and type **TIME FOR A NEW CAR?**

   Visual Web Designer enters your new title. Now run the Web site again.

3. Click the Start Debugging button.

   Visual Studio opens Internet Explorer and loads the Web site. Now a more useful title bar and banner message appears, as shown in the following screen shot:

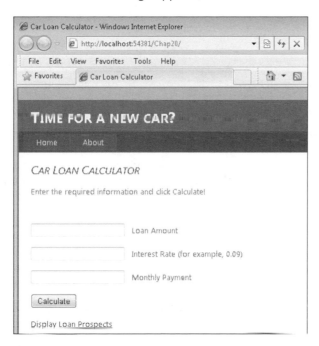

Now that looks better.

4. Close Internet Explorer, and then update the *Title* properties for the other Web pages on your Web site.

5. When you're finished experimenting with the Car Loan Calculator, save your changes and close Visual Studio.

Congratulations on completing the entire *Microsoft Visual Basic 2010 Step by Step* programming course! Take a few moments to flip back through this book and see all that you have learned. Now you're ready for more sophisticated Visual Basic challenges and programming techniques. Check out the resource list in the Appendix, "Where to Go for More Information," for a few ideas about continuing your learning. But take a break first—you've earned it!

Chapter 20 Quick Reference

To	Do This
Create a new ASP.NET Web site	Click the New Web Site command on the File menu, click the ASP.NET Web Site template, specify a folder location in the Web Location list box, and then click OK.
Switch between Design view and Source view in the Web Page Designer	Click the Source or Design tabs in the Web Page Designer. For a mixed view, click the Split tab.
Enter text on a Web page	Click the Design tab, and then type the text you want to add.
Format text on a Web page	On the page, select the text that you want to format, and then click a button or control on the Formatting toolbar. Additional formatting options are available on the Format menu.
View the HTML and ASP.NET markup in your Web page	Click the Source tab in the Web Page Designer.
Add controls to a Web page	Display the Web page in Design view, open the Toolbox (which automatically contains Visual Web Developer controls), position the insertion point where you want to place the control on the page, and then double-click the control in the Toolbox.
Change the name of an object on a Web page	Use the Properties window to change the object's *ID* property to a new name.
Write the default event procedure for an object on a Web page	Double-click the object to display the code-behind file, and then write the event procedure code for the object in the Code Editor.
Verify the format of the data entered by the user into a control on a Web page	Use one or more validator controls from the Validation tab of the Toolbox to test the data entered in an input control.
Run and test a Web site in Visual Studio	Click the Start Debugging button on the Standard toolbar. Visual Studio builds the project, starts the ASP.NET Development Server, and loads the Web site in Internet Explorer.
Create a Web page for a project	Click the Add New Item command on the Website menu, and then add a new Web Form or an HTML Page template to the project. Create and format the page by using the Web Page Designer.
Create a link to other Web pages on your Web site	Add a *HyperLink* control to your Web page, and then set the control's *NavigateUrl* property to the address of the linked Web page.
Display database records on a Web page	Add a *GridView* control to a Web page in the Web Page Designer. Establish a connection to the database and format the data by using commands in the GridView Tasks list. (The Choose Data Source command starts the Data Source Configuration Wizard.)
Set the title displayed for Web pages on the Internet Explorer title bar	For each Web page, use the Properties window to set the *DOCUMENT* object's *Title* property.
Adjust the banner title, menus, and other default values in the master page	Select the Site.Master file in Solution Explorer, and then click View Designer. Adjust the master page's default values in the Designer.

Appendix
Where to Go for More Information

This book has presented beginning, intermediate, and advanced Microsoft Visual Basic 2010 programming techniques with the aim of making you a confident software developer and Windows programmer. Now that you've experimented with many of the tools and features in Visual Basic 2010, you're ready for more advanced topics and the full breadth of the Microsoft Visual Studio 2010 development suite.

If you have your sights set on a career in Visual Basic programming, you might also want to test your proficiency by preparing for a certified exam in Visual Basic 2010 development. In this appendix, you'll learn about additional resources for Visual Basic programming, including helpful Web sites, a source for certification information, and books that you can use to expand your Visual Basic programming skills.

Visual Basic Web Sites

The Web is a boon to programmers and is definitely the fastest mechanism for gathering the latest information about Visual Basic 2010 and related technologies. In this section, I list several of the Web sites that I use to learn about new products and services related to Visual Basic. As you use this list, note that the Internet address and contents of each site change from time to time, so the sites might not appear exactly as I've described them. Considering the constant ebb and flow of the Internet, it's also a good idea to search for "Visual Basic," "Visual Studio 2010," and "Visual Basic Tutorial" occasionally to see what new information is available. (For the most specific hits, include the quotes around each search item as shown.) You might also find some useful information if you search for the product's early code names such as "Visual Basic 10."

http://msdn.microsoft.com/en-us/vbasic/default.aspx

The Microsoft Visual Basic Developer Center home page is the best overall site for documentation, breaking news, conference information, and product support for Visual Basic 2010. (If you're not interested in the U.S. English language site, browse to the Web site and select a different language in the list box at the top of the page.) The Developer Center gives you up-to-date information about the entire Visual Basic product line and lets you know how new operating systems, applications, and programming tools affect Visual Basic development. Features that I like here are the blogs by Visual Basic team members, and access to recent videos and downloads.

> **Tip** Remember that you can also access MSDN resources quickly from the Visual Studio Start Page within the Visual Studio Integrated Development Environment (IDE). The Start Page loads updated articles and news content each time you start Visual Studio, so its contents are always changing.

http://www.microsoft.com/learning/en/us/training/format-books.aspx

The Microsoft Learning Web site offers the newest books on Visual Studio programming from Microsoft Press. Check here for new books about Visual Basic, Microsoft Visual C#, Microsoft Visual C++, and supporting database and Web programming technologies. You can also download freebies, learn about certification, and send e-mail to Microsoft Press.

http://www.microsoft.com/learning/en/us/start/start-right-courses.aspx

This URL leads to the Microsoft Learning Web site for software training and services, including testing, certification, and distance learning. Over the past several years, many Visual Basic programmers have found that they can better demonstrate their development skills to potential employers if they pass one or more certification examinations and earn a Microsoft certified credential, such as Microsoft Certified Technology Specialist (MCTS), Microsoft Certified Professional Developer (MCPD), Microsoft Certified Application Developer (MCAD), and Microsoft Certified Solution Developer (MCSD). Visit the Web site to learn more about current certification options.

http://www.microsoft.com/communities/default.mspx

This site of technical communities for many Microsoft software products and technologies offers opportunities to interact with Microsoft employees and your software development peers. Through this Web site, you can access blogs, newsgroups, webcasts, technical chats, user groups, and other resources related to Visual Studio development. Visual Studio newsgroup topics are currently listed under Find a Community in the Products and Technologies category.

Video Web Sites

The Web has seen an explosion of video content. There are several sites that have videos related to Visual Basic and programming. If you have a few minutes and a high-speed Internet connection, videos can be a great way to quickly learn something new. If you are the type of person that learns best by visualizing, check out some of these sites:

http://msdn.microsoft.com/en-us/vbasic/

The Visual Basic Developer Center has a How Do I videos section with videos that are specific to Visual Basic. These videos cover a variety of areas including new features in Visual Basic 2010, Forms over Data, Office, Windows, LINQ, and WPF.

http://windowsclient.net/learn/videos.aspx

WindowsClient.net is a Microsoft site that has information about writing client applications for Windows. The site focuses on two presentation technologies, Windows Forms and Windows Presentation Foundation (WPF). In addition to technical articles, hands-on labs, samples, forums, and blog posts, this site also has videos. The Windows Forms videos are a great place to continue your learning after completing this book.

http://channel9.msdn.com/learn/

Channel 9 is a Microsoft site that hosts videos and discussions around programming. It has a learning center that has online training videos. Some of the training includes Visual Studio 2010, .NET Framework 4, Windows 7, Office 2010, SharePoint 2010, Silverlight, SQL Server, and Windows Phone.

http://live.visitmix.com/Videos

Mix is a yearly Microsoft conference that focuses on current and upcoming Web technologies. All of the sessions are recorded and posted online for free. The technologies include Silverlight, ASP.NET, Visual Studio, Web services, HTML, Internet Explorer, and Windows Phone.

http://microsoftpdc.com/Videos

PDC, or the Professional Developers Conference, is a Microsoft conference that focuses on future Microsoft technologies. All of the sessions are recorded and posted online for free. The technologies include Windows, Windows Azure, WPF, ASP.NET, ADO.NET, Visual Studio, Visual Basic, C#, and Office.

http://www.learnvisualstudio.net/

The LearnVisualStudio.NET site is a pay site that includes over 500 videos that target beginner to experienced skill levels. The videos cover several areas in .NET including the .NET Framework, Visual Studio, Visual Basic, C#, Windows Forms, WPF, ASP.NET, ADO.NET, and SQL Server.

Books about Visual Basic and Visual Studio Programming

Books about Visual Basic and Visual Studio programming provide in-depth sources of information and self-paced training that Web sites can supplement but not replace. As you seek to expand your Visual Basic and Visual Studio programming skills, I recommend that you consult the following sources of printed information (listed here by category and date of publication). Note that this isn't a complete bibliography of Visual Studio titles, but it is a list that's representative of the books available in English at the time of the initial release of Visual Studio 2010. I also list books related to database programming, Web programming, Visual Basic for Applications (VBA) programming, and general books about software development and computer science.

Visual Basic Programming

- *Visual Basic 2010 Programmer's Reference*, by Rod Stephens (Wrox, ISBN 978-0-470-49983-2).

- *Professional Visual Studio 2010*, by Nick Randolph, David Gardner, Chris Anderson, and Michael Minutillo (Wrox, ISBN 978-0470548653).

- *Programming Windows Services with Microsoft Visual Basic 2008*, by Michael Gernaey (Microsoft Press, ISBN 978-0-7356-2433-7).

- *Practical Guidelines and Best Practices for Microsoft Visual Basic and Visual C# Developers*, by Francesco Balena and Giuseppe Dimauro (Microsoft Press, ISBN 978-0-7356-2172-5).

- *Programming Microsoft Visual Basic 2005: The Language*, by Francesco Balena (Microsoft Press, ISBN 978-0-7356-2183-1). This book covers Visual Basic 2005, but it is still very useful because many of the language features remain the same between versions.

Microsoft .NET Framework

- *Microsoft .NET Internals*, by Tom Christian (Microsoft Press, ISBN 978-0-7356-2675-1). Takes Visual Studio 2010 programmers deep into the architecture and inner workings of the .NET Framework. Offers a tour the core framework and the tools that extend .NET, including Silverlight, WPF, WCF, and WF.

- *MCTS Self-Paced Training Kit (Exam 70-536): Microsoft® .NET Framework–Application Development Foundation*, Second Edition, by Tony Northup (Microsoft Press, ISBN 0-7356-2619-7).

- *Microsoft Windows Presentation Foundation: A Scenario-Based Approach*, by Billy Hollis (Microsoft Press, ISBN 978-0-7356-2418-4).

- *Microsoft Windows Workflow Foundation Step by Step*, by Kenn Scribner (Microsoft Press, ISBN 978-0-7356-2335-4).

- *Microsoft Windows Communication Foundation Step by Step*, by John Sharp (Microsoft Press, ISBN 978-0-7356-2336-1).

Database Programming with ADO.NET

- *Programming the Microsoft ADO.NET Entity Framework*, by David Sceppa (Microsoft Press, ISBN 978-0-7356-2529-7). The Entity Framework allows developers to construct their application model and then map the application model to their database schema. Developers write queries using either Language Integrated Query (LINQ) or Entity SQL. The Entity Framework converts the LINQ expressions or Entity SQL queries into database queries based on the mapping information supplied.

- *ADO.NET 3.5 Cookbook*, by Bill Hamilton (O'Reilly Media, 978-0596101404). ADO.NET 3.5 is part of Visual Studio 2008, but still useful with Visual Studio 2010.

- *Programming Microsoft LINQ*, by Paolo Pialorsi and Marco Russo (Microsoft Press, ISBN 978-0-7356-2400-9). This is a source of in-depth information about the LINQ technology included with Visual Studio 2008. It is still useful with Visual Studio 2010.

- *Microsoft ADO.NET 2.0 Step by Step*, by Rebecca Riordan (Microsoft Press, ISBN 978-0-7356-2164-0).

- *Programming Microsoft ADO.NET 2.0 Core Reference*, by David Sceppa (Microsoft Press, ISBN 978-0-7356-2206-7).

- *Programming Microsoft ADO.NET 2.0 Applications: Advanced Topics*, by Glenn Johnson (Microsoft Press, ISBN 978-0-7356-2141-1).

 Note Books about ADO.NET 2.0 remain useful for Visual Studio 2010.

Web Programming with ASP.NET

- *Microsoft ASP.NET 4 Step by Step*, by George Shepherd (Microsoft Press, ISBN 978-0-7356-2701-7). ASP.NET 4 is the version included with Visual Studio 2010.

- *Programming Microsoft ASP.NET 4.*, by Dino Esposito (Microsoft Press, ISBN 978-0-7356-2527-3).

- *Programming Microsoft ASP.NET MVC*, by Dino Esposito (Microsoft Press, ISBN 978-0-7356-2714-7).

- *Microsoft ASP.NET and AJAX: Architecting Web Applications*, by Dino Esposito (Microsoft Press, 978-07356-2621-8).

- *ASP.NET Internals*, by George Shepherd (Microsoft Press, ISBN 978-0-7356-2641-6).

- *Pro ASP.NET 4 in VB 2010*, Third Edition, by Matthew MacDonald, Mario Szpuszta, and Vidya Vrat Agarwal (Apress, ISBN 978-1430225119).

Office Programming

- *Microsoft Office Excel 2007 Visual Basic for Applications Step by Step*, by Reed Jacobsen (Microsoft Press, ISBN 978-0735624023).

- *Mastering VBA for Microsoft Office 2007*, by Richard Mansfield (Sybex, 978-0470279595).

- *Visual Studio Tools for Office 2007: VSTO for Excel, Word, and Outlook*, by Eric Carter and Eric Lippert (Addison-Wesley Professional, ISBN 978-0321533210).

- *Access 2007 VBA Bible: For Data-Centric Microsoft Office Applications*, by Helen Feddema (Wiley, ISBN 978-0470047026).

- *Access 2007 VBA Programmer's Reference*, by Teresa Hennig, Rob Cooper, Geoffrey L. Griffith, and Armen Stein (Wrox, ISBN 978-0470047033).

In Microsoft Office 2007, a new paradigm was released for writing VBA macros in Office applications. In 2010, a new version of Office is scheduled to be released, but as of mid-2010, no books are available describing VBA and the upgraded technology.

General Books about Programming and Computer Science

- *Code Complete,* Second Edition, by Steve McConnell (Microsoft Press, ISBN 978-0-7356-1967-8). I list this book first because it has been one of my favorite resources for self-taught programmers.

- *Code,* by Charles Petzold (Microsoft Press, ISBN 978-0-7356-1131-3).

- *Writing Secure Code,* Second Edition, by Michael Howard and David LeBlanc (Microsoft Press, ISBN 978-0-7356-1722-3).

- *Software Project Survival Guide,* by Steve McConnell (Microsoft Press, ISBN 978-1-57231-621-8).

- *Data Structures and Algorithms Using Visual Basic .NET*, by Michael McMillan (Cambridge University Press, ISBN 978-0-521-54765-9).

- *The Art of Computer Programming, Volumes 1–3*, by Donald Knuth (Addison-Wesley Professional, ISBN 978-0-201-48541-7). I was given the third-edition, three-volume set (published in 1997–1998) as a gift, and it made my day! If you can afford only one, get Volume 1.

- *Data Structures and Algorithms*, by Alfred V. Aho, Jeffrey D. Ullman, and John E. Hopcroft (Addison-Wesley, ISBN 978-0-201-00023-8).

It is especially important that self-taught programmers acquire a library of general programming books over time that can help them with more theoretical (and non-language-dependent) topics such as fundamental algorithms, data structures, sorting, searching, compression, random numbers, advanced mathematics, networking, and compilers. The books listed in this appendix are only the beginning, and many can be found in used-book stores.

Index

Symbols and Numbers

- (subtraction operator), 143, 147
& (string concatenation operator), 75, 147, 149, 184
* (multiplication operator), 143, 147
... (ellipsis) in menu commands, 100
.gif files, 113
.jpeg files, 113
.NET Framework
  accessing Help files for, 28
  Array class, 288–89
  Exception objects, 236–37
  identifying version of, 496
  Imports statement, 243
  math methods, 152–55
  MSDN Help in, 28
  My namespace, 314–16
  overview, 153
  specifying version in new projects, 39
  StreamReader class, 316–17
  String class, 327
  System.Drawing namespace, 376
  System.IO namespace, 242
  System.Math class, 154
.png files, 113
/ (division operator), 143, 147
@ Page directive, 501
\ (backslash), 147
^ (exponential operator), 43, 147, 149
_ (line continuation character), 75, 187
| (pipe symbol), 113
+ (addition operator), 143, 147
< (less than operator), 161, 331
<= (less than or equal to operator), 161, 331
<> (not equal to operator), 161, 331
= (assignment or equal to operator), 161, 182, 331
= (assignment or equal to), 125
> (greater than operator), 161, 331
>= (greater than or equal to operator), 161, 331
>cmd command, using to switch to Command Window, 223

A

Abs(n) method, 152, 504–05
absolute path names, 89
Access databases, working with, 444
access keys
  adding, 100–02, 119
  defined, 99
  displaying, in Windows, 100
Add connection dialog box, 447
Add Controls program
  creating new Label and Button controls, 363, 365–66
  folder location, 366
  running, 366–67
Add method (List Box), 85, 87, 175
Add New Item dialog box, 248
Add ToolStrip Button button, 109
AddHandler statement, 417
adding
  code snippets, 208
  nonstandard dialog boxes, 117
addition operator (+), 143, 147
address, coordinate system, 376
ADO Faculty Form program, 456–58
ADO.NET, 442
ADO.NET Entity Framework, 442
Advanced Math program, 147–52
AllowFullOpen property, 114
All Windows Forms tab, 67
AllowUserToResizeColumns property, 478
Alphabetical button (Properties window), 15
Always Show Solution check box, 7, 31
Anchor and Dock program
  folder location, 370
  organizing objects at run time, 368–69
  running, 370–71
Anchor property, 368–69
anchoring objects, 368–71, 374
And (logical operator), 167–69

AndAlso operator, 169–71
animating objects
  by using properties, 380–81
  expanding and shrinking, 386–88
  moving on forms, 380–81
  on forms (Sun icon example), 382–85
animation, 380
AnyColor property, 114
applications
  console, 373–74
  datacentric, 439
  deploying, 62–63, 65
arguments
  defined, 131, 257
  in Function procedures, 257
  in Sub procedures, 262
  more than one in a function, 133
  passing by value and by reference, 268–71
Array Class Sorts project, 289–95
Array class, overview, 288–89
array literal, 278
arrays. *See also* dynamic arrays; fixed-size arrays
  assigning values to, 295
  converting strings with separators to, 332, 346
  creating, 274, 295
  declaring, 278–79
  For … Next loops in, 281–82
  overview, 273–74
  processing elements in, 295
  public, creating, 295
  redimensioning, preserving data in, 295
  reordering contents of, 296
  scope of, 274
  setting aside memory for, 276
  sorting, 289–95
  syntax elements, table of, 274
  three-dimensional, 288
  working with elements, 277
As keyword, 125
As Type keyword, 257
Asc function, 330, 339, 347
ASCII codes
  characters, sorting and, 329
  converting, 330, 347

Michael Halvorson

Michael Halvorson is the author or co-author of more than 35 books, including *Microsoft Visual Basic 2008 Step by Step, Microsoft Office XP Inside Out,* and *Microsoft Visual Basic 6.0 Professional Step By Step.* Halvorson has been the recipient of numerous non-fiction writing awards, including the Computer Press Best How-to Book Award (Software category) and the Society for Technical Communication Excellence Award (Writing category). Halvorson earned a bachelor's degree in Computer Science from Pacific Lutheran University in Tacoma, Washington, and master's and doctoral degrees in History from the University of Washington in Seattle. He was employed at Microsoft Corporation from 1985 to 1993, and he has been an advocate for Visual Basic programming since the product's original debut at Windows World in 1991. Halvorson is currently an associate professor at Pacific Lutheran University.

Best Practices for Software Engineering

Software Estimation: Demystifying the Black Art
Steve McConnell
ISBN 9780735605350

Amazon.com's pick for "Best Computer Book of 2006"! Generating accurate software estimates is fairly straightforward—once you understand the art of creating them. Acclaimed author Steve McConnell demystifies the process—illuminating the practical procedures, formulas, and heuristics you can apply right away.

Code Complete, Second Edition
Steve McConnell
ISBN 9780735619678

Widely considered one of the best practical guides to programming—fully updated. Drawing from research, academia, and everyday commercial practice, McConnell synthesizes must-know principles and techniques into clear, pragmatic guidance. Rethink your approach—and deliver the highest quality code.

Agile Portfolio Management
Jochen Krebs
ISBN 9780735625679

Agile processes foster better collaboration, innovation, and results. So why limit their use to software projects—when you can transform your entire business? This book illuminates the opportunities—and rewards—of applying agile processes to your overall IT portfolio, with best practices for optimizing results.

Simple Architectures for Complex Enterprises
Roger Sessions
ISBN 9780735625785

Why do so many IT projects fail? Enterprise consultant Roger Sessions believes complex problems require simple solutions. And in this book, he shows how to make simplicity a core architectural requirement—as critical as performance, reliability, or security—to achieve better, more reliable results for your organization.

The Enterprise and Scrum
Ken Schwaber
ISBN 9780735623378

Extend Scrum's benefits—greater agility, higher-quality products, and lower costs—beyond individual teams to the entire enterprise. Scrum cofounder Ken Schwaber describes proven practices for adopting Scrum principles across your organization, including that all-critical component—managing change.

ALSO SEE

Software Requirements, Second Edition
Karl E. Wiegers
ISBN 9780735618794

More About Software Requirements: Thorny Issues and Practical Advice
Karl E. Wiegers
ISBN 9780735622678

Software Requirement Patterns
Stephen Withall
ISBN 9780735623989

Agile Project Management with Scrum
Ken Schwaber
ISBN 9780735619937

Solid Code
Donis Marshall, John Bruno
ISBN 9780735625921

microsoft.com/mspress

What do you think of this book?

We want to hear from you!

To participate in a brief online survey, please visit:

microsoft.com/learning/booksurvey

Tell us how well this book meets your needs—what works effectively, and what we can do better. Your feedback will help us continually improve our books and learning resources for you.

Thank you in advance for your input!

Stay in touch!

To subscribe to the *Microsoft Press® Book Connection Newsletter*—for news on upcoming books, events, and special offers—please visit:

microsoft.com/learning/books/newsletter